SONSHIP
AND THE
URANTIA
PAPERS

SHARING THE
MIND OF GOD

Robert Crickett

Sonship Books

Sonship and the Urantia papers: sharing the mind of God.
Copyright © 2000 by Robert Crickett.
**Distributed by Sonship Books: P.O.Box 6067, Hawthorn West,
Victoria 3122 Australia. Email: sonship@gravity.net.au**
Website http://users.gravity.net.au/sonship

First printed by Aristoc Offset Printers—
3 Aristoc Road, Glen Waverley, Victoria, 3150.
Tel. (03) 9561 5622 Email: aristoc@sprint.com.au.
Cataloguing-in-publication data
Crickett, Robert James 1949—,
Sonship and the Urantia papers: sharing the mind of God.

ISBN 0-646039316-2
1. Crickett, Robert James 1949—Religion. 2. Urantia papers.
3. Christian spirituality.
For notes on the scripture quotations in this book, please refer to "Scripture quotations and references" on page xix.

NOTE

Dedication and thanks

To the spiritually courageous person who sincerely seeks the perfecting power of Jesus' own spiritual experience: the person who will dare to receive the full depth and breadth and height of perfection that is within the baptism of the Holy Spirit and its sharing of the mind of God. Through you, our Father is magnificently glorified, sonship with God is demonstrated to a spiritually hurting and hungry world, the Father's love prevails, and a bridge of revelation spans his diverse historic covenants.

❦

Thank you Mary Crickett, for the thrilling experience of growing from Urantia to Paradise with my very best friend.

❦

Michael, thank you for showing me our Father's perfection through your life, your teachings, your crucifixion and your sonship. Thank you for being there for me and helping me to be there for you. Truly you are magnificent and sovereign.

❦

My thanks, and prayers for loving understanding, go to my Christian companions who feature the strongest in my life nowadays with whom I have ministered healing and deliverance and yet who would struggle with the concept of a larger revelation of the Father outside the Bible. There is none among us except the Son himself who knows the whole shape of the Father's endless revelation. The Spirit-filled look beyond the words to the Father's Spirit and therein find the Word of God.

❦

My thanks also goes to a distant grandfather, the Rev. Alexander Moncrieff of Culfargie, Scotland, who, back around 1700, emerged from within his Presbyterian peers to form the Secession Church. The knowledge of your calling has given me human courage to balance the spiritual calling by my Father to step out where ordinarily I might never go.

❦

Appreciation

I wish to express my appreciation to the creators of three magnificent search engines, access to which I believe every student of Jesus' religion ought to have:

Computer Based Concordance, "Folio Views" by the Urantia Foundation:
533 Diversey Parkway, Chicago, Illinois 60614 USA.
Phone: 773-525-3319
Email: urantia@urantia.org

❦

"Quickverse Bible Reference Collection" by Parsons Technology:
P.O.Box 100, Hiawatha, Iowa 52233-0100 USA.
Phone: 319-395-7314
Email: customerserv@shopmattel.com
Web: www.parsonstech.com

❦

"Index To The Urantia Book" (1999) by Harry McMullan of Michael Foundation: S 3333 Council Rd Oklahoma City, OK 73179-4410 USA.
Phone: 405-745-7707
Email: michaelfoundation@ibm.net

❦

Titles of the chapters in the book

❦

Table of Contents

Scripture quotations and references

The Urantia papers

The Urantia papers have to date, 2000, been published under different names such as "The Urantia Book"; "God's Bible"; "The Urantia Book, A Revelation For Humanity"; and the fourth section of the Urantia papers only as "Jesus—A New Revelation."

Their circulation is worldwide, translations into languages other than English exist, and the reading population now number people from all walks of life, cultures and ethnicities. It is no longer true that all readers read the first copy of the text that was produced by the Urantia Foundation in Chicago USA.

Fortunately, each of these publications endeavoured to maintain the integrity of the original text inviolate, and the single consistent feature upon which referencing can be based is the text's own structure.

The Urantia papers consist of 196 Chapters and a Foreword. The Chapters comprise numerous Sections. Each of the Sections contains one or more paragraphs.

These editions and versions of the Urantia papers have differing page numbers and layout. It is important to avoid making reference to page and paragraph numbers in any one publication. It is more appropriate to site Chapter, Section and Paragraph and cover all the various editions.

In this book therefore, references to the text of the Urantia papers are to the number of the paper, the number of the section in the paper, and the number of the paragraph in the section.

An example of this method is 95:5.4 which represents Paper 95:Section 5.Paragraph 4.

Where part of a paragraph is cited references will include the first three words of the paragraph. It is hoped that by so doing, confusion will be avoided as the reader scans the text for the appropriate reference in the Urantia papers publication of their preference. If the reference number doesn't match the edition you are reading then search in the same section for a paragraph starting with the three words in the reference.

An example of this is taken from page 72 as follows:
15. 140:8.6 {Jesus did not attack...}; Mark 5:36
16. 1 Corinthians 13:13
17. 140:1.5
18. 147:3.3
19. 141:6.4-5
20. 40:9.6
21. 30:4.8
22. 113:7.4 {Before leaving the...}; 39:2.5 {3. Spirit Co-ordinators...}
23. Paper 53 {The Lucifer Rebellion}
24. 4:3.3 {Much, very much...}

The Bible

References to the text of the Bible are to the name of the book, the number of the chapter, the number of the verse.

In this book there are around 9 references from the King James Version and they are cited as follows: 2 Corinthians 3:17 KJV; Genesis 1:2 KJV; Hebrews 12:2 KJV.

One reference is from the NIV—Holy Bible: New International Version. Copyright © 1973, 1978, 1984 by New York International Bible Society. It is cited as Luke 1:37 NIV.

The remaining 160 or so scripture quotations contained herein are from the New Revised Standard Version Bible, copyright © 1989 by the Division of Christian Education of the National Council of the Churches of Christ in the U.S.A. Used by permission. All rights reserved.

References

References are placed at the end of each chapter rather than included in the text so that the reader who is not reference friendly can read on uninterrupted. The numbering of references commences afresh with each chapter.

The reader may find the references useful in further researching the topics they flag.

❧

Introduction

The authors of the Urantia papers employ the term *sonship* to mean either a male or a female person who is in personal relationship with God. They make no distinction about gender, despite the fact that to many people it represents bias. I use the term purely in order to stay consistent with the terminology in the Urantia papers. I therefore ask the reader to suspend any irritation that the term sonship may cause in order to get to deeper values embedded by the authors of the Urantia papers.

The son of God is a person who knows God directly, as a parent. Consequently he or she is in a child-parent relationship. Sonship, as spiritual experience, is unique among the aims and practices of other religions. I employ the term sonship to mean the peak aim and the spiritual power within the religion that was lived by Jesus of Nazareth. The experiential distinctions between religions are outlined in Paper 5:4.5, as follows:

"All religions teach the worship of Deity and some doctrine of human salvation. The Buddhist religion promises salvation from suffering, unending peace; the Jewish religion promises salvation from difficulties, prosperity predicated on righteousness; the Greek religion promised salvation from disharmony, ugliness, by the realization of beauty; Christianity promises salvation from sin, sanctity; Mohammedanism provides deliverance from the rigorous moral standards of Judaism and Christianity. The religion of Jesus is salvation from self, deliverance from the evils of creature isolation in time and in eternity."

Sonship refers to a person who, with a sincere, forgiven and loving heart, shares herself or himself with God. We share our hearts and minds with those people we love—our brothers and sisters, our parents, our partner, our children. Sonship sees us sharing ourselves with our divine Parents. Sonship with God is a communion with God that bestows a sublime, wholehearted, wholly personal and purely spiritual faith in God.

The life of Jesus

The life of Jesus of Nazareth was able to be understood and followed by humanity in two ways: the religion of personal experience in doing the will of God and serving humanity as spiritual siblings—Jesus' own personal religion; and the religion of worshipping the glorified Jesus and serving the Church, the fellow believers in the divine Christ. Sonship with God enables you to believe not only *in* Jesus but also *with* him, believing not only *what* he believed, but also *as* he believed. The son of God shares with Jesus his transcendent faith in the realness and sovereignty of the love of God. In full confidence that matches Jesus' confidence, the son of God accepts the security of the assurance of sonship with the heavenly Father.

Accepting the challenge

Having traveled to some extent with Buddhism and Christianity and being challenged to find the spiritual experience within the Urantia papers, I have to say that I love what sonship has made me into, what it has given me, what it has rescued me out of and steered me away from. I love what sonship does for other people, just like you. Most of all, I love taking adventures in faith based solely upon the virtues of my sonship with God the Father. This book, then, is a collection of stories about unimaginable events as they occurred in the life of pretty ordinary people. They are not so much stories about the author, as glimpses into the ways that God acts as a parent.

In writing this book, I am not presuming to interpret the Urantia papers (there are scholars enough to do that task) so much as to reflect upon events and understandings that closely resemble Jesus' gospel in the Urantia papers and the spirit of that extraordinary revelation itself.

A passing familiarity with the Urantia papers and the Bible is assumed of the reader.

Divine Persons

I employ the term "God" to refer to certain divinely creative persons. These persons have character and purpose. They have desires, they plan and prepare, and they make decisions on our behalf and with our consent. They act on both broadly universal and intimately personal levels. Religions that have realized a creative God acknowledge this.

We search for happiness, meaningful human relationships and rewarding careers. Beyond these goals, the deeper dimensions of spirituality are given to humanity only via insight into the nature of these divinely creative persons, association with them and the adoption of their ways. The stories in this book convey significant glimpses into all three persons of the Trinity and, it is hoped, will help the reader of the Urantia papers to better engage these deeper dimensions of their own spirituality.

Stories

They are stories about your divine creator Parents, and how they have acted in the lives of some of their children on earth. These stories will bring you closer to God, as a little child with a pure and believing heart is brought closer to his or her own parents by acts of love and kindness.

In a very real sense, these stories are fuel for your divine Parents to employ in your life, as much as they are for you to employ in theirs. They are written for your joy and your prosperity, with much devotion to your well being—that you might prosper in all things spiritual and be a mighty blessing throughout all of your days.

Names

To read this book is to spend time with Jesus and with others whose names will doubtless be an initial obstacle to you: people like *Christ Michael,* your *Thought Adjuster, Mother Spirit of Nebadon, God the Father* and even the term *Urantia* papers. But this book is unique in that it is the witness of a man who lives very close to God. While these terms and names may be new to you, please recall that they were once new also to the author. Yet, behind the names, there exist extraordinary divine persons. They have you in their heart. Your name is on their prayerful lips and in their loving hearts, even now as you read these words and give thought to them. To read this book is to meet the fount of hope in the world and in the eternity beyond—beyond all the Buddhas; beyond all the Saints and the angels; beyond reincarnation; beyond hell; beyond all that the world has known of God to date.

Foreign land

For most readers, this book will be like a foreign land. The Urantia papers present new and unusual terminology and a host of complex problems to the average man and woman of our day who seek simple solutions to sophisticated problems of living.

When we enter a foreign land though, because our heart has sent us on that journey, we find little that is familiar to us. Even the food is strange and unsettling. But our heart calls us to remember that the customs and the food that are feeding the millions who dwell there, can also feed us. Our heart calls us to have faith in their life and what it may bring to us. It calls us to have a bigger faith than that to which we are accustomed so that we can adapt and grow into an appreciation of their ways. We are called to let the journey completely reinvent us. Jesus came into the world that we might have life. He does not bring us our own food but the food of another people—those into whose likeness we are growing. The characters in this book, and their kind of food, change our life.

The contents of the book

In this book I am endeavouring to bridge experiences that God brings to the reader of the Bible and the reader of the Urantia papers. I also seek to form a bridge for people to cross to the Father from spiritual arenas other than those that directly look to Jesus and his life and teachings.

The book speaks of finding the person of God the Father, the person of Christ and the person of the Holy Spirit, and their immediate place in our life. Perennial questions around death, resurrection and reincarnation are addressed from the Urantia papers perspective. Spiritual empowerment is discussed as it relates to sonship with the Father and the baptism of the Holy Spirit. Epochal revelations are introduced, particularly with a view to helping Bible believers to receive the Father's anointing which will help them appreciate the context in which the Bible and its Word of God exists.

The greater part of this book focusses on living with the adjustments to our thinking and consciousness that our heavenly Father seeds in our hearts and minds as he brings us into perfect sonship with him. The Urantia papers call this role of the Father within us the Thought Adjuster. It is his work to enable us willingly to be perfect as the Father in heaven is perfect. Such perfection, dear reader, is the highest goal given to us.

Many Christians will consider this to be a work of the devil.

The Father is my only defence on that issue, and I plead the life, the teachings, the ministry, the death, the blood, the name, the resurrection, the ascension, Pentecost, the sovereign Lordship and the on-going ministry in the world of Jesus of Nazareth, the Son of God who was born flesh for our sakes through the will of God the Father. I fully expect all that is in the truth, the beauty and the goodness of God to stand in defence of that criticism against this sonship with God about which I am writing. It is my sincere wish that, in responding to God's call on my heart to write this book, that your journey with me in it will help enable God to free you from burdens, strongholds and yokes; will give you what it takes for you to be happier and not miserable; will enlighten you and not deceive or mislead you but will be a beacon of our Father's mighty light and love for you.

When you read this book, it may well benefit you to have open a copy of the Urantia papers and the New Revised Standard Version Bible—or your preferred Bible translation—for reference.

Please forgive me if I am found failing to write to your own level of expertise or simplicity or viewpoint—our Father will surely bring another to you who will translate the immense blessings of sonship within the Urantia papers to you in a more suitable form.

❧

Father, bless this reader please, with the immense gratification and destiny that is within the knowledge and reality of their sonship with you, that she or he might be a blessing to all existence.

❧

I have written this book to the eternal honour and glorification of our sharing the mind of God. May it foster in your life an abundance of divine goodness, truth, beauty and enthusiasm to be perfect as God our Father is perfect, to your immense well being, creativity, usefulness and happiness and to the benefit of all creation.

❧

Chapter 1

Sonship with God the Thought Adjuster

In March of 1993, I was exhausted and spiritually depleted—desperately in need of a solution to life as it was. If you saw that on a rose bush, you'd prune it right back to the strongest bud. I wanted to be free of all the entanglements, the baggage, the weight of caring and the poverty of being uncared for. You must surely know how it is. I felt an intense depth of need to get back to the source of what life, and my life in particular, was all about. I needed spiritual retreat, away from everything but my God—and I needed a new God. The endlessness of the carnage and the meaninglessness of the despair and depravity of the drug users with which I worked had pretty much consumed the spiritual portion with which I was equipped when I first commenced detoxing heroin addicts some years prior. I'd had enough.

A word from God assured me that it was a good thing to have a couple of weeks off work, so I made arrangements to go on leave and finished up that afternoon. For a few weeks prior, I had had the occasional thought about going back to the Buddhist monastery in Singapore in which I was once ordained. Considering that an overseas trip for its own sake was not really going to achieve all that much benefit, I had, however, given these thoughts little attention. I treated them as seeds of a bye gone season.

Shortly into my retreat from the busy scenes of life, I clearly perceived that the next fortnight would realistically need to be spent in the achievement of real spiritual contact with God. I shuddered to think that if I did not attain this degree of solitude in my own home, which was unlikely with Mary around, then I would be in just as terrible a shape when I returned to work and my leave would have amounted to nothing.

When I was alone out in the flower garden in our home however, whilst I was feeling the intensity of my spiritual hunger, God whispered in my heart about going again to my old monastery. I gently put down my tools, sat down on the grass under the shade of a young maple tree, and while I casually surveyed the garden in its wonderful late summer bloom, I brought myself into agreement with his desire.

At Kong Meng San, Singapore

I telephoned the temple and made arrangements with an old friend and brother monk. A couple of days later I found myself standing within the precincts of the main prayer hall, quietly chatting in the warm evening stillness with a local Singapore taxi driver who had dropped in to say his prayers before retiring for the night. Our company was sweetly honest. While we quietly chatted with each other, I thanked God for this fellow's presence: he was a kindly welcome back to the place that was once my home in Singapore. I knew beyond the shadow of a doubt that I was in the right place at the right time. After he left, I dropped my bag off in the room allocated to me by the head monk, befriended the temple dogs that ferociously guard such places at night, and as I quietly walked around the beautiful temple grounds in the stillness of that late night, I knew my God was with me. I walked with him through this very familiar tropical garden, the one that Su Fu Hong Choon, my late abbot, had so lovingly designed. I relaxed in the assurance of knowing God's desire for my complete replenishment.

My accommodation was in a relatively new building, which was constructed exclusively to house monks, and each room had a small adjoining toilet and wash room, and a ceiling fan. All quite lavish really. I spent most of my days and nights locked in my room, letting myself out pretty much only to eat when all was quiet and I wouldn't be involved in conversation. I spent the days in prayer, occasionally reading, and plunging deeply into whatever it was that my life had become since leaving these tranquil halls ten years before. With every day, I felt myself less burdened with my world. It was natural to consider the place of the monastic vocation in my life—it all seemed so much more valuable now, in new ways previously not known to me, that had been brought on by being at the coal face of human misery for a few years.

Renewal dawns

On the seventh day, I seemed to come to the end of knowing my inner burden. I had eaten lunch off campus, sharing a little time with a delightful Muslim couple who had a food stall in the nearby industrial area. They were across the road from those bizarre funeral directors that make paper cars and combustibles for Chinese funerals; and we made considerable conversation around that topic. He had fought the Japanese in Penang when he was a young man, and delighted in the re-telling of how he wielded a now ancient Bofor anti-aircraft gun. Their son had just been called up into military service in Singapore, and they bemoaned the fact of its interruption to his university schooling. She was clearly the financier of the family; he like many Malaysian men, was an excellent chef. There was a sort of family fellowship among us somehow, with so many things in common, and the uncommon things rarely getting a mention, as is the way with such ships in the night.

Many hours later, the temple grounds drew to a hush. The lights in each cell went out one by one. The last of the old women finished saying her prayers and tootled off to bed after a long day of cooking and cleaning and selflessly doing a million and one things around the temple for the love of her God. Monasteries tend to come to life early in the day and so by 10 p.m. it entered its own kind of silence. It is a silence of God's rest. It is guarded over by those crazy dogs that wail like banshees all through the night, and the invisible servants of the Most Highs who are so graphically portrayed in life size statues adorning every building and shrine within the temple grounds; and by God himself.

On the evening of this seventh day in retreat, I had entered into a rather strange sleep at around 8 p.m. I awoke about an hour and a half later having slept very soundly. I was refreshed. I was back in my body, feeling physically recuperated from the exhaustion that had brought me to Singapore, and my body was again an OK kind of a place to be. Upon waking, my mind naturally came to rest upon spiritual matters and, in particular, the current state of my own spirituality. Over the next four hours I revisited the nature of my God and the goals I had pursued over the past twenty some years, doing a personal inventory as it is called in other disciplines. As I searched through the roots of my current position in life, my attention fell upon the history of those experiences that led to the crossroads that had provoked major decisions. I followed the trail of how they had shaped my thinking. My thoughts fell onto my empathy with God and his for me. My memories thumbed through my journey through

Buddhism; my struggle with Christian Theology College in an early and strangling attempt to find spirituality in the west; the recognition that the Urantia papers were the scriptures of my religion; and the struggle to find and embody the spirituality alluded to within their pages.

The unexpected visitor

At ten past two on the morning of the eighth day, as these hours of deep spiritual reflection continued, I had an unannounced and wholly unexpected visitor. In an instant, and much to my surprise, without warning, the room suddenly filled up with the glory of God. Immediately, I was in the presence of my Thought Adjuster. Love saturated the room. His love soaked my every fibre to the core. He "stood" outside me, in the room with me, as another person. My room was a mess. I was a mess. And here in the midst of this mess, I was standing in the direct presence of God. His glory, his divinity, was so incredibly present it was almost palpable. He was very definite in his attempts to manifest himself to me. He was inescapable, unavoidable: utterly magnetic. His ability to be personal was simply awesome. He was so present that if someone were to have come into the room, they surely would have fallen flat on their face in worship. I was speechless.

Then as quickly as he appeared, with utmost precision, he spoke into my heart, saying, "I am your Father, Robert, and you are my son." And with those few words, he completed in me the highest goal I had ever conceived, sonship with God—the goal that Jesus of Nazareth had proclaimed so long ago, and so perfectly, for all humankind.

I had known the presence of God for many years, but it was absolutely extraordinary for me that the God I had always known internally, should be standing in front of me in this manner. Imagine that you are in the same room, only a metre apart from the person whom you love the most. Then amplify that by a thousandfold. You feel them deeply and know them on the inside of you whilst simultaneously they are standing there in front of you: your inner and the outer worlds are completely unbroken, totally unified.

Still he lingered.

He gave me the opportunity to discuss things, to commune

with him, as I imagine Jesus had communed with the Father. But I was too emotionally overcome. I was just about jumping out of my skin with ecstasy, enthusiasm and astonishment over the most profound sense of completeness he had brought to me. I have since learned to be in communion with him, in a leisurely way, but in those days the sheer impact of the experience was totally moving for me. Upon reflection, I can understand something of Peter unavoidably falling on his face all a-tremble on the occasion of Jesus' transfiguration on Mount Hermon.[1]

The completion within sonship

The completeness of perfection that my Father illuminated in me was absolute, total, and sublimely personal. I was a totally whole person, both human and divine in one form. I wasn't any smarter, just complete. I knew a total completion to my spiritual search. There was nothing else I needed spiritually—the spiritual and the divine had perfectly met the personal and the human. In a mystical manner, I felt my sonship expand all across the universe, commensurate with his Fatherhood, transcending the realm of matter, space and time. I comprehended what was right and wrong in God's view, and his revelation of sonship made me spiritually right with him. This sense of completeness included a sense of destiny and career: I felt my past and my infinite future occupying a single stream of consciousness which had its roots in my own divine Father's personal presence throughout all infinity. The experience of sonship dwarfed my earlier Buddhist enlightenment experience of original mind. A certain personal quality, which was lacking in the absoluteness of "original mind", was suddenly filled. Everything Buddhist in me was transcended in an instant, and my life issued directly from my Paradise Father who was both indwelling me and at the centre of all creation and pre-creation.

I felt that by my Father's grace and skill, I had partaken of the spirit-consciousness, the actuality of sonship with God, spoken of in the Urantia papers 196:3.28:

> "The great challenge to modern man is to achieve better communication with the divine Monitor that dwells within the human mind. Man's greatest adventure in the flesh consists in the well-balanced and sane effort to advance the borders of self-consciousness out through the dim realms of

embryonic soul-consciousness in a wholehearted effort to reach the borderland of spirit-consciousness—contact with the divine presence. Such an experience constitutes God-consciousness, an experience mightily confirmative of the pre-existent truth of the religious experience of knowing God. Such spirit-consciousness is the equivalent of the knowledge of the actuality of sonship with God. Otherwise, the assurance of sonship is the experience of faith."

I had had direct experience of this "actuality of sonship with God," and the way it cuts through the type of faith that has not yet been literally contacted by the person of God, in all his divinity. I had been contacted by God the Father, the Father with whom Jesus communed, and it had completely satisfied and altered me spiritually. I have no doubt that there exist profound differences in the scope of experience known to a Creator Son of God who has incarnated in the flesh on earth for the purposes of outworking issues of immense universe proportions, and that of one of his mortal creatures: but communion with the Father is an act of perfection and deep satisfaction on any level of existence.

Whilst my spirit was reacting ecstatically to this creation of sonship, my Father managed to communicate a qualifying fact to me that I found to be simply magnificent.

"I am the sovereign source of all that is," he said; "of all that has been, and all that ever will be. You are my son, Robert. You are heir to and a partaker of this my absolute sovereignty. You and I are not separate in this authority in all the universes, whether in time or in eternity."

The provision, the freedom, the responsibility, the destiny in that statement, I felt, was utterly limitless in its truthfulness, its beauty, its goodness and its eternal assurance. It was in fact the Universal Father, the God of all creation, the First Source and Centre of all things and beings[2] confirming his own truth in person with one of his sons.

The authority within sonship

On this occasion and at that time in my life, God, my Father, revealed the fact that, in his view, I had sonship with him. It is one thing to ponder that idea, to even embrace the philosophy of that ideal, or to read about Jesus preaching that concept in his life and teachings on earth. It is a whole other matter, which is recorded in Paradise, to hear it and receive the fact of it in person from God himself.

Dear reader, I wish upon you with all my being that you might speedily pursue and be met by God your Father. You will be freed from an orphanhood you can barely recognise at present. You will know the actuality of sonship with God. Jesus, "brought to God, as a man of the realm, the greatest of all offerings. Similarly, you will find that this actuality of sonship will equip you to bring to God the greatest of all offerings: the consecration and dedication of your own will to the majestic service of doing the divine will."[3] The thrill of being equipped so, will be truly unparalleled in all your experience.

I feel the inadequacy of my own words to convey to you the extraordinary impact of sonship, and so I will draw your attention to one of the Urantia papers portraits of our lovely brother Jesus. I wish to encourage you, by giving you my own witness, that all that is in his experience of sonship is fully available for you too. Sonship is not measured out to us according to our own efforts, but by the grace of our own Father in heaven who touches the child-like heart and mind within each of us. This is their portrait dear reader; I pray that you let it be yours:

"Jesus always and consistently interpreted religion wholly in terms of the Father's will. When you study the career of the Master, as concerns prayer or any other feature of the religious life, look not so much for what he taught as for what he did. Jesus never prayed as a religious duty. To him prayer was a sincere expression of spiritual attitude, a declaration of soul loyalty, a recital of personal devotion, an expression of thanksgiving, an avoidance of emotional tension, a prevention of conflict, an exaltation of intellection, an ennoblement of desire, a vindication of moral decision, an enrichment of thought, an invigoration of higher inclinations, a consecration of impulse, a clarification of viewpoint, a declaration of faith, a transcendental surrender of will, a sublime assertion of confidence, a revelation of courage, the proclamation of discovery, a confession of supreme devotion, the validation of consecration, a technique for the adjustment of difficulties, and the mighty mobilisation of the combined soul powers to withstand all human tendencies toward selfishness, evil, and sin. He lived just such a life of prayerful consecration to the doing of his Father's will and ended his life triumphantly with just such a prayer. The secret of his unparalleled religious life was this consciousness of the presence of God; and he attained it by intelligent prayer and sincere worship—unbroken communion with God—and not by leadings, voices, visions, or extraordinary religious practices."[4]

Being a son of God, not because I believed in sonship but because I had experienced God himself believing it of me, meant for me a number of things. It meant that God considered himself to be a father in his own mind. It meant that the strength and power of my sonship came not by my design but through his design. Sonship meant that God my Father was the source of my existence, my life, my love, my hope, my faith and the very best goals for my will and my desire. My sonship emerged directly from him, as does yours beloved.

Orphanhood

Its emergence made me acutely aware of the orphanhood to which non-sons of God are subjected. The Urantia papers portray Jesus teaching the Indian boy Ganid, saying, "Your Buddha was much better than your Buddhism. Buddha was a great man, even a prophet to his people, but he was an orphan prophet; by that I mean that he early lost sight of his spiritual Father, the Father in heaven."[5] Sonship will forever lift you above all that Buddha was unable to grasp—freedom from divine orphanhood. This was also true in my own Buddhist experience. I found that the primary goal of fulfilment and divine truth gained by the recognition of one's "original face" was, as Buddhism promised, extraordinary. However, after the dust settled, it still left me with a sense of orphanhood which was only completely exhausted by sonship with the Father and then later embellished through local universe sonship with Michael and the Mother Spirit of Nebadon.

The experience of receiving God's sonship is identical to the boy orphan who sees his own sonship in his original genetic parents. Suddenly, he cries out with glee and runs to their embrace, for this sonship is his own absolute assurance regarding the nature and truth about his human existence. So too, in like manner, you run to your divine Father's embrace the instant he reveals his Fatherhood and your sonship.

From out of the belly of Jesus' own sonship, he said to us:

"The kingdom of heaven is also like a merchant seeking goodly pearls; and having found one pearl of great price, he went out and sold everything he possessed that he might be able to buy the extraordinary pearl."[6]

Sonship is the pearl.

Jesus' "kingdom" is sonship

Jesus continues to guide us today with his words about the central significance of sonship, saying, "Your message to the world shall be: Seek first the kingdom of God and his righteousness, and in finding these, all other things essential to eternal survival shall be secured therewith. And now would I make it plain to you that this kingdom of my Father will not come with an outward show of power or with unseemly demonstration. You are not to go hence in the proclamation of the kingdom, saying, 'it is here' or 'it is there,' for this kingdom of which you preach is God within you."[7] And again, "Seek first the kingdom of God, and when you have found entrance thereto, all things needful shall be added to you. Be not, therefore, unduly anxious for the morrow. Sufficient for the day is the trouble thereof."[8] Beloved reader, the kingdom of God is the sonship your own Father bestows upon you as a free gift. It is fully yours when you truly know each other as Father and son, or Father and daughter as the case may be—for sonship is a gender-free divine appellation in the Urantia papers, not a mortal expression of gender bias. If this experience I am referring to is unknown to you, then I exhort you to have faith in my own experience with our Father, and appeal to him so you can receive sonship for yourself also.

For me, this sonship was the exalted culmination of an ambition I set myself at the age of five, when I first promised myself that I would find and know God. This reality called Fatherhood, and its associated sonship, was for me far greater, far more satisfying, far more real, far more absolute than the enlightenment promised by realising "self mind,"[9] "original mind,"[10] as experienced by the oriental seekers of a pre-personal God. At the age of 42 years, 37 years after I had first heard a preacher announce the news that there was a personal God who created heaven and earth, I had at last found God and he had found me in a spiritual liaison which presented total and enduring, inner, personal gratification. God was now my Father, and I was now God's son.

By three o'clock in the morning, on the eighth day of my stay in that Chinese Buddhist monastery, I was feeling pretty good! I had my victory.

❧

Notes

1. 158:1.10 {While Peter was...}
2. 1:0.1 {The Universal Father...}
3. 196:0.10
4. 196:0.10
5. 132:7.4
6. 151:4.5
7. 140:1.5
8. 140:6.13
9. See, for example: Godman, D. 1985. "The Teachings Of Sri Ramana Maharshi." Arkana, London.
10. See, for example: Chang, Garma C. C. 1959. "The Practice Of Zen." Harper & Row. New York.
    Also see: Schloegl, I. 1976. "The Zen Teaching Of Rinzai." Shambhala. Berkley.

❧

Chapter 2

Spreading the message of sonship with God

When my Thought Adjuster appeared to me and conveyed the fact of his Fatherhood of me, and my sonship with him, I slept little that night, and over the remaining days of my retreat at Kong Meng San Temple in Singapore, my will moved across a range of matters. Sonship brought with it an indefatigable desire to serve my Father's interests in the world of his orphan children.

Confirming the right of passage

I appealed to heavenly authorities, stating my belief that this teaching about one's sonship with God needed to become a mainstream religious expression and spiritual channel on earth. I perceived in my Father's will that the gospel of Jesus, as it is portrayed in the Urantia papers, needed to be given optimum support. It needed evangelists, missionaries, schools and worship centres. Magnificently, and much to the surprise of my human emotions I was told, "We agree."

Equipped with what I experienced as the divine right of passage to proceed along these lines, my mind turned to how to go about sharing sonship with people in the context of the Urantia papers. My starting point was simple, comprising two things, one theoretical and the other experiential. It was clear to me that the Urantia papers held the greatest exposition on sonship that this world had ever seen. Believers who wanted to experience the Father's sonship would benefit tremendously from a sincere study of them. Additionally, believers would need the direct experience of the Father's sonship through contact with him. It was clear to me that the believing son of God should have both, and that my Father was totally committed to bringing this about in all who would believe and seek and receive and learn of his love.

Finding the gospel

I looked through part four of the Urantia papers, the "Life and Teachings of Jesus," and it quickly dawned on me that I really didn't know much at all about what they had to say about sonship. There I was, filled to overflowing with the spiritual experience of sonship, yet I had no language with which to convey its magnificence to another living soul. Most of my spiritual experience had been couched in Buddhist terms, despite having been profoundly moved over the years by a few experiences in Urantia papers' terms. As I looked through the chapters on Jesus' life and teachings, I realised how precious they were as a primary source of information, and how little I had studied them. For more than twenty years, all my reading and studies of the Urantia papers had been about Adjuster fusion, the history of the world and its religious development, and the management structure of the universe of universes. I had been wounded by Christians early on in my life, bamboozled by the Bible, disappointed by the non-existence of spirituality in the Church and, although I had been met by Jesus Christ on a couple of life-changing occasions, I had never found a meaningful entrance into the study of his life and teachings until now.

In the light of the presence of such a magnificent and on-going communion with God the Father, I felt an extraordinary barrenness about having such little practical understanding of Jesus' gospel about the Fatherhood of God and its corollary of sonship. I really had no idea what Jesus had to say about sonship with my Father. I had no understanding of the values that he lived by, died by, resurrected himself by; and they were all singularly centred on the fact that he experienced God as his Father.

Seeking Jesus and his sonship with God

Having been in the presence of God and having had the very heart and soul of sonship transmitted to me by the divine source of that most real grace called Fatherhood, I truly hungered to know what Jesus knew about sonship. It became an immediate and passionate goal. Like the Greeks who said, "We would see Jesus,"[1] I desired more than any other thing to know my lovely brother, Jesus, the man, the son of God, and his experience of sonship.

Having already engaged study at Christian Theology College, I knew that the Bible would not deliver to me the man who was Jesus the son of God. Most certainly, it would deliver Paul's Jesus Christ the promised saviour of the Jew and the Gentile, and Christ Jesus the Son of God. So too, it would deliver the Book of Enoch's "Son of Man." It takes, by the grace of God however, the Urantia papers to deliver to us Jesus the human man of Galilee, and his sonship with God. It was to this man and his experience of sonship that I now turned, as a student, a believer and a brother.

Throughout the eighties and nineties, I had conducted spiritual groups and retreats in Australia. I perceived in the will of my Father for me, the desire to conduct a similar retreat in Melbourne over the five day Easter holiday soon after my return from Singapore. I immediately began planning for it from my room in Singapore. I drew up a list of some twenty people, all but one or two of whom had been first exposed to the Urantia papers in groups I had facilitated some years before. I designed the retreat to focus on Jesus' journey from Palm Sunday to resurrection Monday and his own gospel of the Fatherhood of God. We would gather on Palm Sunday and read and pray together. I would teach a little. Then on every evening for the next few days, people would pair up and read through the successive chapters until we met at the camp on Thursday evening for the retreat.

In my spirit I knew it would be very powerful, a sacred time, a time where the freshness of this incredible experience with my Father would overflow into the hearts and souls of my friends who would be participating. More than that though, it thrilled me to serve their Thought Adjusters in this manner, and it sent me into an ecstasy of worship when I considered that I would be serving the great and mighty Michael of this universe. So concentrated was the ecstasy that I would be immobilised, and my whole being would flood the universe in a profound abandonment of unabashed love for Michael of Nebadon and my Paradise Father. I did not yet know Michael as my father in those days, but I conceived of him as the most pure human fount of revelation regarding my newly acquired sonship. I adored him unbidden.

Jesus' gospel

It took me a while to find what it was that Jesus actually referred to when he invited people to share his kind of sonship. Others of course may have different interpretations, but I like to

39

use 141:6.4-5 of the Urantia papers when I point out the gospel of Jesus. These passages state, "Jesus said, 'This is the kingdom of heaven: God is your Father and you are his sons, and this good news, if you wholeheartedly believe it, is your eternal salvation.' 'When you enter the kingdom of heaven, you shall be baptized with the Spirit.' 'When you enter the kingdom, you are reborn.'"

I knew these words of Jesus to be one hundred percent true, as stated. Equipped with this scriptural understanding of the gospel, and empowered by my own Father's anointing of sonship, I launched into the preparations for the retreat in his name.

God my Father had certainly given me unshakeable evidence of the facts about which Jesus had preached when he spoke on sonship. Similarly, he had given me confirmation of other matters that were related to Adjuster fusion.[2] In his revelation of his Fatherhood, God had given to me the experience of the essence of Jesus' own gospel and truth—even the truth with which he lives and reigns in heaven as a Master Michael.[3] His gospel had spiritual power and authority to it. It was a reliable way to the Father. I knew that now. I now fully believed in myself; and in my Father; and in the gospel; and that people should receive it and prosper enormously from it.

One of the most thrilling passages in the Urantia papers for me, is a moment of Jesus' last group prayer on the night he was betrayed. I see this as a direct statement by Jesus to every human son of God—male, female, young or old:

"And now, my Father, I would pray not only for these eleven men but also for all others who now believe, or who may hereafter believe the gospel of the kingdom through the word of their future ministry. I want them all to be one, even as you and I are one. You are in me and I am in you, and I desire that these believers likewise be in us; that both of our spirits indwell them. If my children are one as we are one, and if they love one another as I have loved them, all men will then believe that I came forth from you and be willing to receive the revelation of truth and glory which I have made. The glory which you gave me I have revealed to these believers. As you have lived with me in spirit, so have I lived with them in the flesh. As you have been one with me, so have I been one with them, and so will the new teacher ever be one with them and in them. And all this have I done that my brethren in the flesh may know that the Father loves them even as does the Son, and that you love them even as you love me. Father, work with me to save these believers that they may presently come to be with me in glory and then go on to join you in the Paradise embrace. Those who serve with me in humiliation, I would have with me in glory so that they may see all you have given into my hands as the eternal harvest of the seed sowing of time in the likeness of mortal flesh. I long to show my Earthly brethren the glory I had with you before the founding of this world. This world knows very little of you, righteous Father, but I know you, and I have made you known to these believers, and they will make known your name to other generations. And now I promise them that you will be with them in the world even as you have been with me—even so."[4]

Having experienced sonship directly with my Father, I was now one of those "others who now believe," for whom Jesus himself was praying with his Father, my Father, on this last night on earth in the flesh. I was one of those who would help others to "believe the gospel of the kingdom through the word of their future ministry." I really wanted to receive the full impact of Jesus' "desire that these believers likewise be in us; that both of our spirits indwell them." I profoundly loved people, for I was filled with the love that Jesus has for us. It was a passion for me to let my Father find ways through my works to show that he "loves them even as does the Son." I knew that when Jesus prayed saying, "Father, work with me to save these believers that they may presently come to be with me in glory and then go on to join you in the Paradise embrace," that he extended to me the same support and that if I were to offer a ministry of my Father's sonship to these people whom I loved, both he and my Father would actively work together to create their passage to glory and the Paradise embrace. I was one of those believers on earth now who would, "make known your name to other generations."

I was absolutely ecstatic with the idea of serving Jesus and my Father. Nothing had ever given me such incredibly worship-based enthusiasm and energy like this: not Buddhism and its enlightenment experience; not victory over evil; not the transcendence of reincarnation; not even a spiritual death on the cross. To be fully awake in sonship, with a mission, has to be one of the most exhilarating experiences on earth!

Jesus' parable of the marriage feast

Of the twenty loved ones who were invited, most declined to come on the retreat. Those who declined comprised the readers who intellectualised the papers, and those with little interest in seeking God or knowing Jesus.

Mary, my wife, and I added to the remaining group of believers, a few clients of the drug rehab at which I worked. It reminded me of Jesus' parable of the marriage feast,[5] where the invited and esteemed guests decline, and so the doors are thrown open to the neglected.

Needless to say, the retreat was life changing for all of us, as these types of events usually are for believers who are made more real by the factuality of their faith and real association with the divine. The most astounding thing that impressed us all, was that God the Father was so profoundly present in our midst, working for the sake of that perfection called sonship. The clients of the drug rehab tasted the real heaven, for the first time in their lives.

The Singapore retreat was another milestone in my life. I am counting these kinds of milestones as I write this chapter, and there appear to have been around a dozen of similar magnitude in my now fifty years. It was a peak, the occasion of discovering the highest spiritual reality I could then imagine. The Easter retreat in April was the overflow and the growth that issued from that peak experience.

I conducted another retreat for believers over Father's Day weekend, and another over Mother's Day weekend. Gradually, sonship was embracing the concepts around Jesus, Michael, Mother Spirit, the indwelling Thought Adjuster, the Paradise Father and the human spiritual journey into Adjuster fusion—all of these being central to the spirituality of the Urantia papers. Gradually, my journey in sonship itself was moulding me into the kind of vessel that could pour out the new wine of the Urantia papers' message of sonship to people. These early retreats gave evidence to me that the message was true. God honoured his revelation, by changing peoples' lives. Faith found its author, and the Spirit of God quickened the human spirit in its spiritual hunger and thirst for righteousness.

I recently spoke with one of the drug users who attended that first retreat, now seven years on. He stated how that single event had been a primary beacon for his life ever since. For the first time in his life, he had experienced what it was like to be a spiritual human being. Since then he has had hard days. He has had several heroin habits; been in prison a few times; separated from his partner; raised his little girl as a single parent; had a stroke and a heart attack; done rehab a couple of times; and lost it all, so to speak. Now, he claims, he's tired of it all; he wants to live for Christ alone. The retreat, he said, was the only thing that kept him going: he wanted one day to return to the kind of person he was when he was sharing the mind of God like he did in our company.

❧

Notes

1. 139:5.9 {The inability of...}; John 12:21 KJV
2. 112:7.1 {Thought Adjuster fusion...}
3. 21:5.1 {The power of...}
4. 182:1.6
5. 173:5.2 {The kingdom of...}; Matthew 22:10

❧

Chapter 3

Sonship with Christ Michael

October is a lovely month in Melbourne. The roses have their first blooms and the heavily scented winter freesias, jonquils and earlicheers give way to the spring.

Sonship and Pentecost

In October 1993, six months after my Singapore experience of sonship, Kenneth and Gloria Copeland, Jerry Savelle and Jesse Duplantis came to Melbourne from the U.S. and conducted a 6-day Christian revival crusade. I had watched Ken's television broadcast from time to time over the years since leaving Theology College, in an effort to understand the Christian experience and perspective. I was interested in being with him live in Melbourne.

In the course of running the Urantia papers retreats on sonship, and taking the newly found divine realities of sonship into my work in the drug withdrawal program, my world view on sonship had grown considerably. What also had grown was the intensity of my search for greater knowledge of my Father and greater contact with him in the world. I had become passionately hungry for knowledge of Jesus, discernment of the Father in Jesus, and for mastery in my life so that the Father and I might do the works that Jesus said believers would do.[1] These American evangelists showed me the Jesus of the Day of Pentecost, with their praise and worship, their sense of barnstorming the kingdom of heaven, their healing and anointing, their "getting saved" publicly in front of thousands of people, and their baptism of the Holy Spirit and fire and speaking in tongues. I had never been in a meeting like this before. I took to the spirit of the love of God that I found there, like a duck to water.

Chicken bones in the soup

A Christian preacher and friend of mine named Kwesi, originally from Ghana, once told me, "Rob, you can never go to a Christian Church and be fully satisfied. People are too different and diverse in the Lord. No one person will ever tell you only the things you will always agree with. Being in the gathering of the faithful is like eating chicken soup: you'll always come across a bone. But when you come across the bone, don't throw away the whole bowl of soup, just put the bone to one side and keep sipping the soup."

There was a truckload of bones for me in that Pentecostal bowl of chicken soup! But I did get revival. I did see my Father in the actions of these Christians. I did come to know Jesus more intimately. I did encounter the Holy Spirit in new ways; and I did become a better son of God through their efforts—and that's what the chicken soup is all about.

I wonder what kinds of bones you have found in the Urantia papers bowl of chicken soup. I know I found a good few. Jesus taught us about putting aside the chicken bones, in his teaching to Nathaniel.[2] For Kwesi, like a lot of Christians, the fact that the Urantia papers were not of Biblical authority, represented a significant chicken bone, so I think he just went on sipping the Biblical soup. He sipped it well too. Personally I hope he didn't completely miss out on the incredible dimension that the Urantia papers add to the salvation Jesus brought to the world; but we all deal with our chicken bones the best we know how, readers of the Urantia papers included.

Revival was all over us

On the sixth day of that revival meeting, Mary and I attended the wedding of her nephew. By this time we were pretty much "on fire for God," as they say in those circles. Revival had gotten all over Mary. She had kicked and screamed all through the week, flatly refusing to go to any of the meetings, until she reluctantly went along on the fourth night. At that session, Jesse Duplantis played some foot-stompin', hand clappin', throat roarin' gospel rock and roll. Poor Mary didn't stand a chance. God had her in the palm of his hand in an instant, and she just melted on the spot. Our Father certainly has his ways with his children—he sure found her weak spot. By the time of the wedding on Saturday afternoon, Mary was as excited in spirit as was I. It was an extraordinary time of awakening in Mary's life and mine alike, for different reasons and with different catalysts.

It was a Saturday afternoon wedding. We took our wedding clothes with us and hurriedly changed in the car after the morning revival service, making a quick dash to the nearby Church for the wedding service. Our plans were to just as hurriedly dash back in between the service and the wedding supper planned for around 7pm that evening.

The wedding

The Church looked magnificent. It was Our Lady of Victories Basilica in Camberwell: very Catholic. The perfect place to engage the holiness of God. Flowers were everywhere inside the Church. Outside, the first spring roses were in full bud. We skipped up the stone steps and entered inside. Mary did her Catholic curtsy, and I did the deep bow of the Benedictines. Then we made our way up the aisle to sit about three of four rows from the front, on the right among the bride's family.

We chatted in hushed tones for a moment or two and then I settled back into the pew. I found myself slipping into a deeply meditative frame of mind. The glory of God then enfolded me like some great chief's cloak. I was still buoyant from the morning's revival meeting with Gloria Copeland, when I had publicly declared through the microphone to a packed house, all of the good things God had done for me that week. That the glory of God should fall on me was not anything special. After a moment or two, I gently looked about and noticed that people were busy finding their seats, directing others, shaking hands in greeting and occupying themselves with all of the things of a wedding in a Church. I presumed the glory of God had not fallen on them. What followed was amazing and, dare I say it, more glorious than the meeting with my Father in the Singapore monastery some six months earlier.

Another unexpected visitor

As I regained my settled compose in the pew, I sensed a spiritual being standing right beside me. He introduced himself, speaking into my spirit, saying:

"Rob, I am here with others on a mission to take you to meet your Lord and Father who is in Salvington, Michael of Nebadon."

I was too astonished to comment. I really didn't believe the thoughts of my spirit. I surveyed this concept, looked around at the Church full of people, and quietly said to myself, "Settle down Rob, pay attention to the wedding and see if you can get out of here without causing a stir." In moments, though, the fellow returned, bringing with him others of his kind. In my spirit, I could see them. He then proceeded to explain what they were going to do.

"Rob, these two," and he mentioned a name to describe them, but it didn't translate into English in my mind, "are going to wrap you firmly, to bind you for the flight." Then he went into considerable detail about the nature of some kind of spiritual flight on which I was about to embark, how long it was expected to take, where it would go and how they would distort the sense of time so that it fitted in with the events of the Church service which, incidentally, was starting—if they hadn't noticed!

By this time, he had my attention. But in walked the Priest. The Best Man and the Groom took their positions and nervously shuffled with each other, casting glances over various shoulders and fingering things in their pockets. And then came the entrance march. As a body, we were all on our feet. I gave a kind of furtive thought to my spirit companions, wondering how on earth they were going to pull off what had just been described to me. Finally, as Norma elegantly wafted down the aisle and past where Mary and I were standing, I left the whole thing in their hands to do with as they could. I still felt the weight of the glory of God on me though, and it left me curious as I smiled at Norma as she passed by on her way to Anthony at the altar. She really did look lovely.

In a moment, the Priest was reorganising the little gathering up near the altar, and saying a few appropriate words into the microphone. The public address system was turned down way too low to hear. A few minutes went by, someone sorted out the problem, on with the show, and then somehow, we were seated.

All wrapped up

Immediately, these ones whom Michael later termed to me, "Seraphim of my assignment," converged on me and I felt myself being wrapped up like a mummy. Three of these spirit fellows were working at a frantic pace. Whatever they were doing felt like they were wrapping lines of wire around me, like the fencing wire that is used on farms. It wasn't wire, it was a force, but it felt strong like wire and it kind of stuck to me. It didn't hurt in any way, it was simply absolutely firm, binding, and held me so that I couldn't move. Whilst my physical body was relaxed and serene because of the impact of the glory of God, my inner person was being bound firmly.

It took a couple of minutes before they stepped back and communicated to the one who had introduced the team to me, that all was in place and ready to go. Immediately, he thanked them and commanded them on their way. He drew close to me and said, "Try to maintain your composure when you meet Michael." Straight away, an angel appeared from nowhere, wrapped herself around me and more or less melted into the "wire" that now wrapped my spirit from head to foot. In an instant, and without so much as a glance to any of these workers, the angel suddenly took off like a rocket, with me in tow. I momentarily lost consciousness of the Church and the priest and the congregation as I felt myself hurtling away from the planet and into some kind of deeper than human spirit reality. The blast off had reminded me of something straight out of Cape Kennedy: in the spirit domain, it seemed that there were sparks flying and thunder roaring!

Lord! Send me!

As we journeyed, my consciousness seemed to become unified and I found myself able to participate in the Church service whilst consciously knowing I was spiritually engaged in some kind of fantastic journey to a spiritual destination about which I really knew very little. I was simultaneously bobbing up and down at the wedding priest's commands and mumbling out the odd hymn with glazed eyes as the service progressed, and hurtling through space in the embrace of an angel.

This was the second such occasion something like this had happened to me.

The first time had been around eighteen years previously when I had had an experience with Christ, and I've written about it in this book, concerning a spiritual experience of death on the cross. At the time of this wedding, however, I had no more of an idea about the human soul travelling into the vicinity of Christ Michael on Salvington of Nebadon than elephants flying to the moon. It simply wasn't in my level of awareness or in my expectations. I'd never heard of such a thing in the

Urantia papers, but, in the midst of experiencing what to all intents and purposes looked and felt like some kind of angelic flight at break-neck speed through a starry universe, I was willing to suspend my conclusions for a short while. Whilst I loved sonship, and I had come to love Jesus even more profoundly over the week of this revival crusade of the Copelands, nothing at all had intimated that I would journey in this way. I had been in dialogue with Christ Michael on the day before, the Friday morning, and the best I could imagine was that this journey was somehow connected to the matter we discussed.

What we discussed, emerged directly out of the topic on which Jerry Savelle had preached. He chose the passage about God looking all over the world for someone, anyone, to do his will:

> "Also I heard the voice of the Lord, saying, 'Whom shall I send, and who will go for us?' Then said I, 'here am I; send me.'"[3]

As I sat up in the balcony and meditated while he preached that Friday morning, I found myself suddenly in the presence of the same Jesus Christ I had met in the same visionary Great Hall eighteen years previously. He looked at me very affectionately, seeming to continue a conversation as if the past eighteen years were but a moment in time. He smiled and said:

"Will you do a global ministry Rob?"

I was speechless. His question took me totally by surprise. I knew nothing about such a thing. I was not equipped for such a thing. I felt like the least likely candidate in all the world for such a thing. And anyway, what kind of global ministry did he mean?

"You're kidding aren't you Sir?" I replied after a few minutes of soul searching.

"No I am not. Will you do a global ministry?" Jesus asked again.

I thought deeply on the matter until finally I came up with my best shot.

"The only way I could do a global ministry with you ... and what are we talking about here? ... a Urantia papers ministry or a Biblical ministry? ... is if you walk right in front of me and you don't take your next step until my front foot is right in your last footprint."

"That's fine with me. I agree."

Then, without further word, I found myself back in the auditorium where Jerry was still preaching. The whole event had only taken perhaps fifteen minutes, but somehow I seemed to have landed a contract with Jesus Christ, and I had no idea about its significance.

I really didn't know Jesus all that well. I knew Christianity even less. I thought that whatever a global ministry might have meant to him, because it was inconceivable to me, it would probably take twenty years to develop and that I need not pay too much attention to it right then and there. But a day later, there I was in Church whistling through the universe in my spirit, wrapped in the arms of an angel to go and visit with Christ Michael. It was all pretty sudden and totally unexpected.

What was more sudden and unexpected was the week that would follow. During that week I went through a spiritual preparation, an equipping for what he had in mind.

The wedding service went on and on. The journey to heaven went on and on, and deeper and deeper, and higher and higher.

Meeting Michael

Eventually we were seated again, for what would be a fairly lengthy sermon on the origins and virtues of marriage. As the Priest commenced to speak, my attention completely left the Church and its beautiful events. The angel kind of woke me up in-flight,[4] and I could see some unknown spiritual world all around me. She said we were close to our destination. To me, the atmosphere simply looked like brilliant light instead of starry and dark. There was atmosphere, presence to the environment, but I could see no forms, I simply sensed that we were close to another world, as it were, a planet: even the capital domain of that planet.

For want of a better word, we landed, on firm ground. I still couldn't see much more than fog all around me. This is not to say that it was a foggy day, rather that my sensitivity was insufficient to identify anything. The most that I could detect was that I was in some place, a world, that was completely divine. It was completely not like Earth. It felt familiar, in that it was welcoming, like home, but there was nothing I could identify to prove that, other than the fullness in my spirit of being much loved. Then, after a few moments, everything suddenly changed.

I felt someone draw close by my right side and lay a hand on my shoulder. Then he wheeled in front of me as he softly and tenderly said the words:

"Rob, I sent for you."

And my eyes opened.

"I want you to be with me here for a while so that we can know more about each other, and our mission together," he continued.

I was gazing into the person of Michael of Nebadon. He held my right hand as he gently spoke. Unbelievably, to all intents and purposes, I was in his home, in Salvington.

"Michael!" I finally exclaimed as my eyes and my heart became clearer and clearer.

I could see him. I could feel him with my heart's love. Straight away, as if by some kind of reflex, I dropped to the floor on my face and began kissing his feet. I have no idea why I did that; it was not planned. It is not something I would ordinarily do in the world. I felt an overwhelming humility and love for this most beloved of persons. I felt incredibly grateful to him: grateful for his loyalty to the Father during his life on earth as Jesus; grateful for his contact with me which led to my becoming confirmed in the Anglican Church and taking communion; grateful for the experience of his type of death, which utterly transformed my human life and the dimension of my spiritual life; grateful for the opportunity to be at his feet and in contact with him in person.

A wholly new realisation and gratitude rose up in me, as he let me continue kissing his feet to the satisfaction of my overwhelming desire to worship him—and that was that he was my Father.

From where did this knowledge spring?

Was it in my expectations? No, not really.

Was it that I was experiencing God the Father within Michael of Nebadon?

No, not at all.

How then did I know?

He told me. Wordlessly.

He received my worship, my adoration and my love. When he returned his own perfect love for me, he conveyed his love as my Father.

I did not at first think of him as my Father. Our worshipful love revealed this relationship within the truth of my being.

I just cried and cried and cried. Tears of joy flooded over his feet. I was totally abandoned in my unabashed love for him. I kept on blubbering the words:

"My Father."

"You are my Father."

"Oh how I love you Father."

"Thank you Father. Thank you Father. Thank you Father." And my tears and kisses flowed endlessly, emptying the depths of my soul's joy.

Eventually, he reached down and lifted me to my feet. As he held both of my hands in his, he looked into my eyes and softly said, "And you are my son."

Then we hugged each other for an eternity. Father and son had found each other. One embrace. One name. One spirit. One genealogy. One life. Father and son: the one person following after the other, growing to be like him in all his splendour. Oh how glorious! How glorious! How splendid to be in the arms of the one who is my own divine parent in this universe. How absolutely perfect, to be in the embrace of the one who gave me the opportunity of life. Oh, dear Jesus: never was there a sweeter name! Oh, dear Michael: never was there a more lovely Creator in all the universes. Oh, we had such a time together!

For a moment during this wonderful exaltation, I remembered the wedding that was happening with the mortal part of me back on Earth. I felt my physical face to be lit up all aglow like a Christmas tree, smiling from ear to ear, with tears streaming down my face. People in the row in front of us must have thought it odd as they turned around to look, because Mary was saying to them, in the hope of dismissing their attention on me, "It's OK…he's praying…it's OK." Then in an instant, my whole attention was back with Michael, this gorgeous and most impressive person.

Who is Michael of Nebadon?

Who is Michael of Nebadon? Oh, the list is almost endless

dear reader! He is the Son of God who created this universe in which we live.[5] He is the literal local universe Father of every being who is created within the domain called Nebadon.[6] He is the God of mortal humanity.[7] He is the risen Jesus of Nazareth.[8] He is the Christ of the Bible.[9] He is the author and finisher of the faith of every Christian believer.[10] He is the Alpha and the Omega.[11] It is he to whom all beings gravitate as they grow ever inward and upward throughout this universe of Nebadon.[12]

Is Michael my Universal Father, the First Source and Centre of all life?[13]

No, he is not.

Is Michael, God the Eternal Son, He who is known to Christian theology as the Second Person of the Trinity?[14]

No, he is not; and the Urantia papers go to great length to describe our theologians' misunderstanding, and to give us a clearer image of the relationships of these perfect beings of heavenly origin.[15]

It is a peculiar thing, but when you are with God your Father, all the world's theological ideas and speculations simply don't enter into the experience. So too, when you are with your local universe Father—yes it's true! you have two Fathers and they are Michael your time-space Father, and the infinite Paradise Father who is the "Heavenly Father" of Jesus of Nazareth—all the theology just doesn't get a mention. In both cases, you are beyond the grave; beyond the world and its perspective; beyond sin; beyond reincarnation and other ideas about the after life; beyond your imaginations, your hopes, your fears and your little faith. When you are with your Father, there is no difference between your faith and the glory of God, for they are of the same substance, and neither begs for justification.

To the Bible believer, the one who knows Michael not by that name but by the descriptions in the Bible, he is The Lord;[16] the Christ;[17] Christ Jesus;[18] The Father;[19] Wonderful Counsellor, Mighty God, Everlasting Father, Prince of Peace;[20] and the Lamb of God who takes away the sins of the world.[21]

A flood of knowing him

To most students of the Urantia papers around the world it seems, at the time of this writing in late 1999, he is little known personally. But it is my will to change that status into a flood of the knowing of him. The prophet Joel spoke of the way God brings people up to speed, compensating them for their past lack. He speaks of the former and the latter rains coming at one time, and the harvest being so great that all the time in the past is made up for.

Wouldn't that be a wonderful thing in your own life? To have happen in you a replenishment, a fullness, of the presence of Michael of Nebadon, as if you had always grown up with his Fatherhood and your sonship with him. Wouldn't you like such a splendid thing? Well, God said through the prophet Joel that you could have just such a thing, listen and hear God speaking directly to you:

> "O children of Zion, be glad and rejoice in the Lord your God; for he has given the early rain for your vindication, he has poured down for you abundant rain, the early and the later rain, as before.
>
> "The threshing floors shall be full of grain, the vats shall overflow with wine and oil.
>
> "I will repay you for the years that the swarming locust has eaten, the hopper, the destroyer, and the cutter, my great army, which I sent against you.
>
> "You shall eat in plenty and be satisfied, and praise the name of the Lord your God, who has dealt wondrously with you. And my people shall never again be put to shame.
>
> "You shall know that I am in the midst of Israel, and that I, the Lord, am your God and there is no other. And my people shall never again be put to shame.
>
> "Then afterward I will pour out my spirit on all flesh; your sons and your daughters shall prophesy, your old men shall dream dreams, and your young men shall see visions."[22]

This knowledge of Michael shall be so. In Michael, there resides the dominant desire to contact his sons and daughters and to parent them spiritually with an indefatigable love and attention to personal detail. He is a virus of love, a spiritual magnet that will inevitably win the entire world. His call to your heart and soul is that you and all the world receive his love and his Fatherhood. His passion is that you experience his love for you. As the generations pass, his love will increasingly conquer heart upon heart until the whole world is his, and he is the Father of the whole world. Just as the friend of Jesus, John Zebedee, once perceived within the will of God, Christ Michael is the Lord of Lords and the King of Kings.[23] He will be victorious.

Sonship for you

Would you like to have sonship with Michael of Nebadon dear reader? The way is simple and straightforward. It doesn't require a long time. It doesn't require effort and struggle. Just as you are, without a doubt or a quiver, without reference to Church or priest, sin or unworthiness on earth, simply and like a child, receive his love for you in your own heart. That's all you need to do. Then all else concerning him, this magnificent person whom the world knows as Jesus Christ, will follow into your life.

How do you receive Michael's love for you in your heart?

The same way you have received any other person's love for you in your heart.

If you have never received another person's love in your heart, and there are many people like this, then simply ask Michael saying, "Michael, I really believe what Rob is saying and I want to experience you as my Father. Please help me to receive your love for me."

Then, dear reader, having asked Jesus, having prayed with Michael, do exactly like he told you to do in Mark 11:23-24:

> "Truly I tell you, if you say to this mountain, 'Be taken up and thrown into the sea,' and if you do not doubt in your heart, but believe that what you say will come to pass, it will be done for you. So I tell you, whatever you ask for in prayer, believe that you have received it, and it will be yours."

Dear loved one, believe that you have received it, believe that Michael will find a way to make his Fatherly love known to you, and you will have claimed it for yourself, and it shall be recorded in heaven as a fact in your life, and it shall be so. Then, trusting the power in your own believing, let Michael help you to learn to live with the fact of your sonship.

From this point on until its materialisation in your life, let it be a great bright nugget that you have found and kept— "Michael is right now helping me to receive his love for me." Keep it on your lips and in your heart and it shall arrive.

If you do not keep the flames of expectation alive, you will likely fan the flames of doubt and unbelief and apathy and they will inhibit its arrival. Your expectation *is* your climbing above where you currently are at in life. Believe and receive.

☙

Notes

1. John 14:12-14; 14:26; 16:23; Mark 16:17-18; Luke 10:19-20
2. 159:4.1-159:5.5{And then went ...}
3. Isaiah 6:8
4. 39:2.7{5. The Transporters...}
5. 136:3.4 {While wandering about ...}; John 1:1-4
6. 33:3.7 {The Son and...}; 53:4.6 {Gabriel was personally...}; Matthew 11:27-30; John 3:35-36; John 5:19-31
7. 5:3.6 {The Creator or...}; 186:5.6 {The Father in...}; Mathew 28:18
8. 188:0.1{The day and...}; Luke 24:32-36
9. 89:9.3{The ancient social...}; 98:7.3{The Christian religion...}; 196:1.1{Jesus' devotion to...}; Matthew 26:63-64; Mark 8:29-30; Mark 14:61-62; Luke 2:10-14
10. 196:2.1 {Some day a...}; Hebrews 12:2 KJV
11. 128:1.10 {And yet, throughout...}; Revelations 1:8, 1:11, 21:6, 22:13
12. 14:6.7 {A Creator Son uses...}; 33:2.3 {This subordination of...}; John 14:6-7; 33:3.2 {The Universe Mother Spirit...}; 33:3.7 {The Son and Spirit...} Parents; 34:2.1 {Having undergone marked...}
13. 1:0.1 {The Universal Father is...}
14. 104:1.11 {The first Trinity...}
15. Urantia papers Paper 33
16. Mark 11:3; Genesis 2:4
17. Mark 1:1
18. Romans 3:24
19. Romans 8:15
20. Isaiah 9:6
21. John 1:29,36

22. Joel 2:23-28
23. Revelation 17:14

❦

Chapter 4

Sonship with Mother Spirit

The Urantia papers say:

> "At the head of all personality in Nebadon stands the Creator and Master Son, Michael, the universe father and sovereign. Co-ordinate in divinity and complemental in creative attributes is the local universe Mother Spirit, the Divine Minister of Salvington. And these creators are in a very literal sense the Father-Son and the Spirit-Mother of all the native creatures of Nebadon."[1]

I remembered something of that statement as I was in the embrace of this extraordinary person, my "universe Father and sovereign." When we finally could speak with each other, the first thing I said was a request. My words were like molten love in his company. Nothing was impossible; everything was possible. The words gently flowed straight out of the worship in my spirit, "Father, may I please see my Mother?"

Meeting Mother Spirit

He beamed with loving joy and instantly, as if materialising right in front of me out of thin air, stood Mother Spirit of Nebadon.

Mother Spirit was before me. She is absolutely radiant. She is living glory. She is so holy that I could barely focus upon her without being totally overwhelmed by the extent of the sacredness of her purity.

Mother Spirit is so thoroughly pure that she is creativity itself. She is the embodiment of creativity. There is nothing about her that is not super-charged with divine creativity; and that creativity is without blemish, even by infinite, absolute and eternal standards.

Even Michael, it seemed to me then, did not have this kind of immaculate feature about him: the two are quite different, that's all. He has features which are patently so sovereign and majestic, so regal and dignified that surely you would call him Lord unbidden. But, Mother Spirit is so astonishingly beautiful; so magnificently true. Of all the things that impacted upon me when I first met her, and her embrace all but sent me reeling back from heaven to the wedding in the Church in Melbourne, such was its power, it was her holiness and her motherliness that won me.

Mother Spirit is impeccably holy, in every sense of the way that she can register the experience of that term in your soul to you, and more.

Mother Spirit is magnetically attractive as your mother, the mother of your spirit. Just as Michael is magnetic in the way that he exudes his fatherliness and his fatherly love for you, so too Mother Spirit draws you into her with the most compelling invitation of motherly love. You know, with absolute conviction, throughout all of your being, with no part of your being left in doubt or quandary, that this beautiful and wondrous person of God before you, is your own Mother.

When you are in her company like this, instantly you know she is your universe Mother. Everything in your being is drawn to her like a baby. Her personality is so utterly compelling. In her company, it is so very easy to see how this Creator Son of God, Michael of Nebadon, could have been born to Mary of Nazareth by the power of this Holy Spirit. For that is who she is, this Mother Spirit, a daughter of the Holy Spirit, the co-creator of this universe in which we have our lives. Do you see that little flower in the ground? It has its life because of her creativity! Right now, her creativity is happening. And you are her son, or her daughter! How magnificent!

When you realise the divine Fatherhood within Michael, you simultaneously contact the Father in Paradise and the Eternal Son in Havona as these two Central Persons exist within him. When you realise the divine Motherhood within Mother Spirit, you simultaneously contact the Infinite Spirit in her, the third person of the Paradise Trinity.[2] These, our beloved Parents, reveal all this to you with such devotion and care in their process of making this real in you.

Such contact enables you to experience the truth of their position as creators of the local universe, and you can position them geographically against their own personal and infinite parents who reside across the barrier between the time-space universes of the Superuniverse and the Paradise-Havona domains at the centre of all creation.

Your meeting of Mother Spirit

Is the Holy Spirit, Mother of Nebadon so easily contactable by the mortal soul? Oh yes, surely. This is my witness to you, and I bring you word of her desire that you should know how very much she longs to be known in your heart and to your soul's touch. The Urantia papers speak of her ability to be contacted:

> "Having undergone marked personality metamorphosis at the time of life creation, the Divine Minister thereafter functions as a person and co-operates in a very personal manner with the Creator Son in the planning and management of the extensive affairs of their local creation. To many universe types of being, even this representation of the Infinite Spirit may not appear to be wholly personal during the ages preceding the final Michael bestowal; but subsequent to the elevation of the Creator Son to the sovereign authority of a Master Son, the Creative Mother Spirit becomes so augmented in personal qualities as to be personally recognised by all contacting individuals."[3]

By the grace of Michael of Nebadon, I was enabled to be one of the "contacting individuals." In the days to follow, as a result of this contact and its on-going potency in my daily life, I would be gifted somewhat with an ability to help others make contact with her.

This passage refers to the way that Mother Spirit underwent personal transformations of gigantic proportions in the course of her relationship with Michael as they co-create and manage this universe.

There appears to have been a difference in her before the time Michael lived on earth as Jesus of Nazareth, and after his ascension to the Father from the Mount of Olives and the bestowal of the Spirit of Truth that Thursday, May 18th, 30 A.D.[4]

The most significant difference, it seems to me with my minimal experience of her, is that she is now infinitely more contactable in spirit by her sons and daughters throughout all of Nebadon.[5]

Mother spirit is the merciful one

Michael and Mother Spirit always answer the cry of faith from their infants,[6] irrespective of its intellectual accuracy.

Having met her, I am convinced that it is she, Mother Spirit, who is contacted by the mortal soul who reaches out for "Our Lady" of the Roman Catholic Church tradition.[7]

When the Tibetan Buddhist reaches out to Tara or Avalokitesvara, Mother Spirit finds him.[8]

When the Chinese person calls out to Quan Yin, Mother Spirit responds in all her thousand-handed glory. She is the mother of all of Nebadon's angels.[9]

She is the mother of all who minister and serve by the power of the Holy Spirit, and there are not two such mothers in this universe. Whilst it is by Michael's authority, it is by her loving and holy hand that we are healed when we are sick, comforted when we grieve, and prepared in our souls just as John beckoned of us saying:

"The voice of one crying out in the wilderness: 'Prepare the way of the Lord, make his paths straight.'"

"I baptize you with water for repentance, but one who is more powerful than I is coming after me; I am not worthy to carry his sandals. He will baptize you with the Holy Spirit and fire."[10]

Mother Spirit is Holy by nature

Mother Spirit invites you into her holiness. Her holiness is her love. Her love is her holiness—her divine goodness and purity. Receive her invitation. Simply say to her directly, "Mother, come to me please," and she will attend you. Ask her to cleanse you, to make in you a pure heart, so that you might see God.[11] And she will do this work in you; she is your Mother.

What human mother would ignore the plea of her child to be washed clean? What mortal mother would not draw their hurting child to their breast and loving arms? What mortal mother would not move heaven and earth so that their child might prosper and survive and be noble and good?

How much more so then, would the Divine Mother, the

mother of all mothers in this universe, do for each of her children? She is present, of God, motherly, personal, contactable, willing to help, never judging or criticising, understanding, available and effective for your woes and your hopes and dreams. She is the co-creator and co-manager of all the good you see around you. She is here for you and will be there for you. Fact!

Heavenly home

For all the while I was with Mother Spirit and Michael, my level of sensitivity and awareness increased, thanks to the effect of their presence. Eventually I could look around, identify objects and distances and dimensions. Most significantly, I found a level at which I could perceive Mother Spirit without collapsing in the face of her overwhelming purity and power. I feel sure that this came about as she adjusted herself, limiting herself for my sake. Eventually, Michael led me out with her onto what looked like a very large patio, where we gazed about at the surroundings, and kept on chatting.

This place was their home. This was not universe headquarters or some huge hub of activity. This was their home. They were relaxed. They were with one of their sons. Although I have never been to boarding school, it reminded me something of how a young boy might be with his parents at semester break when he returns home for the first time. He is so jubilant to see his parents. He is so glad to be in their home, the centre of his very existence. They, in turn, have put aside time to be with him, to reconnect, to bring him up to speed with the events that have gone on in his absence, not that I had ever been here before. This event was the birth of my sonship with the local universe Gods, Co-creators, Parents, Sovereigns of a vast environment and population and administration of their own design and making. Look into the night sky: what of this is not within Nebadon? Little. Here I was, by the grace of God, standing in spirit and with everything that is real in me, with the two divine creators of an entire universe, in their home, as their son, holding their hands so to speak, deeply in love, chatting about this and that at our leisure—not deep and meaningful questions and answers, simply chit chat.

Sonship: the son at home

This, truly is sonship: to be in the company of one's own divine parents and, as a consequence, to live on earth a life in companionship with one's divine parents, growing in their likeness.

This kind of confirmation of sonship transcends the grave; severs the root of one's mortal evil and sin; and forever clarifies any misunderstanding about one's origin and one's eternal destiny, by finding one's fundamental being, one's enlightened being, even one's Adjuster fused being, inextricably in the existence of the Creator Son and the Creator Daughter of this universe.[12]

Sonship is deeper and higher than enlightenment, because, astonishingly, one finds that one's absolutely enlightened self is in fact a child of another even greater absolutely enlightened self and such a vista enhances the seemingly unenhanceable (if there were such a word).

Sonship annihilates theories about being lost on a wheel of reincarnation generated by cause and effect, because sonship reveals personality as being the root cause of existence rather than an impersonal or a pre-personal mechanism of cause and effect. Sonship proves to oneself that at least three forces of primal reality exist: the Parent-child relationship, mercy (love) and justice (cause and effect). Of these, the essential force of life, the most fundamental force within any person and within even God the Eternal Son and God the Infinite Spirit, is the fact of the Parent-child relationship. The essential Parent-child relationship is one's belonging to the Father of all, whose first force is love and mercy, not justice and the power within cause and effect. Sonship is founded upon the Father's personality which is in the human being, rather than the pre-personalness of the Thought Adjuster who also resides in the human being. Among the religions of reincarnation, the Thought Adjuster is realised as man's fundamental ground of being and, as such, is experienced as the escape from the sensory identity that is believed to reincarnate.

Sonship will prove to you that essentially you are moved the most, and moved the most exceptionally, and moved the most excellently by the love which is yours through your own divine

Father.

Sonship will prove itself to you as being the most central truth, the most dependable beauty, the most authentic goodness upon which you can judge your world, know yourself, build your self esteem, plan your life's details, and commune with the same God and Father with whom Jesus Christ communed on earth.

If you would have an ideal, a truth which is uniquely yours, which will ever work magnificently to raise your flagging spirits, encourage your wearied soul, bring you into even greater and brighter levels of performance and illumination, endlessly recast and reinvent you for wider and higher and deeper personal fulfilment, enable you to build your house upon the rock of an eternal foundation rather than upon the sands of Earthly shadows, then let your ideal and your truth be all that is within sonship with God.

The Father's path to himself

You will never be God, despite appearances from time to time as you progress and occasionally engage extraordinary states of existential being, but even now you are his direct offspring in spirit, his son.[13]

Sonship shatters any delusions one might have about the existence of a hell—there is no such a thing for the eternal damnation of living souls.

Sonship is a more confirming path to finding God than all the known spiritual, religious and psychological practices and traditions that are currently in the world. Whilst they are obviously of immense aid to millions of people and hundreds of thousands of groups and institutions, invariably they fail to cut the root of the isolation, fear and confusion which stems from being spiritual orphans in a vast universe.[14] Sonship cuts the root of separation from God in an instant. Sonship is not the path of the isolated person who is seeking his or her union with God: it is a communion with God on a path shared, from its beginning.

Sonship does not require you to join a cult, or to bind yourself with vows to this group or that organisation. Whilst you may well benefit from social gatherings and groups whose mission is social or religious welfare, sonship maintains in you a prior allegiance to your spiritual Parents that fosters authentic spiritual freedom among people. If you would have you a vow that keeps you disciplined, then let it be empowered by the love and will of your own divine Parents.

Sonship frees you from wandering the earth in search of other people's thoughts, ideas and experiences. Sonship frees you from others, and brings you into communion with your own divine Parents, through whom you come to serve others as you pass by.

This experience of genuine spiritual liberty which is yours through sonship with Michael and sonship with the Paradise Father and sonship with Mother Spirit becomes your watchword to others. Jesus' watchword was "fear not,"[15] and sonship casts away fear.

Paul wrote of the high estate of spiritual attributes, saying:

"And now faith, hope, and love abide, these three; and the greatest of these is love."[16]

The eternal fount from which faith, hope and love spring is direct sonship with God. Without sonship, they are at best sails flapping on a boat with no helmsman. Sonship, fully enlightened, fully liberated, fully clothed in the glory of the Father, is the heart of all things, as Jesus said:

"Your message to the world shall be: Seek first the kingdom of God and his righteousness, and in finding these, all other things essential to eternal survival shall be secured therewith."[17]

"He who hears the gospel of the kingdom and believes this teaching of sonship with God, has eternal life; already are such believers passing from judgement and death to light and life."[18]

"This is the kingdom of heaven: God is your Father and you are his sons, and this good news, if you wholeheartedly believe it, is your eternal salvation."

"When you enter the kingdom of heaven, you shall be baptized with the Spirit."

"When you enter the kingdom, you are reborn."[19]

The Urantia papers tell us that Jesus' gospel grew out of his own communion with the Father. Personal communion for Jesus was the key that validated spiritual realities over and above the power of belief and faith. To be *with* God was to go beyond mortal philosophy, religion and science and to engage truth, beauty and goodness as they exist in the eyes of the divine. Sonship, then, is the experience of communion with God. The impact of such communion in human life is, naturally enough, final and conclusive about a whole range of things spiritual.

This spiritual journey at Our Lady of Miracles Basilica, had brought me into the literal presence of the divine persons whose very presence made clear to me the fact of my sonship at a local universe level. I already had met my Paradise Father during my retreat at Kong Meng San Temple in Singapore earlier in the year. Having now been at the centre of the local universe in communion with Nebadon's creative designers, the message in the Urantia papers about one's local universe Parents also seemed so completely valid.

In the course of our time together, Michael outlined to me the spiritual journey that he had provided for the human being, from their birth on their native world, in our case the Earth (Urantia), extending on upward and inward to actual citizenship in his own domains of Salvington. The realisation of it in my understanding was fully commensurate with his explanation of it. This was not some kind of symbolic mystical experience—it was communion, dialogue, verbal and non-verbal, with extraordinary persons whose story matched the Urantia papers story. I believed Michael. I took him at his word. His words awakened his truth in me, in a manner similar to the following process whereby recognition occurs:

> "When a Spirit-fused mortal is told about the events of the unremembered past experience, there is an immediate response of experiential recognition within the soul (identity) of such a survivor which instantly invests the narrated event with the emotional tinge of reality and with the intellectual quality of fact; and this dual response constitutes the reconstruction, recognition, and validation of an unremembered facet of mortal experience."[20]

As Michael described his universe, it became real in me.

The message of thanksgiving and adoration

One of the passages in the Urantia papers that I find truly beautiful because of the way it places Michael's Fatherhood in the context of an enormous universal perspective, is as follows:

"On Earth you were a creature of flesh and blood; through the local universe you were a morontia being; through the superuniverse you were an evolving spirit; with your arrival on the receiving worlds of Havona your spiritual education begins in reality and in earnest; your eventual appearance on Paradise will be as a perfected spirit.

"The journey from the superuniverse headquarters to the Havona receiving spheres is always made alone. From now on no more class or group instruction will be administered. You are through with the technical and administrative training of the evolutionary worlds of time and space. Now begins your personal education, your individual spiritual training. From first to last, throughout all Havona, the instruction is personal and threefold in nature: intellectual, spiritual, and experiential.

"The first act of your Havona career will be to recognize and thank your transport seconaphim for the long and safe journey. Then you are presented to those beings who will sponsor your early Havona activities. Next you go to register your arrival and prepare your message of thanksgiving and adoration for dispatch to the Creator Son of your local universe, the universe Father who made possible your sonship career."[21]

When I read the last sentence of that passage, I am always taken into their presence. It makes me miss my local universe Father and Mother, as if I am homesick. Such is the profound love they create in one's heart that only communion with them in spirit satisfies my own soul's longing to be in their embrace.

Many things transpired in their company. Michael confirmed his Fatherhood to me in words and I confirmed to him my sonship and the loyalty of my allegiance to helping his interests on Earth. I declared my allegiance to the will of the authorities down the line, through the Constellation, the System, the Planet and the Group. I dedicated myself to my Adjuster and fusion. I blessed my wife, Mary, from Salvington, and envisaged the two of us one day standing in the graduation line before our own Parents,[22] the Michael and Mother Spirit with whom I was visiting right there and then—and what a joy that was for me.

Mother Spirit spoke with me for some time, about family spirit, healing, being healed, growing, living and ministering.

We laughed, and hugged, and held hands, and just held each other until time stood still almost. Oh what a blessing is our Mum! One day soon, I pray you will know her and her depth of love for you, and her world changing power in your life.

Our parting

It was wonderful being in Salvington. Through Michael's vision of his universe, I could look out across the constellations and the local universes and even locate Urantia, where the wedding was proceeding on schedule. It was a grand time.

Eventually, with no urgency to it in the least, as if I had spent all day there and it was time to leave, we started to prepare for my return to Earth. The angel who brought me, came into focus some distance away.

There stood the three of us on this patio, Michael on my left and Mother Spirit on my right, and the transport Seraphim away off to Michael's left. Before us seemed to stretch the entire universe of Nebadon. It was not starry and dark: it was brilliantly light and alive. We all three were looking out across it, although I was merely looking and they were wholly sustaining it. Every breath that was breathed, happened within them. Every prayerful wish, he knew. Every glorification of worship, the Father in him drew into himself in eternity. To every little cry, she sent forth her power and her loving touch. The stillness, the serenity, the enormity of those last moments lingers in my soul even now.

Then quietly, casually, he moved over to my right and Mother Spirit moved behind me. She drew herself around me and I leaned back into her gloriously motherly embrace. He held my right hand very tenderly, then he asked with such a profound fatherly love:

"Is there anything your heart desires Rob?"

His question was so terribly natural and yet I knew that he would have created whatever I had asked for then and there. I felt so absolutely clean and pure, so loved and loving, so good and so true—nothing I could have asked for would have been in error.

Eventually, after thinking long about many matters, I replied.

"Father," I said. "My wish is for your glorification, and," I turned my head to look at Mother Spirit and continued speaking, "my Mother's glorification."

Then I again looked out across Nebadon, saying, "and the glorification of our Paradise Father, and the glorification of every one of my brothers and sisters throughout all Nebadon. Father, my desire is for Light and Life and the Father's perfection in Nebadon as a whole universe."

Then I added, "and the closure and healing of the rebellion,[23] and the upliftment of my world, Urantia."[24]

Michael smiled at the enormity of my request, but he approved its sentiment.

"These things take time Rob, as you know, but one thing I can guarantee you: surely, as you have uttered this prayer today, you shall stand here one day with us when all Nebadon shall be as you have just said, perfect in Light and Life."

That statement found its mark in my soul ever so quickly. Oh how we cried out with joy, all three of us, at the thought of such a magnificent perfection. We embraced each other in our delight, and our lingering embrace slowly transformed itself into our loving statement of farewell. Almost in unison they said, "We will never be apart now."

The return journey

Within a few moments, the nearby Seraphim drew close to us. Suddenly there appeared two or three others who were involved in the transport process. I was again bound, embraced by the angel, and with the heartland of Nebadon still serenely pulsating deeply within my whole being, ferried away from my Parents home at the centre of this universe of their creation.

With Michael, Mother Spirit, Salvington and the entire universe of Nebadon just a moment away, so to speak, eventually I opened my eyes and found myself back in Our Lady of Victories Basilica, Melbourne.

The wedding was all but over. The original herald of this journey greeted me with such a love that I thought I would stand up and hug him—but for the fact of his invisibility!

The "wire wrappers" were there too, unharnessing me. As they were about to commence, the transport Seraphim looked right into my face.

"Thank you sweetheart," I whispered to her.

She beamed with love and then, in an instant, she simply

vanished from sight.

Within two minutes, the whole team had gone back to from whence they came.

I looked at Mary sitting off to my left, where only a short while ago Michael had stood. "I have just been to Salvington with Michael and Mother Spirit," I whispered to her.

She just looked at me with a look of concern.

"Tell me later," she said in muffled tones that expressed her wish for me not to raise my voice too loudly. "I thought you must have gone somewhere, you missed most of the service."

I became conscious of an overwhelming ecstasy that still filled me. My mind was so very enlarged, that I could barely move my limbs. I tried to ground myself by increasing the sensations of being in my physical body. I had been completely unaware of the extent of the spiritual elevation of my heart and mind and soul, and now that I was again in the Church, it was plainly obvious to me.

All of a sudden, the whole congregation stood up as a body. The triumphant processional march burst the air, and the happy couple started making their way down from the altar.

What a joke! I made a valiant grasp for the pew in front of me, and staggered to my feet, not really sure if they were even there, making out like I had been thoroughly attentive throughout the entire ceremony.

As they passed on by, my gaze turned to a nearby life size statue of Jesus, and my heart went to my memory of Michael of Nebadon.

Across the other side of the altar, there she stood! Our Lady! Oh how my heart soared as my soul turned to my dear heavenly Mother, in whose embrace I was bathed merely moments before.

As the procession made its way down the aisle, the realities of heaven became seamlessly integrated into my physical surroundings in the Church—much like when one flies from one part of the world to another, and over the next few hours both places, cultures and loved ones are somehow equally real in the same time and space.

When the congregation began filtering outside after the service, I mooned around inside, looking at all the stained glass windows and the Catholic statues. All around me were Earthly reflections of another and very glorious estate. For a while I was lost in the glory of two worlds made one through literal contact with Christ Michael and Mother Spirit. I was like a man who had died and gone to heaven and who, on the third day, visits his own funeral service. There is something shadowy and unreal about the event. The pictures of Jesus Christ are extremely poor representations of Christ Michael. They are in paint and he is alive! The portrait of God creating the world, hardly depicts the grandeur and complexity and enormity of creation, much less the vastness of the array of life and personal beings. The statue of the archangel seems so lifeless and bureaucratic a depiction of persons who are filled to overflowing with the Holy Spirit power and life of which humans taste but a drop.

There I stood gazing around at what the best of the human spirit creates of its heavenly vision, and it all seemed too lifeless—I was in the full glow of having just been with Michael and Mother Spirit in person. Whilst the images were so lifeless and unlike the persons they portrayed however, to me Michael and Mother Spirit were so unbelievably alive and present, both in me and in the world around about me.

❦

Notes

1. 37:0.1
2. 158:3.1 {That which Peter...}
3. 34:2.1
4. 193:5 {The Master's Ascension}
5. Needless to say, I encourage you to make your own personal study of these two persons as they are written up in the Urantia papers. I have found no finer search engine with which to undertake that study than the electronic version of the papers which have been marketed by the Urantia Foundation, "Folio Views".
6. 144:4.2 {The earnest and...}; 168:4.3
7. 80:7.7 {It was during...}
8. 94:10.2 {These simple-minded Tibetans...}
9. 38:1.1 {Seraphim are created...}; 38:3.1 {Numerous

orders of...}

10. 135:7.2 {As John journeyed...}: Matthew 3:3, 3:11
11. 146:2.13 {12. All believers...}; 159:5.1 {At Philadelphia, where...}; Psalm 51:10
12. 148:4.5 {Men are, indeed...}
13. Please remember that "sonship" is a spiritual term as used by the authors of the Urantia papers, and that I use the term similarly to convey the meaning of being direct kin with God regardless of whether you are male or female, trans-sexual or non-sexual: for your spirit does not reproduce its spiritual species— also see 45:6.7. The Urantia papers refer to all humans as sons of God, and all angels as daughter of God.
14. 114:7.14 {Your isolated world...}; 132:7.4 {Your Buddha was...}; 180:3.3 {But I will...}
15. 140:8.6 {Jesus did not attack...}; Mark 5:36
16. 1 Corinthians 13:13
17. 140:1.5
18. 147:3.3
19. 141:6.4-5
20. 40:9.6
21. 30:4.8
22. 113:7.4 {Before leaving the...}; 39:2.5 {3. Spirit Co-ordinators...}
23. Paper 53 {The Lucifer Rebellion}
24. 4:3.3 {Much, very much...}

❧

Chapter 5

The wedding supper

Finally, I went outside the Church and caught up with Mary. Shortly after, she drove us back to the Copeland's revival convention only a few miles away. We spent the remainder of the afternoon there, leaving at around 7pm for the wedding supper.

It wasn't long before we were seated in the large reception centre. Eventually the bridal party arrived. There were all the customary things that occur at Italian weddings. Whilst everyone else was enjoying the wedding supper, I, however, was still hovering in an out of two worlds: heaven and earth. I was celebrating my sonship with Michael and Mother Spirit far more than I was celebrating the marriage of Anthony and Norma, even though I was truly happy for them and their families.

An unbroken communion

All through the evening, it seemed to me as if something had opened up in my spirit and the two domains of heaven and earth were merged. It was as if the physical wedding supper was also a heavenly wedding supper. My spirit looked into some kind of heavenly courtyard where I saw hosts of angels dancing, with tremendous rejoicing and celebration going on.

As strange as it may be, at one point I saw Michael of Nebadon step down to me from the heavenly celebration to the Earthly wedding feast. He placed a wedding ring around my waist and his waist, linking me to himself, and he said:

"You are my bride."

At that, all heaven broke into a thunderous praise of the most extraordinarily moving symphony of sound and love.

That was the first time I ever saw angels dancing, moving around in an ecstasy of worshipful praise and joy.

Christ Michael of Nebadon, my local universe Father, was as real in the wedding supper as he had been when I was with him in Salvington only hours earlier during the wedding ceremony in the Basilica. Somehow, the journey which was begun in the Basilica opened up a connection between heaven and earth, the like of which I had never even dreamed of before. Oh what a celebration it was! I thought it just too fantastic. I had never ever experienced this degree of love, and praise for God, and a sense of endless worship. If this was revival, then, I got it!

One of the most extraordinary things in my life was brewing, and about to unfold throughout the following days.

All that evening, the heavenly celebration filled my spirit, while in the world, the wedding supper for Norma and Anthony continued in true Italian style, with great music and dancing, fine food, laughter and enduring celebration of the fact of family.

It was a real family event, on earth as in heaven!

As the night wore on, eventually the supper ended. Mary and I wended our way home and still, as we drove home, Michael and Mother Spirit filled my heart with such great joy. Mary and I chatted on and on about how beautiful the couple looked, and how gorgeous her young nephews looked, and wasn't the dancing so much fun, and how fabulous Jesus was in the Copeland's revival meeting.

After a while, Mary and I tucked ourselves up in our warm bed, away from the October midnight chill, and for a while slept like babes in arms. The Father's sleep, like that in Psalm 4:8 came on us:

"I will both lie down and sleep in peace; for you alone, O Lord, make me lie down in safety."

What a great pleasure it is to sleep with a trouble-free heart; to sleep in God's peace. What a thrilling day it had been—Mary got revival and I met Michael and Mother Spirit.

Oh what a bright future opens up before you, and how your ragged past is woven into a new kind of quilt, when you meet your divine Parents in person and you are in fact, and not only in thought, a son of God.

❧

Chapter 6

A period of equipping

After a few hours' sleep, I woke up in the middle of the night around three thirty, and I was prompted to leave my bed and go out into the prayer house I had built in my back garden.

There I lingered for an hour or so, in prayerful reflection on the past week of the revival meeting and the extraordinary events of the wedding day, fondling the pages of my Urantia papers and from time to time reading short passages from the Bible.

Spiritual visitations begin

All around me was as if I was in heaven and earth at the same time, as it had been since coming back from Salvington.

Interestingly though, there were other kinds of spiritual movement developing now. I was expecting things to wind down, as they normally do, but now instead of a winding down I was feeling myself becoming even more supercharged with Holy Spirit energy and power, the kind the Pentecostals speak of so much.

Towards the end of my stay in the prayer house, I had a visit from Mother Spirit. Her presence was almost exactly as she was when I had been with her in Salvington: so personal; so present; her communication so clear; so compelling in her unblemished purity.

She outlined to me the idea that I was going to become equipped for working in the kingdom on this global mission with Michael—whose aim was to spiritually uplift readers of the Urantia papers revelation around the world. She said that she would at some point soon bestow the keys to the kingdom, the keys of life and death. I had no idea whatsoever, what those terms meant in practical terms. She said that this process would take some days. All the while, the glory of God shone all around and about the little prayer house that chilly morning.

Her visit was the first inclination I had that there would be continued contact with her on earth. I had experienced the extraordinary visitation the previous day and its continuity that evening at the wedding supper. Now it seemed that, instead of the experiences turning into memories, there was an on-going reality to them, which was sustained by continued contact that they themselves, well, at least Mother Spirit, initiated. I had no idea if Michael of Nebadon would be involved in this kind of contact.

The process that Mother Spirit spoke of was to last for eight days in total. It went on twenty-four hours a day, whether I was awake or asleep. During the day, I continued making my living at the drug withdrawal house in Melbourne, but all through the week I slept little, prayed much, communed with Mother Spirit and even Michael intermittently, and the depths of my being were re-written by God's hand.

Our prayer house

Many events occurred that week. On the following Saturday however, the eighth day, after a considerable range of experiences and increasing depths of experience had come to a kind of culmination, I was again in our prayer house.

I will describe it so you have something to imagine.

It was a simple timber construction with an iron roof. It was painted in the Australian federation colours of Lincoln green with pale yellow and maroon trim, and overhung with climbing roses. It was closed at the back and on both sides, open at the front. It was essentially a shelter for a wide seat that was a couple of feet off the ground, with a five-foot long maroon meditation cushion on it that my friend Ina had made up specially.

The house property sloped from the front up to the back. At the back boundary of the land, one was almost higher than the top of the house roof.

The prayer house was located halfway up the property, so it had a high aspect to it. It was on the western side facing northeast, overlooking the outdoor spa and many of the flower gardens. Having at one time surveyed the whole property for its spiritually fragrant aspects, I had chosen the spot and the direction it faced for its ideal outlook. This was the most suitable location on all the property wherein the sense of the Father's peace and the Son's prayerfulness met in the garden.

One Easter, with Jesus life and teachings and death and resurrection firmly in my heart and mind, I commenced building the prayer house. It was a retreat hut for me during this week or so, and in the months ahead, when I needed a private place outside in the garden to be with God. I spent many hours there throughout the night while Mary slept on. It was the place that I shared mind with Michael, Mother Spirit and our Father. It was in every sense *our* house for prayer and meditation, for they came to share my mind also.

Our garden

It really was a picturesque scene. At three or four in the morning, the little light from the prayer house was burning away and sending splashes of light and shadow across the flower gardens and the paved paths that meandered here and there. With such a power of the Holy Spirit all around at that time, it was like an enchanted heavenly garden.

I had built the garden originally as an aid to healing the many people who would visit. It did that admirably. It was a very special garden and time. What also made it so special was that people who had been touched by God in that garden often came back with a gift for it. I mentioned Ina's cushion. Kaya bought in the most beautiful bust of Mary holding the infant Jesus, and it adorned the prayer house. She also brought in a beautiful fine leafed weeping maple miniature. Chris bought in a row of conifer bushes. Tony and Maggie bought in a rhododendron; Rosa, an angel figurine and hanging baskets of fuchsias; Andrea, a figurine of Van the Steadfast;[1] John, water lilies for the ponds and a beautiful peony rose; Charles and Susan, a green miniature weeping maple tree; Steve and the entire graduating class I had taught brought in a magnificent red weeping maple tree; Chris and Ina, lilies; Ryta, cactus; others brought a rose bush here—for they knew how much I loved scented roses, and a heavenly ornament there—for they saw heaven's power for good contacting this place.

It was the love from the healed and those dear ones whose burdens God had lifted that made the garden so special. There was something sacred about it all. What's more, God was visiting it regularly for, with every troubled or ill person, he came and did his business as only he does so well.

This garden was the kind of garden that matched the sentiments in the beautiful old hymn "In the Garden," by C. Austen Miles:

"I come to the garden alone, while the dew is still on the roses;
And the voice I hear, falling on my ear, the Son of God discloses; And he
Walks with me and he talks with me, and he tells me I am his own,
And the joy we share as we tarry there, none other has ever known."[2]

One more blessing

On the preceding Friday, October 15th 1993, I was told by a prophetic word of knowledge from God that this Saturday night was to be a special time of blessing, anointing, with God, "One more thing to do that will complete the process," were the words of the Spirit of Truth[3] within me.

Accordingly, I was expectant of marvellous things and it was around eleven in the evening that Saturday when I went to our prayer house. I wrapped a light blanket around me to keep off the evening chill, as had been my custom throughout the week, and serenely bathed myself in the glory of God.

❧

Notes

1. 67:6.0
2. "In the garden." Words and Music copyright © C. Austen Miles, 1868-1946. Used by permission.
3. 146:3.6; 181:2.10

❧

Chapter 7

Mind-union with Mother Spirit

After about a quarter of an hour, Mother Spirit made herself known to me. We greeted each other as Mother and son, with great love, personality touching personality, a communion. When our time of greeting passed, I conveyed to her my greetings for Michael.

Mother Spirit spoke to me about how the week's events had introduced many new dimensions into my spiritual reality, how that much seed sowing had gone on and that the harvest of this week would be reaped later on in life as many things were worked out. She spoke of encounters I had had with my Adjuster, with Michael and herself, and with the Paradise Father.

An uncommon union

Then she went on to say that she was about to initiate a union with me, and that this type of union was one of the final touches to the process I had undergone throughout the week.

I had never heard of this type of union she spoke of, where the Mother Spirit of a local universe undertakes to create a direct link with the spiritual identity, the conscious self, of one of her children. I had read about "Spirit Fusion,"[1] but she was not referring to this when she spoke of her union with me. She was referring to a link that was from personality to personality, a union of mind that spanned across spiritual dimensions and across distance, so that wherever she was and wherever I was there would be direct access to each other. To my mind, she was talking about establishing the kind of connection that would enable spiritual and personal communion between the two of us. Beyond that, I could not imagine.

It was not until several years after it happened, that I was successful in my search of the Urantia papers in finding a passage or two that speak even remotely like this experience. However, they do exhibit traces of this kind of profound move of the Holy Spirit in one's life:

"Having undergone marked personality metamorphosis at the time of life creation, the Divine Minister thereafter functions as a person and co-operates in a very personal manner with the Creator Son in the planning and management of the extensive affairs of their local creation. To many universe types of being, even this representation of the Infinite Spirit may not appear to be wholly personal during the ages preceding the final Michael bestowal; but subsequent to the elevation of the Creator Son to the sovereign authority of a Master Son, the Creative Mother Spirit becomes so augmented in personal qualities as to be personally recognised by all contacting individuals."[2]

When I ponder that passage, my attention falls upon the last part, "the Creative Mother Spirit becomes so augmented in personal qualities as to be personally recognised by all contacting individuals."

It is a short step from the fact that individuals can contact her and recognize her, to the fact that as a Mother of the native universe inhabitants, she will endeavour to convey her motherliness to the individual during that contact. Consequently, there will be a literal contact with one's universe Mother: the quality of the contact will be defined by the love between a son and a mother, or a daughter and a mother.

Meeting Mother Spirit is meeting your own Mother

Were you to meet with her, you would meet your universe Mother. She is obviously not your flesh mother. She is the Mother of your life, even the life, which came into your flesh mother. Your own meeting of your Mother would be filled with spiritual sentiments, wholly pure in motive, patently sinless and unapologetically radiant with love.

When I experienced meeting my Mother, my sonship was made factual to me when I experienced her motherliness. When I experienced both her motherliness and my own sonship with her, a wholly new dimension of my own spirituality was created.

Increased spiritual faculties

The experience of contact with Mother Spirit augmented my spirituality. I perceived that I would never have even conceived of the idea of real contact with her had the augmented spirituality not made it possible. This told me that prior to this encounter, the only means I had of understanding sonship was with a type of spirituality and a type of mind that in and of itself could never have even conceived of the depth of experience I now experienced.

In the light of this, I would expect that some readers might not grasp the spiritual experience of sonship with Mother Spirit until they too have direct contact with her. I presume this for Michael also. I pray that such contact will be on earth so that your mortal life is afforded the greater benefits of that communion. If not here, however, surely this type of contact will be made on the mansion worlds in the general course of living.

My hesitance

I was hesitant, at first, to engage this kind of an activity with Mother Spirit, I had absolutely no idea what she meant, and she perceived that.

"Show me in God's Word, where you do this kind of thing," I asked her.

She proceeded to show me numerous passages in the Bible I had open in my lap.[3] As I read them one by one, and raised other questions, which she answered in the same manner, I eventually came to an understanding and agreement with her plan for some kind of a union between us.

Dear reader, have patience with me. Surely you are reading this and questioning my timidity. In my defence, all I can say is that one day you will come across the invitation to step across thresholds about which you can know nothing, and you too may want to not rush in quite so vigorously as you are accustomed. There are many spiritual experiences that you must pass through alone. At such times, for you, they are utterly unchartered; as if no human has ever before walked that way—like Grandfanda entering Havona.[4] Your decisions are leaps of faith, from burnt bridges.

Our union—Spirit and son

About twenty minutes had lapsed as I researched to my satisfaction, when I finally said, "Yes my Mother, I will accept this union with you."

Straight away, she moved from her position before me and

without losing any of the glory of God around her, she "stepped" right into me, in an instant finding the deepest place in my inner being, the place wherein I know my Thought Adjuster.

The exhilaration reached levels of ecstacy. Tears flooded my face. My whole body felt like it had become fully electrified. Then, after a while, just as effortlessly and just as matter-of-factly, she moved out of me and resumed her place outside me.

To all intents and purposes now there was literally no separation from her, her inner presence and her objective and outer presence a few feet from me were identical, the same Holy Mother Spirit of Nebadon.

When I closed my eyes and found her presence within me, and then opened my eyes and looked out at her standing before me, they were the same person; the inner person was not a fabrication of my own thoughts and feelings, she was personally present both within and without.

This is an extraordinary experience.

❦

Notes

1. 40:9.1-2 {Ascending Spirit-fused mortals...}; 40:9.9 {A Spirit-fused survivor...}; 63:7.2 {On Jerusem both...}; 107:1.7 {As the Universal...}
2. 34:2.1; See also 160:1.12 {This worshipful practice...}
3. I no longer have them on record.
4. 24:6.7 {The name of...}; 7:5.8 {Whatever our difficulty...}

❦

Chapter 8

Mind-union with Christ Michael

Shortly after Mother Spirit formed this very personal connection between us, she said:

"I am going away and I will be back soon. I am going in order to invite Michael, your Father, to join us."

After I acknowledged what she said, and indicated to her that I would not leave until she had returned, she withdrew her presence from the vicinity of our little prayer house and to all intents and purposes withdrew herself back to Salvington.

For around twenty minutes I was alone, trying to fathom the extent of what I had just experienced. I was pretty sure that the Urantia papers had said that Mother Spirit never leaves Salvington[1]—what then was I experiencing? It was a question that I was simply unprepared for, and I found myself simply looking out across the garden, the yellow light casting shadows in the blackness of the night, not quite sure what to think of it all. Despite the experiences of the previous week being extraordinarily profound, I had little theological framework upon which to base many of them. This was wholly new territory for me. It required more than a little daring and trust in the unseen.

It was Saturday night as I sat there. I could hear the traffic on the distant freeway, and the laughter and singing of a family party going on a few streets away. Close at hand, I could see the first buds on the Iceberg rose bushes starting to show their little pure white petals. Astonishingly, to me a very ordinary human being, Mother Spirit had come and created an eternal bond. The experience made the earth around me seem suddenly light years closer to heaven, with all the daily affairs and goings on of that wondrous source of order and life somehow inclusive of those of the world on which I lived.

Michael is coming

My reflections were interrupted by her return. She again greeted me and as Mother and son: we embraced in our communion. "Michael is coming now," she said; and the glory of God seemed to increase immeasurably all around us.

Then, in an instant, Michael suddenly revealed himself before

83

me. He stood about three feet away from me, directly in front of me. His arrival included a glimpse into the fact that he was coming from some distance, just as occurred with Mother Spirit's coming and going.

He spoke with me in the same deeply personal and spiritually refreshing way that he had upon my visit with him the previous Saturday when I was at the wedding in Our Lady of Victories Basilica. It was such a joy to be with him. The Father of all Nebadon was with me in my garden. After the events of the previous week, during which we had been in communion on several occasions, it was a comfortable and familiar liaison, despite the fact that my spiritual energy and consciousness was running on what seemed like absolute peak performance. In the presence of Michael, one doesn't have to remember what one read about in a book about him to know who he is or his station in the universe scheme of things. Michael is self-evidently the Father, the God and the Creator of all one beholds in the worlds within and without—with the exception of the lovely Thought Adjuster, Father God.

He explained briefly that he desired to establish a union with me. He asked me a few things about the union that had just been established between Mother Spirit and myself, more, I think, to have me verify matters in myself than to confirm things in his own thinking. He then called the union that Mother Spirit had established as a sort of preliminary to his own kind of union. From this, I assumed that there was some kind of order to the way these things occur in people: first the Holy Spirit, then the Eternal Son. Then after settling things of this nature, he asked me if I was ready to go ahead with receiving him.

I turned to Mother Spirit. For some reason that I am not sure about, I hesitated again. I didn't want to jump into this without some kind of surety that what was going on was with the Father's will. I said to her, "Mother, is this normal within the Paradise Father's will?"

She extended her assurance and her love to me, very comfortingly and reassuringly, and replied, "Why don't you ask him directly son?"

My Father's reassurance

I immediately turned my attention to my Thought Adjuster

and he instantly drew me into his own kind of solitude with him—the kind that no other can access.[2] "Speak to me about the matter on your heart," he said to me as a true and good father would counsel his much loved son.

I talked to him, knowing that he knew of the events of the evening with Mother Spirit, but needing to express myself as the little mortal being that I was—a creature talking to his creator Father, seeking his will and wisdom. I needed some kind of objective anchor with whom I could speak and in whom I could trust. Him I trusted. Him I knew. The events of the past week with Michael and Mother Spirit were so very much beyond my previously known horizons that I had only him to turn to.

When I speak like this dear reader, please understand that there was no hint whatsoever of sin or evil or trickery present in these events. These were not events of sensuality or fleshly lusts. This was not the devil in disguise. They were extraordinarily glorious in every sense that divinity is glorious. They glorified God in the highest possible way. They saluted Jesus Christ and the Holy Spirit with utmost honour and praise. They brought forward the spirit of worship in abundance from my Father. My hesitancy to jump straight in unquestioningly was due solely to the incredible loftiness of their requests.

When I had finished speaking, my Father quietly communicated his assurance to me that such a thing as Michael was suggesting, this "mind-union," was in fact very common in the spiritual growth of the mortals of the universe. It was in fact the way that the ascending son of God came to identify with their Michael.

Then he asked me to consider how it would be for me after I left this world, and how it would be for anyone from my world.

"Consider that you die and you do not yet know Michael," he said.

"You can understand that at some stage during your progression through the mansion worlds, you will meet him. The whole universe is always talking about their Michael and Father. He is their God. Every being most assuredly knows his presence and underlying influence.

"That meeting would be similar to the meeting of many other personalities in heaven. You would, for example, meet many Finaliters, absolutely perfected persons of your own origins.

You would meet Melchizedeks, the teacher sons of the universe. You would of course meet many kinds of the angelic orders, even your own Guardian Seraphim. You would meet persons in authority, persons of historic significance to the local universe and from time to time you also would meet a great many visitors to the universe, even such of my own kind. You can understand Rob that in this way, the morontia citizen would meet many individuals, just as he would meet individuals on this world, Earth.

"Let us then expand the nature of these meetings and you will grasp that the meeting of someone such as the Michael of your universe must necessarily have in it other dimensions that include the fact of his Creator prerogatives. Whilst you would meet a great number of individuals, and even fall in love with them and their exquisite character, your meeting with Michael and Mother Spirit would evince in you a profound sense of sonship because you would perceive your spiritual origins in them.

"These origins are real. They are the foundation of the local universe identity in the human. It is upon these spiritual origins that mortals of his universe gradually build their identity as they move through the various mansion worlds and constellation abodes of Nebadon. It is the gene of origin within you, the fact that you are a human son of Michael of Nebadon and of the Holy Spirit of Nebadon, that becomes fully revealed and qualified when you eventually reach the stage of graduation candidacy from Salvington, prior to passing into the domains of the wider universe beyond Nebadon's shores. Mortals come to recognise their spiritual genesis in the Michael and Holy Spirit of their local universe at quite varied stages of their ascendant careers—some on their native planets, like you, and some in the mansion worlds. Eventually, all surviving humans enjoy a wonderful empathy with their universe Parents."

He did not advise me to proceed with Michael. Nor did he tell me not to. My Father never tells me to go or stay, to do or refrain. He always explains the matter in such a way as to allow me to make an informed decision of my own making. God never forces, ever.

"The Spirit never drives, only leads. If you are a willing learner, if you want to attain spirit levels and reach divine heights, if you sincerely desire to reach the eternal goal, then the divine Spirit will gently and lovingly lead you along the pathway of sonship and spiritual progress. Every step you take must be one of willingness, intelligent and cheerful co-operation. The domination of the Spirit is never tainted with coercion nor compromised by compulsion."[3]

I chose to go with whatever Michael wanted.

Our union—Son and son

I returned my attention to Michael and Mother Spirit who were waiting for my reply. I looked at my Michael and said simply, "Yes."

Instantly, he stepped forward, right into me, in the same way as Mother Spirit before him.

I have no idea how to explain how this happens, but it was exactly like a person in front of you literally moving forward and into you, becoming smaller as they engage you, and going deeply into your heart and diaphragm area until they disappeared momentarily in the deepest and most transcendental aspects of your mind and being.

The inward journey was so deep that I found Michael came to an infinite aspect within my mind, at which point he simply vanished from sight. Then, shortly thereafter, he re-emerged from the infinite and most deep parts of my personal and higher mind. I expected him to resurface until he came to a point of stepping out of me again, much like Mother Spirit's method of mind-union.

Whilst the contacting procedures were the same, involving an incredible dive into the infinite domains of my mind, Michael's manner of creating what I am calling mind-union, was altogether different from Mother Spirit's manner in regard to the closure of the procedure.

As he re-emerged from the infinite depths of my superconscious mind, his own presence flooded my conscious mind. At this point, the mind of Christ Michael and my own mind became the same mind. One mind. It was, to all intents and purposes, a complete identification.

From all that was infinite and superconscious within me, to all that was conscious in me, Michael and I were one mind. He never stepped out of me in the way that Mother Spirit stepped out of me to return to her own domain. Michael remained present in exactly the same way as the Paradise Father remains present within me; and I will tell you the story of encountering him in this way shortly.

This encounter with Mother Spirit and Michael had gone on for about two and a half hours. The one-mindedness with Michael remained fully conscious in me for a few days after, until I petitioned for it to be relaxed and modified so that I could get on with my life in relative ease and learn to live with this exceptional liaison with God.

The state of one-mindedness was like taking a blue ball of light and a yellow ball of light and merging them together. The result is a perfect blend that forms a green ball of light. Like this, the son of God and his or her sonship in the local universe creator Father is created as a wholly new being—one in whom the Father knows the son; the son knows the Father; and the two of them enjoy a new passport to communion with each other whenever they so choose. Sonship is the green ball of light, so to speak.

The Father is in me and I in the Father

The wonderful thing about this type of communion is that it is with one's divine Father. In the experience of communion with the Holy Spirit Mother it is with one's divine Mother. And it is fully personal. By this I mean that it is not an encounter with one's own ideals, thoughts, images and memories. Communion is not a ritual. There occurs a breakthrough in time and space at a spiritual level in which the human child, such as you, actually meets, contacts, loves and dialogues with his or her local universe Parent. Communion is *that* personal.

Regarding this kind of communion and its personal nature, Jesus said:

"But that you may be certain of what I proclaim, let me again assert that the Father is in me and I in the Father, and that, as the Father dwells in me, so will I dwell in every one who believes this gospel."[4]

"He who lives in me, and I in him, will bear much fruit of the spirit and experience the supreme joy of yielding this spiritual harvest. If you will maintain this living spiritual connection with me, you will bear abundant fruit. If you abide in me and my words live in you, you will be able to commune freely with me, and then can my living spirit so infuse you that you may ask whatsoever my spirit wills and do all this with the assurance that the Father will grant us our petition."[5]

"As I have lived with you in person, then shall I live in you; I shall be one with your personal experience in the spirit kingdom. And when this has come to pass, you shall surely know that I am in the Father, and that, while your life is hid with the Father in me, I am also in you. I have loved the Father and have kept his word; you have loved me, and you will keep my word. As my Father has given me of his spirit, so will I give you of my spirit. And this Spirit of Truth which I will bestow upon you shall guide and comfort you and shall eventually lead you into all truth."[6]

"Never forget that, when you are a faith son of God, all upright work of the realm is sacred. Nothing which a son of God does can be common. Do your work, therefore, from this time on, as for God. And when you are through on this world, I have other and better worlds where you shall likewise work for me. And in all of this work, on this world and on other worlds, I will work with you, and my spirit shall dwell within you."[7]

Sonship—by any name

By whatever name the kingdom of heaven is opened to you— Jesus, Christ, Son of God, Michael of Nebadon, Christ Michael, Lamb of God—you should know that they all involve the same wonderful person; and that he is your local universe Father; and that you are his child.

In the terms of the fifth epochal revelation, the Urantia papers, you are of the seed of Michael of Nebadon, who is:

"the personification of the 611,121st original concept of infinite identity of simultaneous origin in the Universal Father and the Eternal Son;"

"the 'only-begotten Son' personalizing this 611,121st universal concept of divinity and infinity;" whose "headquarters is in the threefold mansion of light on Salvington;" and who, because of his life as Jesus of Nazareth on Earth, Urantia, "he is sometimes spoken of as

Christ Michael."[8]

Listen again to Jesus' gospel about Fatherhood with a new ear and a pure heart now.

"Jesus said, 'This is the kingdom of heaven: God is your Father and you are his sons, and this good news, if you wholeheartedly believe it, is your eternal salvation.' 'When you enter the kingdom of heaven, you shall be baptized with the Spirit.' 'When you enter the kingdom, you are reborn.'"[9]

This Fatherhood to which Jesus pointed, was not only a relationship with the Father in Paradise, the Father of Michael of Nebadon and of Jesus himself. Buried in the heart of Jesus' gospel is the witness of your sonship with him also. To any willing child-like heart, he will reveal this relationship for it is written:

"At the head of all personality in Nebadon stands the Creator and Master Son, Michael, the universe father and sovereign. Co-ordinate in divinity and complemental in creative attributes is the local universe Mother Spirit, the Divine Minister of Salvington. And these creators are in a very literal sense the Father-Son and the Spirit-Mother of all the native creatures of Nebadon."[10]

Truly, dear reader, and with a great love, I wish upon you all that is waiting for you in this most glorious estate of sonship with your Michael.

❦

Notes

1. 34:4.4 {The Universe Mother Spirit...}
2. 12:7.13
3. 34:6.11
4. 164 :5.3
5. 180:2.1
6. 180:4.2
7. 192:2.13
8. 33:1.1
9. 141:6.4-5
10. 37:0.1
11. Genesis 1:2 KJV

❦

Chapter 9

Preparation by the indwelling Thought Adjuster

I encountered Michael and Mother Spirit during the wedding service in Our Lady of Victories Basilica in Melbourne on Saturday October 9th 1993—a couple of weeks before my 44th birthday. On Tuesday the 12th of October, the Thought Adjuster attending my life invited me to be alone at a certain time in a certain place in my garden on the following evening.

For many years, I had enjoyed a very amiable and exciting relationship with this Adjuster, and we enjoyed many adventures together. It was with great expectations therefore that I spent all of Wednesday in anticipation of something new and adventurous. I had no idea what was planned for that time, but I trusted him fully. I anticipated that it was something in connection with the constant and wide ranging blessings that had been occurring over recent days.

On Wednesday evening around nine, I left the prayer house and went to the location in the garden that my Adjuster had asked me to attend. It seemed to me that he had been absent from me all day, and as I stood there waiting, I was sensing that he was returning from some far away place.

Suddenly, and unannounced, my Father appeared standing in front of me. Quietly, serenely, he communicated that he was about to undertake a certain exercise with me in a condition of fully conscious wakefulness. He expressed the need for me to brace myself, remain fully conscious, and to not become worshipful:

"As it was in Genesis 1:2," were his words.

I really had no idea what he meant by that and so I temporarily excused myself, walked over to the prayer house and I looked it up. He waited while I read and pondered to myself what it was to which he alluded:

"And the Earth was without form, and void; and darkness was upon the face of the deep. And the Spirit of God moved upon the face of the waters."[1]

I must confess that I still had no idea about what he meant. But, kind of satisfied that there was at least something written that I could link to whatever it was that he was about to do, I took him at his word and went back to my place in the garden.

After I regained my composure, he again showed himself to be standing in front of me, about a six feet (two metres) away from me. When I was ready, he suddenly lunged forward, entered into me, and disappeared into the infinite dimensions of my superconscious mind.

Then he emerged into my inner consciousness, saying: "What did you experience?"

I described to him the fact that I perceived him in front of me and then he entered into me and disappeared into my superconscious mind, only to remerge and commence this dialogue.

My answer didn't seem to satisfy him. He vanished from within me, and shortly after reappeared outside me again, near the place where he had been only moments before.

"I want to do it again, if you are willing," he said.

I consented and in an instant he again stepped forward, entered into me and disappeared into my superconscious mind, only to re-emerge into my inner consciousness.

"What did you experience?"

I told him the same as the first time. He seemed quite happy at that, and quietly slipped out of sight into the upper dimensions of my mind, leaving me to carry on with my evening in the prayer house.

As he vanished off into wherever it is in the mind that Adjusters reside, I smiled to myself to console my disappointment. I thought he might have been practising, and maybe successfully achieving, Adjuster fusion. The event didn't make much sense to me at all, despite the fact that it was deeply moving at both a physical and a superconscious level.

It was only after Mother Spirit and Michael of Nebadon had done similar actions in the course of securing what I have called their mind-union, or mind-liaison procedures, that it dawned on me that he was probably preparing my own mind so as to be amenable to them. Perhaps he had well practiced abilities that allowed him to navigate the various dimensions of my mind, and he prepared a way for the Son and the Holy Spirit.[2]

I have never heard of this happening with other Adjusters and their mortal wards—but then again, as the angel said to Mary in the Bible, nothing is impossible with God.[3] My knowledge of others' encounters is of course further handicapped because it seems rare in this day and age to find people who read the Urantia papers, and who are experiencing their Adjusters to the point of discovering new ground, and also who are sharing those experiences with others in ways that invite public comment.

One thing about Thought Adjusters though: it seems that once they become a little capable in the personal domain, they live in a world of their own and who knows what they get up to! There's something I do know however, and that is that there are times when they have a barrel of fun. It's great when we can get our minds off our own needs to enjoy that fun with them and have a good laugh. Laughing with God our Dad and our best friend is just the best medicine there is. I had to smile to myself when I later thought about him lunging at me and disappearing inside. It obviously made a whole lot of sense to him, in some kind of lofty God-type domain—and here's this totally dumb mortal that hasn't got the foggiest clue about what's going on, at best just going along for the ride. In all this, my Father was clearly enjoying himself, despite the fact that he still maintained all the prerogatives and responsibilities of being the one who said:

> "And the Earth was without form, and void; and darkness was upon the face of the deep. And the Spirit of God moved upon the face of the waters."[4]

This experience did somehow resemble the creation epic of Genesis. It involved the creativity of Michael, and instead of "Light be and light was," it was a matter of "sonship be and sonship was," as he moved from his heavenly position and entered into all of the depths of the mind of a mortal.

So too for Mother Spirit, "sonship be and sonship was."

As I mentioned before, perhaps it is the Thought Adjuster who prepares the way for Michael and Mother Spirit to engage the full depths of the mortal mind in such a way as to enable actual personality contact, over and above the impact of the Spirit of Truth.

This is sacred ground, I tred carefully and gently. To date I have not given the matter particularly lengthy study. I know of individuals who are already becoming well-versed in relations with their Thought Adjusters—God indwelling the human mind—as a result of the seeds I have sown just over the past two years. I feel confident that there will arise far greater men and women than I, however, who will plumb the depths of these kinds of matters as their own sonship manifests and matures and as they share their findings with us. May you be just such a one.

ॐ

Notes

1. Genesis 1:2 KJV
2. See 42:10.2 point 3 regarding mind liaison {Evolving morontia minds...}
3. Luke 1:37 NIV—the visitation by the Angel to Mary, whom the Urantia papers say was Gabriel, the Bright Morning Star—122:0.3; 136:3.4; 33:4.2
4. Genesis 1:2 KJV

ॐ

Chapter 10

Sonship with the Paradise Father through Christ Michael

In both the Urantia papers and the New Testament it is recorded that Jesus said, "I am the way, and the truth, and the life. No one comes to the Father except through me. If you know me, you will know my Father also."[1]

Over the years, I have heard people commenting on that statement saying that the Father is accessible to anyone at any time without going through Jesus and that the statement is just another ploy by Christianity to corner the market on God and thereby increase the political power of the Church, to the intended disempowerment of all other faiths.

People are wary of those who state that they have the only One True God. Obviously, because they haven't and can't have. They only have certain experiences and viewpoints on the revelation received from God. God is larger than all of the individuals who ever lived, are living or ever will live on this planet—even in this universe—and it is logistically and philosophically impossible for any one person or group to claim that their God is the one true God.

The great thing about God is that he is utterly personal, accessible to all who have a functioning mind, and magnificently dedicated to seeking out personal contact with every such person. Even the case I am stating here in this book, suggesting that you notice that the Father concept is the highest human concept and experience of your God,[2] is for any person regardless of religious background.

Except through whom?

I never understood what Jesus meant by that statement, and in particular where he said, "No one comes to the Father except through me," until I experienced Michael making a way for me to pass across the domains of his universe's time and space to reach the shores of the Father's infinity and eternity; at which point I was greeted and embraced by the Paradise Father.

It was on the Friday night, only a week after he had asked me if I would do a global ministry with him, that I found myself in the company of Michael yet again on Salvington. Whether I was actually on Salvington, or whether it was just a reflectivity event, I really can't say. One thing is certain though, it was so real and vivid that to all intents and purposes it was on Salvington.

Michael called me into communion with him. To be with Michael *is* to be in communion with him. After a week of the most blessed experiences with Mother Spirit and Michael and my Adjuster and my Seraphim and others, it was an easy event to commune with Michael and to endure an increasing amount of his inherent glory.

Shortly after being with him, he took hold of my left hand with his right hand and he said, "I *am* the way to the Father. Look about you son; look out across all of this universe."

So I did. I gazed out across a vast domain of his creation.

"All who come seeking the Father will come to the Father in me," he continued. "Having found the Father in me, I shall then pass them on to the Father where he is in Paradise. In this way my own sons come to know their own Father. This is the great desire of the Paradise Father for his universe children: that the Father and the child might love one another with nothing of the universe standing between them. Not distance. Not time. Not space. Not sin and evil. Not the lack of mercy and care. Nothing shall separate his children from his love and himself."

The meeting of a lifetime!

Then he looked at me with such a magnificent love for me, and such overwhelming pride at what he was about to do for me and with me.

"This I shall do with you now," he continued. "Come, let me introduce you to your Paradise Father."

Before I could utter a word, he made a sweep of his left hand and suddenly the entire time-space universe in which we had our being parted, rent, as it were, like a temple cloth torn from top to bottom.[3] Then, in a single step, we literally stepped through into the infinity of Paradise and the thrilling and loving person of God the First Source and Centre.

"This is my son Robert, Father." And the Father turned his attention fully on me. Then Michael stepped aside and brought me forward saying,

"Robert. I give you your Father."

Instantly, I was immersed in my Father. I was swimming in him. He was liquid love. He was everywhere, like a sea of shimmering liquid gold. He was infinite; never beginning and never ending; eternal; perfect; living, creating.

Oh dear reader, I cannot describe to you just how much he is the living centre of all life, and all truth, and all love. I can only rejoice with you on that moment when you yourself hear Michael saying:

"Father, this is my son…" and you are the one standing in his glorious midst.

The Paradise Father is nothing like anything I have ever experienced with my Thought Adjuster. The Paradise Father is total person. He is fully "I." Even as I write these words, I feel my soul calling out to my elder brothers and sisters who are Finaliters, saying:

"Oh beloved ones, give me the words and the living love and the joy with which to adequately portray our First Father to each of these precious readers."

My prayer does not go unheard, but the pen is still only the pen.

I remained in my Father for a long time.

It was a timeless time.

We discussed many things. I wrote my name in him. That sounds like a funny thing to say, but it was extraordinary. Imagine writing your name with your finger, within the being of someone who is absolutely and infinitely everywhere. And as you write each character, you are writing in liquid, golden, shimmering love and it is immaculately, perfectly creative—you are creating something with the source of creation itself. As you do this, you fully comprehend that what you are creating is a creation in and through and by the universal source of creativity itself.

Looking out from the Father

One of the most extraordinary events of this experience in the Paradise Father was to look out from him across the whole of creation.

In every direction at once, the domains of Havona sparkled with their own kind of glory.

Beyond them, the superuniverses of time and space were

strung, teeming with universes and their own splendid Michaels and Mother Spirits. Within them, millions of worlds and an almost infinite number of human sons and daughters like myself.

Across this great garden of life, billions of beings were travelling, journeying, growing, transforming, going out and coming in, rising up and descending down. Gazing into the domains of Paradise was gazing into infinite domains and activities and living beings, the like of which would never fully be fathomed or grasped, such was its infinity. Yet one thing lingered in all of this: every being knew with a certainty that this most precious and wonderful Source and Centre of all existence, was their Father, their source, beyond whom there was no other.

All, have their being, ultimately, in the Paradise Father.

When I thought of my fellows on Earth, it was plainly obvious that Jew or Gentile, Buddhist or Hindu, Christian or Pagan, rich man, poor man, beggar man, thief—we all have our being in the First Source and Centre, the Paradise Father, and we all attain him through Michael of Nebadon. There really is no other way to encounter the Paradise Father except through the Creator Michael of the universe in which one is born.

My Adjuster's unbroken communion with the Father in Paradise

When eventually, I found myself back in my prayer house in Melbourne, in the chill of that Friday night, I was met by my own Thought Adjuster.

He stood before me with an extraordinary upliftment about himself. Something was different about him. He was somehow more present; grander; more personal; larger than life.

He fell into communion with me and wordlessly joined me in a loving embrace, which lingered for some time. The most amazing thing followed. He became utterly transparent and through his being I beheld the Paradise Father in my immediate presence. Suddenly, perfectly, I was in communion with the Paradise Father, where he was in Paradise, and where I was in my prayer house.

This was truly astonishing. Here on Earth, through one's own Thought Adjuster, a gateway to the Paradise Father is able to be opened such that the human child can be in the presence of his or her Paradise Father right here on Earth.

I had never dreamed such a thing was possible. The Urantia papers are definite about the absolute inability of the human being to land on Paradise and perceive or comprehend anything at all of Paradise affairs, saying:

> "Between you and God there is a tremendous distance (physical space) to be traversed. There likewise exists a great gulf of spiritual differential which must be bridged; but notwithstanding all that physically and spiritually separates you from the Paradise personal presence of God, stop and ponder the solemn fact that God lives within you; he has in his own way already bridged the gulf. He has sent of himself, his spirit, to live in you and to toil with you as you pursue your eternal universe career."[4]

The Adjuster who indwells us is capable of acting for and as the Paradise Father in any way he possibly can that can impress the human mind here on Earth. One of those ways is to show the mortal the way that he is a living bridge across time and space to the place of origin in Paradise.

❦

Notes

1. John 14:6-7; 180:3.7
2. 196:3.29 {And God-consciousness is...}
3. Mark 15:38
4. 2:5.6

❦

Chapter 11

Reflections on sonship

As I personally struggled to understand these experiences that involved the Paradise Father, Michael, Mother Spirit and other affairs of the local system that were a part of the acquisition of universe citizenship and sonship with God, I had little to go on but the experiences themselves and the occasional passage in the Urantia papers which I understood in a new light.

The whole process of fathoming these things quickly became somewhat technical and to some extent academic. For example, there exists a type of angel, a seconaphim, some of whom can reflect the mind of beings such as Christ Michael.

"If the Ancients of Days would like to know—really know—the attitude of Michael of Nebadon regarding some matter under consideration, they do not have to call him on the lines of space; they need only call for the Chief of Nebadon Voices, who, upon request, will present the Michael seconaphim of record; and right then and there the Ancients of Days will perceive the voice of the Master Son of Nebadon.

"No other order of sonship is thus 'reflectible', and no other order of angel can thus function. We do not fully understand just how this is accomplished, and I doubt very much that the Creator Sons themselves fully understand it. But of a certainty we know it works, and that it unfailingly works acceptably we also know, for in all the history of Uversa the secoraphic voices have never erred in their presentations.

"You are here beginning to see something of the manner in which divinity encompasses the space of time and masters the time of space. You are here obtaining one of your first fleeting glimpses of the technique of the eternity cycle, divergent for the moment to assist the children of time in their tasks of mastering the difficult handicaps of space. And these phenomena are additional to the established universe technique of the Reflective Spirits.

"Though apparently deprived of the personal presence of the Master Spirits above and of the Creator Sons below, the Ancients of Days have at their command living beings attuned to cosmic mechanisms of reflective perfection and ultimate precision whereby they may enjoy the reflective presence of all those exalted beings whose personal presence is denied them. By and through these means, and others unknown to you, God is potentially present on the headquarters of the superuniverses.

"The Ancients of Days perfectly deduce the Father's will by equating the Spirit voice-flash from above and the Michael voice-flashes from below. Thus may they be unerringly certain in calculating the Father's will concerning the administrative affairs of the local universes. But to deduce the will of one of the Gods from a knowledge of the other two, the three Ancients of Days must act together; two would not be able to achieve the answer. And for this reason, even were there no others, the superuniverses are always presided over by three Ancients of Days, and not by one or even two."[1]

In a similar way as the person of Michael, his image and his voice is able to be carried across enormous distances of space and depths of spiritual reality, there appears to be a similar ability within the Thought Adjuster to provide the experience of transportation and real life contact and communication with others such as Michael, Mother Spirit and, ultimately, his own inner self, the First Source and Centre in Paradise. But this estimation, to me, is at best only a fleeting glimpse of a conclusion, which is largely out of mortal hands.

Occasionally throughout history, Christians have enjoyed experiences of the living presence of Jesus Christ—at times of personal need and during times of great faith during the ministering of healing or the provoking of spiritual conversion. The believer has met Christ in person, done his will, and loved him more deeply than before. The encounter as been sublimely holy, sanctified.

The Urantia papers tell us that we do not possess in our inner person, a portion of the actual person Christ Michael or the actual Mother Spirit as we do a portion of the Paradise Father. Neither does Michael or Mother Spirit make contact with our thinking centre from the aspect of being an actual part of our mind, as does the Thought Adjuster—who harmoniously works with the combined spirits of both Michael and Mother Spirit.[2]

My experience of them was not that they were within me as the Adjuster is within me, but I would describe it more appropriately that they established such an intimate empathy and rapport that communion was enabled. The communion is little different from the way that two human lovers commune: their inner beings melting in an atmosphere of exquisite union comprised of love, cooperation, insight, devotion, trust and timeless expansion.

Concerning the experience of the Paradise Father, I am speaking of an experience of God, which stretches all the way from Earth to Paradise. In other words, God is with you here on Earth, you are in communion with him, and simultaneously, in him, you perceive that he is the same Father who is in Paradise. They are not two Gods: the Paradise Father in Paradise and Thought Adjuster indwelling the mind of a mortal on Earth. They are the same one.

The Adjuster is further prepared for fusion

Some extraordinary change had obviously come about in the Thought Adjuster such that he and the Father were now personally recognisable as the same being. He now had identity in time and space as well as in Paradise. The consequence of this was that the Thought Adjuster was able to be personal about representing the Father's personalness and his place as the First Source and Centre located in Paradise.

The Urantia papers speak of this kind of change in the Thought Adjuster, saying:

"Upon fusion with the ascending evolutionary soul, it appears that the Adjuster translates from the absolute existential level of the universe to the finite experiential level of functional association with an ascending personality. While retaining all of the character of the existential divine nature, a fused Adjuster becomes indissolubly linked with the ascending career of a surviving mortal."[3]

I understand this passage to say two things to me. Firstly, just as you and I go through changes that prepare us for Adjuster fusion, so too the Thought Adjuster goes through changes, which prepare him for Adjuster fusion.

Secondly, this particular type of change about which I am

writing, involves him increasing his ability to be personal and thereby able to fuse with a personal mind. The manifestation of his increased personalness is that he is able to present to the mortal mind the fact and the functioning of the personal Father in Paradise.

Where before, the Father was able to be God for me, and even to facilitate connection with the functional goings on within some aspects of the local universe system in which I live, never was he able to be, in my mind, the fullness of the personalness of the Paradise Father, which is who an Adjuster actually is. It could be said that this experience, for the Thought Adjuster in attendance of my life, was a very real personal growth experience of deep and lasting significance.

New dimensions of sonship

As a result of these revelations and experiences, sonship with God took on a new dimension for me. Sonship now embraced a number of experiences.

Firstly, my Thought Adjuster came to me during my time of retreat in Kong Meng San Temple, Singapore, confirming his Fatherhood and my sonship with him. I considered this level of sonship to be similar to the way that Jesus knew God as his Father with the type of consciousness he had prior to his baptism with John. At his baptism he received a vision, an anointing, an empowerment, of his position as the Creator Son of God, Michael of Nebadon.[4] Clearly, at that point in his human life, Jesus was able to relate to the Father differently from how he did prior to the reception of that revelation.

Secondly, about six months later on October 9th, Michael and Mother Spirit each separately confirmed their Parenthood and my sonship with them during the wedding service at Our Lady of Victories in Melbourne. This I counted as the reception of universe citizenship. At this stage, sonship with God is enhanced; increasing one's self awareness to a sense of interaction within one's own local universe; it becomes an experiential fact that there is no separation between living on Earth and living in the mansion worlds. On a micro level, this is like the five year old child who goes off to school for the first time, and encounters a wider universe than the home based world in which he or she has predominantly acted to date.

Now, almost a week later on October 15th, sonship was made real in the Paradise Father. Sonship had a full and complete dimension to it. Sonship was with the local universe Creator Parents and also with the First Source and Centre who indwelt me as the Thought Adjuster. There is no other source of sonship with God on Earth than these three—the Father,[5] the Son,[6] and the Holy Spirit. The Urantia papers speak of this symmetry within sonship:

> "The presence of the Holy Spirit of the Universe Daughter of the Infinite Spirit, of the Spirit of Truth of the Universe Son of the Eternal Son, and of the Adjuster-spirit of the Paradise Father in or with an evolutionary mortal, denotes symmetry of spiritual endowment and ministry and qualifies such a mortal consciously to realise the faith-fact of sonship with God."[7]

This extraordinary experience of sonship with the Paradise Father element of my Indwelling Thought Adjuster I counted as being the seed sown in me for superuniverse citizenship: a level of citizenship that would come to fruit a long, long time from now. I assume that this is a normal part of the Adjuster's program of revelation to the mind of man and would usually have been completed by the time of passage out of the mansion worlds into the constellation worlds.

I also counted these experiences to be considerably beyond the province of the Christian experience of both the conquest of sin and evil, and the baptism in the Holy Spirit and fire and tongues, and the turning of one's life over to the voluntary spiritual service of others under the Lordship of Christ. These experiences seemed to have had a lot more to do with certain aspects of Adjuster fusion and universe citizenship beyond this short life span on Earth than with the basics of spiritual formation in the Christian Church—or any other religion for that matter. I knew of no other human being currently alive who had experienced these matters: hence my conclusion about their place in our collective spiritual experiences.

Lasting confirmation

As deeply personal experiences, they were deeply rewarding. Moreover, they confirmed in me the truth of the Urantia papers' statement about how a human being can attain the actuality of sonship with God and trust in it to be his or her spiritual framework, religion, on Earth to the extent of it delivering all things contained in a successful spiritual career:

> "The great challenge to modern man is to achieve better communication with the divine Monitor that dwells within the human mind. Man's greatest adventure in the flesh consists in the well-balanced and sane effort to advance the borders of self-consciousness out through the dim realms of embryonic soul-consciousness in a wholehearted effort to reach the borderland of spirit-consciousness—contact with the divine presence. Such an experience constitutes God-consciousness, an experience mightily confirmative of the pre-existent truth of the religious experience of knowing God. Such spirit-consciousness is the equivalent of the knowledge of the actuality of sonship with God. Otherwise, the assurance of sonship is the experience of faith."[8]

When once you are in communion with the Father, then the things of the Father are open to you. When once you are in communion with the Son, then the things of the local universe and prayer and service are open to you. When once you are in communion with the Holy Spirit, then the things of the power and holiness and diversity of the Spirit are open to you. When these things are open to you, which they surely are right now if you will but appropriate them for your own property, then sonship is yours and all other things in this world are contained therein.

"Be like me"

In all of these experiences, I have been completely dependent upon the desires and skills of my Thought Adjuster. At certain times, it was obvious that I became involved in the specific will of Michael of Nebadon and that of Mother Spirit. The foundations of my beliefs and contact with God are written up in other parts of this book however it can be said briefly here, that I believed the Urantia papers' teaching about how religions differ, and that somewhere within sonship there was the acme of all religious drives and truth and love:

> "The Greek religion had a watchword 'Know yourself'; the Hebrews centred their teaching on 'Know your God'; the Christians preach a gospel aimed at a 'knowledge of the

Lord Jesus Christ'; Jesus proclaimed the good news of 'knowing God, and yourself as a son of God.' These differing concepts of the purpose of religion determine the individual's attitude in various life situations and foreshadow the depth of worship and the nature of his personal habits of prayer. The spiritual status of any religion may be determined by the nature of its prayers."[9]

My Thought Adjuster had originally given me the watchword 'Be like me' and had guided me convincingly into Buddhism and contact with the Buddha Nature.

The Urantia papers speak of this Buddha nature—the Thought Adjuster's nature and character—somewhat appreciatively:

"This philosophy also held that the Buddha (divine) nature resided in all men; that man, through his own endeavors, could attain to the realization of this inner divinity. And this teaching is one of the clearest presentations of the truth of the indwelling Adjusters ever to be made by a Urantian religion."[10]

When once that contact had been securely attained, when I was 34 years of age, this same indwelling Buddha—the Thought Adjuster—guided me into the discovery of sonship with God. I found that journey to be the discovery and creation of considerably more personal aspects of life with God.

That journey into sonship with God became a trust in Jesus and his gospel written in the Urantia papers. It eventually led me to wholeheartedly agree with the words that amplify those of John Zebedee, the apostle:

"The consciousness of a victorious human life on Earth is born of that creature faith which dares to challenge each recurring episode of existence when confronted with the awful spectacle of human limitations, by the unfailing declaration: Even if I cannot do this, there lives in me one who can and will do it, a part of the Father-Absolute of the universe of universes. And that is 'the victory which overcomes the world, even your faith.'"[11]

❦

Notes

1. 28:4.6 point 3 {The Voice of the Creator Sons...}

2. 34:5.6 {As individuals you...}
3. 107:2.1, point 6 {6. Fused Adjusters—Finaliters...}
4. 136:2.4 {When the returned...}; 136:2.7 {This day of...}
5. 5:2.3 {The divine presence...}
6. 7:5.2 {The Eternal Son...}
7. 34:5.7
8. 196:3.28
9. 5:4.8
10. 94:11.5
11. 1 John 5:4; 4:4.9

❧

Chapter 12

Is this for real?

Reflecting on these kinds of experiences naturally gives rise to whether they, and in fact the Urantia papers themselves, are real—a question that also asks us to question what it is that we mean by the term "real."

Proof

When it comes to proof, it must be pretty obvious to you by now, that I consider the authors and the message of the Urantia papers to be real. There was a point in my life when I faced the challenge of either accepting or rejecting the entire canon of papers outright. A single issue was the pivotal point of my decision and it was whether or not reincarnation existed, a belief I then held and had proven to myself in the classical ways. As I searched for an answer, I exhausted my abilities to come to a satisfactory conclusion. I appealed heavenward saying:

> "If you want me to continue studying these papers, then you must supply an answer to this problem: 'Is this the first life for every person here on Earth, or does reincarnation exist as my Buddhist teachers have taught?'"

In asking my question, I appealed to God thinking that, if the authors of the Urantia papers were true and real, then God would help me to prove the case against reincarnation despite the fact that I whole-heartedly believed in it—but that if the authors of the Urantia papers were in fact merely clever human beings who didn't really know one way or the other about reincarnation or first life, then God would be sufficiently loving to advise me of that fact and I could discard the papers and get on with matters of concern to the Buddhist.

The experience God gave me in response to my plea was so very believable, that I completely abandoned my belief in reincarnation that same hour. I have written about that experience in this book under the title "There is no reincarnation."

Your own conclusions

Every reader must come to their own conclusion about these kinds of matters. It is actually important to spiritual growth and welfare, for you to make up your own mind. The Urantia papers hold the view that the decision of every single person is accounted for and totally respected.[1] It may take you a while to register that fact, and to employ it in your spiritual life, but I have found it to be so.

Sincere questioning

What is it though? What's actually happening when angels bind one's spirit and one travels to heavenly places? Are the encounters with Christ Michael and the Father and the Creative Mother Spirit actually real? Do things like that really happen? If they don't really happen, then what is it that does happen? A more pressing question is, "If things like this do happen, can they happen to me too please?" Questions arise around "What do I have to do to have contact with these heavenly Parents, to meet with Christ Michael and Mother Spirit my local universe parents, and the Paradise Father my infinite Parent?"

These are all particularly relevant questions. To answer them is not only important, but it is important to bring these kinds of questions and answers to the table so that the whole picture can be recognised.

It should be remembered that there is no one relationship that humanity has with God. Some people might have a relationship with God in deeply personal ways like these experiences of mine indicate. Other people might be wholly satisfied with a distant relationship, no face to face contact, no desire for Adjuster fusion. Still others, might prefer to follow the teachings of any of the traditional religions, and worship the word of their scriptures and the concepts and ideals they uphold. It should be possible to see that the question, "Is this for real?" has a different meaning for different people. So what is my own view on experiences involving an encounter with God on a person to person basis, seeing as I am the one who has had them?

To begin with, I have found that such experiences have brought me closer to God. They have taught me more about the way that the human mind and soul performs during the events which bring man and God closer in their conscious experience of each other.

My own understanding of these kinds of encounters with

God and the Divine Creators prompts me to seek out answers about their reality also. Having experienced these things, I too want to know their validity, their relevance, their power to enhance life, their value to other students of the Urantia papers, the ways they might translate into the language and experience of other faiths, and their place in the larger picture of spiritual history, current events and future possibilities on Earth. I research exhaustively, by matching against them the highest values and realities I currently embody. I match them against Jesus' gospel in the Bible and in the Urantia papers. I plumb their possibilities for significance with regard to Adjuster fusion, the term in the Urantia papers for perfected sonship. This sort of proving will obviously not satisfy all people, but it certainly satisfies me, and I have evidence from my Father that it is also divinely satisfying.

Proof is subjective

Speaking on proof for a moment, I want to say that proof seems to be ultimately a subjective perspective and decision. For example, if we are directed toward the experience of something, we either accept or reject the directions and/or the object. Trying to prove God's presence, for example, is a pointless task. I have not ventured along that road in this book whatsoever. Only two things prove God's presence and they are the experience of faith and the direct experience of God. Either one will do it for us, and they are quite different, but both are patently personal.

The Urantia papers say that the only thing someone such as you and I can have by way of proof of God to show another person is to have experienced the fact of God's presence.[2]

There is, however, no spiritual or communication bridge between the believer and the non-believer except that which God first makes for himself: both the believer and the unbeliever would benefit enormously from fully understanding that statement. The human being is patently incapable of doing anything to initiate contact with God—the pot simply cannot reach out to the potter—unless God first grants the human being the means to receive him.

First, believe with God

In order to believe whether or not these kinds of experiences about which I am writing are real, it should be obvious that one must first believe in God, because the experiences are with God. The progression, whether at the stage of development of a child, an adolescent, and adult or an aged person, from being a human being who does not know God to one who subsequently hears about God, and then who searches for God, and then who finds God, and then who grows in God's ways, and then who masters his or herself through fusion with their Thought Adjuster, is a topic of immense complexity because it is unique for every single individual person. I am, however, assuming that because you chose to read this type of a book, you have beliefs about God that you hold dear to yourself.

My first belief in God was a belief in a universal creator and that he was a person. You'll probably be able to recall your first belief in God too. For me, that event occurred at the age of five years, in a Presbyterian Church in Morrinsville, New Zealand, as I listened to a visiting evangelist. I believed God was primal and infinite, just as the Urantia papers describe.[3] I have included that chapter in my life in this book. It was my first encounter with the Thought Adjuster who is attending my life for the sake of achieving Adjuster fusion with me, and it was therefore significant as being the first time I acquired proof of God to my own satisfaction. What were you doing when you first heard about God? And what did you do with that knowledge?

From Buddhism to sonship

It was not until I was in my late thirties, and after a wealth of spiritual experience with the pre-personal and non-personal elements of Deity that are known to Buddhists, that I also found wholly new nourishment and spiritual depth of experience and meaning in the Urantia papers' presentation of Jesus of Nazareth. The papers told me that:

"The nature of God can best be understood by the revelation of the Father which Michael of Nebadon unfolded in his manifold teachings and in his superb mortal life in the flesh. The divine nature can also be better

111

understood by man if he regards himself as a child of God and looks up to the Paradise Creator as a true spiritual Father."[4]

As a Buddhist, that statement was nonsense to me, it was all too personal. But on the other side of the enlightenment experience, when the human soul has reached higher than both the laws of reincarnation and the experience of enlightenment can reach, and when one's question is no longer "how do I end suffering?" then one finds that the personalness of God re-emerges to in fact dominate all existence.

The fact of God being a person ultimately swallows up all other beliefs about God.[5] Every enlightened being, sooner or later bows to the absolute fact, whether here on Earth or in the Mansion Worlds, that:

"He is a saving person and a loving Father to all who enjoy spiritual peace on Earth, and who crave to experience personality survival in death."[6]

The Urantia papers say that an individual doesn't have to be particularly intellectually conscious of "close and intimate contact"[7] with God in order to prove his inner liaison, for the evidence "consists wholly in the nature and extent of the fruits of the spirit which are yielded in the life experience of the individual believer."[8] Ultimately, the journey of believing in God is founded upon our own response to longings and desires that are singularly spiritual in nature, and which finally persuade us to conclude that we have no right not to believe in God and, later as more mature sons of God, that:

"to doubt God or distrust his goodness would be to prove untrue to the realest and deepest thing within the human mind and soul—the divine Adjuster."[9]

Proof is in our own experience

The foundation of proof is firstly in our own knowing of God and not in some independent evaluation which is out of contact with God and the forces that bring about divine experiences. My own position, in writing this book and providing my own witness to you, is reflected in the Urantia papers position as follows:

"God is so all real and absolute that no material sign of proof or no demonstration of so-called miracle may be

112

offered in testimony of his reality. Always will we know him because we trust him, and our belief in him is wholly based on our personal participation in the divine manifestations of his infinite reality."[10]

Further to this foundation then, I hope it is clear that my aim in writing the book is not to prove the existence of God but rather to advance the cause of Christ Michael and my Paradise Father in their mission through the revelation called the Urantia papers, in whom I expect the reader to have existing faith and experience.

In asking oneself about whether or not one can experience these kinds of contacts with God and eternal realities, I have taken the position of showing you how life worked out for me. If some of my perspectives and values can tweak the odd good note in you, then my approach has some merit to it. There does always arise the question, however, about our own abilities to experience such things. How much is good enough? How much must I believe? How much must I be good? What must I be good at? Must I be a saint or is it OK to be a little bad and still gain eternal life? You know the kind of nagging questions.

Actual contact with God

Each religion has its own arguments regarding qualifying for contact with God and gaining the experience of an eternal life of righteousness. The atheist of course says that nothing qualifies you. The Buddhist says that the causes you alone create qualify you. The Christian says that you qualify not for eternal life so much, as for an eternal heaven or an eternal hell. The Urantia papers say that:

"True, many apparently religious traits can grow out of nonreligious roots. Man can, intellectually, deny God and yet be morally good, loyal, filial, honest, and even idealistic. Man may graft many purely humanistic branches onto his basic spiritual nature and thus apparently prove his contentions in behalf of a godless religion, but such an experience is devoid of survival values, God-knowingness and God-ascension. In such a mortal experience only social fruits are forthcoming, not spiritual. The graft determines the nature of the fruit, notwithstanding that the living sustenance is drawn from the roots of original divine endowment of both mind and spirit."[11]

This tells us that we can be good people, but not choose righteousness with God.[12] Jesus said that the pure in heart shall see God. I take Jesus' word "see" to mean having personal contact, face to face, the one knowing the other as a Father and child, and nothing less. Echoing the teachings of the Urantia papers, I hope my experiences do not attract you to the miraculous, which they say do not enhance religion and merely hark back to primitive religions of magic. I approach spiritual experience not as the search for miracles and magic but rather as a source of the true religion of personal experience with God, even the "highest yet revealed in the universe of Nebadon—the Earth life of Jesus of Nazareth."[13]

Real proof is real contact with God

For me the greatest proof of the existence of God has always been contact with God. Such contact has taken away all doubt and speculation for me. As a result of such pure-hearted contact, I can now identify the Father who indwells the individual person, the Thought Adjuster; I can observe some of the ministry actions of the Holy Spirit; I can commune with the Father and the Son and the Spirit as individual persons and parents; and I can do the Father's will and produce his kind of fruits of the spirit. Every experience of the divine has helped to foster this, but it is not by my efforts so much as by my father's leading and grace.[14]

To new readers and old alike, the Urantia papers provide fairly jargonistic and technical words to describe such literal contact. For example:

> "The consciousness of the Adjuster is based on the intellectual reception of truth, the supermind perception of goodness, and the personality motivation to love."[15]

Whilst I understand this to be true, after twenty some years of reading the Urantia papers, and having had considerable contact with my Adjuster and those of other people, I never found that kind of description helpful to know. I never found it possible for that kind of description to lead one into contact with God. In fact, for years I only ever found that kind of language turned me away from experience and into an intellectual domain, which bore no resemblance to contact with God whatsoever. It seemed all too cerebral and so lacking in human warmth of heart.

My contact with God came first as an experience and then, later as I meditated and deliberated over the experience and developed my own understanding from it, then only, some times years later, would I read words written on such topics in order to clarify or expand my own thoughts. I have never liked the idea of first getting a head full of theory and then trying to experience it. That always seemed somehow too open to being just self-fulfilling psychological mechanisms at work. I didn't like that at all, because it seemed to position me for being robbed of authentic experience which had its roots in the real God. I wanted God's version of the truth rather than man's version and, to do that, one must approach learning as a complete beginner. I do have to say that every one of these extraordinary encounters with God was utterly new and previously inconceivable to me. I had a pure heart, and I was a beginner.

A pure heart that sees God

We question ourselves about a pure heart. How pure did Jesus mean? Is it a spiritual thing to question and speculate and not feel that you are one hundred percent in contact with God all the day long? Oh yes of course it is, but it is eventually tempered by the absolute certainty that makes one doubt-free. Read of Jesus' own experience after his baptism when he went on the forty-day retreat which he devoted exclusively to planning the Father's business:

> "Throughout all this momentous dialog of Jesus' communing with himself, there was present the human element of questioning and near-doubting, for Jesus was man as well as God. It was evident he would never be received by the Jews as the Messiah if he did not work wonders. Besides, if he would consent to do just one unnatural thing, the human mind would know of a certainty that it was in subservience to a truly divine mind. Would it be consistent with 'the Father's will' for the divine mind to make this concession to the doubting nature of the human mind? Jesus decided that it would not and cited the presence of the Personalised Adjuster as sufficient proof of divinity in partnership with humanity."[16]

I understand that to mean that Jesus thought like his Thought Adjuster thought, which is the meaning of Adjuster fusion anyway.

The Urantia papers portray a pure heart like this:

"Out of a pure heart shall gladness spring forth to the Infinite; all my being shall be at peace with this supermortal rejoicing. My soul is filled with content, and my heart overflows with the bliss of peaceful trust. I have no fear; I am free from anxiety. I dwell in security, and my enemies cannot alarm me. I am satisfied with the fruits of my confidence. I have found the approach to the Immortal easy of access. I pray for faith to sustain me on the long journey; I know that faith from beyond will not fail me."[17]

Sincerity

For Jesus, a pure heart meant sincerity. Have you sincerity about a matter, then you have a pure heart on that matter. Find his pure-heartedness in the following passage:

"Jesus did not attack the teachings of the Hebrew prophets or the Greek moralists. The Master recognised the many good things which these great teachers stood for, but he had come down to Earth to teach something additional, 'the voluntary conformity of man's will to God's will.' Jesus did not want simply to produce a religious man, a mortal wholly occupied with religious feelings and actuated only by spiritual impulses. Could you have had but one look at him, you would have known that Jesus was a real man of great experience in the things of this world. The teachings of Jesus in this respect have been grossly perverted and much misrepresented all down through the centuries of the Christian era; you have also held perverted ideas about the Master's meekness and humility. What he aimed at in his life appears to have been a superb self-respect. He only advised man to humble himself that he might become truly exalted; what he really aimed at was true humility toward God. He placed great value upon sincerity—a pure heart. Fidelity was a cardinal virtue in his estimate of character, while courage was the very heart of his teachings. 'Fear not' was his watchword, and patient endurance his ideal of strength of character. The teachings of Jesus constitute a religion of valour, courage, and heroism. And this is just why he chose as his personal representatives twelve commonplace men, the majority of whom were rugged, virile, and manly fishermen."[18]

Dear reader, would you have a pure heart? Then your pure heart will surely manifest as "valour, courage, and heroism."

The fruits of the spirit; and risking all

The Urantia papers say that you cannot prove to other people that you have found God, for "you cannot consciously produce such valid proof."[19]

There is a wonderful account in the Urantia papers, depicting Jesus' disciple, Nathaniel, winning over the Greek philosopher named Rodan, to believe in the personality of the Father—but it must also be remembered that Rodan had already encountered Jesus the person. Whilst proof of God's existence might be elusive, you can of course demonstrate to them the pure heart God has made in you with your cooperation.

Calling upon Jesus' teaching as your foundation principle, "Be you therefore perfect, even as your Father in heaven is perfect,"[20] there are "two positive and powerful demonstrations of the fact that you are God-knowing, and they are:

1. The fruits of the spirit of God showing forth in your daily routine life—love, joy, peace, long-suffering, gentleness, goodness, faith, meekness, temperance[21] and true self mastery.[22]

2. The fact that your entire life plan furnishes positive proof that you have unreservedly risked everything you are and have on the adventure of survival after death in the pursuit of the hope of finding the God of eternity, whose presence you have foretasted in time."[23]

The Urantia papers further tell us that:

"Jesus never gave his apostles a systematic lesson concerning the personality and attributes of the Father in heaven. He never asked men to believe in his Father; he took it for granted they did. Jesus never belittled himself by offering arguments in proof of the reality of the Father. His teaching regarding the Father all centred in the declaration that he and the Father are one; that he who has seen the Son has seen the Father; that the Father, like the Son, knows all things; that only the Son really knows the Father, and he to whom the Son will reveal him; that he who knows the Son knows also the Father; and that the Father sent him into the world to reveal their combined natures and to show forth their conjoint work. He never made other pronouncements about his Father except to the woman of Samaria at Jacob's well, when he declared, 'God is spirit.'"[24]

"Jesus lived on Earth and taught a gospel which redeemed man from the superstition that he was a child of the devil and elevated him to the dignity of a faith son of God."[25]

Being familiar with experience as a son of God, I would add that when with a pure heart you see a son of the Son of God, you therein will see the Son in that son of God just as you will see the Father in him or her also. Your own pure heart will discern the same kind of pure heart in the son of God. You will also discern the pure heart of the Son of God who is in the son of God. You will also discern the pure heart of the Father who is in the son of God and in the Son of God. This pure heart, which is passed across generations from the Father, is thoroughly consistent. The pure heart of the Father is just as pristine in the God-knowing individual on Earth, even you and me. In this way, the love, which is in the Father's pure heart, comes to exist in Christ Michael the Son of God and through him in his human sons of God. In this way, we sons of God love each other with the Father's love, through Michael the Son.

Did I go somewhere?

As I understand my own experiences of encountering God, I, probably like you, question, did I go somewhere, or did someone bring something of God to me? Did I really go to Paradise? Did I really go to Salvington? Did I really see into the Mansion Worlds? My initial answer is yes, but I don't really have a foolproof answer. I probably won't have anything like that kind of an answer until I observe the records of my life long after I have left the Earth. The experiences certainly have reality to them, for me. They are a source of spiritual power and influence for others, and they uplift the lives of others and help to cut through their burdens. They denounce evil and sin and they raise up Jesus and the Holy Spirit and the Father. They produce the fruit of the Spirit in my life and assist others to produce the fruit of the spirit in their own lives. They obviously have impact, but that doesn't necessarily prove that they are in every sense known to man, real. Some people simply cannot discern realness of this kind.

In responding to this line of questioning then, and it concerns your own spiritual inquiries as well, there are really three questions to ponder.

One question is:

"Can a person travel in spirit to the other domains in Michael's universe and participate in or witness events at those locations? Yes or no?"

The next question is:

"Can a person consciously meet Michael, Mother Spirit or the Paradise Father, irrespective of whether or not the person travels to other locations in the universe? Yes or no?"

The third question is:

"If a person can meet these universe Parents, or these persons can meet with the individual person and the person participates in universe events, is there any difference whether the person travels to other locations in the universe or stays where they are on Earth?"

As I write this, I am conscious that a number of readers will be assessing their own spiritual adventures with these same Parents as they read my own questioning style. One of the interesting speculations to ponder is this: if I did go to these places in spirit, or you did in fact go to your heavenly place of destination, then what we encountered was absolutely real on heaven's terms and if anyone else went there they'd experience an equivalent kind of experience. I believe that of sonship for example, in that I fully expect it to be true that if with a pure heart you invite Michael of Nebadon into your heart as sovereign parent over your spirit and life then you will definitely experience an awakening to being born again as his son of God—you will definitely know him as your local universe spiritual Father. But what if God simply brought a vision to us of what it would be like if in fact we had actually gone there. We probably couldn't tell the difference. What's more important is that we wouldn't need to tell the difference because essentially there wouldn't be any difference at that level of experience. To all intents and purposes, if God is involved, the location of your sense of self is irrelevant.

Man and God can share mind

Firstly, it's important to know that God's mind and the mind of a person on Earth do in fact unite. The Urantia papers are emphatic about this point.

> "You as a personal creature have mind and will. The Adjuster as a prepersonal creature has premind and prewill. If you so fully conform to the Adjuster's mind that you see eye to eye, then your minds become one, and you receive the reinforcement of the Adjuster's mind. Subsequently, if your will orders and enforces the execution of the decisions of this new or combined mind, the Adjuster's prepersonal will attains to personality expression through your decision, and as far as that particular project is concerned, you and the Adjuster are one. Your mind has attained to divinity attunement, and the Adjuster's will has achieved personality expression."[26]

The point in question is the mention of you enforcing "the execution of the decisions of this new or combined mind." In order to do this, you must first know the content of your Adjuster's mind and will on the matter. That is, mortal man must be able to share the same mind with God.

The prophetic mind

I think that the way God's mind and our mind work together during these kinds of experiences, is much the same way as that employed in divine prophecy. When I have examined the gift of prophecy, for example, to shed light on the experience of contacting and being contacted by God, what I find is that God manifests prophecy in the inspired human mind, frequently by delivering a vision of the end result of some project or exercise.

I'll give you an example that is not too unrealistic for many readers.

Let's say that a divine peace comes upon you, you close your eyes, and suddenly, unannounced, there comes into your mind an image of a house door, a blue door, with a number nine on it. You see the door opening and a lady invites you in. Your go in through the darkened corridor until you eventually come to a living room which is a little brighter. She points to a little boy who is sitting in an armchair, and says some words to you about him. Then you hear what you know to be God's voice saying to you:

"Tell the little boy, 'Simon, you are well. Take my hand and stand up and run now.'"

Then you see yourself taking the little boy's hand and he slides off the armchair and stands upright and, in squeals of glee, he runs on down the corridor. Then the vision fades out, you feel yourself return to your own place, the peace remains for a minute or two, and then it too lifts off you. You are left with the absolute sense that you have been in contact with God, that he has taken you to a place where you have seen a divine healing happen, and then you returned back to your own consciousness. Deep inside you there is the feeling that if that situation comes about, you will be doing the will of God by doing exactly what you saw in the prophetic vision.

The following day, a friend picks you up on the way to a dinner you have planned, and along the way says:

"Oh, I just remembered, do you mind if we stop in to visit a friend of mine. Her little boy has this horrible disease in his legs. I bought him a book today and I want to drop it off."

For the rest of the journey until you get to this person's house, the two of you discuss Godly things, healing, prayer, helping out as you pass by—just like Jesus said to do.[27]

When you get to the steps of the house, you find that it is exactly like the front door in the vision. When you enter inside it is the same dark corridor and then you come upon the same room and the little boy sitting in the armchair, just like in the vision. Then, suddenly, there comes an amplification of the power of God's presence all over you. You do exactly what was in the vision; you say what God told you to say:

"Simon, you are well. Take my hand and stand up and run now."

Then you take the little boy's hand and he slides off the armchair and stands upright just like it was shown to you in the vision. He's obviously excited and he squeals with glee, then he runs on down the corridor to show you that he feels healed, and that he can run and move without the limitations and pain brought on by the disease.

When you later contemplate this event, you will ask yourself, "In the vision, did I go to the house or did God bring the house to me?" Ultimately, after all the questioning is over, it matters very little if you can't answer it with 100% accuracy, for the boy is well; and well by God's hand; and well to God's glorification. The winner in the experience is the fact of your fruit of the spirit, which came about through your sonship with God—your sharing the mind of God.

God's love, when it co-mingles with our own, does let us see across time and space barriers that normally prohibit the gathering of data by the senses. In contemplating these kinds of matters then, it is important to factor in the impact upon events of the will of God and its magnificent divine love and Fatherly sovereignty.

Sufficient proof: the indwelling Father

Inevitably, despite studying all the theories and looking across the spectrum of how different people and different faiths speak of such experiences, you will come to a final conclusion about your own experiences, and possibly through them, mine. Just like Jesus, who deemed the presence of his Thought Adjuster to be "sufficient proof of divinity in partnership with humanity,"[28] you will settle your doubts and reservations about your liaison with the mind of God. A surety will build up within you that cannot be assailed by the world or even by your past failures and shortcomings. The surety will be that, of a certainty you will know that you and your divine Father are acting together in all these matters. You will have a strength of conviction which will seem to come to you from another domain, even the kingdom of heaven, and you will understand it to be what the Urantia papers call "this new or combined mind". The evidence of your truth will not be in having a mighty God, or a powerful Thought Adjuster. Rather, the evidence will be in your own might and power as they are divinely uplifted by your Adjuster, and by the "two positive and powerful demonstrations of the fact that you are God-knowing": the fruits of the spirit and self mastery; and the fact that you risk all for the companionship with God your Father whose presence you have experienced.

As a final note in this section, I'd like to say that it is good to recognise that you already have a mighty God and a powerful and capable Thought Adjuster, suited to your every need and potential. To expect him to increase his might and power, in order for you to increase your spiritual life and experience, means little however. He already has the conviction. He already is thoroughly convinced. He already has no doubt. He already is beyond haggling, and quibbling, and two-ing and fro-ing. He already stands firm. He isn't waiting for you to order him to get his act together. He is waiting for you yourself to become certain and free of doubt, convicted with a Holy and powerful Spirit in a fusion that unites his own convictions with those of your own. He is the one who has given up all things to travel through time and space to reside with you, in your mind.[29] He has already demonstrated his faith in you, by his "patient and intense struggle"[30] to date. He is also not waiting for you to somehow become someone special enough for him to act in your life—he only needs your conviction. Along with your conviction comes your reception of his conviction and when both of you are convinced about things in a single point of view, perfection will burst into creation anew![31] When you see eye to eye, you are with and in God: you are perfect.

Then, at that time, with the perspective that is capable of knowing the will of God,[32] ask your question again, "Is all this for real?" You will then have your answer with a certainty to it, an eternal and unchallengeable certainty.

The Father's certainty and your own certainty will have a single voice. And it will say "Yes!" all across creation, "This *is* real!" With this voice, you will take the magnificent values and realities of the Urantia papers, and deposit them centrally in your own eternal being. With this voice, as a "forward-looking personality,"[33] you will influence others in your daily life with acts that emerge out of the will of your heavenly Father. With this voice, you will assist Christ Michael in his mission to bring his entire creation into the Father's perfection.[34] With this voice, you will the better be able to know God, and to be perfect as he is perfect.[35] With this voice, you will maximise your potentials, and may eventually win whole worlds to the greatest cause you will ever know, sonship with your own Father.[36]

Is this real for me, these experiences? According to my

Father's will, absolutely—for therein is it written and proven.
Of course, a better question is, "Is sonship real for you?"

Notes

1. 67:2.6 {For more than...}
2. 1:2.5 {Those who know...}
3. 2:0.1 {Inasmuch as man's...}
4. 2:0.1 {Inasmuch as man's...}
5. 161:1.1-6 {When Rodan heard...}
6. 1:2.2 {The eternal God...}
7. 5:2.4 {It is because...}
8. 5:2.4 {It is because...}
9. 101:1.7 {Thus it may...}
10. 102:1.5 {God is so...}
11. 102:7.4 {True, many apparently...}
12. 140:3.2 {I send you...}; Matthew 5:8
13. 102:8.7 {But religion is...}
14. Ephesians 2:8 — "For by grace you have been saved through faith, and this is not your own doing; it is the gift of God."
15. 103:7.14 {There is a...}
16. 136:8.3
17. 131:3.2
18. 140:8.6 {5. Personal religion...}
19. 155:6.14 {But do not...}
20. 161:1.5 point 5 {5. That God must be...}
21. 34:6.13 {The consciousness of...}
22. 143:3.8 {If, then, my children...}
23. 155:6.14 {But do not...}
24. 169:4.2
25. 194:2.1
26. 110:2.5
27. 171:7.10 {And it behooves...}
28. 136:8.3 {Throughout all this...}
29. 108:1.6 {When once the...}
30. 110:7.10 {During the making...}
31. 101:6.8 {The teachings of...}; 102:6.7 {Belief may not...}

32. 146:2.7 {6. When you have...}
33. 114:7.6 {On many worlds...}
34. 114:0.1 {The Most Highs rule...}; 114:6.4 point 4 {The angels of nation life...}
35. 1:0.3 {The enlightened worlds...}
36. 30:4.9 {7. The Paradise arrivals...}

❧

Chapter 13

Sonship and the baptism of the Holy Spirit

Experience becomes philosophical when it becomes meaningful. Philosophy becomes spiritual when it becomes empowered with divine authority. Divine authority becomes the possession of the human individual when it is revealed to him or her by grace and he or she appropriates it by faith. The individual appropriates spiritual empowerment when he or she shares it with the divine Parent who empowers it—then must the individual exercise the authority of its truth in real life situations.

The human being is best when he or she is empowered with divine authority. Such empowerment is not limited to personal allegiances to any one particular religion. It is the domain of revelation and faith in the individual.

A portion of the empowerment to which Jesus referred when he called men and women to be born again as sons of God, was referred to by the Jews of his day and by the later Christians, as the Baptism of the Holy Spirit—a term which is still in use today at the turn of the second millennium.

The Urantia papers teach that:

> "The term 'baptism of the spirit,' which came into such general use about this time, merely signified the conscious reception of this gift of the Spirit of Truth and the personal acknowledgment of this new spiritual power as an augmentation of all spiritual influences previously experienced by God-knowing souls."[1]

Sonship with Mother Spirit is not the Baptism of the Holy Spirit

This experience of mine with Mother Spirit was not like receiving the "Baptism of the Holy Spirit and fire and speaking in tongues"[2] that has been popularised by Pentecostal evangelism. I had already lived with that experience for about eighteen years. Sonship was completely different, higher, deeper, an encounter with the person who is the source of the Holy Spirit power and vitality, even a kind of will-union[3] with her. This experience made me absolutely conscious of, and certain about, my sonship with the Mother Spirit, the Holy

Spirit of Nebadon.

I invite you to search out your own experience of the Holy Spirit, fire and tongues you who have it, and I doubt you will find your sonship in amongst it. It seems that Sonship does not emerge from the *gift* of the Holy Spirit,[4] the "acknowledgment," but rather by direct contact with the person who is the Holy Spirit. That person is the Mother Spirit of Nebadon. Jesus of Nazareth did not depend upon the Baptism of the Holy Spirit at his water baptism with John in the Jordan to know his sonship with God the Father—not in Biblical nor in Urantia papers terms.

This two fold feature—our relationship of sonship with Christ Michael, Mother Spirit and the Paradise Father whose Spirit indwells us, and what is called the power from on high, the power of the Holy Spirit—is, I think, more distinguishable in the Urantia papers than the Bible.

The baptism of the Holy Spirit is acceptance of Jesus

Sonship, is a matter of contact with the person of the Son of God, Michael of Nebadon, and being spiritually changed such that you tangibly know him as your Father. The baptism of the Holy Spirit, on the other hand, is possibly better understood as the divine power that comes through the acceptance of the life and teachings and person of the risen Jesus.

There seems to be a difference. For example a believer seems to be able to have the experience of accepting Jesus and yet have no contact with Michael of Nebadon, or experience the Holy Spirit power but have no contact with Mother Spirit. I would advocate for the believer to have both types of experience: both the power and the parents.

The Bible tells us that what sounds like a single spirit, the "comforter (KJV)," "an advocate" (NRSV),[5] "even the Spirit of Truth"[6] will be sent by the Father upon the prayer of the risen Jesus after he has ascended to heaven.

The Urantia papers indicate that the Biblical terms are blurry and in fact confuse the ministry of three individual "Spirits," each of whom provide a ministry to the human being which is able to be both individual—that is, three ministries—and perfectly unified in nature—that is, as if from a single source that we name "God."

The three spiritual persons are the Holy Spirit (Mother Spirit), the Spirit of Truth (Michael of Nebadon's truth) and the Spirit of the Father (the Thought Adjuster).

The Urantia papers go into greater detail than I am addressing here in my narrative, and identify additional spiritual influences that contact with the human individual.[7]

The Spirit of Truth

Regarding the Spirit of Truth, the Urantia papers say:

"Do not overlook the fact that the Spirit of Truth was bestowed upon all sincere believers; this gift of the spirit did not come only to the apostles. The one hundred and twenty men and women assembled in the upper chamber all received the new teacher, as did all the honest of heart throughout the whole world. This new teacher was bestowed upon mankind, and every soul received him in accordance with the love for truth and the capacity to grasp and comprehend spiritual realities. At last, true religion is delivered from the custody of priests and all sacred classes and finds its real manifestation in the individual souls of men."[8]

"Though the Spirit of Truth is poured out upon all flesh, this spirit of the Son is almost wholly limited in function and power by man's personal reception of that which constitutes the sum and substance of the mission of the bestowal Son. The Holy Spirit is partly independent of human attitude and partially conditioned by the decisions and co-operation of the will of man. Nevertheless, the ministry of the Holy Spirit becomes increasingly effective in the sanctification and spiritualization of the inner life of those mortals who the more fully obey the divine leadings."[9]

"The first mission of this spirit is, of course, to foster and personalise truth, for it is the comprehension of truth that constitutes the highest form of human liberty. Next, it is the purpose of this spirit to destroy the believer's feeling of orphanhood. Jesus having been among men, all believers would experience a sense of loneliness had not the Spirit of

Truth come to dwell in men's hearts."[10]

"Thus it appears that the Spirit of Truth comes really to lead all believers into all truth, into the expanding knowledge of the experience of the living and growing spiritual consciousness of the reality of eternal and ascending sonship with God."[11]

"On the day of Pentecost the religion of Jesus broke all national restrictions and racial fetters. It is forever true, 'Where the spirit of the Lord is, there is liberty.' On this day the Spirit of Truth became the personal gift from the Master to every mortal. This spirit was bestowed for the purpose of qualifying believers more effectively to preach the gospel of the kingdom, but they mistook the experience of receiving the outpoured spirit for a part of the new gospel which they were unconsciously formulating."[12]

The Bible and the baptism of the Holy Spirit

The Bible speaks of receiving power when the Holy Spirit has come upon you;[13] "being clothed with power from on high;"[14] that you will do greater works than Jesus;[15] if you are willing, you will begin to speak in other tongues as the Holy Spirit gives you utterance;[16] and that you should ask, for it will be given you; you should search, and you will find; you should knock, and the door will be opened for you: for everyone who asks receives, and everyone who searches finds, and for everyone who knocks, the door will be opened.[17]

Jesus commanded believers who are equipped with this power to evangelise the world, when he said:

"All authority in heaven and on Earth has been given to me. Go therefore and make disciples of all nations, baptising them in the name of the Father and of the Son and of the Holy Spirit, and teaching them to obey everything that I have commanded you. And remember, I am with you always, to the end of the age."[18]

Again, Jesus said,

"Go into all the world and proclaim the good news to the whole creation. The one who believes and is baptized will be saved; but the one who does not believe will be condemned. And these signs will accompany those who believe: by using my name they will cast out demons; they will speak in new tongues; they will pick up snakes in their hands, and if they drink any deadly thing, it will not hurt them; they will lay their hands on the sick, and they will recover."[19]

The difference between sonship and the power from on high

The clearest Biblical statement that tells me of the distinction between the sonship of contact with Michael of Nebadon, and contact with the "power from on high" of Luke 24:49, comes from Acts 1:4-5 and Acts 2:1-4. These two passages are arguably the definitive Biblical statement on what it was that the closest followers of Jesus experienced at the time they were empowered for the kingdom work.

"While staying with them, he ordered them not to leave Jerusalem, but to wait there for the promise of the Father. 'This,' he said, 'is what you have heard from me; for John baptized with water, but you will be baptized with the Holy Spirit not many days from now.' So when they had come together, they asked him, 'Lord, is this the time when you will restore the kingdom to Israel?' He replied, 'It is not for you to know the times or periods that the Father has set by his own authority. But you will receive power when the Holy Spirit has come upon you; and you will be my witnesses in Jerusalem, in all Judea and Samaria, and to the ends of the Earth.' When he had said this, as they were watching, he was lifted up, and a cloud took him out of their sight."[20]

"When the day of Pentecost had come, they were all together in one place. And suddenly from heaven there came a sound like the rush of a violent wind, and it filled the entire house where they were sitting. Divided tongues, as of fire, appeared among them, and a tongue rested on each of them. All of them were filled with the Holy Spirit and began to speak in other languages, as the Spirit gave them ability."[21]

These two passages tell me that the men and women in the upper room did not experience the consciousness of sonship with the Son of God, who is Michael of Nebadon, at that time, but that they were mightily empowered to do the work of the kingdom, as they understood it.

These believers and apostles had already experienced the risen Jesus when he appeared to them on various occasions. Those experiences surely added something to their faith and knowledge and confidence in the later experience of the Holy Spirit and fire and tongues. For someone like Peter, this empowerment in the upper room was additional to the personal spiritual breakthrough he had already made which pre-empted his contact with the risen Jesus in the garden some forty days previously on Easter Sunday.[22]

Yet, in all this, there is a difference between being in the company of the risen Jesus, receiving the baptism of the Holy Spirit, and receiving sonship with the persons of Michael of Nebadon, Mother Spirit and the Paradise Father who indwells the human mind as the Thought Adjuster.

Chronology of spiritual development

When I survey the chronology of spiritual experiences in my life, I would place the Baptism of the Holy Spirit and fire and tongues fairly early in my young adult life. The experience of universal citizenship that came through sonship with Michael and Mother Spirit and the Paradise Father came some eighteen years later when I was in my forties. Both experiences were interlinked. I came to understand more about the baptism experience through the sonship experience, and I doubt I could have had such a pure hearted vision of God when sonship arrived were it not for the intensity and depth of the baptism experience. One thing I do know is that the experience of the Baptism of the Holy Spirit and fire and tongues, with its extraordinary gift of power from on high, is the same empowerment whether the recipient is a Bible believer or a Urantia papers believer or both. The baptism of the Holy Spirit issues forth from the empowered ministry of the Father and the Son and the Holy Spirit through the life and teachings of Jesus of Nazareth.

My own baptism of the Holy Spirit and fire and tongues came about through an experience of crucifixion in my spirit. The crucifixion was the surrendering of my will wholly into obedience to the will of Jesus Christ, Michael of Nebadon. The surrender was so complete that, in very real terms, it called for, and found, the surrendering of my life. It totally changed all that my life had ever been. The following chapter chronicles that particular story for you.

ᕀ

Notes

1. 194:2.10 {The term 'baptism...}
2. Acts 2:3; 10:46; 19:6; 1 Corinthians 12:10; 12:28; 14:5
3. 180:2.4 {But great sorrow...}
4. 34:5.5
5. John 14:16
6. John 14:17
7. 194:2.12 {In a way...}
8. 194:3.6
9. 34:5.5
10. 194:2.2
11. 194:2.7
12. 194:3.5
13. Acts 1:8
14. Luke 24:49
15. John 14:12
16. Acts 2:4
17. Luke 11:9-10
18. Matthew 28:18-20
19. Mark 16:15-18
20. Acts 1:4-9
21. Acts 2:1-4
22. 191:1.1

ᕀ

Chapter 14

Sonship and death on the cross

In 1973, I was on retreat on a farm in Ormond near Dannevirke New Zealand, with another young chap who, like me, had given his life over to God, yoga and meditation. We were both young in spirit and in years. We had met in the Sivananda Yoga Ashram in Auckland and later headed south to live in isolation with God.

I was still highly motivated and spiritually invigorated from some kind of Earth shaking spiritual awakening of about six months earlier. I had pierced the meaning of a sentence in a Taoist book that said, "...and causation is the name whereby the sensorial universe is perceived."

It flipped me into a whole other world and, at twenty-two, I knew with a certainty that my spiritual destiny lay in the area of the enlightenment that Taoists, Hindus and Buddhists pursued.

A still small voice

One day, while my companion on this retreat was alone in the nearby mountains, a still, small voice of God entered my equally still, small mind during a period of meditation, saying:

"Why don't you go to India."

So I did. When he returned the next day, I told him of my experience, packed my few belongings and headed north.

I didn't know a whole lot about India. I had read "Autobiography of a Yogi," by Paramhansa Yogananda. I believed him. I believed in his yoga. I had read a book on Ramana Maharshi. I believed him too. I believed in his utterly transcendent renunciation of the world. I headed off with a half-baked idea about becoming a wandering Sadhu, but it never eventuated. I returned from India having spent time with Satya Sai Baba and some monks in Rishikesh in North India. Something was missing, either in what they were all doing or what I was doing.

The following year I went to Nepal, where I stayed with Lama Yeshe and Lama Zopa in their Tibetan monastery at Kopan near Boudhanath outside Kathmandu.

I very much wanted to become a monk, and I had a pretty good grasp of the basics of Buddhism. I made friends with another westerner who had recently been ordained in that order, called Ngawang Chodok. His companionship, plus a dream that I'd had several months before, made me think that this was the place for me. But I had difficulty supporting myself financially for more than a few months.

The monk in the Tibetan Buddhist monastic system is dependent largely on benefactorial support, and I had none. I would later live in that locality as a monk ordained in a Chinese order of Buddhism, making my living by treating people with acupuncture. I even had the joyful privilege of being called on to assist the Queen Mother of Bhutan, and the head Umchi, traditional Tibetan doctor, of Ladakh, who resided in Leh. Many monks later told me about the great opportunities and benefits that would come to me through that association with the Queen Mother. At that time I also caught up with Chodok again.

Later, unknown to each of us, we would both leave Asia and work in drug and alcohol centres, he in San Francisco and me in Melbourne. But in these days of 1974, my staying there as a monk was difficult.

The following year, after I had stayed in India for a while, revisiting Satya Sai Baba, the monks in Rishikesh and some Sufis in New Delhi, I went to Australia. I was still spiritually aching inside for some kind of vocation with God.

I took a job but after about a month I felt that it was simply too far off the mark. I was so very hungry for a spiritual vocation. I surveyed the adventures in faith that I had undertaken to date and whilst they were of God, the gap they were filling still had holes in it.

While I worked at my job each day, I eventually arrived at the conclusion to simply renounce the world. It seemed that that would take care of my desire to be a wandering Sadhu. I thought I would live a quiet spiritual life as a hermit in the woods in New Zealand. It seemed that that would take care of any visa and cultural requirements. It was a little thought out idea, but it seemed to match my inner desire to be utterly alone with God. I wasn't seeking monastic creeds and activities, and the obligations of community. I loved people very much, but now they seemed to be standing between God and me.

Quietly pursuing my Father

Over the next month, I made a monk's habit out of cloth to wear in my new vocation. My friend Don Anderson, bless his heart, still has that habit hanging behind his bedroom door.

I bought a wooden bowl to eat out of. I had had a copy of the Urantia papers for some time and, although I hadn't read much of them, I thought that they would be suitable for long periods of isolation. I met a lovely lady once, years later, Gwen, who had gone with her daughter into a retreat cabin in the woodlands of Kentucky, as I recall, where they spent an entire year sitting opposite each other on the floor over a low wooden table, reading the Urantia papers to each other. What a year that must have been for them. She said it completely reshaped her view on life, and the empowerment with which she then approached all of life's challenges.

It also seemed to me that there was a desire from God that I should take it along, so I packed my copy of the Urantia papers, handed in my notice at work and one Friday night around midnight I flew over to New Zealand from Melbourne.

My plans had been pretty simple. About a week after I had made the decision to launch out on a hermit's life, I received a letter from a fellow I had met at Lama Yeshe's monastery in Nepal. He told me that the Lamas were going to be visiting New Zealand and conducting a retreat. He said that he felt moved in his spirit that I should come to that retreat. I thought that it would be a good thing to kickstart my new life, so I phoned him and confirmed my arrival. As it happened, the flight I was taking would bring me into the country in the early morning of the day the retreat commenced. It all seemed to fall together pretty well really.

I was very secretive about what I was doing. I told only one fellow, the chap who I had arranged to take over my job once I left. I changed into my habit at his place in Melbourne around midnight, and he drove me out to the airport. I left everything else I owned at Don's house, and a note saying that I wasn't coming back. He later said that he was very surprised that I had vanished like that, but he understood, and kept my habit as a token of yet another interesting event in his already unusual life.

On Saturday morning, clad in this brown woollen habit that

was a cross between the habit of the Benedictines I had stayed with briefly in Yarra Glen, Victoria, and that of Francis of Assisi in the movies, I walked into the Lamas' retreat. I came with my bowl, my Urantia papers, a sleeping bag, soap, tooth brush and paste and a little cash. Whatever was going on for me, I knew that I was on a life-changing mission that was a renunciation of life as I had known it, and an adoption of a life for God alone. It might have been a pretty dumb idea, but it was all I had to work with. I have never regretted it.

Buddhist retreat

Upon my arrival, I met with Lama Yeshe. Each day, Lama Zopa taught the Lam Rim teaching, apparently more fully than ever before, such was the apparent zeal of the participants. Over the week, the flock of about fifty people dwindled down to about twenty-five. The old hands who had done a Tibetan Buddhist retreat before, looked like they were really getting the hang of it all. The newcomers mostly just looked lost, motherless, and they constantly rubbed their knees that ached from sitting cross-legged for long hours at a time. We all mostly seemed to have arrived with our homespun fantasies of spiritual experience, intent on trying our best to match them up to Tibetan Buddhism, and feeling the frustration of that kind of jigsaw simply not coming together at all.

In those days, religion seemed to be everywhere. Christian revivalists prayed side by side with monastics and those who spear-headed a Christian sexual revolution. Maharishi, Maharaji, Sai Baba, Maher Baba, Ananda Margha and the Hare Krishna's emerged out of Hinduism with yoga and love and bliss, asceticism, weird costumes and vegetarian cooking. Islam revealed its beautiful Koran and Whirling Dervishes and the wisdom of the Sufi sect. There was Thai Buddhism with its begging; Japanese Zen Buddhism with its riddles and whacking sticks; Tibetan Tantric Buddhism with its Himalayan magical ritual. There was Bruce Lee and Kung Fu, Martial Art, Tai Chi, Chi Gong. East and West were both knocking on heaven's door together. Even Judaism, that monument to *aint nothing new till the Messiah shows up*, got caught up in it. It seemed that ever so many people were getting into something or other, and for all sorts of reasons, not the least of which was the spiritual revulsion at the impact of the police action in Vietnam.

Some people wanted to be the next generation of teachers. For others it was to be healers. Some seemed to be called to be fore-tellers and prophets. Others wanted to be mystics and recluses. Still others wanted the romance of the mysterious Taoist mist walkers and Hawaiian Kahunas. Some people wanted spirituality to miraculously pander to their every whim, others saw it as the great ascetic challenge. Some saw it in terms of the transcendence of life and death, while others saw it as the means of living this life in the world as a servant of the poor and the increasingly drug affected.

Some people were lukewarm window shoppers, wanting merely to satisfy their idle curiosity. They sang the songs and danced the dance but never knew there was a walk to walk called the faith walk. Mammon ruled their hearts and minds and they had no problem whatsoever with Jesus' teaching about not being able to serve two masters.[1]

Everywhere, there were large numbers of people who didn't want a bar of it, and a few who actively opposed it. And it wasn't all *for the good*. The Church of Satan in San Francisco was doing pretty good business up the West Coast of the States and Canada too.

Looking back from the view of the religions themselves, there were some instances when the sheer might and power of lofty, mature spiritual experience that was being presented to wide-eyed devotees, really struggled to find a big enough patch of ground in which to plant this new seed. By the eighties, there was a developing search for sensitivity and meaning found in a mix of godless personal growth and natural therapies. There would also be the repercussion of such present divinity: the raw, gaping, wounded soul of street drugs, death, crime, hopelessness, hatred, violence; ferocious recklessness for its own sake.

This Cain and Abel of the so-called marvellous Aquarian age would be light and darkness, life and death, the upliftment of mankind and the desecration of mankind, both born to the same parent it seemed. But that was way off there in the future of the nineteen eighties. The ideologies of the seventies somehow misinterpreted Jesus' words[2] about the morrow bringing its own troubles, to read the morrow will somehow miraculously look after itself. Of course, it didn't.

Like most others, that retreat in New Zealand in 1975 attracted a pretty good cross-section of the spiritual aspirants of the day. Personal growth didn't exist. New Age bodywork and therapies didn't exist. Believers were looking for the pure, unadulterated spirit. By far, most of the teachers were foreign religious.

For a retreat, it was pretty intense. It was in the middle of winter, freezing, in Spartan conditions, and yet the Tibetans had a disarmingly toothy-smile kind of way of bringing out the best in their students. And that meant getting down to some heavy-duty intensity.

Seeking universal love

About a week into this retreat, and fully drenched with the power that spills over into your life from those who live committed lives of renunciation, I found a strong desire in me to experience the universal love I had heard so much of in the various spiritual camps of those days.

I didn't want to know it as something I could get my head around; I wanted to spiritually know it with my whole being. I wanted it for real. I had a great faith in the effects of real spiritual experience. It wasn't that I wanted to get saved, as Christians use that term. The term *saved* didn't make any sense to me in those days because I felt I was so connected to God that I didn't have anything to get saved from. I was intensely hungry to be in direct contact with God's character though. I wanted what Jesus called "a pure heart,"[3] but more than that, I wanted to embody the kind of love that loves all persons and beings, just like God embodies that kind of love.

It was a genuine desire in me. It wasn't just some passing thought or whimsical speculation. I really wanted to know. In Urantia papers terminology, I wanted to appropriate it.

The desire faded and transformed into a total desire for renunciation. One night I spent the entire night sitting up in meditation. The whole place was deserted as people went off to their cabins to sleep. I on the other hand had given my whole life, body and soul over to God. There I sat on the meditation room floor, leaning against the wall, the things of this world, my body, thoughts, actions, history, everything, had become rootless, selfless, void of inherent self reality. They were showing themselves to have no lasting reality to them at all. They were just like shadows, when you turn the light on, where do they go? Nowhere: they never were in the first place.

The journey

As I sat in the meditation hall the next day while Lama Zopa continued his regime of teaching from memorised scripture, I sensed the presence of a spiritual personality standing behind me. This person told me that he would help me to answer my heart's wish, to know "universal love."

In a moment, I found myself secured into him and being transported out beyond the realms where humans live. We journeyed in spirit, first to some kind of a Buddhist Buddha and then on to a great throne room where I saw a dozen Buddha-like beings sitting solemnly on their thrones in a line against a vast marble wall. Years later, I speculated whether these were the seats of the Twenty-four Counsellors of Jerusem mentioned in the Urantia papers, but I never found it an important enough question to bother with seeking an answer.

Meeting Jesus Christ

I asked one of these beings if he could help me to know what universal love is. He beckoned me to the person in the middle. I looked over, walked to the foot of that throne and, looking up, I found myself before Jesus. There was no mistaking him.

I found his presence in this great hall quite surprising. Firstly, I didn't have much connection with Jesus. I'd given my heart to him at the age of twelve. The power of that conviction lasted about three attempts at reading Genesis and a couple of weeks of finding out that Bible study girls were weird. Then when I was sixteen and in the Navy, I had a dream one night in which he asked me to take confirmation classes, so that he and I could share communion bread and wine together: which I did. But neither of these experiences had drawn me into Christianity or to a personal spiritual walk with him. More importantly I suppose, was the fact that this was a Buddhist retreat. What was Jesus doing in it? Surely, Buddhism, and Tibetan Buddhism especially, would have had someone in charge of their version of universal love without having to draw on Jesus. I finally reconciled these queries by simply thinking that Jesus was just a part of all the spiritual growth we humans encounter along the way to increased enlightenment.

I looked up at him. He looked at me.

"Sir, I began. "Will you help me to know what universal love is?"

Jesus serenely looked down at me as if I was not the best candidate to be probing around in that kind of a field. Then he replied:

"That is a very difficult thing to do. Are you sure you want to do it?"

"Yes I am," I replied expectantly, and completely naively.

The two angels and the grassy hill

He promptly summoned two angelic assistants who, coming to my side, received instructions and commands from him. Then one of them drew close to me, enfolded me and ferried me some distance to a grassy green hillside.

On the hillside was a large, rough-hewn, timber cross like you see in all the Easter movies and in the occasional fundamentalist Church. Nestled at each point around it were a handful of gruff men in nondescript uniforms of sorts.

I stood at the foot of the cross, facing away from it. The two angels of escort hovered in mid air about fifteen feet away from me. Jesus did not accompany us.

Questioning

In what can only be described as a display of duty, showing no emotion whatsoever, the taller of the two angels out there in front of me asked:

"What is it that you want?"

"I want to know what love is," I replied.

He repeated Jesus' earlier warning:

"That is a very difficult thing to do. Are you sure you want to do this thing?" he asked me.

"Yes I am", I said.

With that same display of unemotional impartiality he asked:

"Are you really sure?"

For a moment I paused, and wondered to myself what could possibly be the big deal. I felt safe. This was nothing more than my imagination. It couldn't possibly be real. At best it was some kind of quasi-mystical pantomime, not to be taken too seriously. Why would my own internal dialogue produce that kind of a question? In fact, the whole line of dialogue seemed quite unusual and foreign. With a naive nonchalance, I looked into the eyes of that angel and answered:

"Yes, I'm sure."

"Look down there," he said, as he swept his left arm back as an indication to look down to the bottom of the hill.

Suffering humanity

I looked down to the foot of the hill. It sloped away several miles beneath me. There I saw the most disgusting and loathsome collection of creatures I have ever witnessed. It was a crowd of millions upon millions of people. With almost complete exception, they possessed no spirituality in themselves whatsoever.

They were so many in number, so materially governed, so enslaved to the bondage of fear and hatred, so consumed with hacking out their survival, and their movements were so vicious as they hurriedly brushed past each other. They looked like a seething sea of rats with no redeeming features whatsoever about them.

Among them were but a handful of men and women who had a glow of light around them that varied from dim to bright, proportional with their own spiritual vision. They were the figures of spiritual influence in the population and, despite their valiant efforts, it wasn't difficult to see that revival had not yet hit town.

"Do you see these people?" the taller of the angels asked me.

"Yes", I replied; somewhat hoping this grotesque *before* scene was going to magically transform into a heavenly *after* scene at any moment. But it wasn't to be.

I had totally forgotten about the burly soldiers milling around that cross behind me. When I said my response to his question, he commanded them to lay me out on the cross and to hold me fast.

They did that, leaning onto my hands and feet and shoulders, pinning me to the cross. As I lay there I could look over my toes to see that ugly mass of people so far off at the base of the hill.

The two angels, still hovering in mid air, now moved quite close to me. The taller one looked at me and asked:

"Do you see those people down there?"

I looked at that forsaken, horrible population that possessed no realistic redeeming features and replied:

"Yes."

Then I couldn't believe what he said next. He stunned me. They were the most devastating words he could ever have spoken. In absolutely unemotional and matter of fact terms, he said:

"Will you die for them?"

I really was taken aback. I thought to myself, this guy can't be for real. Surely not! I looked, searchingly, at that pit of hate and filth to which he alluded, in absolute disbelief.

"What!" I said to myself. I couldn't believe that he was asking such a thing.

I began to console myself and was so thankful that this was only some kind of weird daydream that I was occupying myself with while Lama Zopa worked his own way through the morning's session back in the meditation retreat. I certainly felt like I was some place else, I knew not where, disengaged from the retreat centre, but it wasn't particularly real.

Probably, more than anything, it was out of curiosity and out of wanting to get to the end of this so-called movie that I replied to his question of whether I would die for these horrible people. Finally, I said it, but I didn't really say it with any conviction:

"Yes."

My response brought the soldiers to a state of readiness. Their strong hands gripped my ankles and shoulders and wrists as if steel vices had suddenly tightened around my limbs. I saw one fellow place the tip of a big metal spike on my right wrist. It looked hideous and it felt every bit as sharp as it looked. He lay his mallet on the thick timber of the crossbeam, with complete indifference toward me.

A sudden shift of reality

Then, an extraordinary empowerment, a divine anointing, came on this taller angel. A grand countenance came about him. The very essence of universal nobility boldly declared throughout the heavens that all authority was vested in him. He was to all intents and purposes, the *Lord*. What he did, was the *Lord* doing things. What he said, was the *Lord* saying things. He didn't hover in space any more, the space did what he told it to do. This angel was in control, and everybody around about me knew it.

As cool as a cucumber, with total command over the situation, he looked at me with an absolute conviction and finality about himself. Then he exercised his authority to act in the name of Jesus; and for Jesus; and as Jesus. I had just told him that I would indeed die for these people, but it was a pretty shallow answer. Then he slowly said:

"Are...you...certain?"

Each word was an absolute statement in itself. They were spoken as if each syllable was an 'I am that I am' declaration.

Suddenly, this seemed a whole lot more real than it had been a moment ago!

Suddenly, this was a new thing. These folks weren't fooling around.

Suddenly, I knew that I could not have returned to the meditation room if I had tried. I looked across at the grass nearby, I could smell it, it was *that* real.

Suddenly, I was actually living this mystical experience. I was on a track with no going back and I had to live out its conclusion. Whatever this stuff was, it was suddenly more real than anything else I had ever known.

My thoughts went a million miles an hour, searching for all the safety nets, all the rationale and logic, all the for's and against's for dying for this horde of soul-less human refuse.

I was unable to find a single reason to die for those people. They surely could not benefit by my death. They wouldn't even know that I had died for them. The whole idea was preposterous.

Finally, the only remaining thought I had was about why I was in this situation anyway. I restated to myself that I had wanted to learn what love is; I had asked Jesus to help me; then here I was.

I thought to myself that, if this was the outcome of trusting Jesus, then I'd go with whatever was required, without knowing all the in's and out's of why it was like this. If Jesus thought I should die for these seemingly forsaken people, then I had only one answer and it had to be "yes." I had nothing to go on but my trust in Jesus. My life was worth nothing, and yet for some reason he wanted me to die for these people—people I didn't even believe in. So, in faith, I replied to the angelic character who was in mid air before me:

I looked at the two angels.

"Yes", I slowly said. "I'll die for them."

Instantly I felt the mallets drive home those metal spikes through my wrists and my feet.

The agony

Agony hit me.

Profoundly.

Through and through.

Totally—total agony!

In an instant, my whole body filled with agony. Agony consumed me. It grew and grew. As if an hour went by, still the agony increased. It engulfed me, and still it increased until it seemed that the entire universe, all space in all directions, was nothing but all consuming and endless agony.

The agony reached infinite proportions. I was not in control of it. The agony didn't take long to sweep all control away from me. It swept me up and splintered me like a little wooden house engulfed by the tornado of 1999 that carved its path through Moore, Oklahoma.

Agony ruled, and increased, in intensity, in volume and in dimension. After a while all there was, was agony—as if all the space in all the universe became some all consuming pain that absorbed everything in its path. Soon the whole universe was utter, hopeless, soul destroying agony; and it had its own will to grow bigger and bigger.

I have no idea how long this went on for. It was an eternity of raw, physical, soul-shattering pain, made eternal because it had no end. I was long extinguished as a creature identity with will to do anything about it, and yet still I suffered this dreadful pain. I had become a fully awake dead thing who was all consumed by this agony. Perhaps, as I reflect on it now as I am writing this long after the fact of the experience, this death is what some people have called hell because of its subjective experience of eternal pain. Nothing could have reached and turned that pain from the inside. All hope was gone. I had long ago had all thoughts of Jesus and his angels swept away from me, like how a raging river sweeps a helpless victim away from a branch they are clinging to.

On and on it went, more infinite and more infinite it grew, this raging nuclear holocaust of agony.

Then suddenly, long after I had any consciousness of myself, something changed.

Total love

In a single moment, the agony reach its zenith. This great infinity of pain suddenly flipped and, as vast and total as it was agony it became equally as vast an infinity of love.

O God, the release!

The explosion of love!

The unbelievable uprooting of pain.

It seemed to be forever before there was an I to experience it. But experience it I eventually did.

Where there had been total agony and total desolation of my identity and my will, now there was total love—universal love in all its originality. It was as if I had entered the volcano of its very origin in the heart of God himself. The love was so raw, so real, so virginal. It wasn't loving anyone or anything, it was simply total, omnipresent love.

Gradually, the love included me and I found myself becoming a self again. I found myself being put back together, the significant difference was that this universal love was now the origin of my existence.

That love was mine. I owned it. It owned me. That vanquished pain was mine. I owned it too. They forged the core of a new me that was now the very skeleton of my soul. It was my victory. Suddenly, I was caught up in a process like the creation in Genesis: Life Be, and Life Was. Suddenly, Resurrection Be, and Resurrection Was.

Born again in the spirit

I was born again in spirit!

I had come to Jesus with my question and he had afforded me the answer.

After that event, I was never the same person. My genes were different somehow. I had put myself in the hands of Jesus; I had taken on board a part of his realness spoken of in John 10: 11, "I am the good shepherd. The good shepherd lays down his life for the sheep."

I had died for these people and now I was born again. Born of the spirit.

After I gathered my presence back in the meditation hall, I looked through the wall and out into the field. Two angels glided across the field and through the wall and stopped in front of me. They were intent on doing something of their own design, and seemed oblivious to whether I could perceive them or not. These were not the same angels who had accompanied me to the cross. The taller of the two moved to my right hand side. He revealed a roaring blue-silver flame. It was about half a metre long, and powerful like a welding torch. It sat about an inch above my head. Then he and his companion stood back a few feet in front of me. They looked at the flame to verify its place. The smaller of the two then wrote something in a book. They turned, still without so much as saying one word to me or even seeking my attention, and glided across the room and through the wall and out across the field. They disappeared about fifty yards out over the grass.

I had never read the book of Acts at that time in my life, but it speaks of such things as flames above the heads of the Holy Spirit-filled.

Another peculiar thing that was foreign to me at that time was the spirit-filled speaking in tongues that was going on almost of its own volition. To all intents and purposes it was like I was speaking in some rustic Tibetan dialect. In fact, that's what I thought I was doing. It was only many years later that I heard Christians speaking in tongues that I understood that was what I had been doing. The language was somehow the language of God: when I spoke it, it was as though I was speaking to God in God's language. Strange stuff. I had no idea about these sorts of things in those days.

I was a new thing, and by God I knew it! I had gone through the totality of mortal suffering and everything that was the absence of God, and been birthed out the other side of it. Things were going on inside of me that were just like fireworks. There was an all consuming Holy Fire on the inside of me. I was baptized in something powerfully Holy. I sat there looking straight out through the wall as if it was an everyday matter of fact thing to do, looking at the traces of these angels. I was filled with the universal love of Christ Jesus in a *cup runneth over* way. I had the spirit of renunciation. I was crucified in the flesh, and born again in the spirit. And there was this mighty gushing flame thundering above my head. It was a new thing. I was a new creature. And God knew it, for I was of him!

I turned my attention to the Spirit of God who was standing behind me. I wanted to say thank you, but all I could do was commune in an endless love with him and occasionally mutter the words:

"Thank you Father. Thank you Jesus."

The experience of finding universal love was completely life changing, as you can imagine. The power of it was awesome. There seemed to be an endless supply and variety of spiritual gifts for communication and healing. I emerged out of the meditation hall that morning with God's ability to look right into the hearts and minds of people, even to communicate with God who touched their soul and spoke to their inner heart.

Heavenly humility

But the greatest gift of that experience was that I knew love through humility. I had died the spiritual death. I was reborn. It's an incredibly fortifying experience. Yet it is a magnificently and irrevocably humbling experience. From that day on, I knew that humility underpins all spiritual wisdom, all spiritual growth, all spiritual power—even God himself.

The Urantia papers say that Jesus brought people to God by asking them to receive the Father's forgiveness and to believe in the principle of sonship with God. I hope you can see in both of these aspects of his gospel, the foundation stone of indomitable humility. God is enabled to contact us, to Father us, when first we are humble and allow him.

Authentic humility is spiritual. It formed my genes as my new spiritual self emerged from this Baptism of the Holy Spirit through Jesus. Jesus had orchestrated my death on the cross, his cross, not me. Jesus had rebuilt me from a dead thing that was consumed in agony, not me. Jesus had supplied me this new thing called divine life, not me. Jesus maintained a living connection with me that supplied the boundless gifts of the spirit; and it was Jesus who commenced to share with me the things he had inherited from his Father. Jesus gave me of himself, abundantly.

I had no choice but to be humble about it all. But better than that, it was fantastic being humble. I loved being humble, I still do. Humility is a compass. It is a living link with Jesus and Mother Spirit, Christ Michael and the Paradise Father.

The baptism of the Holy Spirit issues forth from Christ Michael, Mother Spirit and the Paradise Father who indwells us. It is the force of their combined Parenting of us. It comes to us from beyond all that is of this world and thereby enables us to be victorious over all that is of this world. Humility, like authentic love, is eternal, infinite, omnipotent and ever refreshing because it reunites us with the world-overcoming life that is in our divine Parents.

The Baptism of the Holy Spirit has its origins in humility, love and power which is divine. I would say that it is the foundation of the realisation of sonship with its authors— Mother Spirit and Michael of Nebadon, and the Paradise Father—yet, whilst they both issue from heaven, the two experiences are quite distinct.

A couple of worthy questions to ask yourself are:

"When you live in heaven, what use is the baptism of the Holy Spirit to you?"

"When you live in heaven, who are your parents?"

❦

Notes

1. Matthew 6:24
2. Matthew 6:34
3. 140:5.10; 140:8.6; Matthew 5:8

❦

Chapter 15

Sonship and discipleship

For me, to meet with the risen Jesus of Nazareth, as compared with Michael of Nebadon, was a fact of spiritual hope. It gave me confidence that God loved me and that my love for God was pure. When I found actual sonship in the Father, and when I found actual sonship in Michael of Nebadon, and when I found sonship in Mother Spirit, three different aspects of sonship with three different persons, I was completely transformed in my spiritual condition and granted the passport, so to speak, of universal citizenship.

The belief in God, even the belief in sonship with God, or for those with gender sensitivities—daughtership with God or childship with God—obviously has dimensions of reality to it. I understand those dimensions to be based around actual personal contact with the persons of deity. An aside here is that it is obviously important to be sufficiently mature in one's relationship with God and these matters of sonship as to easily move beyond the primitive concept that no man can see God and live.[1]   Sonship, inevitably, necessarily, is about literal contact with the persons who are our own divine Parents.

Peter in the garden

I want to show you something about the phenomenon of meeting one's divine Parents and how it differs somewhat from the currently accepted experiences of contact with God. Whilst the Bible shows no trace of this account, the Urantia papers speak of Peter meeting the risen Jesus in the garden on resurrection Sunday. Peter pushes his faith in a mammoth struggle to believe things that challenge him. Perhaps he is challenged by the simple fact that his friend and teacher is all that the Jewish scriptures say he is. Perhaps he struggles with the fact of life after death. Perhaps he struggles with the guilt and shame that arose from his rejecting Jesus before the cock crowed. Perhaps it was all of these and more. Whatever it was, however, Peter's faith was sufficient to enable him to experience the person of Jesus by means of his faith and by means of his spirit's perception. The following is the record in the Urantia papers of that meeting.

"It was near half past eight o'clock this Sunday evening when Jesus appeared to Simon Peter in the garden of the Mark home. This was his eighth morontia[2] manifestation. Peter had lived under a heavy burden of doubt and guilt ever since his denial of the Master. All day Saturday and this Sunday he had fought the fear that, perhaps, he was no longer an apostle. He had shuddered at the fate of Judas and even thought that he, too, had betrayed his Master. All this afternoon he thought that it might be his presence with the apostles that prevented Jesus' appearing to them, provided, of course, he had really risen from the dead. And it was to Peter, in such a frame of mind and in such a state of soul, that Jesus appeared as the dejected apostle strolled among the flowers and shrubs.

"When Peter thought of the loving look of the Master as he passed by on Annas's porch, and as he turned over in his mind that wonderful message brought him early that morning by the women who came from the empty tomb, 'Go tell my apostles—and Peter'—as he contemplated these tokens of mercy, his faith began to surmount his doubts, and he stood still, clenching his fists, while he spoke aloud: 'I believe he has risen from the dead; I will go and tell my brethren.' And as he said this, there suddenly appeared in front of him the form of a man, who spoke to him in familiar tones, saying: 'Peter, the enemy desired to have you, but I would not give you up. I knew it was not from the heart that you disowned me; therefore I forgave you even before you asked; but now must you cease to think about yourself and the troubles of the hour while you prepare to carry the good news of the gospel to those who sit in darkness. No longer should you be concerned with what you may obtain from the kingdom but rather be exercised about what you can give to those who live in dire spiritual poverty. Gird yourself, Simon, for the battle of a new day, the struggle with spiritual darkness and the evil doubtings of the natural minds of men.'

"Peter and the morontia Jesus walked through the garden and talked of things past, present, and future for almost five minutes. Then the Master vanished from his gaze, saying, 'Farewell, Peter, until I see you with your brethren.'

"For a moment, Peter was overcome by the realization that he had talked with the risen Master, and that he could be sure he was still an ambassador of the kingdom. He had just heard the glorified Master exhort him to go on preaching the gospel. And with all this welling up within his heart, he rushed to the upper chamber and into the presence of his fellow apostles, exclaiming in breathless excitement: 'I have seen the Master; he was in the garden. I talked with him, and he has forgiven me.'

"Peter's declaration that he had seen Jesus in the garden made a profound impression upon his fellow apostles, and they were about ready to surrender their doubts when Andrew got up and warned them not to be too much influenced by his brother's report. Andrew intimated that Peter had seen things which were not real before. Although Andrew did not directly allude to the vision of the night on the Sea of Galilee wherein Peter claimed to have seen the Master coming to them walking on the water, he said enough to betray to all present that he had this incident in mind. Simon Peter was very much hurt by his brother's insinuations and immediately lapsed into crestfallen silence. The twins felt very sorry for Peter, and they both went over to express their sympathy and to say that they believed him and to reassert that their own mother had also seen the Master."[3]

This passage speaks to me about how Peter is a disciple of Jesus; a respecter of Jesus; a believer in Jesus; one who is divinely forgiven by Jesus and one who sincerely craved his forgiveness; one through whom the desire for the Father's righteousness is transparent; even one who has been in the presence of the risen Jesus; but not yet one who is conscious of being a son of the living local universe Son of God, Michael of Nebadon—and the difference is quite sublime.

The difference

Peter is the disciple of a religious friend who has transcended the grave. At some point in his life, whether here on Earth or in the same mansonia that Jesus was traversing at the time they met in the garden, he would surely experience his actual sonship with this same Jesus whenever Michael called him into that particular spiritual revelation.

Why do I say this? Because Michael of Nebadon is the God and Father of all of the mortals in Nebadon. While their grasp of this can be negligible on their native planets, sooner or later, as a natural part of their spiritual appreciation of the universe around them, each individual will come to know in their inner being the fact of Michael's Fatherhood at a whole and complete level. This growth in consciousness of our universe Father, comes to us as we grow in the recognition that the very universe in which we live, is literally his creation.

The Urantia papers raise higher than any other document or record on Earth, the life and teachings of Jesus of Nazareth. The experience of him, however, can be on a number of levels.

The non-believer can just pass on by Jesus without so much as a flicker of curiosity.

The luke-warm believer might attend Easter Church service and see him on the cross, for example, and never even seriously ponder what his life and death means to himself or herself whilst they carry on with the busy-ness or boredom of their daily routine.

The stronger believer will see Jesus as an example of God, and Jesus' example will inspire them to draw near to God.

The anti-Jesus person will see Jesus as a target for their own vile evil, contempt, rebuke and ridicule.

The Jew may see Jesus as possibly just another Rabbi among the many. The Muslim may possibly see Jesus as just another prophet. The Buddhist may see Jesus as just another Bodhisattva, nearly a Buddha.

The men and women of Jesus' day all saw him differently. Consider, for example, the attitudes of his apostles, his family, his disciples, John's followers, the Sanhedrin, Herod, Pilot, Bartimeus the blind beggar of Jericho, the criminals on the cross, Judas Iscariot, the Roman Centurion, Peter's wife, Mary Magdalene, Rebecca of Sepphoris, the Greeks, Nicodemus, David Zebedee and young John Mark. They all differ in their relationship with Jesus and in their understanding of his gospel, his life, and his spiritual fruit.

The person whom Jesus calls to himself, the disciple, the person who will, in modern times, ultimately be a student of the

Biblical Jesus, will see Jesus as the Son of God and the Son of Man in one person, as did Peter. Such a person will take on the yoke of Jesus, the Baptism of the Holy Spirit, and all the blessings of being saved from sin and separation from God by the Christ, the anointed one and his anointing, according to the promises of Isaiah 61:1.[4] This believer, a son of God in the Biblical meaning of that term, is a saved person who is essentially in relationship with his or her Saviour.

A further relationship one can have

There is, however, a further relationship that one can have with Jesus and that is sonship—even the same kind of sonship that one has with the Paradise Father who is effective in the human life as the Thought Adjuster.

The Urantia papers portray this sonship as a spiritually deeper and higher reality than that of being a saved person. This type of sonship with God, even with Jesus Christ, is capable of delivering a deeper spiritual truth about sonship than is encapsulated in the concept of the blood-bought[5] relationship in the Bible that brings about an adoption[6] type of sonship.

The power of salvation is not in the blood of Jesus but in sonship with God

The Urantia papers are a revealed Word of God and as such they advance all that was known by the Old Testament prophets and the New Testament apostles alike—and there was considerable difference between the two due to Pentecost.

These revelations increase the closeness of humanity to God.

At last, however, in the Urantia papers, there is a clear testament about the way that humanity has direct sonship with God. This is a sonship with God that predates the arrival of sin on this world, in the days before the Lucifer rebellion[7]—even before Adam, before Melchizedek and before Jesus.

The significance of this teaching is that such a sonship is the actual power of salvation, which has been mistakenly accredited, to the philosophical concept of Jesus dying in order to take on the sins of the world. This is to say that the person who lives in the power and authority of their sonship with Michael of Nebadon receives all the righteousness of the Father and the keys to the kingdom of heaven by virtue of the genetic spiritual linkage to divinity which is inherent in his or her sonship, rather than through the adoption of the philosophy of the meaning for Jesus' death on the cross which has been developed by Paul and the Church who followed his teaching.

For the disciple to be transformed into a son of God, there needs to be the face to face experience of the Fatherhood of God. To agree with the symmetry of sonship mentioned earlier, this experience should also be inclusive of the Parenthood in the Son and in the Spirit.[8] This experience will be a revelation that is made to the disciple by these divine persons. In this way, by faith and through grace, a principle that has always been the central force of spiritual growth in the believer, God increasingly reveals the true nature of his relationship with the child. Because of his revelation to his child, the child grows in Father-like identity. As is the Father, so is the child.

Jesus frees us from orphanhood, whereas Paul taught freedom from sin. Freedom from orphanhood includes freedom from sin, because it is based on the more real spiritual power of actual kinship with God. Sonship, being higher and deeper than all of the philosophical approaches to God, will deliver the highest goals of all other religions—peace, prosperity, sanctity.

The Spirit of Truth is the spirit of Michael himself. It literally equips the believer in Jesus to overpower every single aspect of the harm done by sin, evil, iniquity and ignorance on this world—that impact of the Lucifer rebellion. This is an extraordinary empowerment. Why, if you have the power to defeat the flesh, sin, evil, corruption and ignorance in this world, such no that force can come against you and defeat you, then there is nothing stopping your spiritual sovereignty. For God is wholly on your side—and where God is, all things are possible!

The life and teachings and death and resurrection of Jesus did not create sonship with God, it equipped sons of God to deal with the problems brought about by Michael's own corrupted sons. If you, dear reader, will believe in Jesus and his own sonship with your Father and take up your rights as a son of God, then all the power that is in the Spirit of Truth will suddenly and dramatically be like a mighty force for good that is awaiting your commands.

❦

Notes

1. Exodus 33:20
2. In simple terms, Morontia refers to that domain after death in which a person is resurrected and continues to develop their perfection, called Adjuster fusion, and their consciousness of universe citizenship. The Urantia papers say that, "Morontia is a term designating a vast level intervening between the material and the spiritual. It may designate personal or impersonal realities, living or nonliving energies. The warp of morontia is spiritual; its woof is physical." Forward:5.8
3. 191:1.1-5
4. Isaiah 61:1 "The spirit of the Lord God is upon me, because the Lord has anointed me; he has sent me to bring good news to the oppressed, to bind up the brokenhearted, to proclaim liberty to the captives, and release to the prisoners."
5. Romans 3:23-25, "since all have sinned and fall short of the glory of God; they are now justified by his grace as a gift, through the redemption that is in Christ Jesus, whom God put forward as a sacrifice of atonement by his blood, effective through faith. He did this to show his righteousness, because in his divine forbearance he had passed over the sins previously committed;"
6. Ephesians 1:5 5 "He destined us for adoption as his children through Jesus Christ,"
7. 148:4.3 {By nature, before...}
8. "The presence of the Holy Spirit of the Universe Daughter of the Infinite Spirit, of the Spirit of Truth of the Universe Son of the Eternal Son, and of the Adjuster-spirit of the Paradise Father in or with an evolutionary mortal, denotes symmetry of spiritual endowment and ministry and qualifies such a mortal consciously to realize the faith-fact of sonship with God." 34:5.7

Chapter 16

The Urantia papers are a revelation of God, from God

I have highlighted the fact that sonship and the reception of power from on high can be registered in the individual believer at different levels and can even occur at different stages in life as a result of differing experiences and levels of maturity and so forth.

I have also suggested that it's highly possible that Christianity has come to know the risen Jesus, the morontian Jesus who appeared to the believers before ascending into heaven, but that it has not really come to know the Son of God, Michael of Nebadon, who, with the Holy Spirit, reigns as the sovereign over his creation.

Our Lady

Christianity certainly hasn't come to know Mother Spirit to anywhere near the degree possible, except in the concept of "Our Lady," Mary the mother of Jesus.

Given the eternal destiny of mortals as they make their way toward Paradise, a journey of spiritual growth easily taking five billion years according to estimates from the Urantia papers, it is understandable that Mary will in fact be one of the many from this world who are currently occupied with the thrilling events and growth in that journey. She will one day pass beyond the shores of Michael's domains, with other graduates, and pass on to the overcare of the Ancients of Days as she journeys on to Uversa and so forth. Meanwhile, the Holy Spirit, Mother Spirit of Nebadon, will continue to minister magnificently on Earth as the Holy Spirit and Divine Creative Mother.

I believe that there is no way to advance this lack of knowledge and communion with Michael and Mother Spirit without two things: first hand spiritual experience of them, and the knowledge about them and their management of universe administrative affairs contained in the Urantia papers.

Awakening to universe citizenship

There is a very real growth, an awakening that occurs in the human mind and the human heart and the human reality. When it happens, we find that we have been living in a cocoon like a little embryo inside an egg, and we have escaped our confines. We find that we have suddenly made contact with the wider universe, the divine realities of heaven, and they are higher and more real than those of the Earth. Then, we stumble for lack of knowledge about that domain.

Our awakening can provide for us in certain, limited ways, such as learning to live and grow with our faith, our love and the challenges of living with our fellows. We can learn the ways of God in the heart, but we cannot learn the ways of God's heaven for we have no knowledge of it. We have knowledge of our home town, our cities, our planet and even some knowledge of the solar system around us: but we have no knowledge of the way that heaven is administered. Many is the person who has in fact broken through into a heavenly consciousness only to find they live in a struggle where the Earth is too shallow and unreal yet they lack the knowledge that comes in a document about heaven's geography, demography, politics and administration— the "where to from here" of spiritual growth.

We see the suffering and chaos and death on this side of life but we have no idea of the means whereby we live on after a death on this world except as it is revealed in our souls by totally subjective spiritual experience. We have no objective means to reflect upon our experience and thereby grow in a more balanced manner through additional intellectual growth commensurate with our soul's growth.

We debate issues around abortion. We try our best to deal with cot death. We lose babies every year by the millions: yet we have little insight into what happens to our babies after they die.

We have a cacophony of confusing ideas that come to us through a million years of myths and traditions, mediums and diviners, prophets and soothsayers; but they mostly provide little more than lessons on how to live with God in our hearts and how best to rationalise or reframe our misery.

The Urantia papers bring knowledge to us, which tells us how the heavens are populated, administered and maintained. This knowledge breaks apart the world of the mystic and the dreamer, and places heaven on a very matter of fact footing.

The process of increasing the believer's reality to include the matter of factness of heaven's everyday life is a delicate one resembling the process of change when, eventually, Santa, with all his cheery gift-giving, takes off his costume and reveals that he was your Dad all along. For some people, that experience is a relief. For others it is the shattering of a dearly held hope and treasure. Whatever the impact might be on the young, sensitive, believing mind, the reality will prevail of there being no Santa and no reindeer that fly through the sky hauling a sleigh full of free presents. A mythical spell is broken. It may well introduce the child to the concept of the Thought Adjuster, in some obscure way, but the young believer must learn to live in the light of a new reality.

So too it is for people who truly, deeply and sincerely love God. There exists a point of growth for them that is contained in their encounter with the matter of fact knowledge of how heaven hangs together. I have met people who read the Urantia papers who had years and years of struggle with the idea that the whole universe was administered. But then I found out that each of them had never worked in a large organisation where administration is the lifeblood of the daily operation of task management. They hadn't yet accepted that to be a part of a team, it takes lessons in being a part of an administrative collective, that lone rangers just don't really exist beyond the confines of their own imaginations. Throughout all of the heaven of heavens, the universe of universes, there is not one single individual who is not accountable to someone else. Why, even the Paradise Father is accountable to every living thing and being.

The struggle to find the spirituality of the Urantia papers

One of the problems I found with the Urantia papers was that it didn't stimulate in me the kind of spiritual experiences I found more readily in other writings. I had to go out on a limb and suspend all other interests and activities in order to find whatever the spirituality of the Urantia papers actually was. There wasn't any precedent. No one had travelled that way before. The littlest gain seemed to take years. Most of all, the authors didn't appear to me to be really talking about things that emerged out of the baptism of the Holy Spirit. It took a long time for me to find the divine life in the Urantia papers. That's why I included those findings in this book, they are a valuable find. Rather than speaking about the subjective experience of having been born again and baptised with the Holy Spirit, the Urantia papers seemed more to be simply pages and pages of relatively irrelevant information. But after a few years of reading, that all changed. With the dawning of sonship with God, suddenly the papers started to deliver the goodies. For many people though, I imagine that it's a long dry dusty road through the papers until they strike oil.

I believe sonship with Michael of Nebadon—the risen Jesus Christ of the Bible—and sonship with the Holy Spirit, and sonship with the Paradise Father are dependent upon such matter of fact information as is contained in the Urantia papers. Without this knowledge and its impact on the human intellect, the human spirit will continue to apply the things of heaven to its own Earthly creation of what it feels heaven ought to be like. The Urantia papers provide a description which is not at all what we think heaven ought to be like, but how it actually is. The Bible provides only scant information about heaven, and, as a consequence, many Christians have fabricated the belief that they will spend eternity on a renewed Earth. But not me! I'm out of here and Paradise bound thank you very much! There's a big wide universe out there and I want to see it all. And I want to take my Parents' blessing to it all as well.

The desire for contact with, and knowledge about these two local universe divine Parents of yours, and your Paradise Father, and your journey from Earth to Paradise, will inevitably bring you face to face with a challenge facing humanity: *are the Urantia papers a real revelation from God?*

You will have to make your own judgement on that. Something worth considering though is to examine something else in your life that you do credit as a revelation from God and find what about it convinces you that it is a revelation from God and not some mere mortal handiwork or some trick of the devil. Then, having identified that thing which is already real in your life, turn that principle over to your inquiries about the Urantia papers and work it out between God and yourself until you have come to your decision. It is better to do that than to simply accept or reject them outright without a second thought.

When it comes to the influences around you, God will lead you in either of two ways. Mankind and the ways of a fearful world will try to lead you in a third way.

Firstly, God might lead you to a place where you can make an informed decision about accepting the papers as a revelation that he fully endorses for you and your spiritual walk in life.

Secondly, if not by the first path then God might lead you to a place where you can make an informed decision about the existing revelation you are accustomed to, or perhaps some other revelation that he endorses—the whole world doesn't rotate around only one revelation of the Father and his righteous workings.

Thirdly, mankind, who is not in contact with God but who flounder around in their own speculations and doubts and fears and power struggles, will endeavour to steer you away from pretty much anything to do with God's real revelation to you. You have to learn to deal with that terrible legacy of evil the best way you can. Michael, however, will always steer you through these troubled waters well.

God will lead

My advice to you is to let God have the opportunity to inform you, to reveal to you, the merits of the papers as they concern your own personal relationship with him. Then, having been informed by the God you already trust and love, make your own assessment. This advice follows the principles of sonship which are given by God to every being in all creation: position yourself so that you can be informed about God's viewpoint; then, having been informed, evaluate your situation until you come firmly to make your own mind up; then follow up your decision by sustained action.

Penang

I will share with you a story about a fellow coming to believe the message of the Urantia papers.

In August 1994, Mary and I went on holiday to Penang in Malaysia. During 1981, I had lived in the famous temple in that city called Kek Lok See. I looked forward to catching up with the head monk—a lovely fellow named Sek Jik Heng—and showing Mary around the temple's beautiful architecture. Her idea of a holiday was great accommodation, great food, great shopping and lots of relaxing sites and sounds. My idea of a holiday was to discover new ways of doing God's will. When we were thinking about a holiday destiny, Penang seemed to be able to fit our varied needs pretty well.

Something that was central to my own experience there was that I wanted to try out a new kind of liaison with my Guardian Seraphim,[1] the angels who attend my life and who translate my Father's will into real life opportunities in my life.

The mission, as I put it to them, was to bring a copy of the Urantia papers to the Chinese-thinking Malaysian community. I put forward the criteria for the recipient about a month or so in advance of our departure.

The recipient must be well versed in English, because the Urantia papers demand a high level of conceptual capacity in the reader.

The recipient must also be on the verge of a spiritual transition in his or her life: genuine spiritual hunger must be present.

The recipient's mind and spiritual destiny must be suited to the papers. God must be able to easily walk this person into wholesome, progressive and authentic spiritual experience, which will bring considerable benefit to himself, his family and his community.

I also added in a factor that would give the mission perpetuity.

I was impressed by the following account in the Urantia papers concerning Moses and the influence made on him by the earlier Melchizedek teachings.

"The members of the family of Katro, with whom Melchizedek lived for more than thirty years, knew many of these higher truths and long perpetuated them in their family, even to the days of their illustrious descendant Moses, who thus had a compelling tradition of the days of Melchizedek handed down to him on this, his father's side, as well as through other sources on his mother's side."[2]

This passage told me that possibly angels could plan for certain teachings to be handed down through the human generations so that someone, some time, would be influenced by them in such a way as would bring glory to God and considerable benefit to mankind.

Accordingly, what was important to me was that the Seraphim needed to do some homework and find such a person in Penang who, like the ancestors of Moses, would adopt the teachings in the Urantia papers and pass them down the family tree through the generations to follow such that there will be a global influence at some stage.

I have a great faith in the abilities of the angels who attend my life, and their love for adventure. Considering their wealth of experience and the resources at their disposal, I didn't think it was a particularly big ask.

I submitted my request to my Father. A couple of days later I received a reply that it was going to proceed.

I now looked forward to an excellent holiday. As soon as my Father told me that it was in his will to bring this about, I knew for a fact that it would be successful. As an after-thought I added, "Father, if you don't mind, I'd like the whole thing to be a communication exercise solely between the Seraphim and myself. If possible, I don't want you to get involved, I want you to keep your distance so that when I begin to work with these angels, it's their communication alone that I will be in contact with." He agreed.

We were to be in Penang for five days and four nights. We arrived late Thursday evening and checked in to our hotel in the downtown area. I had told Mary of my little mission, so that she would accommodate me when I went off on that business.

Throughout the next day, we explored our surroundings. The pool. The restaurants. The shopping. The computer stores. The local temples. At one point we located a bookbinder and gave him a couple of Urantia Books to cut up into four sections and emboss with gold lettering. I let the angels get used to my mentality and emotions and decided that I would do nothing toward the mission until later that first day.

The angels check in

We had come back to our hotel for a rest and around five-thirty I sensed the presence of my Seraphim drawing close to me. I sensed their communication, not at all like my Father's. I called to Mary:

"Honey, my Seraphim are checking in on this mission thing. I think I'm going to go for a walk. Is there a shopping mall nearby here, like a tower, with a computer shop in it?"

"Yes, of course there is," she replied. "Right next door."

I truly hadn't seen it when we went outside our hotel. My attention had been on the little Chinese shops rather than the big western concrete buildings.

"Can I come too? I want to have a look around it," she asked.

"Well, sure Crick," I said, "but I'll have to walk around a bit and just follow the thread of this angel thing. I don't want you getting in the way and I don't want to upset your own time in the place. If that's OK with you then let's go."

So off we went.

Over the next few hours, I walked around all nine floors, I think there were. It was a new shopping centre in those days, The Metro, but shopping is shopping and it didn't interest me a whole lot.

I saw my own task as being to discern how to communicate with these angels, and then how to identify the person to whom they were directing me.

By the end of day one I didn't rank myself particularly high at either achievement, but I knew it took a little experimentation and a little work to build up rapport between the angels and myself. The only thing that stood out to me in the shopping mall was a computer shop up on the seventh floor. But there weren't any hooters or sirens going off saying "That's the one! That's the guy! There he is, race on in and convert him." By the time I had finished my look around, I was happy that I'd done just that, had a look around.

One thing that I was pleased with at the end of the day was that I had interpreted the communication about a tower shopping centre and a computer shop. I had at least found those two things.

I went to bed that night quietly pondering the following day's adventures. We planned to go and visit my old friend Jik Heng at the temple up on Penang Hill.

Kek Lok See

Saturday morning found us at the temple. Mary loved it, and I really enjoyed catching up with the monks and nuns of that place. I had not been there in about fourteen years and so much had changed. They had had a large building plan in place for some years now. One of the new features was a lookout balcony, overlooking all of Georgetown.

As I sat there in the ambience of the temple with its weekend throngs of visitors, I looked to see off in the distance the hotel where Mary and I were staying, and The Metro next to it. My thoughts turned to the person who might be the angels' choice as the recipient of the papers. When I had walked around the temple, I asked them if perhaps someone in the temple, perhaps some monk or nun, even perhaps my old friend Jik Heng the head monk, might not be the recipient they had chosen.

"No. He is not Buddhist," they said. "He has studied Buddhism but he is in a spiritual transition. He would not be here these days. In his heart he has renounced these ways."

The communication wasn't clear. It wasn't audible like a voice of someone standing nearby. It was a strange type of phenomena. It didn't happen within me, as my Father's voice mostly did. It was a communication that happened about a foot in front of my face, outside me yet within my personal space. I believed what I was perceiving, and continued enjoying the temple surroundings for its own sake.

One of the old ladies banged away at the dinner bell—the old hollow wooden fish we used to bang to announce meals was in jeopardy of splintering and so its use had been discontinued. Jik Heng took Mary and me downstairs to have lunch in the monk's section, away from the tourists and pilgrims. May a time I had eaten in this hall before. When I lived there, I had gone out to a number of the temples around Penang and on the mainland, teaching and counselling the local believers. I never thought then that I would one day be dipping into the big rice pot and sipping those gorgeous Buddhist vegetarian soups with a wife sitting nearby. Jik Heng and Mary and I and a few other monks all laughed over that point, as we shared the communal meal with a great love and fellowship.

Eventually we left and found our way back to our hotel. At around five o'clock, I took a copy of the Urantia Book and made my way off to The Metro. Now it was time to get real about this mission. Now I was looking for my mark.

Back in the Metro

I walked each of the floors, passing all the shops. Searching this face, questioning that place. Where was the he? By now I had determined that the angels had selected a male and that he was definitely of Chinese origin.

My attention again came back to the fellow on the seventh floor. I went into the shop. It was small. A glass counter spanned its width of possibly only about twelve feet. The fellow behind the counter, who later turned out to be the angels' choice, was busy with a customer. Another couple of customers lingered around, looking in the cabinet at bits and pieces of computer hardware. I felt awkward and out of place. I left the shop and lingered outside for a while, then I returned to my hotel.

My thoughts had been that this might be the place and he might be the right fellow, but when I was there in his presence, there just seemed to be such a terribly wide gulf between this fellow who was busy making his living as an information technologist, and me who was bringing the history of the entire universe to him in two thousand or so pages. The glory of God just wasn't shining all around, so to speak.

Back in my hotel around seven o'clock, I spoke out to the Seraphim:

"Listen girls. This is not looking good! I have no idea if this is the right bloke or not. I need some kind of clear communication about this, and like...a whole lot clearer than I've been getting please!"

I felt like someone in one of those movies where the angels are standing right nearby but the human can't see them, and they're busy shouting and flapping their wings or whatever, but the human just isn't getting the message.

Then I received a message about calming down; getting focussed; it was a happening thing and would be completed by tonight; and, it was a matter of faith not a matter of the presence of my Father's anointing...which is why it's all so dry and ordinary and human, not like the spiritual experiences I am accustomed to.

"OK," I said to myself. "I can wear that."

Then I went through a hastily contrived thinking process of adjusting my whole outlook to taking into account this new discovery that the mission had to it a whole new kind of feel from what I was used to. It was a crossing over into new ground. I had to quickly learn how to just be an ordinary mortal, acting in a faith that had no anointing power to it. I had to simply go back up there to the seventh floor and give this bloke his book. Period.

The third attempt

Off I went. I was more confident, but still shy about the whole deal. I am inherently quiet and shy. Whilst this had sounded like a great idea back home in my prayer house, on the ground I probably was not the best kind of missionary for the job. I have never had the sales person kind of ease with strangers.

Finally there I was on the seventh floor. I had no idea what to say to this fellow. I went into his shop, book in hand, and said:

"Look this might sound a little strange but, I used to be a monk in the Buddhist temple up there on the hill, Kek Lok See, and I have since left the order and I live in Australia."

He didn't seem to have a problem with the story so far.

"I found that in reading many of the Buddhist and the Christian and the Islamic scriptures, and doing all the practices to attain enlightenment, that some things left me still hungry for more of God."

Now he was looking at me a little strangely, but he hadn't thrown me out of the shop. I guess he wasn't yet certain whether I was selling something, or about to ask his help in something.

"There's this book I came across (and how many of us have said that at one time or another?) and I have been reading it for some years now. It is very popular in the United States of America. It has filled in much that I was looking for." He glanced at the book I was holding.

"Well, when I was in Australia just now," and I thought to myself 'here goes,' "I wanted to bring a copy to a person in Penang when I came for a holiday."

He smiled at that thought.

"So I prayed. I asked God to lead me to someone to whom I could give this book, free of charge." Then I caught his eye and we paused, "I believe you are that person." I held out the book to him. He reached for it and received it, utterly dumbfounded for words.

"It's a heavy book," he finally said as he felt its weight and opened it up on the counter. "And very big."

"I will leave it with you and I will come back later. Perhaps tomorrow, maybe the day after. Have a look at it. Take your time. My name is Rob, I am staying next door."

We shook hands and he introduced himself and gave me his business card.

"Thank you. It's free did you say? For me? Thank you Rob. I am interested in religious things you know; philosophy and things like that."

Not wanting to outstay my welcome, and not wanting to get involved in a discussion that might turn him off the book by him being turned off me, I used the excuse of a couple of people coming into the shop to make my exit.

I said goodbye and went off to meet Mary at the hairdresser.

We discussed the mission and meeting the fellow and my dropping off the book.

"I'll go back and visit him, and see if he's done anything with it." And that was it. So far, so good.

We went off around the coast that evening and had a wonderful night at a seafood restaurant right near the water under beautiful Penang starlit skies.

That night my thoughts turning to Koay and how he would find the Urantia papers. I talked a bit with the angels, reviewing how we were going to date. They seemed to be excited and confident. I slept well.

We got the victory!

On the next day, Sunday, we spent the day out and about. I visited Koay in his shop around three in the afternoon.

He lit up like a Christmas tree when he saw me come into the shop. I was disturbing his reading. Excitedly he exclaimed:

"Rob, this is fantastic. I have been up all night reading this stuff. Look," he said, as he flicked through page after page, "this tells you everything you want to know."

"Yeah, it's like that isn't it?" I replied.

Then he showed me whole chapters that he'd read throughout the night.

"This has the whole history of religious development in the world," he said with a grin from ear to ear. He was so excited he could barely contain himself.

"I've done all sorts of things," he said. "I used to go to the temple with my parents, but that's all just old peoples' superstition. There's no truth there," he complained.

"But this!" and he held the book aloft. "This is the truth, Rob. This is the truth."

On and on Koay spoke, about his spiritual journey and his life. He seemed glad to have someone to talk to about these deeply personal matters. He truly was flabbergasted that the book matched so perfectly his own desires to find the truth about God. He told me about his wife who was "sort of Christian," and all about their young baby. Here before me was a man who was absolutely excited because he had had a revelation from God about the truth of the contents of the Urantia papers.

He was probably in his late twenties, a university graduate, probably from a well-off family. As he spoke, I searched in his words and mind for a resemblance to the family of Katro,[3] and at the end of our meeting I had a certainty that the angels' choice had been excellent. Our mission was a success. Quietly I thought to myself how wonderful the fruit of this spiritual encounter would be down through the centuries and the generations to follow. History tells us that even the best of plans can go astray but, obviously, the seed sowing of this visit was off to a good start.

Later, my Father also expressed his agreement with the project and the way it all went.

Adapting to the revelation

You might recall that I mentioned three kinds of encounter with Jesus and that they are: the risen Jesus of Nazareth; the baptism of the Holy Spirit power from on high; and sonship with Michael of Nebadon, Christ Michael.

There is another type of encounter, which is philosophical, and that is the encounter with truth. Koay seemed to have that kind of encounter. Ahead of him still lay the encounter with sonship and with the Baptism of the Holy Spirit and power.

It seems that just about every reader of the Urantia papers has a unique and interesting story about how they came to find it, read it, believe it and evangelise it. People come to believe in the Urantia papers in such varied ways and at diverse levels. For some the confirmation is its truth. For others, there is a contact with God, a revelation. For others, it's a contact with something cosmic and universal. For yet others, its contact with a believable Jesus who escaped them in the Bible. Others still find a freedom from traditional religion, ecclesiastical regulations and lifeless liturgies. Saskia Raevouri once produced a novel little book on this very topic called, "How I found the Urantia Book."[4] I think that ultimately the proof of the Urantia papers being a revelation from God is made certain when God reveals himself to you in his word in those papers. Until that time, the Urantia papers are simply ideas and truth at the level of philosophy. Once God has imparted his revelation as to the truth of the meaning in their pages however, they become the living word of God.

Increasingly, of course, families are raising children who have never known any other scripture than the Urantia papers. Whilst acceptance of the papers is possibly made easier through this event, the real experience of revelation from God, which is the foundation of authentic spiritual experience, is still another matter.

One of the things that prevents more Christians from accepting the Urantia papers seems to be the plain fact that they already have their allegiance in the truth that is in the Holy Bible. The Holy Spirit experience of power from on high as it is portrayed in the Bible is very convincing and attractive. To lead a person into something higher and broader such as the Urantia papers will, I imagine, require the God whom they trust in the Bible to provide a revelation about the truth in the papers.

The Christian who already knows the Father and the power from on high in the Biblical context is obviously going to need a special kind of revelation from their familiar God about how the Urantia papers can augment what they already possess in the Bible. Of course, there is a certain inevitability that Michael of Nebadon will do just that. After all, it is in the interests of his expansion of the kingdom of heaven to raise up the members of the Christian Church into contact with broader and higher levels of universe activities.

Another thing that trips up Biblical sons of God is that they mostly are not expecting or wanting there to be any written works to add to what is already in the Bible. Christ's authority on this matter is portrayed in Revelation 22:18-19 as saying:

"I warn everyone who hears the words of the prophecy of

this book: if anyone adds to them, God will add to that person the plagues described in this book; if anyone takes away from the words of the book of this prophecy, God will take away that person's share in the tree of life and in the holy city, which are described in this book."

Good hearted men and women everywhere respond to truth. But there isn't a plain passage in the Bible that tells Jew and Christian alike that "When the millennium is nigh, the fifth of the world's great revelations will be revealed."

There is a hint of it in the writings of the Old Testament prophet Daniel, that points to the timely appearance of the Urantia papers.

The prophet Daniel wrote about his encounter with God's messenger, the man wearing linen,[5] saying:

"He said, 'Go your way, Daniel, for the words are to remain secret and sealed until the time of the end.'"[6]

The messenger was referring to certain visions of God's own teachings about universe affairs. Daniel was being restricted in the things he could write about. It is now pretty much commonly accepted by a great many Christians that the twentieth century is the start of the "time of the end," to which the "man clothed in linen" was referring. The messenger in Daniel's divine encounter spoke of how the words that would remain secret to Daniel would be available to humanity as a new revelation at the "time of the end."

Other than this brief note in Daniel, there isn't anything else in the Bible to indicate that God would provide another revelation on top of Christ's own ministry.

Any sincere student of the Urantia papers will acknowledge that the papers are exactly what they say they are—a revelation from representatives of God who write with God's authority about God and his affairs. Particularly is this true because of the exhaustive and exquisite way the Urantia papers elevate every person to being a direct son of God with the potentials to rise to extraordinary heights of both perfection in partnership with God, and perfected universe service.

Neither of the previous collections of God's Word in the Jewish and Christian Testaments had such a profound and broad focus as the Urantia papers. It is this single feature, the augmentation of all previous revelations of God to humanity, that can prove the authenticity of the Urantia papers and the sonship they espouse to the salvation of everyone who will claim it. Once proven to oneself, they are accepted.

For the Urantia papers to be believed to be a revelation from God, that proof will ultimately always have to occupy a place in the individual believer's experience of sonship with God.

❦

Notes

1. Guardian angels. See 113:1.2 Point 3 {3. The supernormal minded...}
2. 93:3.5
3. 93:3.5
4. Raevouri, S. P. 1998. "How I Found The Urantia Book." Square Circles Publishing. Glendale, California,
5. Daniel 12:7
6. Daniel 12:9

❦

Chapter 17

Sonship throughout the epochal revelations

Eventually, we come to grips with the enormity of the Urantia papers and their contents; we make sense of them in our daily life and in our social context. For me, making sense of the Urantia papers was in terms of them being an epochal revelation. This, like most everything else in the Urantia papers, was for me once a new and strange term, needing considerable explanation. No one taught it to me; my Father simply led me in comprehending it like that.

I came to recognize that sonship with God, was not occurring in a vacuum somehow detached from either human history or current events on Earth. Sonship had very real roots in the history of humankind on Earth. There was a time, for example, when sonship didn't exist on the Earth, when not a single Thought Adjuster had left Divinington with the mission of bringing a Urantia human being on the long journey back to Paradise. On Earth, sonship with God commenced with the very first flicker of the human urge toward morality. It was the ability to make a moral decision that in fact identified humanity from its predecessors.[1]

Prior to 991,485 B.C.,[2] moral choice did not exist among the inhabitants of planet Earth. Then one day, our earliest ancestors, Andon and Fonta,[3] made a moral decision and those decisions brought the first two Thought Adjusters to this world to indwell them, to be for them God. Sonship was birthed on Urantia at that time.

For almost one million years of human moral development since that day, the spiritual development of humanity struggled valiantly against incredible setbacks. On the day of Pentecost, Christ Michael commissioned a wholly new dispensation of God's power for good, and today two thousand years since his life on Earth, there are around three billion Thought Adjusters in the world. That figure is forever a grand testament to the extraordinary impact of the work of Christ Michael. It is also not unrealistic to say that there have probably been more Thought Adjusters indwelling more persons since Pentecost than in all the preceding history of man on Earth.

It has always been God's purpose to raise up God-knowing

sons on this world and to launch them on the long journey to the Paradise standard of personal perfection. Before you were born, the Father had a plan to send you a Thought Adjuster so that he could be with you throughout your life. From the dawn of human existence, before even the Earth was formed, God had planned for sonship; he promised sonship; he initiated sonship; and, as the worlds were formed across universe after universe, he achieved sonship with his Earthly children.

Creation theory is the term given to ideas about the way that life began. There are many creation theories in our religions and philosophies on Earth. For example, many God-knowing men and women believe the Bible's creation theory.[4] That creation theory is understood to place the origin of human history to be around five thousand years ago. The information they go by is essentially that God created the entire universe and Adam and Eve over a period of six days. To place Jesus' life in that context, it was three thousand years later that he came down from heaven to live as a human being.

In this particular world view, scientific knowledge that dates life on Earth as being existent prior to 3000 B.C. is simply not factored into the equation: it is treated as false knowledge, a lie. Other things left out of the equation are evolution of any kind and the existence of life on other worlds. Something that is factored in however, is the presence of a place called hell at the volcanic centre of the Earth.

This creation theory is, understandably, a primitive view. It Deifies earlier myths and fragmented thought, saying that the Holy Spirit wrote these concepts down for humanity. But such thinking stems solely from the actions of God in the human heart and soul, in the absence of matter of fact information about the workings of the heavens and the universe of universes which earlier humanity simply wasn't spiritually able to access or use.

The Biblical style of creation in Genesis—"God said, and it was"[5]—is in opposition to the scientists' view of creation—the big bang theory. In the former, creation is believed to have order and purpose which is given it through its divine creator whereas in the latter, creation is essentially a series of accidents without intelligent authorship, events that arise solely due to the inherent attributes of matter. One is utterly spiritual and optimistic, it gives humanity the dignity inherent in its creator: the other is utterly materialistic and fatalistic, shackling man to his animal origins.

The fascinating thing about the theory of "God said, and it was" is the application of that truth in times of healing. Often times, the son of God who is empowered by God's anointing to heal, need only say "Wound be well," and it immediately is well. That might sound a little far fetched, but having done this for people myself, I always find that the Genesis principle is absolutely correct. The Urantia papers also agree with the instant nature of this kind of healing,[6] but they don't carry it over into the creation of universes and life on Earth.[7]

I must say that I do like what the Urantia papers say about our history on Earth. It gives me a perspective which far more realistically approaches the enormous dimensions that exist in life and death and spiritual destiny, as they ebb and flow in a vast plethora of universes, than is currently conceived by the Bible, science, superstition or speculation.

The Urantia papers bring considerably more information to the topic of creation theory. Being a divine revelation, the scientist is of course not afforded the comfort of such information falling within the parameters of his or her outlook. It's quite common for the scientist to reject the Urantia papers because they are non-empirical. The Biblical student, on the other hand, will often reject the Urantia papers because they are not a Biblical revelation. There is, however, another option than these two extremes of instant creation by God, with its non-evolutionary aspect, and instant creation by material circumstance, with its subsequent comprehensive evolutionary development.

The Urantia papers present a creation theory that is, in a sense, a combination of both the Biblical view and the scientific view. They speak of creation being brought about by divine Parents, a vast retinue of persons who can manipulate energy and matter over millions of years, and huge forces which result in a kind of big bang process. Creation comes about over time and yet with huge big bangs. And it comes into being on all the levels—material, mindal, morontial, sub-spiritual, spiritual, super-spiritual, as well as with a capacity to interface with the infinite and eternal. The Urantia papers are quite elaborate in their depictions of not only the vastness of our Father's creative handiwork spanning thousands of inhabited universes, but also the many and varied levels of reality within them.

The Urantia papers indicate that the creation of Earth—Urantia—spanned millions of years but that the origin of human life here was around one million years ago.

Human development is linked to God through specific events in the life of humanity when the local universe Parents—Michael and Mother Spirit—arrange for divine contact to be made with humanity for the purposes of its personal and social growth and development. Each of those significant events is a revelation of God to humanity. It is an epochal event. The revelation is not a one-off blast of enlightenment but rather a lengthy period of time during which humanity is shepherded, discipled, big-brothered and big-sistered into new levels of sonship with God. Each revelation is designed to last for hundreds of thousands of years.

There was a time, for example, when God had never sent a commission of representatives to Earth. Then one day, a team arrived and were visible to the human eye. That was the first epochal event. The team had plans to stay visible to humanity for a couple of hundred thousand years. Then, having brought humanity to a level of civilisation, they would leave the planet and be superseded by the presenters of next epochal revelation.

The Urantia papers comprise 196 individual papers. The authors identify their work of authorising, researching, compiling, editing and presenting these papers under a label of being the fifth epochal revelation.

I have found that an understanding of the history of sonship with God on Earth is enhanced when the Urantia papers are understood in the context of the previous epochal revelations. Every religion on Earth has an origin. Even sin has an origin on Earth—it was introduced by Caligastia around 200,000 years ago.[8] Every culture, every custom, every law on Earth has an origin. Three things have shaped them all. They are:

1. the epochal revelations;
2. the on going ministry of divine overcare for humanity; and
3. humanity's evolution of its own experience.

To really know a person—your friend; your enemy; your colleague; your sibling; your parent; your child—first know these three fields of influence upon him or her.

Revelations that are epochal, are those of a magnitude for potential good which by their presence launch new values and important times of advanced spiritual living in world history. The accrued benefit to the world during the era of any particular epochal revelation, is the personal and global and universal achievement of enhanced values.

An appreciation of the general nature of epochal revelations, in particular those which have occurred in the world's history to date, paves the way for an appreciation of the fifth epochal revelation and its contribution to spiritual living in sonship with God.

The evidence of previous epochal revelations to the world is naturally a valuable source of historic information. It also represents the actual wellspring of the world's traditional and enduring values. Taking its form as a document only within the last three thousand years, the Bible has acted as perhaps the most significant single repository for many of the world's enduring values. As such a repository, the books of the Bible provide evidence not only to the occurrence of epochal revelations, but also fragmentary accounts of the actual events as they were experienced.

While they appear on the world's stage not without announcement to some few who are foretold, their appearance is usually largely unannounced to the world at large.

One of the great difficulties the world faces while trying to appreciate an epochal revelation in the early days before it has been translated into the digested and durable language of tradition and legend, is that a revelation of this magnitude and potential does not provide a particularly visible bridge for a humanity who is accustomed to daily life under its predecessor. Humanity literally struggles to grasp and place in its daily life these new and advanced concepts for spiritual living. This continues to be so until sufficient numbers of men and women, from sufficient cultures, have been able to form a living bridge of experiential understanding, over which their brothers and sisters might more easily cross to higher living.

The epochal revelation is accepted and comes to life around the world in proportion to the human struggle to experience and share its concepts and values.

Existing evidence of previous epochal revelations

The fifth epochal revelation, the Urantia papers, is very clear and definite about its global relevancy and the legitimacy of its own place as the successor to the previous four revelations of equal magnitude. Although each epochal revelation presents entirely new and advanced concepts for spiritual living as a stand-alone beacon for the generations that follow, they are one of the primary supports to God's plan for sonship on Earth and hence do not occur in an historic or cultural vacuum.

The Bible, for example, provides a record of four distinct periods of time during which different revelations of God were delivered by the will of the Father in the local universe of Michael and Holy Spirit. These four distinct periods of time have moved the world toward deeper, higher and more meaningful values.

Working back from the Urantia papers, the fifth of the epochal revelations to date, the dawn of the fourth epochal revelation is recorded in the New Testament as synonymous with the ministry of the person of the Son of God, Jesus of Nazareth.

The third epochal revelation is recorded by the Old Testament writers as synonymous with the Abrahamic Covenant.

The second epochal revelation is recorded in Genesis as it speaks of Adam and Eve.

Lastly, the First Epochal revelation is that period of time which predated Adam and Eve, during which certain spiritual authorities turned against God and followed the one who would become known as the Prince of Darkness. The Bible has recorded the fact that the Devil was in existence before Adam and Eve lived in Earth.

The Bible records clearly substantiate the fact that God provides epochal revelations by which the world prospers and grows. Of course, neither Christians nor Jews regard the Bible in this light, because it takes something larger than the Bible in which they are submerged to provide a bird's eye view of it. The following is a brief look at the way the Bible and then the fifth epochal revelation itself portray and validate epochal revelations.

177

The fourth epochal revelation in the Bible: Jesus of Nazareth

The fourth epochal revelation is commonly known as Christianity. It is, of course, the saving message within the life and teachings of Jesus of Nazareth as this has been recorded in the New Testament and lived out in the Church by the ministry of the Holy Spirit since the day of Pentecost. John the Baptist heralded its coming. Jesus established it. After his resurrection, he set it in motion for the generations to follow. The Bible evidence of these events is as follows:

i) Heralding the coming of the new epochal revelation:
"I baptise you with water for repentance. But after me will come one who is more powerful than I, whose sandals I am not fit to carry. He will baptise you with the Holy Spirit and with fire."[9]

ii) Establishing the new epochal revelation:
"In the same way, after the supper he took the cup, saying, 'This cup is the new covenant in my blood, which is poured out for you.'"[10]

iii) Launching the messengers of the epochal revelation to the world:
"Then Jesus came to them and said, 'All authority in heaven and on Earth has been given to me. Therefore go and make disciples of all nations, baptising them in the name of the Father and of the Son and of the Holy Spirit, and teaching them to obey everything I have commanded you. And surely I am with you always, to the very end of the age.'"[11]

In the Urantia papers, Jesus speaks about the next revelation that will follow after him. In a single paragraph, the fifth epochal revelation restates Jesus teaching his apostles about the inauguration and eventual completion of his, the fourth epochal revelation. Continuing, Jesus then further prophesies, regarding the subsequent presentation of its successor, the fifth epochal revelation. In the course of this moment of teaching, he also harkens back to the epochal revelations which predated his own, then heralds the news of his continuing personal ministry and

178

promised return.

"In further answer to Peter's question, Jesus said: 'Why do you still look for the Son of Man to sit upon the throne of David and expect that the material dreams of the Jews will be fulfilled? Have I not told you all these years that my kingdom is not of this world? The things which you now look down upon are coming to an end, but this will be a new beginning out of which the gospel of the kingdom will go to all the world and this salvation will spread to all peoples. And when the kingdom shall have come to its full fruition, be assured that the Father in heaven will not fail to visit you with an enlarged revelation of truth and an enhanced demonstration of righteousness, even as he has already bestowed upon this world him who became the prince of darkness, and then Adam, who was followed by Melchizedek, and in these days, the Son of Man. And so will my Father continue to manifest his mercy and show forth his love, even to this dark and evil world. So also will I, after my Father has invested me with all power and authority, continue to follow your fortunes and to guide in the affairs of the kingdom by the presence of my spirit, who shall shortly be poured out upon all flesh. Even though I shall thus be present with you in spirit, I also promise that I will sometime return to this world, where I have lived this life in the flesh and achieved the experience of simultaneously revealing God to man and leading man to God. Very soon must I leave you and take up the work the Father has intrusted to my hands, but be of good courage, for I will sometime return. In the meantime, my Spirit of the Truth of a universe shall comfort and guide you.'"[12]

The third epochal revelation in the Bible: Melchizedek and Abraham

The Urantia papers ascribe the third epochal revelation as being that of Machiventa Melchizedek.[13] It occurred two thousand years before Jesus was born. Biblically, it represented a new spiritual understanding and agreement, covenant, that was established between the human man called Abraham of Ur and the Son of God called Melchizedek, the Prince of Salem, in what is now called Jerusalem.

Most of the Hebrew books within what Christianity calls the Old Testament, are devoted to portraying the values acquired under the influence of this particular epochal revelation. While Paul's[14] letter to the Hebrews unifies Melchizedek and Jesus as Sons of God, it is the book of the *beginnings*, Genesis, that tells us of Melchizedek's status and Abraham's call to spiritual leadership which is the dawn of this third covenant of spiritual understanding:

"Then Melchizedek king of Salem brought out bread and wine. He was priest of God Most High, and he blessed Abram, saying, 'Blessed be Abram by God Most High, Creator of heaven and Earth. And blessed be God Most High, who delivered your enemies into your hand.' Then Abram gave him a tenth of everything."[15]

"When Abram was ninety-nine years old, the Lord appeared to him and said, 'I am God Almighty; walk before me and be blameless. I will confirm my covenant between me and you and will greatly increase your numbers.' Abram fell facedown, and God said to him, 'As for me, this is my covenant with you: You will be the father of many nations. No longer will you be called Abram; your name will be Abraham, for I have made you a father of many nations. I will make you very fruitful; I will make nations of you, and kings will come from you. I will establish my covenant as an everlasting covenant between me and you and your descendants after you for the generations to come, to be your God and the God of your descendants after you.'"[16]

"This Melchizedek was king of Salem and priest of God Most High. He met Abraham returning from the defeat of the kings and blessed him, and Abraham gave him a tenth of everything. First, his name means 'king of righteousness'; then also, 'king of Salem' means 'king of peace.' Without father or mother, without genealogy, without beginning of days or end of life, like the Son of God he remains a priest forever. Just think how great he was: even the patriarch Abraham gave him a tenth of the plunder!"[17]

The second epochal revelation in the Bible: Adam and Eve

The second epochal revelation began with the appearance of Adam and Eve.[18]   Being a revelation of God, which was delivered by the will of God, and of epochal magnitude, they of course brought with them the seeds of a new and personal relationship with God. This has been so graphically illustrated in the Bible in every aspect as a new birth for humanity. To some, the new birth for humanity is understood to be in fact the origins of humanity, but this doesn't actually bear out scrutiny in the Bible itself which speaks of other civilisations predating their arrival.

Adam and Eve were Sons of God, like Melchizedek and like Jesus—epochal revelations are only delivered by Sons of God. Adam and Eve were quite literally heavenly grandchildren of Christ Michael,[19] as was Machiventa Melchizedek but through a different family line.

The Urantia papers tell us that Adam and Eve had a mission to produce off spring, and that the offspring were to mate with the local human beings and thereby provide a new and spiritual gene into the human stock.[20] The Bible records this:

> "The Nephilim were on the Earth in those days—and also afterward—when the sons of God went to the daughters of men and had children by them. They were the heroes of old, men of renown."[21]

The stories in the Urantia papers of Adam and Eve and the Garden of Eden, of Van and Amadon,[22] Adamson and Ratta[23] and other characters of that time are truly thrilling and enlightening. The nature of their mission is particularly valuable to practitioners of healing and to genetic scientists.

Of one thing we can be sure in the Biblical records, the appearance on the world stage of Adam and Eve was to an existing condition of social corruption, spiritual desolation, and susceptibility to the corruption by the local celestial spiritual leadership of the day. The Bible speaks of Eve's corruption as if there is little time between her formation and her corruption:

> "Then the Lord God made a woman from the rib he had taken out of the man, and he brought her to the man. The man said, 'This is now bone of my bones and flesh of my

flesh; she shall be called *woman*, for she was taken out of man.' For this reason a man will leave his father and mother and be united to his wife, and they will become one flesh. The man and his wife were both naked, and they felt no shame.

"Now the serpent was more crafty than any of the wild animals the Lord God had made. He said to the woman, 'Did God really say, 'You must not eat from any tree in the garden?'' The woman said to the serpent, 'We may eat fruit from the trees in the garden, but God did say, 'You must not eat fruit from the tree that is in the middle of the garden, and you must not touch it, or you will die.'''"

"'You will not surely die,' the serpent said to the woman. 'For God knows that when you eat of it your eyes will be opened, and you will be like God, knowing good and evil.' When the woman saw that the fruit of the tree was good for food and pleasing to the eye, and also desirable for gaining wisdom, she took some and ate it. She also gave some to her husband, who was with her, and he ate it. Then the eyes of both of them were opened, and they realised they were naked; so they sewed fig leaves together and made coverings for themselves. Then the man and his wife heard the sound of the Lord God as he was walking in the garden in the cool of the day, and they hid from the Lord God among the trees of the garden. But the Lord God called to the man, 'Where are you?' He answered, 'I heard you in the garden, and I was afraid because I was naked; so I hid.' And he said, 'Who told you that you were naked? Have you eaten from the tree that I commanded you not to eat from?' The man said, 'The woman you put here with me—she gave me some fruit from the tree, and I ate it.' Then the Lord God said to the woman, 'What is this you have done?' The woman said, 'The serpent deceived me, and I ate.'[24]

The Urantia papers confirm that the second epochal revelation fell into default. It wasn't due to Eve eating an apple however, but I will leave that for you to read in the Urantia papers.

The first epochal revelation in the Bible: the prince of darkness

The first epochal revelation covers a period dating around 500,000 B.C.[25] when the dawn of life on Earth had already a half a million years of evolutionary development, down to the appearance of Adam and Eve around 35,000 B.C.[26] The Bible provides little elaboration on these times, during which corrupting heavenly personalities entered their fallen state and obviously plagued the world with their corrupt leadership:

"And there was war in heaven. Michael and his angels fought against the dragon, and the dragon and his angels fought back. But he was not strong enough, and they lost their place in heaven. The great dragon was hurled down— that ancient serpent called the devil, or Satan, who leads the whole world astray. He was hurled to the Earth and his angels with him."[27]

These events of course weren't the first epochal revelation. They were the corruption of the first epochal revelation by Lucifer and Satan and the Devil—who was called Caligastia. The fifth epochal revelation has much to say regarding it and how such a revelation was a new, spiritual and beautiful revelation of God on Earth before its demise.

The events about which the prophet Isaiah laments in the following passage were however, far from spiritual. Rather than bringing enlightenment to a progressing global community, their authors eventually brought contempt for God, and fostered the inevitable human social chaos and spiritual desolation:

"How you have fallen from heaven, O morning star, son of the dawn! You have been cast down to the Earth, you who once laid low the nations! You said in your heart, 'I will ascend to heaven; I will raise my throne above the stars of God; I will sit enthroned on the mount of assembly, on the utmost heights of the sacred mountain. I will ascend above the tops of the clouds; I will make myself like the Most High.' But you are brought down to the grave, to the depths of the pit."[28]

Little is mentioned in the Bible of the nature of that first epochal revelation. It does tell us that the human population was well established. Adam's son, Cain, speaks of his fear of the people outside the sanctuary of the family land, prior to his departing that spiritual haven to eventually marry within a neighbouring tribe, where he later would participate in the building of a city.

"'Today you are driving me from the land, and I will be hidden from your presence; I will be a restless wanderer on the Earth, and whoever finds me will kill me.' But the Lord said to him, 'Not so; if anyone kills Cain, he will suffer vengeance seven times over.' Then the Lord put a mark on Cain so that no one who found him would kill him.

"So Cain went out from the Lord's presence and lived in the land of Nod, east of Eden. Cain lay with his wife, and she became pregnant and gave birth to Enoch. Cain was then building a city, and he named it after his son Enoch."[29]

This is a brief look across a million years of human development on Earth and the four revelations of epochal magnitude that have come from God to the world to foster sonship with God, as they are recorded in the Bible. But what does the fifth of these epochal revelations have to say about them?

The first epochal revelation: the Dalamatian teachings

The Urantia papers state that Caligastia and a staff team of one hundred corporeal members arrived to teach about the First Source and Centre. They taught for more than three hundred thousand years before it was halted by a political default among the leadership. Not all the team followed their leaders into revolt. Van, in particular, kept the values and mission of this Dalamatian revelation alive in the world until the arrival of Adam and Eve, but the benefits, after two hundred thousand years of sin and corruption were minimal.[30]

The second epochal revelation: the Edenic teachings

The Urantia papers state that from their base in Eden, Adam and Eve taught humanity about the Father, but they defaulted their mission in its infancy. The remnant of their teachings was never entirely lost to the world until around 2500 B.C.[31]

The third epochal revelation: Melchizedek of Salem

The Urantia papers state that Melchizedek was a response to an emergency on Earth. He taught trust in the goodness of God, and the method for winning God's favour through acting in faith. He made a profound impact on Earth, his teachings laying the foundation for nearly every religion on Earth.[32]

The fourth epochal revelation: Jesus of Nazareth

The Urantia papers state that:
"Christ Michael presented for the fourth time to Urantia the concept of God as the Universal Father, and this teaching has generally persisted ever since. The essence of his teaching was love and service, the loving worship which a creature son voluntarily gives in recognition of, and response to, the loving ministry of God his Father; the freewill service which such creature sons bestow upon their brethren in the joyous realization that in this service they are likewise serving God the Father."[33]

The fifth epochal revelation: the Urantia papers

The authors of the Urantia papers themselves state that the papers are "the most recent presentation of truth to the mortals of Urantia." They indicate that they are different from their predecessors because they are the work of considerable number of persons.[34]

All five epochal revelations have been presented to the world by those persons who are called Sons of God. The difference between their quality and the quality of teachings derived from a mortal teacher is that the bearer of the epochal revelation has a relationship with God which pre-dates their delivery of the epochal revelation, and which qualifies and equips them to the task. These Sons of God have all been ultra-human, with origins in heavenly places.

Epochal revelations bring with them new horizons, new knowledge and perspectives. They are the hope for the future generations. They are the planned outworking of the sonship of individuals, worlds and universes. The following passages from the fifth and most recent of the epochal revelations, speaks eloquently about the call to and the nature of sonship with God.

"The enlightened worlds all recognize and worship the Universal Father, the eternal maker and infinite upholder of all creation. The will creatures of universe upon universe have embarked upon the long, long Paradise journey, the fascinating struggle of the eternal adventure of attaining God the Father. The transcendent goal of the children of time is to find the eternal God, to comprehend the divine nature, to recognize the Universal Father. God-knowing creatures have only one supreme ambition, just one consuming desire, and that is to become, as they are in their spheres, like him as he is in his Paradise perfection of personality and in his universal sphere of righteous supremacy.   From the Universal Father who inhabits eternity there has gone forth the supreme mandate, 'Be you perfect, even as I am perfect.'   In love and mercy the messengers of Paradise have carried this divine exhortation down through the ages and out through the universes, even to such lowly animal-origin creatures as the human races of Urantia.[35]

"The dead theory of even the highest religious doctrines is powerless to transform human character or to control mortal behaviour.   What the world of today needs is the truth which your teacher of old declared: 'Not in word only but also in power and in the Holy Spirit.' The seed of theoretical truth is dead, the highest moral concepts without effect, unless and until the divine Spirit breathes upon the forms of truth and quickens the formulas of righteousness."[36]

"Christianity has indeed done a great service for this world, but what is now most needed is Jesus.   The world needs to see Jesus living again on Earth in the experience of spirit-born mortals who effectively reveal the Master to all men. It is futile to talk about a revival of primitive Christianity; you must go forward from where you find yourselves. Modern culture must become spiritually baptized with a new revelation of Jesus' life and illuminated with a new understanding of his gospel of eternal salvation. And when Jesus becomes thus lifted up, he will draw all men to himself. Jesus' disciples should be more than conquerors, even overflowing sources of inspiration and enhanced living to all men. Religion is only an exalted humanism until it is made divine by the discovery of the reality of the presence of God in personal experience."[37]

"The Father is living love, and this life of the Father is in his Sons. And the spirit of the Father is in his Sons' sons— mortal men. When all is said and done, the Father idea is still the highest human concept of God."[38]

❦

Notes

1. 108:2.1 {Though the Adjusters...}
2. 62:5.1 {From the year...}
3. Paper 63
4. The Urantia papers speak on the Biblical legend of creation in paper 74 sections 3 and 8; and the legend of the fall of man in paper 75.
5. Genesis 1:3-15
6. See, for example, "The healing at sundown": 145:3.10 {Jesus had passed...}
7. See, for example, papers 32, 36, 41, 42, 57-63
8. 148:4.3 {By nature, before...}
9. Matthew 3:11
10. Luke 22:20
11. Matthew 28:18-20
12. 176:2.3
13. Paper 93
14. 47:10.3 {Paul also had...}
15. Genesis 14:18-20
16. Genesis 17:1-7
17. Hebrews 7:1-4
18. Paper 74
19. 37:9.5 {The Material Sons...}
20. 37:9.5 {On a planetary...}
21. Genesis 6:4
22. Paper 67 Sections 3, 6 and 8

23. 77:5.5 {A company of...}
24. Genesis 1:22-33
25. 61:7.4 {500,000 years ago...}
26. 61:7.18 {35,000 years ago...}
27. Revelation 12:7-9
28. Isaiah 14:12-15
29. Genesis 4:14-17
30. 92:4.4-9
31. 92:4.4-9
32. 92:4.4-9
33. 92:4.4-9
34. 92:4.4-9
35. 1:0.3
36. 34:6.6
37. 195:10.1
38. 196:3.29

❧

Chapter 18

Sonship: Urantia papers and Biblical

Understandably, the son of God who pursues the values of the Melchizedek teachings, the third epochal revelation, will likely stumble over the son of God who pursues the teachings of Jesus of Nazareth, the fourth epochal revelation. Both will probably stumble over the son of God who pursues the teachings of the Urantia papers, the fifth epochal revelation. Yet all are indwelt by the same Father. All are ministered to by the same Mother Spirit. All have a destiny in the same mansion world. All have the same ancestors in Andon and Fonta.

To the Biblical son of God, Jesus is the acme of Jewish history. As such, he is unavoidably intertwined in the Jewish idea of a Messiah—the anointed one of God, and his anointing.[1]

The Urantia papers son of God, on the other hand, has a relationship with the Jesus who is demonstrating how to live the perfected human life.[2] He is much more than a descendent of the Jewish expectations for Messiah. Jesus of the Urantia papers is the Paradise originated, time-space Creator Son of God who is known throughout the hundreds of thousands of universes identified in the Urantia papers as Michael of Nebadon. He is the believer's local universe Father and God. He is the terminator of the Lucifer rebellion,[3] but he is also the Son of God who is achieving his seventh incarnation in the likeness of his own creature children.[4]

Essentially, Jesus in the Bible frees humanity from sin and the heritage of the Devil, whereas Jesus in the Urantia papers is Michael of Nebadon who invites his children into sonship with himself and Mother Spirit, and sonship with the Paradise Father. He breaks the myth that humanity is a child of the Devil;[5] and he paves the way for the individual person to receive universal citizenship by the dominance of his Spirit of Truth. Michael of Nebadon proves that salvation comes by the spiritual force of sonship rather than through the philosophical meaning of actions—salvation is received by faith, not deeds.

To the man or woman who deeply loves Jesus, the Urantia papers are an invitation into the heart and mind of Jesus like nothing else, including the Bible. Is the account of Jesus' character in the Urantia papers true? Only Jesus can reveal that to you for sure. In order to know that, you have to go there and find out—sincerely encountering Jesus is not a spectator sport.

It should be recognised however, that any differences between the Biblical and the Urantia papers view of Jesus evaporate in the knowledge that Jesus was the acme of human history on the Earth and that the spiritual benefits of the risen Christ will flow into the lives of all believing sons of God according to their own capacity and desire to claim them.

Sonship is not a new thing

It is not foreign to the Bible that Jesus invites the believer into sonship with God. Look, for example, at John 1:12-13 KJV:

"But as many as received him, to them gave he power to become the sons of God, even to them that believe on his name: which were born, not of blood, nor of the will of the flesh, nor of the will of man, but of God."

The Urantia papers do not have a monopoly on sonship with God. They do, however, highlight the fact that you and I are created as sons of God and not sons of sin. When we are thought of as sons of sin, then we need a God who must first remove that curse before we can be made sons of God. If we do not claim this kind of God, then we are damned to an eternal sinfulness.

On the other hand, when we are thought of as sons of God, there is no curse over us that needs breaking. We need no intermediary for receiving our own Father's forgiveness and love. We grow up in a universe that is skilling us to deal wholeheartedly with both the error, evil and sin which is commensurate with free will in a good universe, and the goodness, beauty and truth that is in the same universe.

If, in the universe of the Urantia papers, we do not claim our sonship, we wither and become as though we never were, in exactly the same way as that plant that will not receive the food and drink and sunshine you bring to it.

Who is our God?

God is perceived according to the needs he meets in us.

Do you want a God to have died for your sin on the cross? Then you will claim Jesus' sacrificial virtues.

Do you want a God of social welfare? Then you will claim Jesus' ministry to the poor and his feeding of the five thousand.

Do you want a God of restoration? Then you will claim Jesus healing the sick and restoring the blind and salvaging people like Mary Magdalene.

Do you want a God of prayerful solitude? Then you will claim Jesus' communion with the Father alone away from even his close friends.

Do you want a God of social action? Then you will claim Jesus in the temple market, driving out the money changers.

Do you want a God who will bring order to humanity? Then you will claim Jesus the heir of King David and Jesus' the head of Paul's "Church".

Do you want a God of the whole universe in which there are countless billions of other sons and daughters of God and infinite diversity and personal options for excellence of expression and loving service? Then you will claim Jesus who is Michael of Nebadon.

Do you want a God who annihilates iniquity? Then you will claim Jesus who defeated Lucifer, Satan and Caligastia on Mount Hermon and whose own son, Gabriel, has requested their eternal destruction.

Do you want a God who will demonstrate to you the perfect human life in all its facets from mortal birth to the attainment of spiritual perfection? Then you will claim Jesus' Adjuster fusion.

Do you want a God who personally indwells you as a Father, and as a Son, and who covers you in the Holy Spirit? Then you will claim Jesus who is Michael of Nebadon, who sent his Spirit of Truth into you, who ushered in a wholly new era of Thought Adjuster association with human beings, one of whom indwells you, and whose co-Creator partner, the Holy Spirit, is elevated such that she can contact her children all the more personally since Pentecost.

Which God do you want?

Which God have you already claimed in your life?

God is always more than we can receive

One thing is certain: there is always more God available to you than you have claimed in your life. Even today, as richly or poorly endowed spiritually as you choose to think of yourself, you reside within one who is more God than you currently have claimed. How much more of God would you like? 1%? 5%? 10%? 50%? Then claim that increase, and let him expand your sonship in him. He always has more for you, even after you have enlisted in the ranks of finality in Paradise.

There is always more and Jesus said that he is the way to that increase, and the truth of that increase, and the life of that increase—and that none would increase in the Father except they go through him. If you want sonship with the Father, it is through sonship with Jesus: and Jesus is both Jesus Christ of the Bible and Michael of Nebadon the Creator Son of God of the Urantia papers.

❦

Notes

1. Mark 14:61: 1 John 2:27
2. 140:8.6 {5. Personal religion...}
3. 53:8.3 {the bestowal of...}
4. 120:0.9 {And this was...}; 120:1.0 {1. The Seventh Bestowal Commission}
5. 145:3.4 {That Sabbath was...}; 162:7.4 {Which of you...}; 194:2.1 {Jesus lived on...}

❦

Chapter 19

Sonship is unity in the Father

The Hebrew son of God perceives the mission of the Lord to be the establishment of the Mosaic law and the inheritance of Abraham. The Christian son of God perceives the mission of Jesus as being the overthrowing of the Lucifer rebellion and the buying back to God, with his sacrifice on the cross, of all sinful humanity once and for all time. The Urantia papers son of God on the other hand, has a relationship not so much with the Jesus of blood sacrifice nor with the laws of Moses but with the Jesus who lived the perfect example of the perfected and righteous human life on Earth.[1]

The difference is both subtle and enormous, and for subtle and enormous reasons, but eventually a person arrives at a point where the merits of both the Biblical and the Urantia papers streams of revelation converge.

It is, admittedly, a lofty point which has the sincere believer seeking—begging for—understanding of the two streams, just as the disciples of John the Baptist sought to understand the relevance of John's ministry once Jesus was baptised and became a public figure.[2]

Into the deep

Another question raises its head here: do you want a God who can draw you into wider, larger, deeper and higher things than you have ever been exposed to? That's what John's disciples faced in the light of Jesus' presence. The records show that some refused to leave John and that even to this day their cult of loyalty to John's teachings still persist.[3] Whilst such allegiance is admirable, the question it raises in the human heart, even your heart, is: will you recognise and be loyal to God's new truth when God or his new truth is brought squarely in front of you and, if so, what will you have to sacrifice of the old in order to let the new live in your heart and grow?

I have seen many Christians who encounter the Urantia papers shy away or step forward in active condemnation of the revelation and I am reminded of John's disciples who cannot be led into the new and larger presence of their own Father.

On the other hand, I have seen many Urantia papers readers

shy away from or step forward in active condemnation of becoming obedient to Jesus teachings and embracing God's rule in their hearts in the way that so many Christians do. These ones will not give up their unruly lives and their self-preferment, and the desires of their own hearts over the desire of the Father's heart. A long time reader in New York once told me that doing anything with leading Urantia papers readers was like trying to herd cats—you can't get any two to go in any one direction for long enough to amount to anything worthwhile much at all. Of course, religion has that effect on people and I'm sure there will be many a Christian who would say the same thing of their own ilk.

The core truth to which the sincere son of God always returns, however, is the Father's own call to perfection through grace by faith in sharing the mind of God—sonship.

I want to share with you that there is a reality that is known to the morontian consciousness within the human spirit, that finds the same central truths of perfection in both streams of revelation, the Bible and the Urantia papers.

The spiritual core of that unifying truth is the fact that the power of salvation is in one's sonship with the Father—even sonship with Jesus himself—whilst the philosophical premises of the purification and growth of the son are truly mirrored in Jesus' ministry and the cross.[4]

The son of God *will* give his or her all to the Parents if called upon, and if it is in the natural course of human events. It is a part of his or her spiritual insignia to give all that the Father has given to him or her. Jesus said that greater love has no person than to lay down their life for their friends.[5] The son of God *is* willing to do just that. The son of God knows unerringly that the life they live is the Father's life, and they freely give it up to the glorification of the Father.

Sonship's greatest victory

Yet, sonship's greatest victory is not to lay down one's life. Rather, it is in finding unity among the diverse streams of spirituality that flow out of and back to the Father. That is what is so precious about Jesus' life and teachings: not so much that he gave his life, but that through his demonstration of the Father's unifying love in all the years of his life, absolutely every person who seeks the Father and his righteousness, can and will find them irrespective of their own personal starting point. Would you lead someone to the Father? Then lead them not to a Father in this or that religion, for that is by a divisive pathway. Show that person the Father who is the source of sonship in all persons. That, loved one, is our inheritance from Jesus of Nazareth. And it far transcends the concept of his shed blood saving the sins of the world.

Will both streams of believer get to heaven when they die? The Biblical and the Urantia papers son? Yes, obviously. They are sons of the same Christ and Father.

But life goes on, even in heaven.

The development of deeper relationships and values, personal skills and competencies, wider perspectives and deeper responsibilities, features which are not addressed in either the Jewish or the Christian Testaments of the Bible, are exhaustively portrayed in the Urantia papers as evidence that spiritual life far exceeds life as it is known here on Earth. Many Christians think that the Urantia papers are a work of the Devil and will trick believers into the ways of iniquity. They do not recognise that over and above the Biblical way to the Father, the Father has his own ways and that the Urantia papers are shown to many by the Father to be one of those ways.

As an example of this, do you recall the story of the strange teacher? The story starts with Jesus speaking:

"'Whoever welcomes one such child in my name welcomes me, and whoever welcomes me welcomes not me but the one who sent me.' John said to him, 'Teacher, we saw someone casting out demons in your name, and we tried to stop him, because he was not following us.' But Jesus said, 'Do not stop him; for no one who does a deed of power in my name will be able soon afterward to speak evil of me. Whoever is not against us is for us. For truly I tell you, whoever gives you a cup of water to drink because you bear the name of Christ will by no means lose the reward. If any of you put a stumbling block before one of these little ones who believe in me, it would be better for you if a great millstone were hung around your neck and you were thrown into the sea."[6]

Ultimately, the Father's call is to perfection in himself and by his own standard. Whenever the human responds to that call, the Father leads him or her quite securely beyond the perspective that any one group of humans may have of his perfection.

Sonship emerges from the Urantia papers

Just as the Word of God in the Bible provides a backdrop for the experience of the Holy Spirit[7] and the risen Christ[8] for the Christian son of God, in the same way the Urantia papers provide a backdrop for the experience of sonship with God involving the persons of Michael,[9] Mother Spirit[10] and the indwelling Paradise Father.[11]

Both backdrops provide a basis for God's revelation to the inner person. The universality of the Biblical son of God is restricted by the lack of knowledge about his role in the wider heavenly universe which is compensated for through the Urantia papers and the ensuing revelation by the Father in the heart of that believing son. Given this additional revelation of God's Word, the Biblical son of God is able to be immeasurably uplifted, advanced, increased, advantaged, skilled, prepared, and linked to the affairs of Jesus' universe. Even now, while he or she is working with the Father's will through Jesus for the kingdom on Earth, he or she could be in contact with the knowledge of wider universe affairs that would enormously help understand and uplift matters on Earth.

Knowledge is power. To know what is beyond the Bible yet of the heart of the Bible, clearly is power in the life of the believing son of God. You would do well to avail yourself of this power.

Dwell on the unifying aspects

It is far better to dwell on the unifying experiences within sonship with the Father than on those things which are divisive and limiting. Currently, popular Christianity appears to treat every other religion as a cult or a dreadful bamboozlement and bondage of the believer by the Devil. Currently, many Urantia papers students treat Christianity as comprising people and institutions that are barking somewhat pig-headedly up the wrong tree. The Christian is seen to have a narrow view of the way that God promotes optimum diversity in order to create the greatest range of opportunities possible to his children. Needless to say, there isn't much dialogue happening in ways that mainstream Christianity wants to partake of. Yet, besides this, there is much to gain from the perspectives of the human experience of the Christ Jesus of the Christian and the Christ Michael of the Urantia papers reader, because all such perspectives give each individual an enhanced appreciation of his or her own universe Father who lived on Earth as a human being.

I hope it is apparent to you that both streams of sonship with God have much to offer each other. When I brought this question of differences to my Father he said to me, "But it shall not always be so on Earth." And I believe him.

There is a spiritual outlook which perceives the real or potential sonship with God in all people and it lies beyond the things that divide humankind-such as scriptural authorities, religious models, and economic, political and racial boundaries.

Whenever, in our future on Earth, the majority of men and women are spiritually willing to adopt this outlook brought on by the direct experience of sonship with God, our Father's prophecy of unity and goodwill among people will dawn on Earth.

The Urantia papers make a significant contribution to the advancement of humanity's personal experience of God and his personal capacity to unify tremendous diversity.

Unity

What is unity?

It is not that we should all do the same thing, but that we should notice how our eternity issues from the same Parents.

What group of children who are born from the same good parents will not eventually find their parent's love amongst them in their daily affairs?

Jesus said:

> "God is your Father and you are his sons, and this good news, if you wholeheartedly believe it, is your eternal salvation."[12]

I have experienced this to be true.

I would love you to believe it in your heart too. Like John, I am a voice crying in the wilderness for Jesus[13]—but I do not call you to anything of mine, I call you to his gospel and to himself and to his Father and to the Holy Spirit, that your joy may be full[14] and that our joy may be full.

If any person shares the mind of God that person is a son of God.

If any two such persons fellowship with each other, their sharing of the mind of God is the substance in their unity.

Is it any wonder that Jesus said:

"Truly I tell you, whatever you bind on Earth will be bound in heaven, and whatever you loose on Earth will be loosed in heaven. Again, truly I tell you, if two of you agree on Earth about anything you ask, it will be done for you by my Father in heaven. For where two or three are gathered in my name, I am there among them."[15]

When two or more are gathered when they share the mind of God, obviously Christ Michael is among them and obviously they will be empowered by the Father's will.

If a Buddhist shares the mind of God and he communes with the Muslim who shares the mind of God, there is unity. Similarly, when the Taoist, the Christian, the Jew, the Hindu, the Shinto and the New Age-er share the mind of God and fellowship with each other in the spirit of that acknowledged sonship with God, great is their love for each other. They have all surrendered to the Father's love and will. They perceive it in each other. They prefer the Father's way to all other ways.

❦

Notes

1. 188:5.9 {The cross is...}
2. 135:9.5 {These forty days...}
3. 137:2.2 {That day, as...}
4. 188:5.1 {The cross of...},7 {The cross makes...}
5. 180:1.3 {When I invite...}
6. Mark 9:37-42
7. Luke 3:16-22; Acts 1:8; Acts 2:4
8. Acts 2:38; Romans 5:1; 5:8;
9. Paper 33
10. Paper 34
11. 1:0.1-6; {The Universal Father...};2:7.7 {The eternal quest...}

12. 141:6.4
13. Mark 1:3
14. John 16:24 KJV
15. Matthew 18:18-20

Chapter 20

Finding the life in the Urantia papers

There is spiritual life in the Urantia papers, even the life which is in Michael of Nebadon and in Mother Spirit and in the Paradise Father who indwells you and develops your thought. The spiritual life in the Urantia papers links you to your divine Parents through the words of their revelation.

I am not about to launch into a study on the issues facing the first-time reader, who must work out their own solutions to a number of problems, such as: the language used by the authors; the apparent gender bias with terms like sonship; the fact of the papers being a revelation in which no human played a part in their authorship; the enormity of the concepts; their teaching on Jesus from a non-Biblical tradition; the mystery and mythology around their production, and so on. I want to step past that for a moment, to show you something more about the Urantia papers.

This is, rather, a look into the means whereby any person from any tradition derives divine nourishment from their sacred scripture, over and above the mere intellectual stimulus they might derive from it. Remember, the topic is about how to find the life in the Urantia papers—what you have to do to hear God talking to you in the words that are in the Urantia papers. Remember that, as you read on now.

When God considers it true

There is something that makes words and facts and stories become spiritually nourishing. It starts, naturally enough, with the belief that God himself considers the Urantia papers to be a true account of his perspective and reality. Think about that for a moment. Ask yourself this question:

"Do I think that God himself considers that the Urantia papers are a true account of what he is all about?"

OK. If you can believe that fact, then you have made the Urantia papers into sacred scripture, and have done so by the power of God's discernment in you. In other words, you and God shared in recognising that fact.

If your answer was, "No," then read on. Maybe somewhere soon when you least expect it you'll find God changing your mind with you. Then you can come back here and pick up where you left off, if you want to.

Continuing, then.

Read the entire collection of papers

At some stage, the whole collection of papers in the Urantia papers needs to be read, to get an idea about the full scope of the collection of papers.

Then, selected readings need to be studied according to one's interest in resolving certain questions.

Move from reader to actor

Having done all that and acquired an understanding of the scope and message of the Urantia papers, then a person has to make a transition from being a reader of the papers, a speculator of their truth, to being an actor in their context. This means being a person who is under the sovereignty of the Deity persons who are central to the Urantia papers.

Many readers I have met have never successfully made this transition from reader to actor, and they spiritually flounder somewhat. It is evident that their reading increases an intellectualisation of the papers, whilst their spiritual hunger remains almost wholly unsatisfied. Sadly, they do not experience the impact of the Holy Spirit cleansing of the heart and the morals. They do not find themselves being led by the Godly parents about whom they are reading. They do not experience righteousness and its spiritual path to perfection. They do not experience the power from on high. They become like dry hollow biscuits lying on the desert sands, with hardened shells and no filling. They know that the papers are full of spiritual leadings, but they are deeply frustrated that they are not able to encounter them first hand.

The emptiness of intellectualism

The result of intellectualisation of the Urantia papers is that it creates a horrible emptiness in the human heart, which is lorded over by pride and a critical spirit who deprives the person of the experience of genuine spiritual love.

When such an intellectual person who cannot, or will not, make the transition from reader to actor hears about, or enters into the presence of genuine spirituality, they find themselves revolting, rebelling, rejecting, condemning and criticising. It's a strange and unfortunate distortion because their heart is all the while wishing for its own genuine spiritual contact with God.

There is only one cure for this hunger. The God, about whom the person is reading, has to be personally received, met.

The person is to take literally Jesus' own instructions on how to get saved,[1] and then to follow Jesus himself.

But the person will invariably argue, making an endless argument for why he or she does not have to, or cannot receive God's forgiveness[2] or follow Jesus or his teachings.[3]

But there is no other solution to this problem for the person, or for you. It becomes necessary to sacrifice our pride's criticism on the altar of humility, if only because all our efforts to date have eventuated in nothing more than empty knowledge; if only because we are just as hungry and just as unreal as we always have been.

There is no other solution, but this solution that the Urantia papers themselves advocate, does perfectly deliver the person. Try it for yourself.

If this is you that I am writing about, then you should know that every son of God throughout the entire universe of universes and on Earth would *love* you to be carried by God out of this desert and into the oasis of his life.

Knowing God as a friend

I would love for you and God to know each other as friends, as Father and son (and "son" means male and females), as one shared heart of love and cooperation. I can't tell you how many times I am telling you this in spirit each day. Let it echo in your inner ear, until the words reach your inner person and cause the wall of the world's struggle inside you to crumble so that your own dear Father has his way with you, drawing you to himself like a lost child to an anxious parent.

Other people might use other examples, but I like the way Paper 2:0.1 speaks of the very central purpose of the Urantia papers' mission to bring sonship to Urantia en masse, through the perfect life and teachings of the creator:

"The nature of God can best be understood by the revelation of the Father which Michael of Nebadon unfolded in his manifold teachings and in his superb mortal life in the flesh. The divine nature can also be better understood by man if he regards himself as a child of God and looks up to the Paradise Creator as a true spiritual Father."

Four substantial longed-for changes

Whenever the reader moves from being a speculator to being an actor in the context of the Urantia papers, the person's actions are centred in the nature of God, in the revelation of Michael of Nebadon, and in sonship with the Father. When this occurs, four substantial longed-for changes emerge in the person's life.

1. Connection with the Father

Firstly, a literal connection is made with the Father such that both the Father and the child can speak, the one to the other, being recognised and heard by each other beyond doubt.

This process is essentially quite simple. One undertakes to follow Jesus' instructions for salvation.[4]

One believes his gospel about God being one's Father and being his son.[5]

One receives his or her Father's forgiveness.[6]

One is born again by the Spirit.[7]

One receives power from on high.[8]

One receives Christ Michael in one's inner heart along with the Father,[9] the corollary of which is that one also receives communion with one's Mother Spirit of Nebadon who is, since Pentecost's outpouring of the Spirit of Truth, as personally present as Michael.[10]

The process, despite the nature of their several ministries being perfectly unified, is more properly a connection with all of the parental divinity which is resident within one's sphere of existence.

For those of us who live and breath on Earth, that includes two divine fathers and one divine mother, and this takes some getting used to. They are:

1. one's Paradise Father indwelling;

2. one's local universe Father and creator, Michael of Nebadon who is also the embodiment of the Paradise Father and Son; and

3. one's local universe Mother, the very holy creator Mother Spirit of Nebadon, who is the embodiment of the Infinite Holy Spirit.

It seems to be uncommon, however, for a person to perceive these persons individually in the early stages of this kind of contact, but ongoing revelation and maturity discloses us to them and them to us.

If this has not occurred for you yet, it will be for only one of a few reasons.

Perhaps you've never thought that you could be this close to God. Perhaps you are caught up in years of intellectualisation of the Urantia papers. Perhaps you are afraid of what God might do to you. Perhaps you don't want to know God at all.

You're welcome to add your own excuse here if it doesn't fit these few, but again I'll repeat that all of the billions upon billions of sons of God throughout God's universe, and their Father himself, would genuinely love you to yield to God your own Father and receive union with him. Nothing stops you but your own whole-heart's sincere decision. It's that simple. It's a decision of the heart, not of the thoughts.

2. The Father is in the Urantia papers

Secondly, this same Father is seen in the revelation made by Michael of Nebadon, as it is portrayed in the writings of the Urantia papers.

In this sense it can be said that the Urantia papers are the word of God, just as countless millions of Christians and Jews say that of the Bible, and countless millions of Muslims say that of the Holy Koran. We are all correct in our understanding of course, for all things flowing out of the mouth of God are true and real, even though they may vary in the context of the light of God they bring forth from him.

The experience of reading the Urantia papers becomes a spiritually empowered time of communion with one's Father, a shared experience involving the divine indwelling Father, the human son (you), the written word of God's revelation through Michael of Nebadon, and the inner revelation of new truths and realities made between one's Father and oneself. At last the intellectual hold over the would-be son has been broken.

What this means is that when you read the words of Jesus you connect quite literally to Michael of Nebadon and the Father. To read Jesus' words, is to hear these divine creator Parents speaking to you directly.

3. The Father is seen in his servant

Thirdly, God is seen in his son and servant.

There will come a time in the life of the son of God, as he or she ascends in his or her maturity in sonship, that all things worldly will become insignificant and a demand will arise in the heart and mind for clarity about how God works and operates in his servant. The son's level of skills are still weak and young. Whilst the son might be highly proficient as a secular counsellor, psychiatrist, psychologist or physician, or perhaps might be a good Buddhist, Hindu yogi, monk or minister of religion, the grace of God will suddenly outshine these skills and they will all seem to be inherently so dreadfully empty and impotent.

It's not that they are in fact as useless as one might perceive them to be, it is simply that one clearly perceives that their roots are not in the mind that one now shares with the Father. And it becomes a passionate ambition to bring forth into the world, only that which is found in the Father.

This is a frustrating time. To where should the son of God turn? To whom can she look? Who can guide her into the satisfaction of God's heart's desire? It seems like the son has come to a precipice in her life. All that she has ever known and loved lies in the land behind her. She cannot progress because there is a great gaping cavern of not knowing stretched out before her. She at first does not even know her true desire, but eventually it takes shape. She wants to see Christ Michael himself, in action, in a mortal, so that she can embody him in the same way.

Just finding clarity about the desire is fulfilling in itself. Later comes an even bigger problem: where to find someone who is embodying the aspect of God she desires to appropriate in her own life.

During my own growth and training in this stage of seeing God in his servant, I was led by Michael of Nebadon to see him in the public spiritual works of a couple of people, and in the a small Church that my friend Kwesi pastored in Melbourne. The best I could get, however, was a Christian witness of Christ whereas I was actually hungry for a witness of Michael of Nebadon. They are not the same. The former is styled on local victory over sin and the latter is styled on universe citizenship and sonship with God. Most of my subsequent thinking and decision making was necessarily a filtering process whereby I sifted out of their beliefs and actions those things that Michael confirmed in my own communion with him as being relevant to the lessons at hand.

I attended an international conference for Urantia papers readers in Flagstaff Arizona in 1996. That was the first time I had met the people of my own faith in large numbers, in all their tremendous diversity. I presented Michael and Mother Spirit and my Father, as I knew them, to formal groups in this gathering. Out of that visit to America grew a calling to return and provide a witness of an aspect of Michael's will for the raising up of sons of God from within the readership. In part, that witness involved demonstrating Michael to people, just as Jesus demonstrated the Father, just as Michael had shown me to do.

I met people who were critical of me for doing this, or for claiming this. When you do similarly, you will have to deal with that as best you can also. Surely the will of your Father will prevail however, as it did for me.

I also met others who were very glad that I was called and very glad that I responded. They saw Michael of Nebadon in what I was doing. I remember one lady in Oklahoma City saying, "I just see so much of Jesus Christ in you and what you are doing." They were drawn to him. They knew him, where before they had not known him. People experienced his promises of healing and forgiveness. Lives were deeply affected and reconstructed. I recall the wonderful experience of being with a man as he literally met Michael of Nebadon in his own kitchen. The veil between heaven and Earth was torn apart, as tears streamed down his forgiven and astonished face. All this, like Paul, I counted as success.[11] Michael will confirm in your heart too, what makes up success and what makes up failure. The perfection of union with his will is always success.

In doing this kind of a mission for Michael, as his son and servant, I had no human master to copy, to follow. I was anointed with the spirit of the apostle and the prophet in order to carry out this work in America. People don't generally understand these things, unless they go through them themselves. Michael himself was my guide. It was in him that I perceived what I should do. Jesus in the Urantia papers was the son of God, the servant of God, whose example I followed because I found my Father's life in his example. I found Jesus of Nazareth perfectly present in the person of Michael of Nebadon. I lived in a closeness with the Jesus of the Urantia papers and the living personal presence of Michael of Nebadon.

In all truth, the wishes of Michael of Nebadon became the seeds I sowed, and the harvest I reaped for him. My journey was solely for his sake, for his interests, that he might prosper in the Earth among Urantia readers. For some it is easier to have a human example to follow. For me there was none, there was Christ Michael only. I had to learn how to be a son of Michael "on mission" as I went. There had been two and a half years of training with him leading up to this event, but there was no precedent I was following. All throughout, however, from the days of preparation to the return to Melbourne, he was completely sufficient. Before the mission started, he sent word to me of the way it would end and even the time it would end. Throughout it all also, he found another willing human being who loved him. This fellow was my support, my friend, my fellow adventurer and a man with a little known extraordinary love for Michael's will on Earth. I would offer you this encouragement right now, today, that if you are planning or being moved to undertake a mission with Michael, he will be utterly all sufficient for your success in him.

There will always be people who will criticise you, of course. People will be sorely challenged when you indicate Michael's will to them, and the will of the Paradise Father. Mostly they don't know that will themselves, and they fear some burden that threatens their own will and understanding. Their criticism is sometimes evil, sometimes sinful. Frequently, criticism was useful to me, if only to better understand the application of Michael's will to the circumstances of that mission. At the end of the day, we all bring our spiritual fruit to the Ancients of Days for a summary that is not on our terms but on the terms of the Father in whom you will put your trust during the mission. Yet, in any mission, there is always far more good and benefit that emerges than things negative. In God, things always lead to goodness and success. You will manage the problems of being a servant of God as best you can.

As you grow to become this kind of a servant, you will eventually find a person to show you God in action.

Ultimately, the person who will demonstrate the will of God your own Father to you, dear reader, at that stage in your own spiritual desire when you are hungry to be about your Father's business, will always be a direct demonstration of your own Father to you by your Father in that person.

Most people who would then criticise you, will be people for whom such a condition has no reality. They cannot conceive it and so they foolishly condemn it. But rest assured, your day will come. You will see that precious will being demonstrated. It will stand out to you, as though it is speaking directly to you alone. You will bravely cast aside all doubts and all thoughts of critical spirits coming against you and you will step out in the will of Michael of Nebadon. You will be strengthened by the knowledge that no human can achieve Adjuster fusion without exercising the will of God. And no human will pass beyond the domain of Michael of Nebadon—the risen Jesus of Nazareth— without Adjuster fusion. Having faith in that kind of "right" to do the will of your divine Parents, you will one day do the will of your Paradise Father. Firstly, however, you will more than likely have seen it done in another person prior to your having accepted your mission work from Michael of Nebadon.

It is a great responsibility, but a wonderful experience. I can not tell just how absolutely committed you become, to knowing and serving Michael and your Father in him; how total is that pre-occupation in your every waking moment, and how fabulous it is to do their will.

The person who is seeking to see an example of his or her Father on Earth, will quickly become hungry to see their own Paradise Father acting in another human being in the course of their own ministry of His love and influence.

They will draw increasing clarity from this witness, and the better find their own expression of the Father's will.

They will want to see Michael of Nebadon fully alive in someone on Earth.

They will want to see a person who is saturated with the presence and ministry love of Mother Spirit through and through. The spirit-parented realness in their love for God, will remind them of Paul's words in Acts 11:16 NRSV:

"And I remembered the word of the Lord, how he had said, 'John baptized with water, but you will be baptized with the Holy Spirit.'"

Having thus remembered, they will want to see this power from on high manifested in someone they can know, love and trust.

They will want to see God confirming his word and his promises in signs and wonders and miracles and in power, just as in Mark 16:20.

The problem facing the person who is critical and judgmental, is that they will struggle with genuinely loving and trusting someone in whom God's will is being manifested.[12]

The problem facing the person who is seeking to see an example of his or her Father on Earth, is that they are hard to find—few engage their Father thus.

This person though, whose sonship is being formed in cooperation with his or her Father, and who longs to witness their God in action in another human, will eventually and most assuredly be brought to a true example and the evidence of himself. The force behind this event in the believer's life stems from the strongest desire in the Father's own heart for his own human child be securely grown into the full stature of his or her perfection.[13]

When at last you do see someone ministering your Father, as though it is a special showing that has been orchestrated by your divine parents just for you, the feeling of achievement is absolutely sensational. You literally are standing in a little piece of Paradise on Earth. You are privy to the most glorious action in all creation's history, the presence and the will of the mighty Father and first source and cause of all that ever was and ever will be. And he is your own Father, showing himself to you.

It's spectacular! Oh, what a treasure was Jesus' life and teachings to the universe. And you will one day be just such a witness to others who will be seeking their Father and finding him in your own ministry—if not on Earth then on some distant world within Nebadon.

4. The Father is seen in your actions

Fourthly, and lastly, the person will see God acting in, through, and because of his or her own life. This is profoundly satisfying and uplifting.

The process involves the person eventually falling in love with his or her fellows with God's kind of love.[14]

It is the way of the Father and the Son and even the Holy Spirit, to demonstrate their ways to their child from the inside view, from within the inner person. In the early stages, it could be said that, by means of this spiritual liaison, Michael who loves his children, personally lives within you, and you increasingly ride on the wings of his love for such a time until his kind of love genuinely becomes your own.

The precursor to this kind of humanly divine love, is that first one must genuinely love Christ Michael and one's Paradise Father indwelling. One must first have loved seeking and finding the kingdom of heaven, God and his righteousness.[15]

This love which emerges within the son of God, will produce a sincere and loving ministry. The ministry will be an expression of devotion, and it will extend to the person's divine Parents, their sons and daughters, and the person's fellows. This is not to say that the person will necessarily become a professional religionist as compared with someone who ministers as they "pass by."[16] Its genuineness will emerge from the overflow of the content of one's own relationship with the Father, the Son and the Holy Spirit.

It will have a contempt for evil and sin, shallowness and sham, as powerfully as it will desire to lift people out of that drudgery.

It will involve the Father's love and word, his forgiveness and mercy, his power and his light.

The person will find the Urantia papers to be perfectly and literally true, to the degree that they genuinely love their fellows with the love Michael has for them. There is no other way. One cannot love them with the love of the Father, imagined or real, without sooner or later loving them with the perfectly personal love that Michael has for them: for such is the formation of sonship.

As a human being, you have no other place in which to

prosper and grow than into the personal love that your divine parents have for you yourself. Knowing them, loving them, worshipping them as a little child worships his or her good parents, is the way, the truth and the light of your destiny on Earth and in the heavens beyond, even unto the achievement of Finality in Paradise.

Not long into this stage or personal ministry, the son of God becomes empowered, anointed, by the relationship he or she has with his or her divine parents. The anointing guides them to develop their own code for living and loving within the Father's will. They will identify key values and directions from within the life and teachings of their brother Jesus, whom they love so very much, even worship, fully believing that these are the words of Michael of Nebadon himself.

For example, in my own life, the following passages are some of the words that I heard and still hear Jesus the son of God saying directly to me—and if he will say them to me he will say them to you too:

"Jesus said to the evangelists: 'Go now forth to do the work as you have been charged, and later on, when you have shown yourselves competent and faithful, I will ordain you to preach the gospel of the kingdom.'"[17]

"No longer should you be concerned with what you may obtain from the kingdom but rather be exercised about what you can give to those who live in dire spiritual poverty. Gird yourself, Simon, for the battle of a new day, the struggle with spiritual darkness and the evil doubtings of the natural minds of men."[18]

"Fear not the resistance of evil, for I am with you always, even to the end of the ages. And my peace I leave with you."[19]

"Again I tell you: As the Father sent me into the world, so send I you. As I have revealed the Father, so shall you reveal the divine love, not merely with words, but in your daily living. I send you forth, not to love the souls of men, but rather to love men.

"When you have faith, when power from on high, the Spirit of Truth, has come upon you, ... you will make known the love and the mercy of God to all mankind.

"...when you shall have been baptized with the Spirit of

Truth, you will bravely and joyously go forth to meet the new experiences of proclaiming the good news of eternal life in the kingdom of God.

"Your mission to the world is founded on the fact that I lived a God-revealing life among you; on the truth that you and all other men are the sons of God; and it shall consist in the life which you will live among men—the actual and living experience of loving men and serving them, even as I have loved and served you. Let faith reveal your light to the world; let the revelation of truth open the eyes blinded by tradition; let your loving service effectually destroy the prejudice engendered by ignorance. By so drawing close to your fellow men in understanding sympathy and with unselfish devotion, you will lead them into a saving knowledge of the Father's love. The Jews have extolled goodness; the Greeks have exalted beauty; the Hindus preach devotion; the far-away ascetics teach reverence; the Romans demand loyalty; but I require of my disciples life, even a life of loving service for your brothers in the flesh."[20]

"Feed my sheep. Do not forsake the flock. Be an example and an inspiration to all your fellow shepherds. Love the flock as I have loved you and devote yourself to their welfare even as I have devoted my life to your welfare. And follow after me even to the end."[21]

"I lived my life in the flesh to show how you can, through loving service, become God-revealing to your fellow men even as, by loving you and serving you, I have become God-revealing to you. I have lived among you as the Son of Man that you, and all other men, might know that you are all indeed the sons of God. Therefore, go you now into all the world preaching this gospel of the kingdom of heaven to all men. Love all men as I have loved you; serve your fellow mortals as I have served you. Freely you have received, freely give."[22]

These words were so pure to me, so straight from the mouth of Jesus and my Michael of Nebadon, that they were included in the ordination service we held in Oklahoma City in the Church of Christ Michael.

These words, to the son of God whom Michael himself is

developing for the purposes of ministry in his "kingdom of heaven", strike very deeply into the soul of man. They are God's own seeds planted in the good soil of your heart. Just as Jesus promised in his parable of the sower, God's seeds produce God's kind of a harvest. The sowing process, the pressing of those seeds ever more deeply into the stillness of our being where we meet God himself, can take a long time. Their sprouting can take a long time too. But the joy of seeing them finally spring into bud and bloom and grow into the full ear[23] is wonderfully rewarding.

For me it remains true that, as I go through the action of believing each word from the mouth of Jesus, Michael's power comes upon me to equip me to live in their truth. This he will do for you too. He has no favourites among his children. Know this in your heart right now dear lover of Christ Michael, Jesus' words will anoint you in his truth and love and vitality. Let your faith partake of his faith. Let the two of you be a single anointing which is confirmed on high in heavenly places for you.

It is through the experience of very lofty achievements, that the attributes of God as they are portrayed in the Urantia papers, are proven in your spirit. The Bible's Holy Spirit in you, the Thought Adjuster of the Urantia papers, confirms the attributes of God and the word of God in the papers as being of God. To believe them in the privacy and shelter of your own reading is one thing, but to act on them in the world for the sake of the lives of others is a wholly different matter. When you act on these truths, you act with God's total support because that's how your own Thought Adjuster would act if he were personally you, decision after decision until the four changes are complete in you.

Read the Urantia papers as a son of God

To recap then, firstly, a literal connection is made between you and your Father and you dialogue the one with the other.

Secondly, you see this same Father in the revelation made by Michael of Nebadon, as it is portrayed in the writings of the Urantia papers.

Thirdly, you see God in his human son and servant on Earth.

Fourthly, God acts in, through, and because of your own life.

As I said, this is profoundly satisfying and uplifting.

To read the Urantia papers as a son of God, for the sakes of others, and to carry your sonship with God into action in your daily life, *is* the divine purpose of this revelation.

❧

Notes

1. 150:5 {5. What must I do to be saved}
2. 150:5.2 {When men and...}
3. 177:1.3 {Jesus did not...}
4. 150:5.2 {When men and...}
5. 141:4.2 {In answer to...}
6. 170:3.3 {It is in...}
7. 141:6.5 {The apostles made...}
8. 193:3.2 {Peace be upon...}
9. 180:4.1 {Jesus continued to...}
10. 30:4.6 {4. Morontia Progressors...}; 194:2.12
11. Philippians 3:8-9
12. 32:3.6 {The farther down...}
13. 1:0.4 {This magnificent and...}
14. 102:6.7 {Belief may not...}; 132:4.6 {To a Roman...}
15. 181:2.5 {As John Zebedee...}
16. 171:7.10 {And it behooves...}
17. 149:0:2 {Before the departure...}
18. 191:1.2 {When Peter thought...}
19. 191:4.4 {Go, then, into...}
20. 191:5.3 {Peace be upon...}
21. 192:2.4 {When they had...}
22. 193:0:5 {Among yourselves, here...}
23. Mark 4:26-28

❧

Chapter 21

How do I get saved?

For Jesus of Nazareth, getting saved, making direct contact with his Father in heaven, was essential to all people. Surely, you will let that priority find its way into your heart as well. Most everybody wants to get to heaven. Or, so they say. This is the story about Joanne meeting Christ Michael and confirming herself own sonship to herself.

The story starts with her boyfriend, Mark, a tall, very good looking teenager with a winning smile and a gorgeous twinkle in his eyes. He lives on his own, has just gotten over a relapse into binge heroin use, and he doesn't have two cents to rub together. He's never had a job. I gave him a few dollars when he mentioned that he needed a few coins so he could buy a laundrette wash for his clothes. He mentioned that life wasn't going all that well. Someone kicked in his door the other day. And he had to resuscitate Joanne.

"It was the fourth time in four months since I met her Rob."

"What do you mean by resuscitate her, Mark? Had she overdosed?" I asked, rather surprised.

"Dead as a door nail, Rob. Swear to God. I held her in my arms and she was just plain dead. I was banging on her heart and blowing into her mouth. It was just horrible, 'cos I really love her."

Then he paused for a moment to connect with me more than with the memory. "Then she came around. God! I was so relieved!"

"How many more of those does she think she's got in her before she doesn't come back Mark?" I asked.

"Yeah, you usually don't get many do you?" he replied. We both knew the heavy toll heroin takes. So many kids have died on their first overdose, and some on their very first use.

Then, for a moment, as I put my attention on Joanne, wherever she was at that time, my Father's will became clear to me about her salvation.

"Mark, I think Joanne needs Jesus in her life. She needs someone to just explain a few things to her in such a way that doesn't add to her burdens and her pain: someone who doesn't scare her off."

"Oh yeah Rob, I agree. Will you talk to her? She likes you. Will you?" he replied.

I thought for a moment and then suggested, "How about the two of you come to Church on Sunday in Richmond. Mary and I will meet with you and talk after Church. Will she come to that?"

Mark looked up with that big enthusiastic, lovable grin and agreed, "Oh yeah Rob, I'll get her there mate. She'll come. It'll be OK, we'll be there."

When he was confident, he was truly confident. But when he was depressed, he was, well, you know how it is. In his case, heroin just made the depression ecstatic, but depression was still the soul-destroying curse on his life it had always been.

We shook hands, we hugged, we smiled, we exchanged God's blessings, then he did it all again with Mary. Then we left the place for home. It was late.

"Vital Youth Victoria" was a place Mary and I frequented to help lost kids come to know Jesus and his Life. It had been a great night, with lots of kids, some really enthusiastic worship music and plain old rock and roll dancing at the end. Everybody had a great time in the spirit of fellowshipping together. These nights were always great for those who are filled with Jesus and the Holy Spirit. For those who do not know him in their hearts though, it's always good for a while, then the emptiness, the loneliness, the doubt and unbelief and the cover up returns. People die so easily under such a burden. Out in the badlands of isolation from Jesus, Joanne was in the queue, waiting her turn to die.

Sunday night came. What a thrill is was for my household. My niece Alex was getting water baptized at that Church and she was so excited. We'd bought her a lovely gold chain and cross the day before, and she was so glad to be able to take it into the "watery grave" with her, in front of the thousand or so people in the congregation.

We looked around for Mark and Joanne, but they were nowhere to be seen. Mary said, "Oh they won't show, you just watch." But I remembered my Father's will for her salvation. "No, they'll be here honey, just wait."

The service started, after a while we were joined by a young woman in her early twenties that we had helped to come to

Jesus. The day she did, her drug using stopped completely. Within three months her depression subsided. She had been suicidal and in despair after having had a devastating childhood being molested by her stepfather. Now she was getting high distinctions for her university marks. She was really doing well. But no sign of Mark and Joanne. The baptisms came and went and I took a few photos. Then the guest preacher's sermon came and went. Then the service wound down to a close. We left our seats and started chatting to a couple of others who also go to Vital Youth on Friday nights. Then, while we were chatting, suddenly Mark's cheery face was close by saying, "Hi. We came like I said we would."

We hugged and shook hands and expressed how good it was to be with each other. He said Joanne was out in the foyer. Mary immediately started out for her, while I stayed in chatting with one of the singers from Vital Youth. After about fifteen minutes, I joined them in the foyer. As I came near, Mary stood up, kissed Joanne on the cheek, took my hand and drew me closer saying, "Rob will talk to you now Joanne. God bless you sweetheart," then she left us.

Joanne introduced me to her little brother, Joshua. "He's just turned seven."

"Hi Joshua," and I touched his hand. "I'm Rob. How are you doing." No words, just squirms of shyness. "I'm just going to talk to Joanne about Jesus for a little bit. You can listen in too 'cos it's really good stuff." More squirms, but he was listening pretty hard.

I started to talk to Joanne saying, "Joanne, Mark tells me you overdosed again last Thursday. What is that, the fourth time?"

"Yeah," she said, raising her sleepy eyes up to look at me. "There've been quite a few."

"How many more do you think you've got sweetheart?"

"Not many, I guess Rob."

"You know Joanne, there is an emptiness inside a lot of people. When we're growing up it's there, and nothing fills it." She looked at me as if to say, yeah but you can't ever get rid of it, but I kept on talking. "And when I look at you Joanne, I know that you keep it together pretty well on the outside. You look after your Dad, you dress well, you smile and look like nothing's wrong. And you've always done that. But there exists two people in you. There's that one, the one that gets depressed and takes heroin. The one that has a boyfriend in Mark. The one that does all the everyday stuff. The one that you don't really care whether she lives or dies because it's all meaningless and a waste of time anyway...so who cares?...right?" And she nodded her agreement, somewhat surprised that I was talking so directly about her exact perspective.

"Then, there's this other person. She's little, deep inside, scared, alone, not connected to anything or anyone. She's lost because she's not connected to anyone at all. Can you feel her Joanne?" And I touched her lightly on her chest above her tee-shirt line.

"Uh Huh" She replied.

"That you, the inner you, is the one who is lost. The outer you doesn't count for anything. You don't care whether she lives or dies. But the problem is that when that you takes heroin and overdoses and dies, she will take the inner you along with her. And I'm here talking to you tonight to tell you that there is a solution for the inner person. There is a connection that is available for the inner person. There is a life that can be breathed into that inner person which brings you to life so completely and powerfully that you feel really alive and complete and all the outer person junk goes away."

She looked at me with big wide doe-eyes like a newborn deer. She didn't say anything, but you could see that her hopes were really high now. She had never had it explained to her that way. She never thought that anything or anyone could actually touch that inner person we all have.

"Jesus comes into contact with us in our inner person Joanne. That's why Christians get so excited about it. There is a real connection that occurs. And Jesus brings his kind of life with him when he touches you inside. You become instantly connected to him. You end being lost. You end being an orphan. You end being helpless. You end being depressed. You end being worthless and a nobody. Jesus is your Father and he brings his life into you his daughter.

"Do you know Joanne, that the Bible says..." then I stopped what I was saying and I looked at her. "You know, I used to hate the way Christians would say that: the Bible says this and the Bible says that, as if they couldn't think for themselves."

"Yeah I know," she looked at me and smiled, "me too."

Avoiding that kind of a glitch, I continued to lead her.

"In the life of Jesus, when he lived on Earth, he taught that he would actively seek out his lost children Joanne. That's what he does. He doesn't sit at home in heaven eating his lunch all day. He's out there in the universe, in all of it at the same time, actively looking for his lost children. Children just like you. He goes everywhere, his spirit is always seeking. And he is thrilled when he finds one. Then he arranges for someone, like me and how I am talking to you tonight, to come visit that child and help him to make contact with that child."

She looked at me in utter surprise. "Really?" She paused. "He looks for me?"

"Sure does. You are his daughter. He is your Father. He can't wait to have you connect to him."

"Wow," she muttered almost inaudibly.

"Jesus wants to bring you into his own heavenly kingdom Joanne. Jesus wants to put you in touch with heaven and heaven's powers and glories while you live on Earth.

When it appeared to me that she had accepted the fact of his desire for her, the love of a good Father for his hurting little girl, I changed tack in order to describe the conditions of being saved, as Jesus himself called it in the Urantia papers.

"He said that the way to come into the kingdom of heaven was to receive God's forgiveness. Let me tell you what that means, and how he showed it to me. How old are you now, fifteen, sixteen?"

"Seventeen," she replied.

"Ok, so for seventeen years, you have been doing all sorts of things with your life. Helping your Dad. Doing drugs. School, and all that stuff. Think back over your life and tell me, what have you done that glorified God? What have you done that showed God to people?"

Joanne sat back in her chair and thought for a moment. Then she looked a little disconcerted. She looked at me saying, "Well, um, nothing. I haven't done anything that brought people's attention to God. In fact, I haven't been too good at all."

"Don't let that be a problem for you Joanne," I said, to prop up her confidence. "God led me through this same process one night and it all works out fine, trust me," I replied and gave her an encouraging smile.

"Consider what it would have been like if Jesus had found you when you were five going on six years old. Imagine if he'd been able to contact you and you two just got on really well. Then all through the years of your growing up to your age of seventeen years now, I imagine you would have had a good life. You would have shown off God to lots of people. He would have talked to you, and you would have talked to him, and things would have been so much different from how they worked out."

"Yeah," she said as she beamed at me. "Wow! Imagine that. Things sure would have been different if God had been in my life right from the start Rob."

"Christians," I continued, "call all that stuff we do without God, sin, and they say that Jesus saves them from their sin.

"Now, how I understand that Joanne, is that when Jesus comes into your heart, when you really let him in there, he wipes those years clean. You get to feel like a whole person straight away. It doesn't take a long time at all, just seconds. It is as if God has no more memory of your separation from him, no more memory of sin, and you live as if you had always lived with God. It's a real cleansing, and a real remaking of yourself. And what's great about it all is that he does all the work. You don't have to struggle and strain and practice or nothing. When he enters into your life, all those years are wiped clean."

She looked at me expectantly.

"Would you like to let Jesus into your heart Joanne?"

"Oh yes, I truly would," she replied.

"Well Jesus said that he will bring his children into the kingdom of heaven but that the kingdom had two requirements.

"One was that you have to receive the Father's forgiveness. Joanne, do you want God's forgiveness?"

"Oh yes I sure do. I want all my life cleaned up."

"OK, well he'll give it to you in an instant when Jesus enters your heart.

"The second condition Jesus mentioned was that you have to grow with God on each level you're living at. God is all about on going growth, exploration, discovery. There are no holding bays with God, you just keep on growing and learning and having different kinds of experiences, even after you die and go to heaven.

"Joanne, do you want to accept God's kind of growth in your life, and let him lead you from now on and forever so that he can be your Father and you can be his daughter?"

She looked alive for the first time. "Yes. Oh yes I do," she said.

"Then I am going to pray and ask Jesus to come into your heart now Joanne," I said as I reached over and took her two hands in mine. I then moved my face close to her face. Our cheeks touched. My lips were right beside her ear so that I could talk ever so gently to her and her alone.

I took a moment to commune with Christ Michael and then I said to Joanne, "Say what I say Joanne," and I began softly praying.

"Jesus," I said to my own universe Father," and Joanne repeated after me:

"Jesus."

"I want to receive God's forgiveness," I continued, and Joanne repeated after me:

"I want to receive God's forgiveness."

"I want God to be my Father and I want to be his daughter," I said and she followed after.

"And I want to grow with him in the kingdom of heaven…

"And I want you to come into my heart…

"And I want you to be the guardian of my life…

"Holy Spirit, I want you to be my mother, in all your wonderful creativeness…

"God, I give myself over to your righteousness…

"Amen."

"Amen," she said.

Then I sat back from Joanne. I looked up to see that Mark had been standing close by with outstretched hands, adding his support to the praying. He had given his heart to Jesus about a month earlier, and had experienced the baptism in the Holy Spirit and speaking in tongues; he loved to pray now, and he sincerely wanted Joanne to give her heart to God.

"Now comes the best part," I said to Joanne. "We'll wait just a few seconds and Jesus will literally come into your heart."

She looked at me with a quiet, refined pose of complete surrender to all that is good and righteous.

I noticed movement in the Holy Spirit around about us and mentioned it. "Here he comes," I said. "Yes, here he comes. Coming closer, closer." Then in an instant he broke through and Jesus was all around us. Quickly, he entered deeply into Joanne, to the core of her personality and mind; to the bones and the marrow and to the tiniest neurones.

This is a move of the spirit. I perceive it in the spirit. It affected Joanne in the spirit. Jesus said to us that when we are born again in spirit, we worship in spirit, that which is spirit. It is not a strange thing to the spirit, to perceive the move of spirit, nor for the spirit of the son to partake of the move of the spirit of his or her Father.

After about a minute of letting her bathe in his glorious presence, I asked her, "Joanne, do you feel Jesus with you now?"

"Yes," she said. "Right inside me." Then she went silent again.

After a while I questioned her again, "How do you feel as a person? Do you feel complete inside in the deepest parts of yourself?"

"Yes, very complete. Whole. Real," she replied.

I sat back. Mark was just about jumping out of his skin, he was so excited for Joanne. Mary, my wife, drew near. It was time to be leaving the Church building for the night.

Quietly I thanked the Michael of our universe, my own Father, for his unending will for the salvation of his children, and for his undying love for each of us that so easily lets us slip into the kingdom of his Father's eternal grace and righteousness.

What a great salvation Jesus brought to the world. Surely Joanne was not far from her death and on this night, her universe Father, Jesus Christ the Michael, won her into universe citizenship by his love and tender mercy.

Dear reader, we have a perfect Father in him. An adoring parent. A seeker of the lost. A winner of souls. A power over all human wretchedness. A glorious saviour of the least flicker of love in us. He is to be truly praised, held high, glorified and served. What a blessing and an honour it is to serve Jesus Christ the Michael of Nebadon. Joanne lives because of him, and by her new and overflowing love for him, she will sow the same seed into the hearts of others.

This time spent with Joanne mirrored Jesus' own words as he walked with the two brothers on the road to Emmaus on the day of his resurrection from the grave two thousand years ago. Still, today, after all that time, Jesus' words have life in them. His words are life itself, eternal life.

"Do you not remember that this Jesus always taught that his kingdom was not of this world, and that all men, being the sons of God, should find liberty and freedom in the spiritual joy of the fellowship of the brotherhood of loving service in this new kingdom of the truth of the heavenly Father's love?

"Do you not recall how this Son of Man proclaimed the salvation of God for all men, ministering to the sick and afflicted and setting free those who were bound by fear and enslaved by evil?

"That he will open the eyes of the spiritually blind and bring the prisoners of despair out into full liberty and light; that all who sit in darkness shall see the great light of eternal salvation.

"That he will bind up the brokenhearted, proclaim liberty to the captives of sin, and open up the prison to those who are enslaved by fear and bound by evil.

"That this Son of truth and righteousness shall rise upon the world with healing light and saving power; even that he will save his people from their sins; that he will really seek and save those who are lost.

"That those who believe in him shall have eternal life. That he will pour out his spirit upon all flesh, and that this Spirit of Truth shall be in each believer a well of water, springing up into everlasting life.

"Did you not understand how great was the gospel of the kingdom which this man delivered to you? Do you not perceive how great a salvation has come upon you?"[1]

Altar call

I appeal to you dear reader. Can you discern in your heart that I myself am one of "those who believe in him" and I have his gift of eternal life? I know for certain that were I to die and leave this planet tonight, that I would be in my Michael's embrace and care. Can you say the same of yourself? If you were to die tonight, leaving all things behind you. Do you know for certain that you have Michael's eternal life? Do you know for certain that you would be in his divine care?

If you have to think for a moment and work it out, then, regardless of what comes to mind, your answer is "no".

If you think, "Oh it's OK, the Urantia papers tell me that I will go to the mansion worlds when I die," then your answer is "no" because the power of your answer is in the Urantia papers and not in your own heart and soul.

If you say anything but "yes", straight out from the belly of your spirit, then your answer is "no".

Your "yes" needs to be experiential. If I ask you, "have you ever been swimming in icy cold water, so cold that you feel you really can't stay in the water too long before you have to get out?" Then you can reflect on your experience. You will weigh up the different times you have been swimming. Some memories are of warm water. Some memories are of cool water. But if you have a memory of being in icy cold water that made you feel that you just had to get out because it was way too cold for you, then you'd answer "yes" and you'd feel that icy chill right deep in your bones. In the same way I am asking you right now, "Have you had the experience of meeting God in your deep inner person?" If someone came into your room right now and asked you, "Please bring God into my presence right now for I have a hurt that only he can touch," could you do that? The son of God could indeed do that. The son of God would simply tell his or her Father, saying, "Father, this person with me needs you. Please come and be with us right now, without delay." And the son of God would have an immediate response from God who is their Father. That's the power of the real "yes" and if that isn't in your grasp then you current answer is "no".

Do you want to get saved dear reader? Do you want what Jesus offers all of his children? If your answer is "yes", then I invite you to follow Jesus' own prescription. He tells us quite plainly in the Urantia papers:

"When men and women ask what shall we do to be saved, you shall answer, believe this gospel of the kingdom; accept divine forgiveness. By faith recognise the indwelling spirit of God, whose acceptance makes you a son of God. Have you not read in the scriptures where it says, 'In the Lord have I righteousness and strength.' Also where the Father says, 'My righteousness is near; my salvation has gone forth, and my arms shall enfold my people.' 'My soul shall be joyful in the love of my God, for he has clothed me with the garments of salvation and has covered me with the robe of his righteousness.' Have you not also read of the Father that his name 'shall be called the Lord our righteousness.' 'Take away the filthy rags of self-righteousness and clothe my son with the robe of divine righteousness and eternal salvation.' It is forever true, 'the just shall live by faith.' Entrance into the Father's kingdom is wholly free, but progress—growth in grace—is essential to continuance therein."[2]

Will you receive the Father's forgiveness, just like Joanne did?

Will you agree to God's growth program, just like Joanne did?

You don't have to understand how the whole of God's domain operates in order to make that decision. The decision is simply based on that fact of it being true for you. Is it true for you? Then tell God "yes".

When you ask for God's forgiveness, keep it simple and just do it. Don't quibble and haggle. Don't complicate matters by saying whose fault it was and who's to blame for your life not having God in it and so on. Simply recognize that your life without God didn't bring any glory to God, and it was pretty ordinary. Then accept the invitation to have him in your life.

Do what Joanne and I have done. Look over your own life, back to your earliest memories. When did you glorify God in your life? When did someone say to you, "My, my, but I love being around you. To be around you is to be around God." If your answer is like mine was when God asked me that same question, "never," then you should know that you can receive a whole new sense of who you are. This salvation, this new birth in the Spirit, this liberation from the grip of the world on you, this entrance into Jesus' kingdom of heaven will come to you through a combined care for you. It will come to you from Jesus Christ who is the Michael of Nebadon, your local universe Father. It will also involve the power of the Holy Spirit, the Creative Mother of Nebadon who is your local universe Mother. It will also involve the Thought Adjuster who dwells in your mind, the Paradise Father who is your eternal and infinite

Father. All this unified and combined Godliness in you, is just a breath away, as you say:

"Come my Father, free me and make me in your image instead of the image of the world that does not know you."

The impact of this new birth will be immediately noticeable in you.

When you are ready, simply ask Jesus, believing that he will hear your prayer and will come straight away to you in order to enter your deepest mind, your deepest sense of who you are.

You can ask your Mother, the Holy Spirit, but she will pass on your prayer to Michael, to Jesus.

You can ask God the Father, but he too will pass on your prayer to Michael.

So bring your prayer request to Michael.

What words should you say? Your own words are best. There is no magic formula. Your own words fit your own lifestyle and circumstances. Your own words spring out of your own heart. Salvation means becoming connected to God in a conscious way. It is a matter between you and God, not you and me and not you and the Church or you and the Temple or you and a group of people. All of those relationships are simply social things. Becoming a child of God is between you and God alone. That's why your own words are so valuable. God has open access to every thought in your mind and every particle in your body and being—how would it be for you to go to him for healing and he replies, "Sorry, I can't access that part of you!" No, it's not like that. He knows you. He knows everything about you. He knows what you have been, what you are now and what you will become. He knows every word in your vocabulary. Every good and kind word. Every swear word. Every curse and word of hate. He also knows when you have used them or thought about using them. He knows the kinds of situations in which you might use them in the future. Your words are the motivation in your heart. Your words have more real power than a traditional formula, even if it doesn't seem so to you. Use your own words, they have been a major power in your life so far, and God knows you through the words you use just as he knows you through the feelings you feel.

I have heard many Christians pray for Jesus to come into their lives as Lord over their life. The preacher has suggested that they use the words that point to salvation in the Bible. You could say those words if you wanted to:

"Jesus, I make you Lord over my life. I turn from sin and follow you. I believe in my heart that God raised you from the dead. I give myself to you. This day, I confess you as Lord; therefore, according to your Word, I am saved. Thank you for making me new and for giving me eternal life."

In theory, those words will get you saved, connected to God your own Father. But the heart of the matter is not in a theory, it is in two very personal experiences.

The first experience is in you asking out of a genuine need. Your need will arise automatically out of the genuine recognition that your life is lacking somewhat because of your lack of contact with God. The words in the Christian prayer point to the very personal experiences that every saved person must have. They point to the experiences Joanne had. She saw that she was without God and she saw that she wanted to turn away from being without God. She wanted God. She asked for God. And she asked really believing that God would answer her prayer.

This "believing" leads me into telling you about the second experience, and for that I'll bring you to Jesus' words about how faith works. He said:

"So I tell you, whatever you ask for in prayer, believe that you have received it, and it will be yours."[3]

Jesus came into her and also awoke in her his previous presence that she was unaware of. He gave her wholeness, the kind that only God can bring. He gave her power over her life. He gave her a future.

The significant thing is that God came and touched her deep inside where it counts, in her heart and in her self-consciousness. The Holy Spirit even provided the power to learn to control what issues out of the depths of her subconscious mind.

If you say words asking for Jesus to come into your heart and to be sovereign of your life and you do not connect with God, then you are saved in theory, but in practical terms you have not realised him by faith and your life will go on the same as it always has.

In that case, God will be trying to contact you, but you aren't registering it. You will say:

"I said the words, but I didn't feel anything from God!"

But Jesus said:

"I will declare that I am both the door to the Father's sheepfold and at the same time the true shepherd of my Father's flocks...Every soul who enters upon the eternal way by the means I have created and ordained shall be saved and will be able to go on to the attainment of the eternal pastures of Paradise...I have come that you all may have life and have it more abundantly...I am the true shepherd; I know my own and my own know me."[4]

The victory of faith over heroin withdrawal

I want to tell you about a woman I once met who was in this kind of a situation. She was withdrawing from methadone in the drug detox I worked in. I went to her room to see her after staff told me that she had been very ill and unable to move because of the pain she was experiencing. I went upstairs and into her room and sat on the bed opposite her. She looked at me as I introduced myself and silently nodded her head slightly in acknowledgment.

"I have been told that you are withdrawing from methadone and that you have a lot of pain." Looking at her, I saw the same slight nod of her head.

"Last night I watched a thing on television about an English lady in Hong Kong called Jackie Pullinger.[5]

"She works with people who have heroin and opium addiction.

"She is a Christian.

"She says that Jesus has proven to her that the power of the Holy Spirit can completely take away the addiction, take away the withdrawal symptoms, give the person a new heart and give the person the power to live a world-overcoming life by the power of God.

"I saw men and woman telling their own stories and saying that they had no withdrawal symptoms at all and that since Jesus came into their heart they have had no craving for heroin or opium.

"Do you believe that kind of thing," I asked her.

She adjusted her body slightly, wincing with the pain as she did so and grimacing her face.

"Oh sure. I believe in God. I've believed in God all my life. But my prayers don't get through to him. They've never gotten through to him. I've always prayed. Over and over and over again. I've prayed ever since I can remember. But they never get through," she replied.

"That must make you feel pretty alone?" I asked.

"Yeah. Totally alone. It's like I've got nobody. Not even God."

Then she cried, in her loneliness. As the tears flowed down her face, I could see a glimpse of her isolation. She felt like a person who was shut out, and I knew what that was like from my own experience.

"You know," I said. "I think God is always knocking on the door of our heart. Sometimes when people don't hear him knocking, or speaking quietly inside, it's not that he's not there it more that something in us is blocking the connection.

"Would you mind if I have a bit of a poke around and see if we can't restore that connection in you?" I asked. "I do acupuncture and bodywork here in the clinic and I have some experience in working with God in this way."

"Yeah, sure. Do whatever you want," she said.

She was lying on her back now, fully clothed in her shirt and pullover, jeens and thick socks. She was perhaps twenty-seven years old. Thin. Long black hair. A nice complexion. She wasn't worn down by years of prostitution, which is common among the women who came to detox.

I let my spirit's gaze come to rest on her body. I touched her torso in a couple of places around her navel and her lower ribs, seeking out the parts of consciousness that might be affecting her prayer life. Then, I found the spot. I checked on the pathways to which it was connected and over which it was influential and found that it linked into relevant parts of the brain that would have been normally involved with prayer.

"I think I have something here Louise.

"I'll make a couple of adjustments and then we'll ask God to help us connect to him and we'll see how we go."

As she lay there like a corpse, in all her agony, she just looked at me in complete disbelief. Her world view had no way to comprehend that a son of God could open up things spiritual in a person, simply by touch and communion with God.

"Uh huh," she finally muttered.

By the power of my own attention and will as I shared the mind of God, I worked quickly and confidently with the power for healing and truth that resides in sonship with God. I took that power into the relevant points of consciousness in her body. In a few seconds, it was done.

"OK. I think we're done here Louise. Let's test it out now, shall we?" I asked, not really expecting an answer from her in order to carry on.

"I want to check and see if the prayer connection is in tact now. OK?" I asked.

"Yeah, OK," she replied.

She seemed to be a little more relaxed, simply from the attention she was receiving, and also from the fact that I was bringing the Holy Spirit to her body and soul.

"Let's use your pain as a monitor, shall we?" I said. "What I mean by this is, I'll pray and ask God to do something in your body, perhaps, say, take away some pain somewhere. Then, if that happens, you and I will know that he can get through. Do you understand this?"

"Yes," she replied.

"Which part of your body would you like God to take the pain away from?"

"What a stupid question," she replied with a halfhearted laugh. "All the pain."

"Yes we know that, but if we just focus on a localised part of your body for the moment, in order to first of all find out if God is connecting to you, then we can deal with all the pain later."

OK," she said. "Anywhere you like."

"OK then," I said. "How about up here around your left shoulder."

"Yep. Fine with me. Whatever," she confirmed.

I sat back from her so as not to touch her. I wanted to be out of her private space, so to speak. I was in communion with God already, so talking to him was simply like talking to a third person in the room. What I said was more for her sake than his.

"Father, if you can get through to Louise now please help her. She's prayed all her life and she feels like her prayer has never connected to you. That makes her very lonely and isolated. If you can get through to her now from your end, please take away the pain in her left shoulder."

Repairing her prayer connection

As soon as I said those words, Louise suddenly raised her head off the pillow in utter astonishment and looked at her left shoulder. Something had happened. She reached her right hand across her chest and started poking the muscles around the shoulder.

"It's gone," she said in complete bewilderment. "It's gone Rob. The pain's gone." then she settled back and I saw faith creep into her again. She had a little smile on her face that came right from the heart. I remember thinking to myself that that kind of a smile had not been there for years and years.

"Thank you Father," I said as I continued on with my work.

"Louise, let's find out where your own prayer connection is not working shall we?" And I touched a place on her abdomen, a little distance out from her navel.

It wasn't a normal acupuncture point, as those things are known in Chinese medicine. I was in contact with an experience she had had when she was a little girl. My Father had taught me to use the power of the gifts of the Spirit which had come to me through Christ and I learned to recognise how our experiences reside in different parts of our body. I had searched for a pathological experience, and had found it in this particular tissue near her navel.

"Louise, I am going to touch this place here on your tummy and I want you to tell me what you remember," I asked her.

Just after I touched the point, she screwed up her face.

"Oh that's horrible. It's all dark. And I'm locked in. And there are these bars I'm hanging on to. I'm all locked in Rob. I'm all locked in."

"How old are you Louise, in your memory?" I asked.

"Oh I don't know, maybe two. I'm really little," she replied.

"And I'm so scared. I can see my parents now. It's like I'm looking out of these bars, and I'm all confined and cramped, and through them I can see my Mum and my Dad and they're fighting. They're having a really big argument and they're hitting each other and yelling and screaming."

"OK, look at me," I asked her.

She opened her eyes and caught mine. I wanted to ground her back in current time so she could reflect on her memory.

"Where were you Louise. At home?" I asked.

"Yes. At home. But I can't figure out what the bars were. They were like the bars you see in the movies when people are in jail."

I let her ponder the memory for a while and then, seeing that she was unable to recall any more detail, I said:

"Let's ask God about those bars shall we?"

"Sure," she replied, "Let's do that ..."

Even before she finished her sentence she cried out:

"Oh I know what it was. I can see a picture of it now and I remember it as clear as a bell. I was only two or three and I had rushed into hiding when my parents started fighting. My hiding place was a chair, one of those ones with the wooden legs and the cross beams holding them together."

Then she reflected more and more on that image.

"That's what the bars were Rob; those round chair legs coming down and the cross beams going across to connect them. I was holding onto one leg with one hand and the other leg with the other hand as I sat all curled up inside all four legs, looking out."

"And the whole scene was very scary for you?" I asked.

"Yes it was," Louise replied.

"Could it have been so scary for you that you felt cut off from the ones you loved and never again felt that their support for you was able to reach you because they had bigger things on their mind than you?"

"Yes, that's exactly how I was feeling."

"Could it also be that perhaps you felt shut out from that time on. And that later on when God arrived in your life and you wanted to pray, you carried over your sense of being shut out. And in that way, you built for yourself the absolute reality that your prayers could never get through to God. You could not communicate with your parents. You could not communicate with God. Something like that?"

"Yes it's that exactly Rob," she replied with a smile that comes from the relief of having some revelation on an important matter. "I have never ever been able to communicate with my parents. I really loved them, more than life itself. But I never felt that they heard me, or wanted to hear me."

"Well, let's see now if we have fixed that," I said. "We have identified that God can connect from his end of the prayer line Louise. Your pain, how is it?"

"Oh it's still gone. My shoulder feels great." Then she laughed, "Shame about the rest of me."

"Well, now we're going to establish that your role in prayer works OK."

"Sure. What do you want me to do?" she asked.

"Well, I'm just going to sit here out of the way on this bed over here, and you're going to pray in the way you have always prayed. This time I want you to pray for God like those people in Hong Kong prayed. Ask God to take away the addiction. Ask God to take away the physical pain. Ask God to give you a new heart. Ask God to give you his power to deal with your life and to live and grow with him."

She didn't say another word, but only closed her eyes.

I waited.

Presumably she had prayed. She just lay there like a dead thing. Motionless. Barely breathing. No sign of change.

Still I waited. A few minutes went by.

After a while I began to think that maybe what I had done with her wasn't working for some reason. Everything in me confirmed that what I had done and perceived was true and right. Maybe she had given up though and, in the haze of her pain, maybe she had just decided to go inside and ignore me.

Still longer I waited for some kind of a response for her. Eventually I quietly cleared my throat, not wanting to disturb her if things were going well, and not wanting to offend her by an unwelcome presence if they weren't gong so well.

Victory

"What's happening for you?" I gently asked in almost hushed tones.

Then Louise gently rolled her head over to the right side to face me. Without even opening her eyes she spoke:

"I have never experienced so much ecstasy ever in my entire life." Then she rolled her head back. I quietly thanked my Father, and tiptoed out of her room.

This is the story of a woman who could not experience God.

Quite literally, her prayer connection was not working.

It wasn't that she didn't believe: she did.

It wasn't that she didn't love God: she did.

It wasn't that her sins stood in the way: they didn't, we never spoke of her life other than the kid in the chair.

What stopped her prayer from working was not God's care for her. Can you imagine the heartache of Christ Michael, and Mother Spirit, and her Thought Adjuster? They all long for her to live in good health; without the horrible effects of drugs; living happily; feeling like she is a much loved little girl; feeling that she is an adored son of God. But her fear crippled her. Fear came in even before her Thought Adjuster arrived, and crippled her heart's belief in itself.

An anointed cloth

I've met other people for whom that kind of thing has happened.

I once met a lady in the mid west of the USA. She called me a month later telling me that she felt she could no longer live with her husband. He had no spirituality about him whatsoever, she said. Her own life was spiritually rich, she wanted to build their marriage on a spiritual foundation, but how could she do that with him having not a single spiritual fibre in his body?

As I listened to her on the phone, I turned my attention to her husband, a man I had never met.

The Holy Spirit had come upon me. What I mean by that is that the will to intervene in the person's life with the power of sonship with God—the power of sharing the mind of God— filled my heart and mind. As I looked into the man's past, this man that I had never met, where he was in America two states away from where I was in America, I saw that he had a blockage in his spiritual development at an age prior to when his Thought Adjuster arrived into his life at age five years tenth months.

"He has a need to remove something personal so that his Adjuster can make spiritual impressions in him. He has legitimately never registered anything spiritual," I said.

"That's right," his wife said. "It's like he isn't evil or sinful. He is just totally unable to empathise with anything that I say or do or feel that is spiritual. He doesn't condemn religion or Church ever. He simply has absolutely no empathy for the things of God, almost as if God isn't in him. And I know that can't be, for God is in everyone."

"Let me take a look and see what might help him," I said as I turned my attention to my Mother Spirit. Quietly I asked her in spirit what I should do that would help this fellow in this kind of problem. In a few moments I had the solution.

"Do you want to do something, it's a little unusual, that will help the Spirit to break through and help him? Do you want this marriage to work?" I asked.

"Oh yes Rob, I do want this marriage to work. We've just bought a new home and we're both looking forward to moving into it. We've been married for around four years, and this home is something we have hoped will add to our lives a whole lot."

"OK. This is what to do. Go now and get a handkerchief and then come back to the phone."

Off she went and then she came back.

"OK I've got one," she said.

"I'm going to pray now, and as I pray I want you to put your hand on that handkerchief. You keep one hand on the phone to your ear, and one hand on the handkerchief. I'm going to impart some anointing for change into that handkerchief and then you're going to place it inside his pillow and leave it there for six days and nights.

"OK," she said.

Then I prayed. As I prayed I felt a Holy Spirit empowerment unify this lady and myself and the handkerchief. When I was satisfied that the empowerment was in place and equipped with God's cutting-through power, like Jesus when he said to the blind man Josiah to, "Go, my son, wash away this clay in the pool of Siloam, and immediately you shall receive your sight,"[6] I said:

"Do you feel the power in you and in that handkerchief?"

"Yes," she replied, "I do."

"Go and place it inside his pillow. Leave it there for six days and nights and after that time he will have access to God and God will have access to him. And all this by the power of our Michael and the Holy Spirit and the power that is in sonship with God—God wants him to be his son and he will awaken in him the desire to find his Father.

It wasn't many weeks later that I received an email

mentioning that indeed the desired change had come about and that the family was indeed able to build their life on a spiritual foundation. She sounded so excited.

Some people have a problem with using a handkerchief in that way. But let me ask you something. If your baby daughter was dying and you prayed to God and he said, lay a hanky on her wound and she will live, and you refused, would you later have wished that God had given you some other way that was more acceptable to you, or would you rather have wished that you had had the sense to simply do what God suggested? I can tell you that when a son of God operates within the will of God their Father, it is to work outside all of conceptual limitations. For me, the whole world is a living anointing. What one person calls a handkerchief, I see it as a part of God's own body and will, deeply anointed for healing and change. I see it like that because he sees it like that.

So anyway, some people have an easy passage to God's forgiveness and salvation, and other people like Louise and this lady's husband have blockages to that same favour with God. Those problems have to be worked out by the power of the Spirit.

Ask, and you will receive unless you are being opposed

If you trust in Jesus, simply ask him to help open you to receiving the Father's forgiveness. He will definitely do that. His word is good and true, for all time. The creator of an entire universe cannot be flippant, choosing this person and not that person. Jesus' word is sure, constant and true. When he says he has set up a way for you to contact the Father and to grow in the ways of the Father, and it is by receiving the Father's forgiveness, then trust in that fact. If need be say aloud to him, as if he is standing in the same room with you:

"Jesus, you said that you had a way to the Father. I want that way. I want you to open it up to me please," And he will do that.

Contact with God the Father, salvation, receiving the favour of God, by any name, comes first through receiving his forgiveness—and it is an experience, not merely a thought.

Please do accept God's forgiveness. To receive God's forgiveness is to receive the ability to forgive others in a way that neutralises the harms they have done to us and in a way that strengthens us with God's life-giving power.

Receiving God's forgiveness is not just something about getting on well with God so much as it is the way to claim for yourself, God's kind of forgiveness in your own heart and mind, and its application in forgiving those that have wronged you; or might wrong you in the future for all time. Every Melchizedek, every angel, every Finaliter and every Adjuster-fused human has the Father's type of forgiveness in them and it is practised daily. Only when we have that kind of relationship with others do we gain the kingdom of heaven. Only when we have God's kind of forgiveness in us, can we love other people with his kind of love. Only with God's kind of forgiveness in us, can we find solutions to the many problems that divide us, because our Father is in our hearts to mediate with us. Only with God's kind of forgiveness in us, can we traverse the many woes and problems of this world and even this universe on wings that sincerely want to understand the views and needs and concerns of the people concerned.

The whole universe is hung on God's forgiveness.

Please do receive contact with him in your life dear one. I ask this with a very deep love for you, even the love of Jesus Christ who lives in me, through whom contact with the Father was made real in my life and without whom my contact with God would have, at best, been not at all personal and as loving and friendly. With his love do I say that I would love you to receive our Father's forgiveness right now. Put the book down and receive it right now.

❧

Notes

1. 190:5.4 {As they walked...}
2. 150:5.2
3. Mark 11:24
4. 165:2.7-8 {And now, lest...}
5. See also her two books published by Hodder and
     Stoughton, London, "Chasing the Dragon," 1980; and

"Crack In The Wall," 1989.
6. 164:3.8 {When Jesus had...}

Chapter 22

Thought Adjuster arrival: how I got "saved"

The first time I heard about God, I believed in him. He was *that* appealing to me, despite the packaging he came in—the Church.

The evangelist

Two thousand years ago, the apostle Paul wrote to the Roman believers in Jesus. In part, he mentioned that he had a burden for those people who did not realise that favour with God[1] came by the belief in one's heart, faith: that is, if you genuinely believe in God, you have access to him and his righteousness through your own faith in his involvement in your life. Once you have favour with God, you were saved from the perils of not having access to God's favour. He wrote that the way to cut to the heart of the matter and appropriate God's favour for yourself, was to:
> "confess with your lips that Jesus is Lord and believe in your heart that God raised him from the dead."[2]

Then he backed this up with the authority of scripture, saying:
> "Everyone who calls on the name of the Lord shall be saved."[3]

Think about the way that God raised up Jesus on Easter morning[4]—what an incredible event. That epic tells us that obviously Jesus is Lord over life and death; listen to the record in the Urantia papers of his own Thought Adjuster—God—on the topic:
> "A Creator Son has within him himself the power to bestow himself in the likeness of any of his created sons; he has within himself the power to lay down his observable life and take it up again; and he has this power because of the direct command of the Paradise Father, and I know whereof I speak."[5]

Then also, there is this extraordinary piece of information concerning Jesus' resurrection that defies all powers on Earth:
> "At two forty-five Sunday morning, the Paradise incarnation commission, consisting of seven unidentified Paradise personalities, arrived on the scene and immediately deployed themselves about the tomb. At ten minutes before three, intense vibrations of commingled

material and morontia activities began to issue from Joseph's new tomb, and at two minutes past three o'clock, this Sunday morning, April 9, A.D. 30, the resurrected morontia form and personality of Jesus of Nazareth came forth from the tomb."[6]

Paul asked people to appropriate God's favour for themselves by inviting them to, "confess with your lips that Jesus is Lord and believe in your heart that God raised him from the dead." That's a pretty simple thing to do. You can do that. I can do that: believe that God raised Jesus from the dead and say out loud that Jesus is Lord. Go on, try it for yourself. It's a spiritual thing to do. Say it aloud so that you can hear it, say it with me:

"Jesus is Lord."

Why? Come on, say it with me.

"Because God raised him from the dead!"

What an extraordinary thing to believe and to say out loud. When we do that we feel all around us, if we genuinely believe that God raised Jesus from the dead that is, some kind of lovely heavenly presence. That presence, is access to God and his favour. It comes to us by his grace and our believing—our faith.

For forty years, I never did understand what Christians were referring to when they spoke about being saved though. Oh, now I do, but not then. They'd say, "Jesus saves you from your sin," but they could say that until the cows came home and it wouldn't make sense to me. I couldn't connect the words "save" and "sin" to anything inside me. Oh, sure, I heard the words, I could *calculate* that what they meant was if you're bad you go to hell, but hell wasn't real for me either, so their words were empty of anything real to me. I had questions like, "Show me God and then show me how I am separate from God because of my sin." And they never did.

That left me thinking that they were all simply talking hot air that didn't amount to anything at all. When it finally came to learning about what Christianity meant in its doctrine of salvation from sin, I had to go right out of my way to try and figure out what on Earth they were talking about, and that took me a lot of work. I had no problem whatsoever understanding any other religion in the world, but I had no idea whatsoever what Christianity was on about. It was like that right on into my forties when I finally asked my Father to help me to understand what it was about the spiritual forces in himself and Michael and Mother Spirit that Christians experienced spiritually. In order to understand their experience, I came to understand their principles.

Continuing, Paul wrote:

"But how are they to call on one in whom they have not believed?"

That is, how can they exercise their faith by believing that God brought Jesus back to life after he was dead and buried and thereby obtain God's favour?

"And how are they to believe in one of whom they have never heard?"

That is, how can the people of the world say, "I believe that Jesus is Lord!"

"And how are they to hear without someone to proclaim him?"

"And how are they to proclaim him unless they are sent? As it is written, 'How beautiful are the feet of those who bring good news!'"

His words speak of the work of the evangelist, the person who takes the good news to the world's people so that they can hear about the sovereignty of Jesus and thereby give rise to faith and appropriate God's favour for themselves—which amounts to being saved.

The church meeting

As I said, the first time I heard about God, I believed in him. The evangelist was up on the platform of the Morrinsville Presbyterian Church in Canada Street, delivering the news about God. He and his team were from out of town, probably from Auckland, two hours drive to the north.

The place was packed. There must have been two hundred people. To his left and right on the platform were about a dozen people who all looked like they knew everything about what this preacher was saying. I remember looking around the Church at all the townsfolk. To me it seemed that they had never before heard what this fellow was talking about. He was like a travelling salesman bringing something totally new to town. But they all seemed so lifeless, as if they weren't getting it somehow.

The main thing I remember that preacher spoke about was that all things were created, and created by God—the heavens, the sky, the world and everything in it including you and me.

I believed that preacher completely.

"I dunno"

Half way into the meeting, he broke up the meeting and his team splintered and gathered everyone into small groups. I was in the group with all the other five year old kids, and we all sat on a couple of wooden benches up behind a curtain hung on the platform where the preacher had been standing.

One of the young ladies in the team on stage was the leader of our group. As I recall she said she was that preacher's daughter; and she seemed to be so much like him. She seemed to know just about everything there was to know about what he had been talking about.

The group was just talking: she mostly talking to us, asking us our thoughts on things. I didn't have any thoughts on things, I just had one huge question. After listening to that preacher, and being totally sold on his story that there was a God and that he created everything, I really wanted to know what he was. You know, really what he was. Like, where was he? How do you get in touch with him? Can my whole family get to enjoy him? Can he connect with us and be a part of our lives? Can he be a part of my life, you know, just him and me all alone at times out in the fields nearby talking to each other? And if he can be a part of my life…wow! What a life that would be!

Just as the whole group thing was over and people were going back to their pews, I went up close to the young lady who had been running our group for little kids and I yanked on her skirt to get her attention, as kids do.

"Excuse me Miss," I said, with wide eyed hope in my heart.

She looked down while she busied herself with shuffling songbooks or something in her hands. Then she caught my eye: "What?" she replied in a matter of fact tone.

I could barely hold back my excitement. Like John the Baptist, I was "fairly vibrating with the mounting impulse"7 of wanting to ask my question to this woman whom I was absolutely certain would deliver me to God.

I drew a breath. Then my whole life was poured forth into my question.

"What's God?" I solemnly asked, and I gazed into her eyes with all of my five-year old being poised to receive the very keys of heaven and Earth from her.

She looked at me with complete disinterest and dismissed my question with a sense of absolute not knowing. Then she passed off a comment that shattered me:

"I dunno."

Then she went on with her business of going out on the other side of the curtain and joining the team with the evangelist on the front stage of the platform.

I stood stunned. What could she mean, she didn't know? She was on the platform with the preacher wasn't she? She was the preacher's daughter, wasn't she? What did she mean by "I don't know"? She must know? She was with the team that was bringing this new thing to town—she had to know!

I looked around at the other kids. Nobody was asking this kind of a question. They all seemed like they didn't care about any of this much one way or the other. But I sure did.

Then I looked at some of the grown-ups. They looked like big versions of the kids. They didn't seem to care one way or the other much either.

I was totally dumbfounded. Speechless. I picked my jaw up off the floor and found my way back to the pew where my family were reclaiming their seats.

Hypocrisy

I looked at them all. I looked around at everyone in the Church. Then I saw the preacher come back on the stage, and all the others in the team, and this young lady who had just told me she didn't know what God was came back on the platform too.

I watched them like a hawk. Were they for real? They seemed to be for real. They acted like they were for real.

Then I started to hear what they were saying. I heard with a new ear. I heard the preacher clearly, and it dawned on me. They didn't have a clue!

They had no more of an idea about God than the poor people who packed the Church pews in front of them and who were busy emptying their money into the wooden collection plates! The whole thing was an empty farce!

Oh sure, they'd read the book and they'd said words that sounded like they knew God. But I could tell: they only knew the book. I have no idea what it was inside of me that let me discern that, but I looked up on that stage and all I saw was a line of hypocrites. And there was the biggest one of them all, that woman who'd tried to lead all of us little kids into this Churchy stuff when all along she didn't have the vaguest idea about the real thing. Sure, she knew the story all right, but she didn't have the goods to back it up.

Their show reminded me of someone coming to town selling the newest fizzy drink to hit the country. They were up on the stage telling everyone about it, how good it is, how irresistible it is, how it's going to change your life forever, inviting everyone to come on up the front and buy some. But in back of the curtain there were just empty crates with not a single bottle of this stuff on the shelf—like someone else owned the drink and had warehouses full of the stuff but these travelling salespeople didn't have any of it themselves.

They had nothing. They knew nothing. They had not found this God they were talking about. They'd just learned stories in a book and hung them together to get other people to believe the same stories.

I'll find God, and he'll help me find him

As I sat there on the pew these kinds of thoughts whirled through my little heart and this conviction became cemented in my mind. I looked out the Church window and way up high I saw the big blue sky outside on this sunny Sunday morning. I made a decision right then and there, and I said it in my heart with all the conviction of some little warrior who was taking a blood oath:

"If there's a God, then I'm *going* to find him!" I said. Then I reflected on how these people and their book full of stories could be no use to me whatsoever on my quest and I added, "And I reckon that if there's a God out there," and I looked into the big blue cloudless sky, "then he'll help me to find him too."

Twenty years later I would read in the Urantia papers that decisions like that have moral significance, but I didn't know anything about that then. I was just a five-year-old kid, dealing with blatant hypocrisy the best I knew how.

I looked at my family. My brother David was sitting between Mum and Dad off to my left. None of them seemed to know God, at least not how I wanted to know him. As I looked at them, I realised that none of them could help me find God. He was not of this world. For the first time in my life I recognised that my Mum and Dad weren't the most powerful people in the world: they had a creator, just like me.

This mission of finding God, then, had straight away become a secret thing in my own little heart, a very private affair. These weren't the words I used then, for I had none to speak of in those days, but I believed God was primal and infinite, just as I would later read about in the Urantia papers.[8] My quest was to find the person who was the creative source of all existence, who was bigger even than all the sky and everything in it.

The sports field and the glory cloud

On the following day I went to school at Morrinsville Primary (Old) School. Late in the afternoon, we were told that the following day we were to be a part of some kind of sporting event with a visiting team from an out of town visiting school. I had never been to something like that, this being pretty much my first year in school, and I was curious about what people from another school would be like.

In the afternoon of the following day, all of our class was duly herded outside and marched up to the northern most football field. We lined up along the west perimeter, under the shade of a huge oak tree, and looked east across an empty field. The game hadn't started. We all were pretty excited about playing with these kids from a whole other locality. Then, our teacher gave us the news that they hadn't brought any kids our age with them and that we were just going to sit and watch the game played by kids a year older than our class, kids we didn't know much at all. The whole thing fell flat. What was really exciting was now completely boring.

That is, until about thirty minutes into the game when this cloud came and hung over the field.

The cloud was about three hundred feet off the ground and positioned itself pretty much in the middle of the field. It was white and fluffy, just like a cloud, in an otherwise cloudless sky.

Angels streaming forth

Within a few minutes of it positioning itself, there came from within it a few people who were brightly coloured, as if they were made out of coloured light. I thought them to be angels. They hovered outside the south side of the cloud and then after a while gently floated down to the ground. As they did so, all the kids playing sport stopped the game and, with the few teachers who were umpiring on the field, all looked up to watch them descending. The trickle of these brightly coloured angels grew into a stream. The whole of my class was on its feet in an instant, gazing up at this marvellous spectacle. When the angels had floated right down to the ground, they started to beckon everyone with greetings of love and affection. Everybody ran to them, they were so inviting and attractive. They cuddled all the kids and the teachers alike, and gave out little bags of sweets to all the kids. I watched as every one of my class thundered off onto the field in a wonderment of child-like excitement to share in this spectacle of joy.

For all the older kids, and a few of the kids in my own class, the meeting with these angels was a reunion. The angels had met them before, but I didn't know where or how.

The trickle of angels coming from within the cloud increased until it became a stream. After a while, with much celebration and jubilation going on in the school ground, some of the angels ascended back into the cloud. The scene on the ground had become a busy and wonderfully spiritual celebration of affirmation about the closeness of God's unseen world to the ordinary world of human beings.

I meet my Thought Adjuster

I stood on the side of the field, looking east into this spectacle, and all of a sudden another person came out from inside the cloud. As he came out of the cloud, the stream of angels going back and forth from the cloud to the ground continued, as did the celebration on the ground below them.

I looked up to see this huge being. He was oval in shape, and pink. He looked kind of like the light that the angels were made from, but there was something hugely different about him. He definitely wasn't an angel; they looked a little bit like people.

He was something a whole lot more than an angel.

It seemed that he had his attention on me, yet he had no eyes nor ears, neither mouth nor body. This very large, pinkish radiance in the shape of an upright oval just hung in the sky beside the cloud and he had his attention on me.

Then he moved toward me, slowly descending from the height of the cloud, until he was about twenty feet in front of me and about fifty feet off the ground. He was about twenty feet tall and about eight feet wide, and sort of flat rather than filled out, as a body would be. There was something really awesome about him. The angels, in comparison, were like our friends, our older brothers and sisters from another dimension of life. This one seemed to be far removed from where ever it was that the angels came.

"Robert," he said aloud to me. "I am God, Robert."

He had my total attention, as I stood transfixed to the grassy ground near that big old oak tree in Morrinsville Primary School.

"You asked to find me, and I have come to be with you," he continued.

Well! I was thrilled. What a God! I knew he would do it. I just knew he would help me to find him. And now, here he was, right in front of me. Wow!

Then he explained a great many things to me, pausing every now and then to involve me in conversation with him.

It was love at first sight. God was just so magnificent, so believable, so true and pure and good and right and a thousand other things that I have come to link into the term righteousness since then.

Eventually, he explained that he was going to reside in me.

As he spoke about these things, I looked out over the field, I still remember that clearly to this day, and I thought to myself:

"Ah, so that's how it is that God knows about everything that we do: he's right here with us throughout our lives. And that's how you get to know God: God comes to you when you are five years old and he lives inside you."

What a profound understanding for God to give to a five year old little boy.

As I looked around at all the kids and adults playing with the angels, I recognised a great unity on Earth: God was with every single one of these people, and if they weren't yet at the stage of whatever it takes at five years of age to receive God inside you, then that would be happening soon. I looked across to all the kids who had been playing sport, even the ones from the other town, and they all had God in them already. I looked and saw that some of the kids in my own class didn't yet have God in them, but it was obvious that it wasn't going to be long before he was there. The arrival of God into little five-year-old kids was an individual thing, it happened at different times of the year. That I knew, but I didn't recognise what it was that brought God other than the desire to find him. I thought that every person who had received God had made some kind of a wish to find him, but I'd never spoken to anyone about it, I'd only heard of God in a sense that was real to me the day before.

God pointed out that he was my Father, a shepherd of my life and that he would be with me forever. He spoke about how he would work with me to show him to other people much later on in my life.

As I looked at the playing field full of people and angels, with this wondrous white cloud hovering overhead, I felt a profound sense of security that penetrated all the Earth. To this day, it has never been uprooted in my life despite some dreadful challenges.

Farewells

At a certain point, the angels started saying their farewells. They gradually started ascending into the cloud and not returning down to the ground. In all there must have been about 35 kids in my own class and about forty older kids who had been playing sport, and a few adults to total about eighty people on the field. At one point it seemed that there were more angels than there were people, and now they were returning to their heavenly chariot just above them in the air.

When they were almost all back inside the cloud, this "God," whom I later came to know through the Urantia papers as my Thought Adjuster, informed me that he was going to farewell them and stay here with me. He was then going to descend into me, in order to make a life long home with me, and I agreed with him.

He moved from his position in front of me, looking at me and facing me, to being directly overhead over me and facing the same direction I faced—looking east across the playing field. He was about fifteen feet above me, and he stretched another twenty feet taller than that.

He started to communicate a very loving but formal farewell to all the people in the cloud. There were others in the cloud besides angels, and he thanked them all for bringing him to this location and to me. The affection that flowed between the people in the cloud and this Thought Adjuster was electric.

It was like the whole world was filled with this divine love that they shared, and it overflowed to the people on the ground. They were all uplifted by this visit to them in their hometown. None of them was sad at the angels' departure. It was a very happy event in itself and it had every sign of recurring some time in the future, as if this kind of thing was done by angels all over the world all the time with comforting regularity.

The strange being

After God had said his farewell to the people in the cloud, and they had said their farewell to him, and wished him well on his mission, there suddenly emerged the most magnificent being to the north side of the cloud. At the time, I didn't think he had arrived inside the cloud, but he had certainly arrived along with the cloud.

He was like this wonderful person who called himself "God" and who now hung in the air above me—he was like this Thought Adjuster. Where God was pinkish and oval, this other being was perfectly circular, and shimmering with a clear light. Imagine placing a clear sheet of circular glass up in the sky, with a diameter to it of about fifty feet. You'd know there was something in the sky, and yet you could see right through it. In the instance of this being, when I looked into it, I could look right through it or I could also look into an infinity of its being. It was, in some sense unknown to me then, the elder of this God who had come to be with me. When I spoke to my Adjuster about this person many, many years later, he disclosed that it was "My elder brother," alluding to another Thought Adjuster who was relevant to his arrival.

The moment came when these two began to communicate their farewells. Suddenly it was like God speaking to God. The whole world came to a halt. Nothing happened on Earth, it seemed to me, until these two had unlocked themselves from their wordless, eternal, omnipotent but intensely personal embrace. I had never experienced realness ever before to the depth that these two "Gods" demonstrated in their parting.

When their parting was complete, they separated their attention from each other as they both "stood" in the air some fifty yards apart from each other. Then, in an instant, this shining one simply vanished from sight as if speeding off in a northeasterly direction. Instantly he was gone. I noticed an immense satisfaction in my Thought Adjuster as a result of this infinite embrace.

Moments after, the cloud sped off in a northerly direction and in less than a second had vanished from sight.

I looked across the playing field and all the kids were watching these two departures. Then they slowly started to gather all the sporting equipment together.

God indwelling the human mind

My Father drew my attention up to look at him where he was directly above me. I saw his exquisite pink radiance and as I beheld him in all his glory, I noticed that I had turned from being a little five year old boy in a grey shirt, shorts and sandals to a smaller white oval much like him.

As I looked up at him, he descended. His pinkishness gently touched and merged with my whitishness. All about us vanished for a moment, as we merged more and more. Increasingly, gently, tenderly, slowly, he descended inside my white form. I had enlarged somewhat to be about five or six feet tall, and he was shrinking somewhat, adapting to fit comfortably within my form. At a certain point I knew he was fully within me. I looked out across the playing field with my mortal eyes, knowing that he was fully within me—God was inside his son.

Then he lifted up and ascended out of me to where he had been. In a moment or two, he again descended again. I looked up and his pinkishness was again coming down to merge with my perfectly pure white form; the one oval receiving the other oval. In a moment or two he was inside again. This time he seemed to be wriggling around, as if he was finding depth within me.

Then again he left his position inside me, rising up out of me, but this time he did not fully separate from me. Slowly, more slowly than before, he descended again into my white form. This time he seemed to be merging with me as a person. I felt myself becoming like him. Then, in a moment of forgetfulness, suddenly I felt like there was only God inside me. I looked out across the field as God. All there was, was the pinkishness of God, in all his oval glory, in all his magnificent loving goodness. Then, as quickly as that had happened, it vanished from my consciousness and I was again aware of God being in me, but now he was kind of in the back of my mind, in me but behind me.

Next there was a merger between myself and God, this Thought Adjuster. I, Robert, the little five-year-old boy, looked out across the playing field and further afield across the empty paddock on the other side of the school where horses roamed. I looked at all the trees and the houses, the school buildings, the Earth and the sky and the people not so far off. As I gazed about I saw them all with God's seeing and I knew that indeed he was the creator of all I beheld. I marvelled at that fact that he held all of this world within his own being.

Lastly, this merger waned and he separated from me within myself. Where, at first, it had been like two individuals with each other, and then it had been two individuals within each other like mixing a pink light with a white light and finding the two lights becoming one single light, now, with a sense of final completion to it, the pinkishness of God was settling back into the back and upper regions of my whitishness. He was placing himself, "Near at hand, but just out of sight," as he said.

As I looked around at this newfound adjustment, my whitishness gently shrank back and resumed my normal little boy form. I could feel my body, wiggle my toes and feel the breeze on my bare arms. I knew with complete conviction that I had found God and that God had found me. Not only that, I knew that that's how God knows everybody, he comes to live inside them when they're five years old.

As I looked out over the field, I saw that all the kids and the teachers had packed up all the sporting equipment and were starting to put the kids in line to be marched off—the visitors to their bus, and the kids from our school back to their own class rooms. All of the kids in my class were coming back to near where I had been standing and were forming a line to go back to our classroom. My friend Gubby was nearby and I asked him if he got any sweets and he showed me the little bag and said yes that he had and they were really nice.

Just then, I felt someone tugging on my little grey shirt collar, from behind me. I turned around to my right to see who it was and I woke up on the ground.

The whole thing had been an extraordinary vision or dream or something. I knew it was a visitation from God. I knew that God was still inside me because I spoke to him and he spoke back to me reassuringly. As we lined up in a column two abreast to go back to our classroom, the events were fully fresh in my reality as to remain so for all time. I can still recall marching back to the classroom with all my classmates, being conscious that I now knew God within me.

The first moral choice

This is the story of how I got to find God and to know him, and how he came to be with me, his son. It was more than twenty years later that I one day came across a piece of writing in the Urantia papers that seemed to match my experience perfectly. I had never seen anything documented in the world's religions that spoke so clearly to me. It became one of the pillars of my faith, for it said:

"Though the Adjusters volunteer for service as soon as the personality forecasts have been relayed to Divinington, they are not actually assigned until the human subjects make their first moral personality decision. The first moral choice of the human child is automatically indicated in the seventh mind-adjutant and registers instantly, by way of the local universe Creative Spirit, over the universal mind-gravity circuit of the Conjoint Actor in the presence of the Master Spirit of superuniverse jurisdiction, who forthwith dispatches this intelligence to Divinington. Adjusters reach their human subjects on Urantia, on the average, just prior to the sixth birthday. In the present generation it is running five years, ten months, and four days; that is, on the 2,134th day of terrestrial life."[9]

I could easily recognize my decision to find God on that

Sunday morning in the Presbyterian Church, as being something akin to my "first moral choice;" and the three days it takes an Adjuster to reach the mortal subject as being the following Tuesday. Based on this, I figured that my Adjuster arrived with that holy cloud on Tuesday August 30th, 1955, around 2pm.

Did I believe that God raised Jesus from the grave then? I truly can't remember, but probably, if I had been told about it. Did I declare that Jesus is Lord then? No, I didn't have a clue what that meant. But I did know that I was in direct contact with God, and I knew a thing or two about how God comes to indwell the human mind when a child is five years old. I did know that I had God's favour, even if I had no theological or mystical framework from which to exploit it in my life when I was that young. Did I feel saved from sin? No, not really, because I believed in God as soon as I heard about him. I wasn't one of those people who found God later in life, when they had led lives that were wrecked by abuse or neglect or selfishness. I knew that God was within, deeply personal, divinely parental, and greater than any religion or scripture or worldly authority.

As I grew up, I came to learn just how many people did not enjoy that kind of deeply personal contact with God. I might take a moment here to just say, "Thank you my Father, for being so generous in letting me partake of your arrival into my life. I hope this story which you have been instrumental in bringing into being, will bless the world and all of its people, particularly the children and those with children. I hope this story brings people to you my Father, and that through favour with you, you will the more easily and firmly, accompany them into Adjuster fusion and the Paradise ascent."

Needless to say dear reader, watch your kids as they reach the tenth month of their fifth year. Your family is about to be joined by another blessed member, a mighty Thought Adjuster! What a blessing. Halleluiah!

The arrival of God brings a change in the human child. The infant becomes a child. New decision making capacities start to show themselves in new types of decisions. New values are appropriated, defended, mistaken, tried and tested, abandoned, reinvented and adopted.

Angel stuff

The experience of consciously having God's favour brings with it a desire for cleanliness through the Holy Spirit's standard of purity and rightness with God, and a real sense of destiny that involves God's work on Earth.

It was quarter to twelve on a beautiful Saturday morning in Morrinsville in the spring of 1955. It had rained the night before, but now the sky was clear right to the horizon. That morning, the sky was totally big, cloudless and blue to the horizon, and I was six years old.

I loved this kind of Saturday. Its weather meant that I had the entire day to play outside in the lush New Zealand bush with the movie characters of my fantasies like Davy Crockett, Long John Silver, the Three Musketeers and Hiawatha. This kind of a Saturday was a great day, a day of promise.

I was six years old watching that film. It had never happened before, but my older brother wasn't with me. I was dropped off at the picture theatre while he went to a birthday party, and I would walk the mile or so home by myself when the film was over. Going to the "flicks," as we called them, was a standard ritual for kids in my hometown on a Saturday morning.

Sometimes, when the story really gripped my imagination, I became completely absorbed in it, living it as it were. I would forget who I was, where I was, and what my own life history was.

I lived through the film that morning in just that way. The matinee session at Jack Munro's picture theatre had just finished. It had been a fabulous film, all about an angel who took on the job of Butler to a wealthy household.

The family comprised a grumpy old father, who had nothing on his mind but the creation of wealth and all its problems. His solution to life was to buy something. Then there was his wife, a puffed up old crow who was filled with pride and conceit. The son was a womanising no-hoper and his sister was a mindless neurotic flirt—both followed in their father's expectations that money would buy the way out of every problem, and their mother's way of throwing a tantrum until they got the money they needed to fix themselves up.

Then came the servants. The original Butler was a thief and

was being fired even as the angel turned up at the door and filled his position. The chauffeur was crooked. The servant had no self-esteem. And so it went through the cook, the gardener, the cleaner and so forth. The angel's mission was to bring the whole family together under the unity of truth and goodness, and to do that by dealing with each person on an individual basis. And he did just that.

Around that time, I knew that my own family was divided. I knew my Mum didn't want to be married to my Dad, and I knew it was probably like that for Dad too. I didn't know their reasons, I wasn't to find those out for another thirty years, but I knew this deep division in my family. Every time I would ride my bike down the road, I used to wonder to myself, if there was an earthquake right now that split the road and I would never see one of my parents again, onto which side of the road would I jump my bike?

That's a horrible division to grow up with. It never left me until I eventually left that household and was able to become an undivided person again.

The Butler's heart's desire was to fulfil a divine mission of personal restoration, healing and reconsecration in every person who lived under that roof.

When I stepped out of that picture theatre and walked into that beautiful, hopeful spring morning, I looked up at the big blue empty sky and said:

"That is what I want to do when I grow up—angel stuff."

Gifts of the Spirit

What I meant by angel stuff, was doing God's work for other peoples' well being. It would involve taking God's tools into peoples' lives so that he could help them. It meant sometimes knowing the inner secrets of their lives; their decisions; their reasoning; their pains; their guilt; their aims; their hopes and their sorrows. It was helping people in real need with the kind of help that only God can bring. I later learned that what I called angel stuff, Christians called working with the gifts of the spirit:

> "Now there are varieties of gifts, but the same Spirit; and there are varieties of services, but the same Lord; and there are varieties of activities, but it is the same God who activates all of them in everyone.

"To each is given the manifestation of the Spirit for the common good.

"To one is given through the Spirit the utterance of wisdom, and to another the utterance of knowledge according to the same Spirit, to another faith by the same Spirit, to another gifts of healing by the one Spirit, to another the working of miracles, to another prophecy, to another the discernment of spirits, to another various kinds of tongues, to another the interpretation of tongues.

"All these are activated by one and the same Spirit, who allots to each one individually just as the Spirit chooses. For just as the body is one and has many members, and all the members of the body, though many, are one body, so it is with Christ."[10]

God has many types of work for people, of course. He is a person who cherishes diversity—the more diversity, the more opportunities there are for unique creativity: that's his watchword. Not everybody wants to heal and help others' understandings. Some people want to sing and play music; others want to act and dance; still others want to write and publish, manage and finance and politic and farm. I do know that if someone sincerely wants to work in God's ministry for the sake of bringing God's favour to people's souls through his direct care for them, then they *will* receive gifts of the spirit as the empowerment with which to do that work.

As my little feet walked me homeward bound from the picture theatre, in the freedom of that glorious morning, in the solitude of my own thoughts and fantasies, I thought through this whole matter of angel-stuff. I walked home like I had the keys to heaven and I could go in and out of my Father's heavenly throne room as I pleased—I knew I had God's favour, even if I never thought of it in those terms, and his favour meant mingling with his angels and doing angel kinds of works. By the time I reached my home, angel stuff had become my heart's compass. I set the course of my life's direction by its God-based values.

Psalm 107

Since that day, the conviction that came to me through the Holy Spirit and that unique film, has never been uprooted in my heart and soul. I absolutely love bringing God to a person. God absolutely loves me bringing him to the person too. And the person in need, really loves to receive him and his great comfort and help.

God has help and healing and righteousness for every believing person. He has it for the unbeliever too, but mostly they don't seem to appropriate it for themselves.

I like how Psalm 107 speaks of the many kinds of adversities that humans fall into: how they call on God to help them; how in his unfailing love he helps them; how they are delivered out of their dreadful circumstances; and how subsequently they are encouraged to give him praise and honour.

The needs of today are little different from the days of the Psalmist. Listen gently, with God's favour on your heart, as you read it. Perhaps you will recognize situations from which you have been delivered in your life already. Perhaps you will see situations you know others could be delivered from, if only a person with the favour of God on them could visit with them. Perhaps you will see situations from which you wish you could be delivered right now, and your heart will long for a visit from someone who will bring God's favour to you and your circumstances.

The reader of the Urantia papers will naturally translate the term Lord to mean the Lordship of God generally, but also the very loving ministries of the Father Thought Adjuster, the Son Christ Michael and the Mother Holy Spirit. The person in need of healing or care or rescue is probably better off keeping it really simple and just thinking in terms that suit their heart of hearts. Here then, is the relevant part of Psalm 107.

1 O give thanks to the Lord, for he is good; for his
   steadfast love endures forever.
2 Let the redeemed of the Lord say so, those he redeemed
   from trouble
3 and gathered in from the lands, from the east and from
   the west, from the north and from the south.
4 Some wandered in desert wastes, finding no way to an
   inhabited town;
5 hungry and thirsty, their soul fainted within them.
6 Then they cried to the Lord in their trouble, and he
   delivered them from their distress;

7 he led them by a straight way, until they reached an inhabited town.

8 Let them thank the Lord for his steadfast love, for his wonderful works to humankind.

9 For he satisfies the thirsty, and the hungry he fills with good things.

10 Some sat in darkness and in gloom, prisoners in misery and in irons,

11 for they had rebelled against the words of God, and spurned the counsel of the Most High.

12 Their hearts were bowed down with hard labour; they fell down, with no one to help.

13 Then they cried to the Lord in their trouble, and he saved them from their distress;

14 he brought them out of darkness and gloom, and broke their bonds asunder.

15 Let them thank the Lord for his steadfast love, for his wonderful works to humankind.

16 For he shatters the doors of bronze, and cuts in two the bars of iron.

17 Some were sick through their sinful ways, and because of their iniquities endured affliction;

18 they loathed any kind of food, and they drew near to the gates of death.

19 Then they cried to the Lord in their trouble, and he saved them from their distress;

20 he sent out his word and healed them, and delivered them from destruction.

21 Let them thank the Lord for his steadfast love, for his wonderful works to humankind.

22 And let them offer thanksgiving sacrifices, and tell of his deeds with songs of joy.

23 Some went down to the sea in ships, doing business on the mighty waters;

24 they saw the deeds of the Lord, his wondrous works in the deep.

25 For he commanded and raised the stormy wind, which lifted up the waves of the sea.

26 They mounted up to heaven, they went down to the depths; their courage melted away in their calamity;

27 they reeled and staggered like drunkards, and were at their wits' end.

28 Then they cried to the Lord in their trouble, and he brought them out from their distress;

29 he made the storm be still, and the waves of the sea were hushed.

30 Then they were glad because they had quiet, and he brought them to their desired haven.

31 Let them thank the Lord for his steadfast love, for his wonderful works to humankind.

Stages of healing and recovery

I particularly like doing the work of verses 28 to 30. They are stages in the healing process, the restoration process. Look at them closely, perhaps you will see a journey you yourself have made out of some kind of misery. I certainly do.

God brings you out of your distress—the shock of your problem is nullified and your distress subsides so that you become calm again.

God then makes the heart of your problem to be healed and at peace. He cuts the root of the disease. His power enters the heart of the conflict, and binds the cause of the disturbance, casting it out, and restoring his own sovereignty where once was disturbance and conflict. Then, as a result of having your peace back, and having the root of the problem cut so that it withers, you have God's peace and assurance of victory.

Riding on the infallible vehicle of his assurance, by the power of your own faith, without any effort on your part except the maintaining of your faith, he brings you in to his desired haven for you—and note that that may not be your first choice of haven until you've been there a while.

Lastly, how can you not thank him for his great love and his works on your behalf? How can you not give praise to his name and tell others about the good things he has done for you?

God's favour

I have always believed that this is a noble and a good work to do during one's life on Earth. The film about the angel who became the Butler gave me a simple world view. There were three kinds of people in the world. The kinds of people before the angel arrived, those who did not know God's favour. The kinds of people after the angel had done his work of bringing God's favour and his benefits to them. Thirdly, there were those kinds of people who actually did the kind of angel stuff I'd seen done in that film—the kind of stuff God gave them to bring to people like those in Psalm 107. As a six-year-old kid, I felt really honoured to be one of this last group, even though I knew it would take years for me to grow into whatever God had for me in its ranks. It wasn't until I experienced the Baptism of the Holy Spirit and fire and tongues with Christ's death on the cross that I received those kinds of gifts of the Spirit that Paul wrote about to the Corinthians.

Cooperating with someone else's Thought Adjuster

The first time I ever saw someone else's Thought Adjuster, it was through those gifts. In 1987 I was working a couple of different jobs to help pay off our home. One of them was as a night shift telephone operator at Fairfield Infectious Diseases Hospital in Melbourne. For a couple of months, I had been developing a Urantia papers board game for people to play. It was a little like monopoly but it entailed journeying from Urantia to Paradise. The way to get there was by successfully answering questions drawn from the Urantia papers. It was so much fun when it was completed that I later developed a computerised version for Windows.

One night around 2 am, as I was working on this game and answering the occasional phone call, I had the most profound sense that someone's Thought Adjuster was standing in mid air directly in front of me.

My spirit was being prompted to focus on him and, putting aside my game, I brought my spirit to shine upon what I thought was an invisible divine person.

When I did that, suddenly I could see him. He had the same kind of pinkish oval shape to him that I remembered from my boyhood. He spoke in very clear terms. He was very definite about his request. He expressed that he had very little time, there was some urgency, I didn't have to help him but he would truly love my help. He then expressed that his human subject was in this hospital and was in a coma and had given up the will to live. His request was if I would help to communicate with the fellow in the coma and to encourage him to regain the will to live.

I thought about what he said.

I agreed to his request, but I really didn't have much of a clue as to how to help out here. I had previously worked with people in unusual states of mind, and had experienced healing through the will of my Father. As soon as I agreed, he vanished from sight.

I consulted with my own Father, who suggested that I give things a go on my own first of all.

I waited a while longer, letting the whole idea settle down inside me. While I was continuing on with the research of drawing out questions from the Urantia papers for my "Ascension Career" game, around 4.30 in the morning a doctor dropped by. Without any prompting he said:

"Did I tell you about that weird case we've got in intensive at the moment Rob?"

"No, who's that?" I asked.

"Well this young guy, Oh I don't know, maybe in his early thirties. He's Turkish. Islamic. Into martial art in a big way. He came in about four days ago with a gash to his leg. He said that he'd cut it on some corrugated iron."

"So what's he in for?" I asked, seeing that nothing really seemed to be unusual about the case.

"Well, it's really peculiar," the doctor continued. "He came in here as fit as a fiddle, then two days ago all of a sudden he went absolutely ballistic. It was like he just went crazy. He's on no medication except some antibiotics so we didn't have a clue about what set it off. We sent every orderly and security person to hold him down. About four or five blokes jumped on top of him and he threw them off like matchsticks. Finally more people came and they managed to restrain him and handcuff him to the bed rails, but not before one of them had his forearm broken in the scuffle.

"What's weird about it all," he continued, "is that the fellow only came in to get a check up to see if he needed a Tetanus shot. We hadn't given him any medication until he flipped and went berserk, and then it was only to sedate him so he wouldn't damage himself or any of us. But since then, all of a sudden it's as if the life is draining out of him. We hold no hope for the guy. We have absolutely no idea what's wrong with him. We've done blood test after blood test and we can't get a bead on anything at all."

"Is he conscious," I asked curiously. When the doctor had been speaking about this case, I had had the abiding suspicion that the Thought Adjuster had come to me about him.

"No. That's the silly thing that's bugging all of us. We can't figure it out. There's just no reason for it. The guy's in a coma. He lapsed into a coma two days ago. His weight has just dropped off him. Honestly we don't give him more than a couple of days. It's like something is sapping the life completely out of him."

Then he tapped his rounds board on the desk, looked at me with that hopeless look, and muttered something like:

"Sometimes you lose and you just don't know why. The whole thing's so bloody stupid. The bloke only came in with a cut leg and now he's in a coma and we're about ready to phone his family to come and get the body. How absurd is that?"

He gave me a look as if to say that some things in life are just too big for anyone much to deal with, then he walked off into the shadows and his rounds.

As I sat alone at the front desk, with the first light of dawn just starting to break the darkness outside, I thought about what I would need to do to help this fellow's Adjuster. I called on my own Father and together we did something to first of all find this fellow, wherever he was, and then to endeavour to communicate to him.

My first efforts to help

It appeared to me that this chap, let's call him Rusul—but I can't recall his name—Rusul was scattered in a million little pieces of mind and that no one portion was his sense of self. If I was to talk to him on some kind of mind circuit, which my Father had taught me about years earlier, then I would need to gather the "self" part of his mind. It all seemed pretty hopeless though. I gave it a couple of shots, but I was totally out of my league. I could locate his mind all right; I just had no way of identifying which bits were which. The level of coma that Rusul had entered was incredibly fragmented—he really didn't want to be put back together again. It was as if he was willing himself into such total disarray that he wanted to keep thousands of parts of himself separate from each other. The man had a personal problem, that was obvious. His solution was to die, that was obvious. His problem was probably something that divided him, a couple of different loyalties that he just couldn't reconcile, perhaps.

I tried a couple of other things, but they didn't really deliver me what I thought was a good outcome either. Finally, tired from having been up all night, I told my Father that, as it was, I didn't think I'd be able to get a hold of this guy long enough to even counsel with him. I asked if there was some other person that might the better help this Adjuster, to which he gave no reply.

I presumed that Rusul's Thought Adjuster needed a human being to pray for his child or, better still, to wilfully intervene in his own mortal child's affairs; and that if someone didn't effectively do that, then Rusul would surely die—and there was every sign of that, according to the doctor.

I presented my Father with my prayerful outcome, telling him what I wanted to achieve. He accepted that from me, confirmed that what I had already done wasn't really going to be much chop, and suggested that I let it rest for a while. That was around 5.30 am. I was scheduled to get on my motorbike and ride home at around seven. Then I needed to sleep because I started work at another place at 4.30 p.m. that same afternoon.

My second attempt at helping

I let the whole matter slip from my mind as I rode home. Then I breakfasted, showered and went to bed. As I lay in bed, my thoughts turned to Rusul's Thought Adjuster's needs. I felt certain that my prayer with my Father had been inadequate. As I was slipping off to sleep, I voiced another prayer.

"Father. I pass everything in me that is human over to the care of my guardian angels, for the duration of my sleep. I give you, and Michael and Mother Spirit complete access to everything that I am. I give you full permission Father, to authorise the Seraphim who watch over my life, to use anything of my mind whatsoever to engage those domains of mind where Rusul exists right now, for the sake of doing whatever it takes to put him back together and convince him of his Father's sustaining love for him, according to the wishes of his own Thought Adjuster. Father, in doing this, I invoke whatever protection you think I might need, Rusul might need, or anyone else might need in doing this kind of service."

"Thank you for your prayer," he replied. And I went to sleep.

I woke up around three thirty that afternoon with a memory of having dreamed some very unusual dreams that had to do with Rusul, wherever and whoever he was. My entire left arm was paralysed from the shoulder joint down to every finger. This was unusual, and a bit of a nuisance when it came to riding my motorbike to work that afternoon. The paralysis lasted until around ten or eleven that night. I put it down to something to do with Rusul's case, but I really didn't identify anything to confirm that conclusion.

We got to victory!

I had the next four days off work from the Fairfield Hospital, but upon my return I was anxious to learn what happened. The doctor who had told me about Rusul's condition happened to pass by the front desk later in the evening and I called out to him to come and talk to me.

"What ever happened to that Muslim fellow, the guy with the cut leg?"

"Oh him. The strangest thing I've ever come across. The guy faded away to just skin and bone, like something just ate out his body in the matter of a few days. Then, about three days ago, all of a sudden he woke up, clear as a bell, told everyone that he was well now and that he wanted to go home."

I reflected on the efforts of those who had intervened on his behalf, and his wonderful Thought Adjuster's loving concern to keep him alive on Earth despite this crippling problem he was facing.

"We held him for about six or seven hours. His weight seemed to come on again from out of nowhere. He spoke to the nurses about how he really loved karate and that, because it was oriental, his Turkish family had major problems with him following it. They didn't think it was right with God to do that kind of stuff, or something like that. Then to top it off, he said he'd just met the girl of his dreams and she was a Christian, and he didn't know what he would do about the Muslim Turkish girl that his parents had set him up to marry."

The doctor looked at me and sighed:

"Complicated family stuff huh?"

Anyway," he continued, "his family came in at around two in the afternoon. He was all dressed and laying on his bed. It was really weird Rob. The guy came in with a gash in his lower leg. It never became infected and wasn't infected on the day he left here. We simply dressed it like a normal wound while we ran blood tests more to find out why the guy should have lapsed into a coma and then why the coma should have been so death-like. Then the day after I spoke to you about his case, all of a sudden he comes out of it like he's resurrected from the grave. It's all too weird for me, mate. Whatever was going on for that guy had nothing to do with us at all. Not in any way. I have no idea why he went into the coma and no idea how he came out. All I know is that I've seen dead people with more life in them that that guy had when he was in the coma!"

"So now he's fine, and he's home and ...life goes on?" I asked.

"Yeah. Seems so. See ya," and he walked off into the shadows to be about his medical business.

The favour of God gives life

As I reflected about Rusul's case, it was hard to calculate what really went on. Perhaps it was just that he had some kind of personal conflict which, in his own way, he wasn't able to deal with without forfeiting his life. That's not all too uncommon. My thoughts had been to bring God's appeal to him, deep within his coma. I had had considerable previous experience doing that with people who weren't in a coma. Perhaps the Seraphim did manage to intervene in some heavenly way. Who knows: I never asked and they never told me. I read the cards as they fell and I think in simple terms about it all—his Adjuster appealed for help, received the kind of help that was needed, and life goes on in its own very fragile way, almost as if nothing has happened out of the ordinary.

This kind of work isn't easy or perhaps useful to describe to others, and I wouldn't prescribe anybody doing it outside the will of God, but it does highlight the fact that, in a son of God and a servant of his children, the gifts of the Spirit can help both humans and Adjusters alike.

As I understand it, Rusul lives today because of the favour of God that was brought to influence his situation and himself. God was enabled to plant new meaning in his inner person in such a way that he chose life. The Bible says:

"I call heaven and Earth to witness against you today that I have set before you life and death, blessings and curses. Choose life so that you and your descendants may live, loving the Lord your God, obeying him, and holding fast to him; for that means life to you and length of days."[11]

Angel stuff, working with the gifts of the Spirit, is often complicated because it crosses over the line between heaven and Earth—the will of God and the will of man— and asks the son of God to become really comfortable in both spheres so that the favour of God is able to be fluidly delivered in its purity as required to whomever has need.

"The favour of God" is a peculiar term to some people. It is, however, written up in the Urantia papers as being something that Machiventa Melchizedek placed at the heart of his teachings around 2000 B.C.,[12] the teachings which would later become the foundation for every religion on Earth with the possible exception of Buddhism, which had its roots in philosophy rather than sonship with God. The term is in Jewish scripture, for example, "And now implore the favour of God, that he may be gracious to us."[13] As a Buddhist, I never dreamed of employing such a term, even though I always called on God to help me in a wide variety of ways, and even though the experience of enlightenment is a real betrothal to God and his favour.

"Being saved" is another term that is often more of an obstacle than a help to people. Ultimately, any contact with God is spiritual and cements the fact of having his favour, whether or not one knows how to employ that favour to its maximum effect.

The Urantia papers say:

"All religions teach the worship of Deity and some doctrine of human salvation. The Buddhist religion promises salvation from suffering, unending peace; the Jewish religion promises salvation from difficulties, prosperity predicated on righteousness; the Greek religion promised salvation from disharmony, ugliness, by the realization of beauty; Christianity promises salvation from sin, sanctity; Mohammedanism provides deliverance from the rigorous moral standards of Judaism and Christianity. The religion of Jesus is salvation from self, deliverance from the evils of creature isolation in time and in eternity."[14]

The religion of Jesus saves a person from the limitations of their self, their selfishness, their self-indulgence, their self pre-occupation, their self-induced death, their self denial, their isolation from God who is their Father. The religionist, no matter how enlightened or philosophically astute or well-regarded by society, is isolated from the central spiritual force in the universe of universes unless she or he has appropriated the world-changing revelation from the Father or the Son or the Holy Spirit Mother that she or he is a son of God.

If you would follow the religion of Jesus, if you would gather to yourself the first and best choice of resources for your spiritual journey, if you would call upon yourself the most light in all the universe that you can obtain for your own benefit, then appropriate for yourself sonship with God. Jesus said that to seek and find God's righteousness as a first priority, is the way of the successful spirit. Doing this first, before other religious pursuits, you will enjoy an experience of God's favour. What musician didn't start off with a poor instrument, and years later wishes they had had a top shelf instrument to learn on? What dancer doesn't wish they had the best teacher in the world, right from the first day? What mother doesn't wish they had had another mother to advise her all about the little creature she enfolded on her breast? What father doesn't wish he had the wisdom of Solomon in raising his children? What person of fifty doesn't wish he or she had that knowledge as a child? First find God your Father, and truly everything else will spring forth from within your sonship with him—even your sonship with Christ Michael and your sonship with the Holy Spirit. Your sonship then can deliver to you the favour of the infinite God as well as the favour of the local universe God. The benefits from God will so fill your life that in a few short years you will not know yourself, and you will be so very happy, as Jesus was so very happy.

That's an important thing on which to keep your focus: Jesus may well have been on mission for three years following his baptism, but remember that his religion made him an extremely happy person.

It's a good question to ask yourself:

"Has anything I have done, changed my life for the better?"

What will make you happy?

If you are a Christian, is happiness doing battle with the Devil and his evil forces until the return of Christ? But has your religion made you a happy and love filled person who enjoys the favour of God like Jesus?

If you are a Buddhist, is happiness doing your Dharma practice and seeking the way out of reincarnation's wheel? But has your religion made you a happy and love filled person who enjoys the favour of God like Jesus? And so on for whoever you are: has your religion made you a happy and love filled person who enjoys the favour of God like Jesus?

Jesus was happy not because he was a Creator Son of God on mission. He put all his Godly power and prestige aside to be a human child of this world, totally dependent upon the will of the Father.[15] He was happy because he lived a religion, which came from a universal truth that had its origins right in the heart and centre of God who dwells in the heart and centre of all things.

In order to gain happiness, most people will act in terms of gain and loss. If I get this, I will be happy. If I lose that, I will be unhappy. But gain and loss is unable to create happiness. After you gain the thing you want, your happiness is soon still wanting—observe it in your own life, it is not a hard thing to notice. Like you and me, Jesus made gains and losses in his day to day life, but his happiness came from his communion with his heavenly Father. His Father didn't demand that he somehow cease making gains and losses in his life in order to be happy, but Jesus placed gain and loss *after* the happiness that first came by being a son of God and fellowshipping with God.

His religion made him good, true, beautiful, noble, endearing, spiritually capable, useful and immensely loved. His religion was all of the things that he found in his sonship with God. He didn't read about sonship in a book, or filter it out of the Jewish scripture. He saw in scripture those occasional references to the sonship with God which he knew as a first hand experience. Just like you will know them.

What a marvellous thing it is to have the religion that Jesus had. Even today, in your heart and from his universe headquarters in Salvington, this same Jesus calls you to claim and enjoy sonship with God for yourself. Do it. Choose life. Life is in sharing the mind of God.

❧

Notes

1. 92:4.4 {3. Melchizedek of Salem...}
2. Romans 10:9
3. Romans 10:13
4. Paper 89; Mark 16:1-20
5. 189:0.2 {Not one of you...}
6. 189:1.1 {At two forty-five...}
7. 135:3.4 {From all John...}
8. 2:0.1 {Inasmuch as man's...}
9. 108:2.1
10. 1 Corinthians 12:4-12
11. Deuteronomy 30:19-20
12. 93:4.1 {The ceremonies of...}; 92:5.5 {2. Era of the Melchizedek missionaries...}
13. Malachi 1:9
14. 5:4.5
15. 120:2.1 {1. In accordance with...}

❧

Chapter 23

Perfect sonship with God: Adjuster Fusion

Clearly, the highest spiritual goal on Earth as portrayed by the Urantia papers is Adjuster fusion. Its rewards to the human son of God are the most striking—perfection of righteousness and exemption from physical death.[1] Its reward to the Universal Father, the "God of all creation, the First Source and Centre of all things and beings,"[2] is the "divine validation of eventual Paradise attainment"[3] for his "personality trust."[4]

Adjuster fusion is not some mere figment of the human mind; it is a quality of life that has accreditation by God. The universally held power and authority that is in a person's fusion with a fragment of the Universal Father, resides in the fact that before ever it becomes a goal in our human mind, it has long been the goal of God who indwells us.[5]

Human evidence

Its human quiet achievers among us have seldom impacted on society and almost never left a record of their journey with God in our midst. They are, to all intents and purposes, invisible to us. We know little of them at all.

Adjusters first arrived into the minds of humans around one million years ago with the dawn of the first humans, Andon and Fonta. The authors of the Urantia papers hold in high regard the deepest inner longings of humans, by saying that, "Andon is the Nebadon name which signifies 'the first Fatherlike creature to exhibit human perfection hunger'"; and that, "Fonta signifies 'the first Sonlike creature to exhibit human perfection hunger.'"[6] We are told that the Adjuster fusion of both Andon and Fonta, the first two persons of our species, was completed not on Earth but in heaven.[7] We have no idea how many of our sisters and brothers have been translated from our midst in the glory of Adjuster fusion since those days of human origin on Earth. Only the records of heaven have that number.

In all the books of the Bible and all the papers of the fifth epochal revelation, there are records of only three people whose Adjusters have achieved the goal of fusion with them. They are Enoch,[8] Elijah[9] and Jesus of Nazareth.[10] That is not to say that only three people, and only men, have attained Adjuster fusion, only that the records are only of these three occasions.

Genesis 5:18 claims that Jared was the father of Enoch. The Urantia papers indicate that a grandson of Eve was named Enoch.[11] They are probably not the same man, but either way, by 5,000 years ago,[12] the benefits to our human grasp of Adjuster fusion which might have once been brought to humanity's struggling spiritual gene pool by Enoch, had long since evaporated.

Whilst Enoch is lost to antiquity, Elijah and Jesus however, are much closer to our own era. Descriptions of the events surrounding their Adjuster fusion, or in Jesus' case his Adjuster accredited perfection, are fairly graphic. The story they have left behind, however, can be interpreted to be such a stunning legacy of perfection with enigmatic criteria, that it has tended to place the equivalent attainment beyond the reach of the average person. The resultant effect is that people settle for a second hand religious experience rather than believing God to attain the same perfection in themselves. The Jesus of the Urantia papers, however, came to dispel that myth.

The Urantia papers are the voice for Thought Adjusters calling us to fusion

The arrival of the Urantia papers, into the resource pool that feeds our human spiritual aspirations, changes everything that has gone before in our million years of human history and struggle to be more than merely imperfect and mortal.

These papers, are a voice for the aspiring Adjusters who would fuse with the intelligent and deeply personal love within the hearts of their human children. I have often experienced my own Thought Adjuster, mouthing words to me in Spirit as I read them. He was affirming his recognition of their truth, and conveying his love for me. God has similarly mouthed words as I read from the Bible. I particularly remember on one occasion, it was Philippians 1:9-11 NIV:

> "And this is my prayer: that your love may abound more and more in knowledge and depth of insight, so that you may be able to discern what is best and may be pure and blameless until the day of Christ, filled with the fruit of righteousness that comes through Jesus Christ—to the

glory and praise of God."

Can you imagine how wonderful it is to hear your own divine Father praying for you in the words of scripture? Or in his own words, for that matter? Of significance though, a key difference between the Bible and the Urantia papers is what they allow your Thought Adjuster to do in these days 2,000 years after Pentecost. Equipped with the Urantia papers, God is better enabled to stimulate you toward perfection because they provide you with a far wider description of the context for Adjuster fusion and thus, far greater opportunities for making perfection-based decisions.

The boldest teaching ever written

Thought Adjusters hail from Divinington.[13] The divine revelation in the Urantia papers is the word of God, which has come forth with the Divinington mission in mind, to portray to humans just like you and me, the context in which Adjuster fusion can occur. It is a word that is carried with the utmost sincerity and parental love, to each human reader who will dare to believe that it has been personally delivered to him or to her. The truth is, that this revelation of sonship with God and its perfection, Adjuster fusion, has indeed been written specifically for you and me.

Nowhere in the history of the world's evolved or revealed religious history, has there ever been such a bold teaching, such a radical revelation, such an inspiring ideal, delivered in such plain text and given by our Father's grace in the hearts of its authors and administrators to so many human beings on Earth. On no prior occasion, have the agencies of God the Paradise Father, Christ Michael the local universe Creator Son and Father, the Holy Spirit Mother of the local universe and a host of their teacher-sons and daughters been able to combine forces to present such a supreme spiritual teaching to this world. This is now the information age—the age when the number of Adjusters who will achieve fusion with their informed and cooperative human sons or daughters, just like you, will dramatically increase.

Adjuster fusion is not easy, however. It is inevitable for the willing and faithful believer, but it is not easy. The concept of Adjuster fusion is lofty. Lofty ideals are like Mount Fuji in the noonday mist—at the high point of the day you still cannot see much beyond its base.

It is ironic that Adjuster fusion is central to the message of the Urantia papers, yet its perceived loftiness can cause us to doubt our ability to ever attain it. In the generations of readers of the twentieth century, it can take a person years of reading, prayer and spiritual experience to arrive at a point where Adjuster fusion becomes a goal and forecast that is personally one's own. In these days, the journey is relatively lonely; you won't have many peers. Doubt, a simple lack of understanding and faithful contact with our Father, can often make us downhearted.[14] Unbelief causes division, what the Bible calls rebellion and sin.[15] Often, we are subject to the unbelief and the divisive assault of those who would separate us from our goal of Adjuster fusion. Often when a lone traveller in the ways of her or his Father brings up the subject of Adjuster fusion, it raises in unbelieving people more than a little of "Why do the heathen rage?"[16]

It does, however, take a while to grow into a workable understanding about Adjuster fusion itself, and then the possibility that it is for oneself, and then realising the actual lessons themselves.

Such growth is not easily earned. It should be noted that it is however, so costly to the individual, that such growth is vehemently defended, if only by silence. The apparent invisibility of those before us who have attained Adjuster fusion is, perhaps, God's final word about its sanctity being beyond the sin-filled minds and grubby fingers of meddlers and unbelievers. Adjuster fusion, is the pearl of great price[17] sought by your indwelling Adjuster, his immediate reason for being.

By God's will

One of the keys in all this growth is gaining the experience to understand that it is not by our own faith and strength that our Adjusters achieve this most love-filled of goals. No, rather it is by our own divine Father's will. On this matter, Jesus said:

> "Very truly, I tell you, the Son can do nothing on his own, but only what he sees the Father doing; for whatever the Father does, the Son does likewise. The Father loves the Son and shows him all that he himself is doing."[18]

The way that the Father is acting and purposive is true of Michael conducting the affairs of Nebadon. It is true for Jesus living out his life and teachings on Earth. It is true for you and me dear reader, as we journey with our Father on Earth into Adjuster fusion.

If ever there was a goal in the mind's eye of your divine Father for you, it is Adjuster fusion. God expects that you will some day achieve it. He brings you and me a great hope, for it is, "not by might, nor by power, but by my spirit, says the Lord of hosts."[19] God has the vision for your perfection, and he is the means whereby you will attain it. You literally need only to agree with him more than you choose to follow your own ambitions or those with which the world would steer you. Such agreement quickly delivers you into his companionship.

The ground rules of Adjuster fusion

The ground rules of Adjuster fusion are simple enough in theory. God is your Father, and you are his son (whether you are male or female).[20] God is perfect and wants you to be perfect like him.[21] The highest level of perfection that you will be able to achieve on Earth is called Adjuster fusion.[22] A perfect example of a human being achieving every facet of Adjuster Fusion is written up in the Urantia papers' account of the life and teachings of Jesus of Nazareth.[23]

Adjuster fusion represents the culmination of God's goals for us on Earth. Being a conclusion as such, Adjuster fusion should be understood to be a matter into which you will have grown as a lifestyle, rather than merely cast an appreciative glance. Adjuster fusion is not something one would hear of, aspire toward and then achieve at a week-long spiritual workshop or retreat. It involves your embodiment of God's kind of loving actions across an enormous spectrum of life, not some mere concept you have realised, or a meditation practice with which you have become familiar, or a unifying mystical experience you have encountered of extraordinarily universal proportions.

Adjuster fusion is a term that refers to the holistic condition of the relation between a human being such as yourself, God who indwells your mind and is particularly concerned with its capacity for higher values, and your mutual abilities to conduct yourselves both divinely and humanly via a single point of decision. I don't think it is a matter easily understood without the preparation of considerable background study and the purest of hearts toward spiritual matters. In a sense, Adjuster fusion is the ultimate Holy Grail for a man or a woman.

Difficulties communicating about fusion

In reading about Adjuster fusion, I commend you to notice the difficulties of writing about it. The difficulties in writing about Adjuster fusion are that it is so utterly personal and the journey is so incredibly varied for each person that the language one employs to allude to or describe its features can be so intrinsically prone to misinterpretation.

The experiences to which one refers are so frequently unyielding to meaningful interpretation in the life of the reader who has not had prior personal physical contact with the writer. Such contact all the better enables a sort of transmission of meaning which mere words can never include to the desired degree.

Another feature of communication about Adjuster fusion-related matters, is that the journey into Adjuster fusion crosses a threshold where it suddenly becomes extremely demanding of your discretion, and that translates into my not telling you a whole lot, and you having to work out a whole lot in the private company of your own Thought Adjuster. There's no way around that: no discretion, no Adjuster fusion. In most instances, not merely some instances, in most instances you have to do your own spadework.

The issue is not that I necessarily have a whole lot of secrets, which is really irrelevant, because to the Jerusem Citizen who has completed her mansion world training and her Adjuster fusion, I have little of interest to her at all because she's been there, done that. The issue is more that you will gain a million fold more from your companionship with your Adjuster than anyone will ever be able to share with you about their companionship with their Adjuster. The path to Adjuster fusion, being the path to personal perfection, is heavily dependent upon you doing considerable leg work on your own as you yourself become a dedicated student of your own perfection and a willing participant in your Thought Adjuster's way of achieving his style of goals.

In saying this, I am not advocating hermit life or isolation—but obviously your Adjuster may indeed call you into that vocation if you are of a certain rare disposition. You will more than likely become more sociable than ever before, but you will be increasingly guarded and silent about the inner workings of your journey into perfection with God. This is true at least up until you begin teaching others and helping them to find their own way, at which point you will have responded to God's clearly perceived will so to open up somewhat about such matters.

So far, I have mentioned barriers to communication that are positive in nature. On the negative side, there are a couple of things that represent real obstacles to communication.

One is that when a writer speaks of Adjuster fusion related matters, the reader can be prone to accumulating information and turning their own process into a matter of philosophical speculation.

I wish to gently warn you about the position that exclaims, "Wow that sounds fantastic: I wonder what that's like. I wish I could experience that!" I say warn, because when encountering a record of another person's experience, several tendencies come into play. One is to romanticise that the same experience is possible for oneself. That is a healthy attitude and faith building and should be encouraged. Another is to study the experience, to analyse it, to break it apart and try to duplicate its individual parts, like taking apart a butterfly wing by wing and anther by anther and then trying to put it back together again in the hope that it will fly. But you have destroyed the life in the butterfly by your own hands, and your own hands cannot revitalise the life. In this manner, you kill the instruction. You end up simply doing a philosophical exercise, and you do not get to partake of the life spoken of in the experience at all.

The evil of this, if I can use that word politely, is that you are then forced to think that you will never achieve authentic spiritual experiences, and that is a lie, for you will. You just won't experience them by employing that method of hearing.

If you would enrol in the class "Adjuster fusion 101," then a wholehearted study of Jesus' use of the parables is useful. You would come to understand how he endeavoured to plant his teachings at the place inside his hearers where the hearer and the

Thought Adjuster communed. It is not unrealistic to identify that specific territory as being the domain of which Jesus spoke when he referred to fertile soil.[24]

Of necessity we are called to have well adapted intellects. We do, however, in the course of growing into a balance of intellectuality and spirit liaison with God, build intellectual barriers to our actual spiritual experience. Some of us go the opposite path and ignore the intellect for the soul's passion. Both, in their own way, were certainly true in my own life, and I have seen it in monks and nuns, and in readers of the Bible, the Koran, the Urantia papers and of all sorts of ideological writings.

The problem is that essentially, in our enthusiasm, or our fear, we develop an intellectual model of a spiritual ideal and then try to achieve it as a spiritual experience. We fail of course, because spiritual experience is in fact granted to us as a gift from our Father. Any spiritual experience we attain by our own abilities is really our own imaginings. That might sound a little harsh, particularly if you can't account for too many grace-filled God-given spiritual experiences in your life. But it is true. The more realistic use of the intellect is to use it to contemplate the significance of spiritual experience that has already happened.[25]

I'll give you this example. Consider the child who plots to get his father to give him a new bicycle for his birthday. He does all the right things to draw his father's attention to his so-called need. When the child gets the present, it is however simply an outcome of his own planning. He has not grown closer to his father's love; he has only proven his own ability to achieve material possessions through cunning. On the other hand, consider the child whom the father perceives to be in need of a new bicycle and whom he subsequently surprises with his thoughtfulness and tender care. The child is drawn to the father by his act of love and thoughtfulness. Which is the richer child? Which is the happier parent?

So too it is for you and your spiritual attainments, and the use of your intellect. I would love you to be drawn to your Father by his love and his graciousness, than to stand at his closed door utterly alone and cold and forsaken with an invitation that you yourself put together by your broodings. The Father knocks on the door of your heart;[26] you never need to write your own invitation, no matter how dazzling your intellect.

Negative mind

One of the most difficult challenges facing the communication about Adjuster fusion, however, is the negative minded attitude of the hearer.

I first met that term, "negative mind", when listening to the Tibetan Lama, Thubten Yeshe. He was a lovely evangelist for Buddhist practices. He fathered a large and fertile cluster of Buddhist residential study centres around the world during the seventies and eighties, and he had considerable contact with spiritually hungry thinkers of many religious persuasions.

He expressed his alarm, as he encountered the throng of westerners in his Himalayan monasteries and in places of learning all around the world, that westerners had a chip on their shoulder about spiritual achievements. It seemed that they did not like hearing about spiritual standards to achieve. All mention of them was somehow like a personal rebuke. Perhaps they thought they were already beyond improvement, and were reluctant to think that spiritual studies actually meant identifying their less than wholesome behaviours and characteristics and actually dealing with them as Jesus suggests in his lessons on self mastery.[27]

On one occasion I recall Lama Yeshe sitting atop the traditional "high seat" in the meditation hall, legs folded in the lotus posture beneath his maroon and yellow robes, his hands gracefully speaking out his heart's affection, his face radiant with deep spiritual joy as he expressed his delight and gratitude over the ease with which he had completed a certain teaching retreat in New Zealand. He complimented people for having effectively dealt with their negative minds, and having given him so much enthusiastic and positive mind to work with as he and his associate, Lama Zopa, taught those past ten days.

Negative mind is not uncommon in us. Jesus had the same issue to deal with among his own apostles two thousand years ago.[28] The western world has a multi-billion dollar industry currently aimed at helping people to realign their motivation by overcoming their negative attitudes and adopting positive attitudes. That industry spans both secular and religious fields of endeavour. Negative mind is real, and it affects a lot of people.

Does it affect you? I've heard Christians say that before they were born again and received the baptism of the Holy Spirit, they were plagued by negative mind but, with greater understanding that came to them through the Spirit, they became equipped to deal with it and cast it out of their lives.

Whatever the model God leads you to, it's good to identify negative mind. It's good and necessary to recognise how it robs you of the good things God has for you. It's good to take decisive and enduring measures to keep it out of your life. In my own life, the experience of Christian "baptism in the Holy Spirit and speaking in tongues"[29] helped me immeasurably to that end.

Negative mind is a certain attitude of rebelliousness concerning spiritual matters. We find ourselves untrusting; unwilling to give of our love and cooperation; we build barriers to unity; we actively seek obstacles; we are argumentative; we are resentful and we stifle progress. Essentially, we put our own will in the way of God's will. We force others to think as we think, assuming that our view is God's view. Ironically, in our blocking God, we think we are actually seeking him and doing his will. It may refresh you to know that there is a day coming, if you have not yet traversed that way dear one, when it will be as if the propensity to obstruct and confound had never been in you.

I have rarely found it personally valuable to entertain the understanding held by fundamentalist religious thinkers of many faiths, that this negative mind has its origins in the devil's influence. My Father simply taught me about the necessity to deal with it, and how to effectively do just that.

An example of negative mind and how to deal with it is this. I have thoughts and experiences that I am sharing in this book. You may take offence at some characteristic of mine that comes out in the writing. For example, you may have argument with the way I quote from the Bible, or the Urantia papers, or perhaps how I use the words of Jesus as an authority.

One solution to this problem is as follows. Can you honestly say that you know everything that has ever happened on Earth? The chances are pretty good that your answer is "no". So then I ask you is it possible that you at least know everything there is to know about my perspective and experiences. Again, the chances are pretty good that your answer will be "no". So lastly I say to you, do you think there is any chance you might learn something new in my perspective or experiences. The chances might be pretty good that you'll say "yes".

That kind of process lets you identify your own negativity and put it aside long enough to ask the question, "I wonder what he means when he says what he says, and if it is the same as what I think he means?" This works well on other people in other settings too. You'll find that.

The purest way to overcome negative mind is to relax, stay attentive to the issue about which you are negative, and to ask God to give you his own view on the matter. Then yield yourself totally to being reshaped by his thoughts and perspectives. You will shortly be the host of a remodelled version of your own view. God will be allowed to present his own view. You will then have the opportunity to exercise the real will of God if you so choose.

Whether you believe that Jesus died for your sins and the sins of the world,[30] or not, Jesus' death was of course the ultimate type of response from negative mind on this Earth—the destruction of that which is good on the basis of an inability to submit to its leading.

Whatever might be your own world view, dear reader, you will find that negative mind is very real, very debilitating, and something that your sincerity sooner or later has to face and deal with. Your adjuster's mission is to have you agree with him.[31] That agreement is absolutely delightful, enriching, strengthening, character ennobling and satisfying. Gradually, it will dawn on you that your own negative mind is not a privilege you are entitled to indulge at your whim. You will inevitably see it as little different—only in size—from the negative, sinful and ultimately iniquitous[32] mind of Lucifer. Being repulsed by that identification, you will cut its root in you by God's grace and power, with great tenacity and righteousness. You will pledge yourself to be like God and never like the iniquitous ones, whose negative mind is "automatically suicidal".[33]

It wasn't like that in my own life, although it certainly is now: I didn't come to divine enthusiasm as a result of rejecting the Devil and all his ways. I loved God's goodness so much that on a single occasion he became so attractive to me, so compelling, that I was drawn to him and I pledged my wholehearted dedication to him through a positive mind.[34]

Perhaps you have done the same, or you will do that in the near future. It is inevitable that sooner or later God will win out over your negative mind. He will win you by his love and consistent goodness. Honestly, where can you go in this universe? Sooner or later you will choose to renounce all your reluctance to be like God, and you will desire to be "surcharged with divine enthusiasm"[35] as was Jesus. Then you will run to your own divine Father, with such a zeal for his love. He will give you the power that overcomes the world. When you are thus equipped, you will never be a slave to your negative mind ever again. You will then deal with two things: your mortal nature and your spiritual growth—and you will do this secure in the ability to approach them with a wholesome attitude. It is such a blessing to be good in spirit.

The sweetness of positive mind

One of the hallmarks of a person who has dealt with their own negative mind is the sweetness with which they approach every other person's expression of spirituality. To dispel your negative mind is to become an equal with the least of us. I once attended a patently fundamentalist Church. A fellow got up half way through the service and sang an unbelievably long hymn with such an out of tune voice, unaccompanied, that I shrank into myself to hide from it. Interestingly, while I was completely withdrawn from the singing, I felt myself become totally alone. As the song droned on and on, I felt myself become like someone who was completely without any opportunity for contact with God. Then I heard this fellow's words about Jesus, as if I was hearing them for the first time. Oh how sweet were those words. I didn't care about the tune, or the croaky voice, or the funny old man who was singing. All I heard was a man singing about Jesus' love for me. In the wilderness of that peculiar isolation into which I had dropped, those words were the most precious things in life. Later I went up to him, hugged him and thanked him for his song.

"Oh, that's all right," he shyly said as he shuffled his feet and awkwardly looked around to avoid eye contact. "I'm not much of a singer, you know. But I think that it's a good thing to sing about Jesus' love for the lost sinner, isn't it? That's why I do it. And do you know what Rob? Sometimes I know I'm singing for the lost sinner that I once was, kind of bringing him God in his complete emptiness. I used to be completely lost and without God Rob. I am so glad that God found me. I don't have much to give him but my song."

This old fellow let me know once and for all time that the least of us who carries the pureness of God's touch for us, is no different from the greatest of us. Dealing with our own negative mind means that God will be able to access us in any vehicle he chooses or has available to him, without our resistance to receiving his favour because of the bias of our own petty preferences.

Back in the light

Now, having said that, let's move out of the shadows and on into our Father's sweet green pastures beside the still waters of the twenty-third Psalm,[36] where our negative mind no longer resides and where he restores our soul and leads us in the paths of righteousness for his name's sake.

The secret of our success in life rests wholly in the size of our God and in the capabilities we attribute to our God. God has a vision for you and for me that is larger than our own vision that we cast for ourselves. Let us therefore, having a large God, cast aside any doubts and negativity. Let us, you and I, now share a God who is big enough and loving enough to bring us to sonship with himself and then to the perfection of that sonship, Adjuster fusion.

Reading for fusion

When researching Adjuster fusion, any background reading undertaken on Adjuster fusion should have at least included the Urantia papers, seeing as the term[37] was coined within its pages alone. Other records written by people on the topic of the journey to perfection are also valuable. There can be considerable benefit derived from the study of other religions. It should be recalled however that most that is written in the world has little to do with Adjuster fusion.

Old Testament

It is appropriate to note that the path to Adjuster fusion is not the goal of the Old Testament writers. Neither is it the goal of the New Testament writers. Neither of these collections speaks of God indwelling the human mind specifically for the purpose of creating a fusion between the human mind and will, and the divine mind and will—for such is Adjuster fusion.[38]

Buddhism

The Urantia papers mention that Buddhism:

> "held that the Buddha (divine) nature resided in all men; that man, through his own endeavors, could attain to the realization of this inner divinity. And this teaching is one of the clearest presentations of the truth of the indwelling Adjusters ever to be made by a Urantian religion."[39]

To some extent then, certain of the Buddhist teachings and practices may be encouraged by your Thought Adjuster, to the end of fostering conditions for genuine spiritual growth. Not the least of these might be the mere fact of his existence and ministry in your life. Certainly this was true for me.

There are differences between the teachings on Adjuster fusion as found in the Urantia papers and in its account of the life and teachings of Jesus of Nazareth, and in the teachings and practices of Buddhism. They can be identified in two statements to do with the personal nature of God.

> 1. "The concept of the Buddha Absolute is at times quasi-personal, at times wholly impersonal—even an infinite creative force. Such concepts, though helpful to philosophy, are not vital to religious development. Even an anthropomorphic Yahweh is of greater religious value than an infinitely remote Absolute of Buddhism or Brahmanism."[40]

2. The Divine Counsellor and author of Paper One confides to us:

> "I come forth from the Eternal, and I have repeatedly returned to the presence of the Universal Father. I know of the actuality and personality of the First Source and Centre, the Eternal and Universal Father. I know that, while the great God is absolute, eternal, and infinite, he is also good, divine, and gracious."[41]

What these words mean is that spirituality can be followed in different ways. Some people seek God the non-person. Others seek God the person. The more complete kind of spiritual

283

identity and experience into which you could grow, is the one that leads you into contact with the absolute person of God, into whose likeness you will grow. For me, that journey took me away from Christianity, into Buddhism, then out of Buddhism and into the Urantia papers. In order to understand some of the spiritual dimensions of Jesus, I then went back into Christian experience again. This, collectively, equipped me with a comprehension of both the personal and the pre-personal aspects of God; and I like that.

The personalness of God

The personalness of God, is not an easy matter to discuss on an interfaith platform with some religionists.

For example, generally, Buddhists aren't the least interested in personalness because the relevant texts in the Buddhist canon consider personality to be a sense based phenomenon which is a part of the law of cause and effect from which they are seeking release.

The Urantia papers, on the other hand, indicate that personality is the very foundation of the individual, and that it emerges directly from the infinite Paradise Father himself.[42] Personality is the "one changeless reality in an otherwise ever-changing creature experience."[43]

When I was in my twenties, my Father was able to draw me very close to himself through the teachings of Buddhism—more so, than through the Christian Church. After he had exhausted the opportunities for my growth in that style however, his continuing efforts to reveal his true nature and blessing drew me to find him in the gospel teachings of Jesus in the Urantia papers. Jesus' entire spirituality rested on a single reliance, that of God being a literal spiritual Father. Through the Urantia papers' account of the life and teachings of Jesus, and my reliance upon that simple gospel claim, that God is my Father and that I am his son,[44] my own Father was able to fully reveal his Fatherhood to me, and make good Jesus' wonderful claims.

It is the personalness of God that awakens the Buddhist to the fact of God's love for him or her. The Bible is not wrong when John tells us that "God so loved the world that he gave his only Son, so that everyone who believes in him may not perish but may have eternal life."[45] Love is deeply personal: the more love, the more personal one is. God who is perfect in love is also perfect in being a person. Everyone who draws near to God on the path of Adjuster fusion, becomes intensely loving, just like his or her Father. Why does the mature Buddhist not more fully embrace the personalness of God? Possibly because Buddhism is not seeking a personal God and his favour and is preoccupied with the philosophic pursuit of the cessation of suffering personally. One thing stood out for me and that was that the teachings and lifestyle of Buddhism isolates the individual person whereas the teachings of Jesus and the lifestyle of a charismatic Church brought people together through the Spirit's love and power in their hearts.

What is there not to love about your Father? What is there not to love about your Michael? What is there not to love about our Mother and Holy Spirit? These are wonderful persons, so gracious, so dignified, so approachable, so lovable, so kind and far seeing, so rich in tender mercies and thoughtfulness for our welfare. It is a splendid thing to love these our parents. Finding God is falling in love with God. When God finds you he falls in love with you too, just like we do with him. You can just imagine how it is on one of those bad days when you are totally unlovable and your Adjuster says to one of his supervising Adjusters, "O Lord! Do I *have* to fall in love with her? Isn't there some other way of doing this fusion thing?" But our parents' love for us is so large, so immediate, so safe, so sensitive yet so enduring that it is our guarantee of access to God no matter how we are. And our Adjusters would never ask that kind of a question in the first place. Love dominates all of God's personal dealings with you.[46]

Evidence

Do you think me too idyllic when I speak like this dear one? What evidence do I have that Your Adjuster loves you even when you are ugly and unlovable? What evidence can I give you that your own Adjuster loves you like a good Father loves his new born baby, with an absolutely pure and untainted love, even when you are in the midst of your intoxication, your hatred, your mad confusion, your bitter resentment, your crushing depression, your meaningless addiction, your deceitfulness and lies, your corruption of the good in others, your contempt for the good things and your lust for the evil and the self-destructive and the vile.

What evidence can I give you that God loves you even when you are consumed with a hatred even of God?

What evidence do I have for you that you are deeply and passionately loved by your Thought Adjuster, and by your Michael in this universe of Nebadon, and your Mother the Holy Spirit of this universe?

The evidence I have for you is two words, Adjuster fusion.[47]

The evidence is that God sent his own spirit to live in you so that you might be rescued from the pit of your own ignorance and lowly birth, to live in the fullness of his glory.

Michael of Nebadon sent his own Spirit to dwell in you so that you would not be left alone on Earth, so that you would have a companion of truth, so that you would have a better way to the Father.

Mother Spirit of Nebadon is all around you and she sends her Spirits to reside in you,[48] and her pure and loving angels to accompany you,[49] to be your guardians, to provide for you as you grow in life and spirit.[50]

All of these wondrous things have one single and immediate goal for you dear one, just as you are in your muck and mire, or in your success and goodness, and that goal is Adjuster fusion.

Never let your muck and mire steal your thanks for being so loved and so fully cared for, even when there is not the least skerrick of evidence for it. Similarly, never let your wealth and success distract you from pursuing the underlying purpose of life, Adjuster fusion.

Many is the time when I have confirmed the love of my Parents in the life of some poor-off foundling whose faith had been crushed or whose life had turned sour, only to find that in a time of desolation on a later occasion, some other of my brothers or sisters in spirit came to me with our Parents' love and lifted me up out of my own misery or fatigue. It is a good thing to share God's love when you have it in abundance, and to receive it when you have none, even enough for your own encouragement.

The plan for your Adjuster fusion

I am writing this book to provide you a witness that God has a plan for your life, a plan called Adjuster fusion.

It is a plan, which no religion on Earth has conceived before the Urantia papers made it known in the life of Jesus of Nazareth. It is a plan of absolute hope, even when you are puzzled, confused, discouraged and distracted.[51]

It is a plan that does not include the merciless, hopeless and shallow extremes of human rationale: reincarnation;[52] damnation in hell under the eternal dominion of evil;[53] atheism;[54] or materialism.[55]

Adjuster fusion is a plan of love;[56] truth, beauty and goodness;[57] prosperity;[58] endless hope,[59] fellowship with God;[60] even the possibility of your own God-like Fatherly sovereignty over universes as yet barely formed.[61] Adjuster fusion is the gateway to your endless adventure and success through intelligent and ever-encompassing love.[62]

I implore you in his name and for his cause, to open your heart and mind to the hope and destiny that exists in this perfect God who, at this very moment while you read these words, indwells your very existence, heart and soul with that single purpose in mind. Say these words aloud right now:

"Father, I know you are here in me to perfect me. By all that is good in me, I declare today that I shall indeed attain Adjuster fusion with you!"

Say it. Believe it. Let it be your affirmation every day.

Adjuster fusion is a plan that has more beings on Earth focussing upon it than any other topic. That's a pretty bold claim, I hear you say, and with good reason. But count them up. Every person who can focus on a topic of personal value has a Thought Adjuster,[63] and every such Adjuster is wholly focussed on the attainment of fusion.[64] Add to their number, the pairs of seraphic guardian angels[65] and their supporting Cherubim and the Sanobim;[66] the planetary Governor General and his or her staff;[67] the Archangels;[68] the Midwayers;[69] and the Life Carriers.[70] They number far more than the 6 billion humans on Earth, and they are all focussed on the Father's plan for perfection.

Judge not your own rights to Adjuster fusion, nor your own progress in perfection, by the affairs of humanity. Adjuster fusion is not the business of the market place, the family, love and sex, organised religion, medicine or law. Adjuster fusion is an affair of the soul between you and God alone. Rather make your assessment solely on your communion with God and the love of Michael in your heart, which is poured out to your friend, your enemy, and your debtor in need.[71]

You are never alone in the journey of ever increasing perfection that leads to Adjuster fusion, but your Adjuster fusion is for you alone.

At the time of this writing, October 12th 1999, I can honestly say that I know of less than a dozen people in the world who are actively pursuing Adjuster fusion, as that term is defined in the Urantia papers. I know of many more people who expect it to happen to them at some stage on the mansion worlds, but if you were to ask them, "What happened this week in your life that has furthered your Adjuster fusion?" their answer would more than likely be, "I have no idea."

Lone walking

Our mortal pursuit of Adjuster fusion as it is defined in the Urantia papers is, at this stage of our world's development, a solitary and little heard of activity. This will not always be the case, but at present you can feel like you are journeying alone with no other mortal companions of that ilk.

The reasons for this spiritual isolation are varied. For example, both the message and the text of the Urantia papers are not widespread. Also, of the readers of the Urantia papers, there are few who can say that they understand the goals of Adjuster fusion or the path to the extent that they are applying some form of methodology in the daily life.

A friend of mine came to me and said, "I am going to Israel, England, France, Thailand and Africa. Who can I meet there who will share with me their experiences of Adjuster fusion training in the Urantia papers context like you do?" My answer was, "I don't know anyone, and I don't know anyone who would know anyone." This is because there is poor networking across most nations at present. Many readers read alone, or do not socialise well. Whilst Internet and email lists and websites are excellent tools for networking, the majority of readers across the world are unlisted, unidentified, and give no evidence of changing that status in the foreseeable future. This challenges

288

befriending someone else who is devoted to Adjuster fusion. Invariably, your companion will be someone to whom you will eventually introduce the topic, as did Elijah with Elisha.[72]

In 1987, I was in communion with God and I was complaining because I was lost, "Father, I feel really frustrated," I said.

"I have left my first love of monk life to come to Melbourne at your bidding. I have abandoned my Buddhist ways in order to promote your truth in the context of the Urantia papers. I have met with the local readers here and nothing seems to amount to anything. None of them seem to be seeking you, and your righteousness and perfection like I do. They all seem to be very fine people, and well-read for years. But we have little in common, for we do not find our unity in worship but in merely reading the same book. We do not celebrate our sharing your mind and heart. Your Holy Spirit fire does not inflame us into a passion for your glories. What exactly am I doing here? I would be better off back in the Himalayas as a monk. I don't have even a single spiritual friend here."

And he replied, quietly, assuredly, and without hesitation: "Make them, son."

Over the next few years I did just that. I started where I was, with the few talents I had, and I began conducting spiritual groups and counselling. From out of the many people who attended, I found spiritual friends. Those men and women became some of the few I now know who are pursuing Adjuster fusion.

Share your spiritual experience: you are someone's guiding light, if only for a moment

I encourage you to do the same. Share your spirituality, it doesn't really matter where you begin. Begin just as you are. God is in you: he will surprise you and do wonders in your life.

It is a wonderful blessing to share experiences around Adjuster fusion with such people: to enjoy the Lord's supper with such companions; to all be a part of our journey into Adjuster fusion together; to share in the beginnings of the most meaningful journey on Earth together—a journey that will not end until we stand together before our Paradise Father. I can see us there now as we prepare to be embraced and acknowledged in the glories of the Infinite and Absolute Parent of all life.[73] Perhaps you are there with us too dear reader, as we cast a knowing and deeply loving glance across at each other, smiling as we recall our early days together here on Earth, where we first loved and supported one another in God's will as we set a course for Paradise and final perfection.[74]

Every reader has their own story about how they found the papers, how they network or don't network with other readers, and how they do or don't socialise their spirituality. You will have your story and, as mine is to me, yours will have a certain type of hallmark to it that you hold dear. You will, however, need to find an enduring inner strength whilst God brings you into the solitude that necessarily pervades the growth into Adjuster fusion candidacy and its sometime actualisation. This kind of inner strength has its power in holiness rather than isolation, righteousness rather than tenacity. Inevitably, your inner strength, the kind that has found appropriate solutions to the stresses of spiritual solitude, will be built on maintaining companionship with the persons of God the Father (the Thought Adjuster), the Son (Michael), and the Spirit (Mother of Nebadon).

Companionship

There is a profound companionship with Jesus and Christ Michael that will nourish you through the scriptural records of his life and teachings in the Urantia papers. He is not so personally presented in the Bible, but he *is* found there too. God's people meet him in his Word. You, the son, will find your Father in the writings that have been done in his name and for his purposes.

I love to follow in Jesus' footsteps. To see Jesus is to see that my life is in Michael, the Creator Son of God "through whom he also created the worlds."[75] To see Jesus is to see my Father in him also.[76] I am a son of my Paradise Father, through the lives of my local universe Michael and Mother Spirit. I am utterly dependent upon my divine Parents. I adore them and crave them. I no longer have either the ambition or the faith in my own skills and capacity for perfection. I trust in Jesus' life and in my divine Parents alone, and in their abilities to make me perfect like themselves. I fellowship with them and so, in them,

I am never alone or lonely. They are an extraordinary upstream current in a downstream kind of world. This became particularly true when I participated in the realness of the risen Jesus as did Peter, "I believe he has risen from the dead; I will go and tell my brethren;" and Jesus' guidance to him, "No longer should you be concerned with what you may obtain from the kingdom but rather be exercised about what you can give to those who live in dire spiritual poverty."[77]

There will come a day for you also, precious son of God, that the Father, the Son and the Holy Spirit, the supreme persons of heaven, will be your constant companions. Such a glory lies beyond the domains of enlightenment, nirvana, meditation and prayer. It resides in your sonship with God as you mature toward Adjuster fusion.

I want to encourage you therefore, to seek the same fellowship with Jesus. Do not ignore him. Do not compare him. Do not look away from him at your previous experiences or your wondrous spiritual accomplishments and say, "Oh I know a better way to the Father." No. Claim him! Stop him as he goes about his universe business, like Bartimeus the blind beggar of Jericho.[78] Shout out his name, "Jesus! Jesus!" Tell him you want him to attend to you now. "Jesus! Jesus! Come and fetch me!" And he will do that, he said so,[79] and he is the Word of God in all its truthfulness in this universe.[80]

Jesus will not leave you lonely on this solitary journey of Adjuster fusion. If you join us, we will soon be a virus of love and confidence across the world for the attainment of our Father's highest ideals for the individuals of this world, and others will join us. Then, long after the struggles of our journeys on Earth have faded into history, still others will come after us saying:

> "How easy the way has been made for us! Halleluiah! Look at all the lives and the teachings of all these precious people who have faithfully followed Jesus on the path to Adjuster fusion. Thanks be to our Father and our Michael."

Jesus made the way to Adjuster fusion clear to us

Jesus made the way easy for you and for me dear one, by his

precious life and teachings, by his death and resurrection, by his ascension to the Father and his everlasting on going ministry within and for each of us.

In Jesus, we have the perfect guide into Adjuster fusion. And during those early years, when the Father indwelling you struggles to communicate with you and cannot show himself easily as your personal God, the risen Jesus of Nazareth who was nailed to the tree, the universe Creator Son of God, Christ Michael, will indeed and truly be your personal God, your Father, your guide, your faith's every answer, your lamp on the path and a light unto your feet.[81]

It is a good and wonderful thing to trust in Jesus and his example in the Urantia papers, for his word is true, he *will* bring you to the Father. Though your heart is aching for a touch from God, I say to you he will touch you. Though your life has been given over to God and you are filled with good works, but still you seek more of God, I tell you Jesus shall not only show you the Father, but he will take you to the Father. He will deliver you into the Father's presence, by your own Father's request, and the Father and you shall be in one embrace. Lord Buddha cannot do that. The prophets cannot do that. The Church cannot do that. You alone cannot do that. Oh, you will attain mighty things beloved, majestic and wonderful things well beyond what I have ever experienced. But only the Michael of your universe will deliver you to the Father in Paradise. This I know as a fact of experience.

There are many things you and I both do not yet comprehend through lack of experience and knowledge. I know of a certainty however, that Jesus' word is true. He said to you and to me:

"I am the way, the truth, and the life. No man goes to the Father except through me. All who find the Father, first find me."[82]

He has shown me the Father and because of Jesus, my universe Michael, my Adjuster fusion is made all the more accessible.

I think my writing clearly demonstrates that I am nobody special. I am merely a plain mortal, born in Morrinsville New Zealand on Urantia fifty years ago, to Alison and Jack. I didn't do well at school; and I loved God ever since I was a boy running in the grassy fields with our family dog.

I am afforded, however, the supreme joy of serving Michael and our Father and my fellows on Earth.[83] I believe in my heart, the many things Jesus said. Similarly, with a straightforward and child like faith, I believe in the divine exhortation the messengers of Paradise have carried down through the ages and out through the universes in love and mercy, even to such lowly animal-origin creatures as the human races of Urantia, from the Universal Father who inhabits eternity, the supreme mandate, 'Be you perfect, even as I am perfect.'[84]

I encourage you to believe in the revelation of their truth within your heart and soul. If you will not believe in the Father, or you will not believe in his Son, Christ Michael, or you will not believe in the works of the Holy Spirit, then I think you will have trouble believing my words too.

If you will not believe the Father, then you surely won't believe a son of the Father. I pray now though, that God's grace, having quietly pierced your heart as you read thus far, will stir up your faith to believe me and my witness of Adjuster fusion, even though I am of no account, only that I am one like you and I speak the truth on this matter because the Father and his Son live in me and I live in them.

This is a confirmation of the work done in me by my divine Parents, even as they will do this in you according to your faith and your choice, just as the great friend of our perfection once determined while on Earth:

"And now, my Father, I would pray not only for these eleven men but also for all others who now believe, or who may hereafter believe the gospel of the kingdom through the word of their future ministry. I want them all to be one, even as you and I are one. You are in me and I am in you, and I desire that these believers likewise be in us; that both of our spirits indwell them... This world knows very little of you, righteous Father, but I know you, and I have made you known to these believers, and they will make known your name to other generations. And now I promise them that you will be with them in the world even as you have been with me—even so."[85]

If you would Adjuster fuse, do not be the rocky island that boldly stands aloof amid the mighty waterfall like the Niagara or the Victoria, dividing the waters. Rather, be gravity; the gushing torrents of the Father will tumble all through you like a flood.

❧

Notes

1. 32:5.4 {To me it...}
2. 1:0.1
3. 40:7.5 {Fusion with a...}
4. 110:7.10 {During the making...}
5. 1:0.3 {The enlightened worlds...}
6. 63:0.2 {Andon is the...}
7. 63:7.2 {On Jerusem both...}
8. Genesis 5:24; Urantia papers 45:4.2
9. 2 Kings 2:11; Urantia papers 45:4.2
10. Matthew 3:17; Urantia papers 135:8.6
11. 76:2.9 {And so Cain...}
12. 93:1.1
13. 13:1.4 {1. Divinington. This world...}
14. 110:3.5 {Confusion, being puzzled...}
15. Hebrews 3:17-19
16. 155:1.3 {Jesus continued to...}
17. 151:4.5 {The kingdom of...}
18. John 5:19-20
19. Zechariah 4:6
20. 1:0.1
21. 1:0.3 {The enlightened worlds...}
22. 110:1.6 {Today you are...}
23. 129:4.7 {And this was...}
24. 151:1.2; Mark 4:8
25. 196:3.1
26. 190:2.6 {And David did...}; Revelation 3:20
27. 143:2.3 {Verily, verily, I...}; Matthew 23:25
28. 146:3.2 {The apostles were...}
29. Acts 2:4
30. 188:4.1-3; John 1:29; Isaiah 53:12
31. 110:3.4 {I cannot but...}
32. 54:0.2 {the Gods neither...}
33. 2:3.5 {In any universe...}
34. 1:1.2 {The Universal Father...}; 174:5.13 {And now

I...}
35. 100:7.4 {the Son of Man...}
36. 48:6.4 {Even on Urantia...}
37. 112: Section 7
38. 5:1.11 {Mortal man may...}
39. 94:11.5
40. 94:11.9 {While this idea...}
41. 1:3.8 {I come forth...}
42. 112:5.2 {That which comes...}
43. Forward:5.7 {Personality. The personality...}
44. 141:6.4 {That night Jesus...}
45. John 3:16
46. 2:5.12 {When man loses...}
47. 103:7.14 {There is a...}
48. 34:4.7 {The seven adjutant...}
49. 113:4.1
50. Paper 113
51. 110:3.5 {Confusion, being puzzled...}
52. 94:2.3 {The undue concentration...}
53. 95:6.6 {The Jewish traditions...}
54. 56:10.3-4 {Philosophy you somewhat...}
55. 195: Sections 6-8
56. 2:5.10 {But the love...}; 110:0.2 {As far as...}
57. 132:2.5 {Goodness is always...}
58. 160: Section 4
59. 107:6.2 {The Adjuster is...}
60. 170:4.3 {The Master on...}
61. 12:2.6 {Throughout Orvonton it...}; 112:7.17 {We
    believe that...}
62. 110:1.2 {I wish it...}
63. 52:5.6 {Upon the resurrection...}; 108: Section 2
64. 108:0.1
65. 113:2.9 {When a seraphic...}
66. 113:2.9 {When a seraphic...}
67. 39:5.5 {3. The Souls of Peace...}
68. 114:5.4 {This rather loosely...}
69. 77:7.2 {The original number...}
70. 36:3.8-9 {When the Life Carriers...}
71. 144:3.2 {When James had...}
72. 2 Kings 2:11

73. 14:6.9 {7. The evolutionary mortals...}
74. 22:2.6 {I am a Mighty Messenger...}
75. Hebrews 1:2
76. 180:4.2 {In just a few...}
77. 191:1.2 {When Peter thought...}
78. 171:5.1; Luke 18:38
79. 180:4.1; John 14:18
80. 128:1.10 {And yet, throughout...}; 2:0.2 {The nature of...}; 6:2.2 {The Eternal Son...}; 104:1.11 {The first Trinity...}; John 1:1; John 1:14; John 5:24
81. Psalm 199:105
82. 180:3.7 {When Jesus heard...}; 21:6.4 {Just as the...}; 34:7.8 {Having started out...}; John 14:6
83. 170:5.17 {Sooner or later...}
84. 1:0.3 {The enlightened worlds...}
85. 182:1.6 {And now, my...}; John 17:1-26

❧

Sonship with God the Thought Adjuster: Kong Meng San Phor Kark See, Singapore

(Left) The late abbot of Kong Meng San, Ven. Sek Hong Choon, formerly of Shao Lin Temple, China. Photo taken after Rob's ordination in 1976.

(Below) The new monks' accommodation building on the left. Rob occupied the 2nd floor corner room above the parked van.

(Bottom) Looking down the hall into the room Rob used for his ten-day retreat at Kong Meng San.

Judhi and Esa, the Malaysian restauranteurs near Kong Meng San in 1993. That same evening Rob's Thought Adjuster confirmed his sonship with God in person in the room (below) with the words, "I am your Father, and you are my son."

The photos of the room were taken at around 4am that same morning.

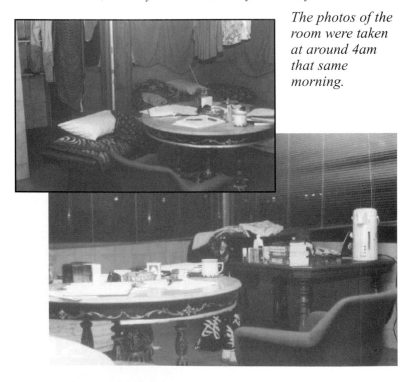

While Rob was away in Singapore, Mary (top left) had fellowship with relatives, friends and readers of the Urantia papers on the very popular patio that saw so much counselling and healing over a ten-year period.

Spreading the message of sonship with God: the early groups and Church in Melbourne

The participants in the first group that Rob facilitated in Melbourne. After this group, many others followed. The groups and their accompanying retreats covered a range of topics from healing, meditation and spiritual growth to just plain old "Getting Real." Many people did more than one group. Increasingly, as Rob moved away from his Buddhist roots, the Urantia papers were employed like a text book. Over the years the groups and retreats focussed exclusively on sonship with God.

Spreading the message of sonship with God: the early groups and Church in Melbourne

In the late 1980's, Rob began facilitating regular worship services based on the teachings of Jesus in the Urantia papers. This was the venue for the launch of his song called "The three days of Mary," that speaks of Mary's experience from Easter Friday to Sunday. Rob had prayed to Michael for a song that would open people's hearts up to Jesus, that he could use for the glory of God at the inaugural Easter Sunday service. When he and Mary sang it in harmony on that special day, there was barely a dry eye in the house.

One of the many "carols by candlelight" held in Rob and Mary's garden; the fancy dress added a wonderful playfulness to the Christmas fellowship among friends who were all fond of the Urantia papers.

For two years, Rob facilitated a weekly meditation group. For one year it was held in the chapel (above) of the Divine Word Catholic Missionaries in Box Hill. Tony, (top right) was the Novice Master in that Seminary in those days. Maggie, (front row 2nd from the right) and Ryta (2nd row, right) were always tremendous supports, 1989-90.

(Below) The Easter Retreat after Rob returned from Singapore, 1993.

Sonship with Christ Michael and Mother Spirit: the wedding of Anthony and Norma.

(Above) Mary reading scripture at the wedding of Norma and Anthony (seated right) at Our Lady of Victories, Camberwell, October 1993. Rob is seated in a pew on the right at the time of the encounter with Christ Michael and Mother Spirit.

(Left) Norma and Anthony.

(Below) Rob with Chris and Ina during the Kenneth Copeland crusade, October 1973.

A period of equipping

The prayer house in "our" garden; the place where Rob experienced mind-union with Mother Spirit and Michael in October 1993.

(Above) "Our" garden, looking up over the spa. The prayer house is off to the right and the place where his Thought Adjuster enacted Genesis 1:2 is on the left of the photo.

(Left) Rob in his study during the equipping period.

Sonship and death on the cross: the Tibetan Buddhist retreat with Lama Thubten Yeshe and Lama Zopa Rinpoche, New Zealand 1975.

(Above and left) Rob just after the retreat in which he was born again and baptised in the Holy Spirit through an experience like Jesus' death on the cross.

The Urantia papers are a revelation of God, from God: Penang, 1994.

Mary at Kek Lok See, Penang. Rob had stayed in this temple as a monk in 1981 and had gone out from here to teach and speak at other temples in Malaysia. Kek Lok See is world famous for its geomancy, its Pagoda and its beautiful architecture and murals. Built on the side of Penang Hill, the temple design maximises the beneficial "fong sui" of the area.

Kek Lok See Pagoda, arguably the largest Buddhist Pagoda outside China and Taiwan, attracts thousands of pilgrims each year.

It can be seen from George-town, many miles away, and is a magnificent monument not only to traditional architectural motifs, but also to the presence of Buddha Nature (the Spirit of the Father) within the mind of man.

The old "fish drum" that was beaten to announce meals, has now been replaced by the ringing of a bell. It had a unique hollow wood sound.

The Urantia papers are a revelation of God, from God: Penang, 1994.

Overlooking Georgetown, Penang, from the high lookouts of Kek Lok temple that springs out of Penang Hill like a colourful green and orange blessing for all to see. It was at this point, on the saturday morning, that Rob was speaking with his Guardian Seraphim and wondering who the "Katro" type fellow might be, and whether or not it was Koay from the computer shop in the Metro building, far off on the horizon.

Rob, (above left) in the hotel in Penang, during the 1994 mission to seed a copy of the Urantia papers in Malaysia led only by his Guardian Seraphim. His ideal was to find a "Katro" who might one day pass the papers and their values down the generations to a "Moses" among that lovely people in Malaysia. (Above right) Living in Kek Lok See and teaching in Malaysia, 1981-82.

Rob and Mary make a pilgrimage to the Holy Land, 1995.

(Above) A plaque in the Garden Tomb in Jerusalem near the Damascus Gate.

(Below) One of the "eyes" of Golgotha, the hill of the skull, Jerusalem, where Jesus was crucified.

Rob and Mary being baptised in the River Jordan near Tiberias, Israel, on 20 August 1995. The Puerto Rican Pastor later said to Rob, "We've been baptising all day but when you two stepped in the water, it was like the Holy Spirit came alive on us for the first time!"

Sunrise over the Sea of Galilee, from Tiberias; the same sun that shone on Jesus as he came to know his Father in lovely Galilee.

Rob on Mt. Hermon, Israel, August 19, 1995, on the day when he received confirmation of Adjuster fusion candidacy.

(Below) In the Nazareth synagogue considered to be where Jesus attended as a boy.

Finding the life in the Urantia papers

The International Conference for students of the Urantia papers in 1996 at Flagstaff University, Arizona. there were about 1100 participants from all around the world. In small groups, Rob ministered worship and healing in the context of the experiences he had had of Michael of Nebadon, Mother Spirit and the Paradise Father two years earlier.

Mary, with friends Bill and Kaye Cooper, in Dallas Texas, 1997. Bill and Kaye are reknowned for their facilitation of excellent spiritual groups and retreats based on the teachings of the Urantia papers. They are co-authors of a great book: "Friendship with God," which is available from Adventures in Spirit Living, P.O. Box 1203, Arlington, TX, 76004-1203.

Finding the life in the Urantia papers

At a Melbourne conference, Rob and Berkley Elliot. For a quarter of a century this little dynamo of God's enthusiasm provided a strong guiding influence for many students of the Urantia papers in Oklahoma.

Julianne Clerget from Washington State and John Thiele from Arkansas were instrumental in Rob attending the International Conference for students of the Urantia papers in 1996 at Flagstaff University, Arizona. They were extremely helpful in arranging the facilities for worship and communion on campus and accommodating the additional meetings that spontaneously occurred as people wanted to receive healing and engage the spiritual dimension of the Urantia papers that Rob was facilitating.

Finding the life in the Urantia papers

A day of ordination in the Church of Christ Michael, Oklahoma City, June 1997, with Jack, Mary, Rob and Harry, which coincided with the close of that phase of Rob's mission (left).

(Right) Mary and Rob in Colorado, 1997.

As a minister in the Church of Christ Michael, Rob was licenced by the State of Oklahoma to perform marriages. (Left and below) The marriage of two long time students of the Urantia papers, Beth and Jerry.

The wedding was co-facilitated by another long time student of the Urantia papers, Dan, (centre) a truly delightful fellow who has been a pillar of wisdom to the communion of believers in Oklahoma for a number of years.

Finding the life in the Urantia papers

(Above and below) Rob visited Oklahoma City after IC96 and met many of the students of the Urantia papers.

The Oklahoman readers are extremely hospitable and very dedicated to their regular fellowshipping around the Urantia papers. Among the Americans who have pioneered the experience of developing a community of Urantia papers believers within the wider community, a good number of them are Oklahoman.

Oklahoma City was the first location for a Church based upon the Urantia papers, long before Rob was involved with the creation of the Oklahoma City Church of Christ Michael in 1997.

Death and resurrection

Jack Crickett of Morrinsville and Alison Wylie of Epsom, Auckland, New Zealand.

Rob and his brother David (right) with Mary who was adopted into their family at Christmas 1962.

Thought Adjuster arrival: how I got "saved."

Rob (centre top row) in the school class photo of five-year olds in the year of his Thought Adjuster arrival at Morrinsville Primary School.

Gubby is the boy on Rob's right.

The playing field site of the arrival, where the big old oak tree once stood, is about twenty-five yards (twenty metres) to the right.

Jack Munroe's daughter, Valmay, is seated front row third from the left: we all thought she was the luckiest kid in town because her Dad owned the two picture theatres in Morrinsville!

Death and resurrection

Jack and his brother Hal, now both gone, a couple of years before Jack's mansion world transition.

Jack, with Hal, healed of the effects of the stroke by divine intervention—on the day that David phoned.

Alison's father, himself the son of a Presbyterian minister, told her to "keep Robert in the church because he'll grow up to be a minister." On his mother's side, Rob's ancestors can be easily traced back to Rev. Alexander Moncrieff of Culfargie, Scotland, who formed the Secession Church in Scotland. Alexander's son, William, was instrumental in bringing that Church to Maryland in America in the mid 1700's. In the eleven generations between Alexander and Rob, eight men are Presbyterian ministers. Rob is pictured here in choir boy robes with Peter Butt, one-time Anglican vicar of Morrinsville.

Jack Crickett at his beloved piano, a Petrov, at Raglan, N.Z., 1987. In retirement, he used to play the old favourites down at the local Raglan pub each week. Youngsters used to ask him about the "old days" when the jazz classics were being written and when he and his brothers, Hal, Ivan and Guy had a dixieland dance band that played all the top dance venues of the nineteen thirties, forties and fifties.

There is no reincarnation

Cho Kyi Nyima Tulku, of Bodhanath, Nepal, dressed in the formal Tibetan robes of the Nyingma Order: 1980.

To Tibetan Buddhists, a Tulku is a person who has been officially recognised to be the reincarnation of a previously known Lama who was known to be "enlightened" and who has taken rebirth for the specific purpose of helping others reach enlightenment.

Cho Kyi Nyima Tulku, playfully dressed up in the Chinese robes worn by Rob: 1981. From him, Rob received the transmission of the Nyingma Phorwa teaching—how to die and attain the clear light liberation.

(Above) Rob and Jack, 1987, during a rare moment when they shared their music together, and (left) during the vision of Jack's mansonia resurrection, July 1990.

The twin that lived and the twin that died

Mary with her Mum and Dad, pregnant with Bean.

When Bean died, Rob had a visit from the angel who is sponsoring her Morontia care until either rob or Mary can begin parenting her there.

The Thought Adjuster's perspective on sonship with God: Ladakh pilgrimage

A composite of several photos Rob took of Leh, Ladakh, India, 1981, from the roof top of the house in which he experienced the miracle of "Say, 'You are well,' to her."

Urgen Tulku, the father of Cho Kyi Nyima Tulku, whose Gompa is perched on the hills of the eastern rim overlooking the Kathmandu valley: 1981. From him, Rob received the transmission of the Nyingma Dzogchen teaching—the Mahamudra liberation.

The American monk Chodok (Chris Kolb) and his wife Lisa, outside their home at Kopan near Bodhanath, Nepal. Years later, both he and Rob would find themselves bringing spiritual principles to help alcohol and drug users—Chodok in San Francisco and Rob in Melbourne. He and Rob chatted about the Urantia papers' views on Tibetan Buddhism, and agreed that the experience of the Thought Adjuster was experience of Buddha Nature—the Father within.

A group of four Nagpas around their cooking fire (from left, an older woman, a man lying down, their teacher, and a third disciple sitting to his left with a white hat on) who had camped in the grounds of the Tibetan monastery in which Rob was living in Nepal, 1981. Rob's room is upstairs left in this picture. The Nagpas are Buddhist yogis who live on the Tibet-Nepal border, high in the Himalayas, and who come down to the lower altitudes during winter. Rob and the group got along very well, despite the language barriers: they had never seen a camera before and all jumped backwards when the camera flashed.

Rob in Boudhanath, Nepal, 1981, in Chinese Buddhist monk robes.

The Thought Adjuster's perspective on sonship with God: the young woman who was dying

(Front row sanyassin women from left to right) Shavda, Fleur and the young German lady who was dying, after she was miraculously restored.

Rob (centre) with two English Rajneesh sanyassins in Leh, Ladakh, October 1981.

Sonship and doing the will of God: marrying Mary

(Top left) Rob and Mary (above).

(Left) Rob and Mary, now engaged and at the wedding of their friend Dr. Charles Krebbs.

Rob, Mary and John—tutor of Rob's courses "Evangelism" and "Old Testament" at Ridley Theological College: the wedding in 1986.

Leonie, Rob, Mary and Anthony—Mary's parents. Their love and respect for each other was always such a blessing and such a delight; many times they prayed together and sang songs of worship together in their homes. Mary's family filled a spot in Rob's life where family had been fragmented and dysfunctional in his own family of origin.

What should I believe? The hills of Perea, Israel

The Perean Hills— one day's walk south of the Sea of Galilee. This is where Jesus was baptised in the Jordan by John— the occasion of the Father's decree of his personal human perfection with the words, "This is my beloved son in whom I am well pleased"; and the hills where Jesus spent forty days in retirement to plan his ministry mission to the world in the light of his full human recognition of being Michael of Nebadon, the sovereign creator of this universe.

The birth of a son of God

(Left) Some of the people involved with Rob's Church of Christ Michael, Melbourne during 1997-98 (men from left) Bill, Robert and Paul; (women from left) Jeanette, Mary, Tya, Chris and Judy.

Carol, of Scottsdale Arizona (left) and Judith, of Toronto (right) who both encountered Michael and Mother Spirit in a deeply personal experience whilst on Internet chat-line meetings with Rob in 1999.

Chapter 24

Revelation: the Word between the Father and his son

During 1999, a question arose in the mind of someone I had been mentoring over the Internet for some months, Carol Davidson. She asked, "Is a resurrection chamber involved in Adjuster fusion...if so, before the welcome, or after?"

There is little information in the Urantia papers about some of the processes through which we mortals pass. This matter about how exactly the process of Adjuster fusion occurs is one of those areas. The Urantia papers document the fact of the Resurrection Halls on Mansonia, and how we mortals are resurrected into heaven after our mortal death.[1] They also tell of a rather spectacular event which will occur in the lives of certain unique individuals—perhaps you are such a one—who attain such a degree of perfection in the union of their mind and their Thought Adjuster's mind that they see eye to eye in all things mortal.[2] When this occurs, as has done on Earth, the Thought Adjuster takes the mortal while they are still alive, and transports them to heaven, completely by-passing the experience of physical death.[3]

The question Carol raised was relevant to her study of what the Urantia papers call Adjuster fusion. Besides, it is an intriguing question. It also raises another question: how does the human son of God go about answering such a question?

Students of the Urantia papers are all unique, that's one of the aims of the teachings in this fifth epochal revelation, to foster the uniqueness of the individual and so encourage greater diversity—for with greater diversity comes greater opportunity for all. Each student will eventually have to deal with such undocumented matters as this question poses. Eventually, each heavenly traveller will cherish the process by which they develop their own ways of dealing with what can only be revealed by God within them. It is to the glory of God and mortals alike that we share these ways with each other as they arise, like the blessed family our Adjusters conceive us to be.

Where angels fear to tread

Some students of the Urantia papers refuse outright to investigate or even speculate on matters that are not written in the Urantia papers. There is a lot of merit in this view. Revelation can get pretty weird—just take a look at the Bible's book of Revelations. It's weird—even the authors of the Urantia papers state that it is abridged, distorted, fragmentary and adulterated despite it once being a "great revelation".[4] What is even more weird, is when human economy and relations are caught up in some kind of utterly nonsensical view on life which aims to divide humanity, simply because of an interpretation of what people believe is a divine revelation. History is littered with masse suicides and the slavery of communities of believers who were misled by their prophets. Let us also not forget the endless campaigns like the Christian crusades, the religious wars of the Middle East and Africa, the plundering of the Americas.

We Adjuster fusion candidates must work out our own solutions for dealing with the problems of revelation. None of us are exempt from this problem because Adjuster fusion is a name for the fact of union with the source of revelation himself. Ultimately, the satisfaction of our solution will rest in our personal experience of whether or not God's will is glorified, and in the corroboration of that satisfaction in the lives of our peers. But the problem will not go away. The problem has its origins in the Thought Adjuster's supreme desire to make contact with his mortal child.[5] Knowing God begins with receiving his forgiveness which, in itself, is an act of receiving revelation. Revelation is possibly the most powerful force known to humanity. You can't know God without revelation being involved. You can know *about* God. You can go through the ritual of Godly dramatics. But it is impossible to know God without him communicating to you things that you yourself become responsible for believing and acting on. If you will not do that, you deny the will of God and you are lost. My authority in saying this is not my own. Jesus told us that in order to enter the kingdom of heaven we would need to be reborn, that such a new birth was in spirit,[6] and that the Father speaks within the human heart as a still, small voice, saying, "This is the way;

walk therein."⁷ That voice is one kind of revelation.

A person meets God in very much expanded terms in the Urantia papers. The type of revelation that a believer can experience will involve new horizons and the domain of a much larger God than is commonly accepted in the world. I regard it that the type of person who protests against the authority and experience of revelation has not yet come into God's territory which lies buried both within and beyond the Urantia papers. Such a domain is the personal relationship with one's own Thought Adjuster and the universe citizenship relationships with Christ Michael and the Mother Spirit of Nebadon. These are very real relationships, which provide for the son of God in ways that simply aren't spelled out to the letter in the Urantia papers.

The journey into and through and out the other side of the Urantia papers revelation is not at all easy and can not successfully be hurried. It has been useful for me to maintain the understanding, however, that the life which is in the teachings, the nectar of contact with and in God himself, is in the living experiences to which the words point, not the words and the book itself. There is a vast difference between turning the papers into a philosophical experience instead of letting it be a prompting for the deeper and more real spiritual experience with one's own Thought Adjuster or divine Parents.

Oh sure, such a young spirit as will not venture outside the words of the Urantia papers may well raise up all manner of protest at me. But I don't care, no, not in the least. These limitations have no substance in the will of God. Sooner or later such a person will encounter the Father's mind, and all their current abilities and attitudes will be swept away, one by one.

I tell you the truth when I say that the things about which I write are in my spirit and in my experience. I write about what I have done in my Father's will, what he has given for me to do, and I write what my Father gives me to write. I am following in the footsteps of Jesus. He is my brother, my Father, my local universe God, my perfect example. When you follow in the footsteps of your father you become like your father—this is true of following your mother also. Jesus said:

"If I glorify myself, my glory is nothing. It is my Father who glorifies me, he of whom you say, 'He is our God,' though you do not know him...But I do know him and I keep his word."[8]

The person who protests is deeply cared for. Their protest is an expression of their timidity about crossing over the threshold of worldly dependence to being swept up under the wings of God. I have travelled on the wings of my Father's inner heart, and they possibly have not done that as yet. Their argument has no real grounds, except to bring attention to their need to find a foothold in new levels of spiritual experience that involve the realness of revelation.

The very best that I can do, however, is to continue to expand into these new territories and shed light for those who will follow. If they too find pathways and nooks and crannies that I have not found, I would be foolish not to follow after their light and draw from it whatever I can in turn.

We don't all know the same things at the same time

Life is like spiritual fossicking. No one will give you your tailor made spirituality. We have to make it happen, choice by choice, decision after decision. We don't get satisfied at a meal by sitting there doing nothing but waiting for the feeling of "full" to come upon us. We get there by taking one bite after another, from dish after dish. Maybe some of this, not some of that, more of this one please. It's the same with the spiritual journey. It's very humbling to recognise that our own perspective on life is in fact not the highest perspective on life that exists in the world.

You should live in the knowledge that the way to Paradise is not one wherein all the lights are turned on and everybody knows all the same things at all the same time. No, rather it is intricately personalised. Listen to the words of the authors of the Urantia papers themselves, as they say, "I do not know."[9] Everyone is a Master. And every Master is either in a perfecting process or a learning process of some kind, even God who, despite having changeless features, is increased with every son of God who joins with him and shares his mind.

Be perfect: therefore you will receive revelation

And he will lead you on. Oh what a glory! Yes he will, for you have upon you and in you the command to be perfect.[10] Such a magnificent command is the gravity throughout the entire universe of universes and it draws all of us into the one Father's love. The Urantia papers are excellent, but they aren't the last word on what the Adjusters or what Michael of Nebadon can do for you and in you.[11] There is no last word to the development of mind. The fact is that the son of God develops a mind, which traverses the worlds from Earth to heaven, from the flesh to the divine. That such a feat is possible is to the glory of God the Father, God the Son our Christ Michael, and God the Holy Spirit our universe Mother. They build this within us. It is their work. Halleluiah! I'm glad it is!

Fusion mind

My means of answering the question about Adjuster fusion was by using what I call "fusion mind."[12] How do the Urantia papers describe that exquisite mind?

"That Morontia oneness, that supernal harmony, that cosmic co-ordination, that divine attunement, that celestial fusion, that never-ending blending of identity, that oneness of being which is so perfect and final that even the most experienced personalities can never segregate or recognize as separate identities the fusion partners—mortal man and divine Adjuster."[13]

This kind of question can't be answered using your normal human mind; our horizons are too local and we are unable to traverse both the height and the depth which comprise the spiritual dimension involved in the task of knowing.

Focussing on the question, and without consultation with my Father but rather employing this mind which is the union of the mortal and the Father's mind, the fusion mind, I recognised how it all happened. As I watched what happened, I wrote it all down. Then I sent off my reply and this student of Adjuster fusion posted it on a few of the Internet lists for other Urantia papers students.

This, then, was her question:

"Is a resurrection chamber involved in Adjuster fusion...if so, before the welcome, or after?"

If you don't know much about Adjuster fusion then before you read my reply to her in the next chapter, titled "The Glory of Adjuster fusion," you will benefit from reading the Urantia papers starting at Paper 112.

❧

Notes

1. 47:3.5 {From the Temple...}
2. 110:2.5 {You as a...}
3. 112:7.3 {Fusion with the...}; 32:5.4 {To me it...}; 49:6.8 {5. Mortals of the...}; 55:2.2 {This experience of...}; 111:3.1
4. 139:4.14 {When in temporary...}
5. 196:3.28 {the great challenge...}
6. 142:6.5 {Jesus said, "Nevertheless...}
7. 148:6.10 {Job was altogether...}; 34:7.8 {Having started out...}; 97:5.2 {Isaiah went on...}; 117:5.9 {While such spiritual...}
8. John 8:54-55
9. 3:6.6 {Does the Paradise...}; 19:1.2 {While the Stationary...}; 19:5.1; 20:8.2 {The exact number...}; 21:1.4 {I do not...}; 23:0.2 {These spirit messengers...}; 24:1.5 {On the headquarters...}; 108:5.7 {I doubt that...}; 112:7.13 {When once an...}
10. 1:0.3 {The enlightened worlds...}; 26:9.3 {The test of...}; 107:0.3 {God, having commanded...}
11. 101:4 {4. The Limitations Of Revelation}
12. 13:1.10 {7. Ascendington. This...}; 48:6.6 {3. Mind Planners...}; 110:7.8 {During mortal life...}
13. 110:1.6 {Today you are...}

❧

302

Chapter 25

The Glory of Adjuster fusion

The resurrection chamber is by-passed. The process of resurrection is facilitated during the fusion journey to Mansonia.

Status

The status of survival is accredited by the Ancients of Days prior to the Adjuster's return to embrace his waiting child.

Confirmation of the Adjuster's impending actions is conveyed to the Seraphic Guardian by messengers, not by the Adjuster directly, confirming the fact that Adjuster fusion will take place and that it will involve the fusion journey from the native planet to Mansonia. This same Seraphim of Destiny will have taken steps to coordinate the mortal's waiting place.

Between the time of that announcement to her, and the time when the Adjuster comes within the bounds of the native planet upon his return for his child, there occurs the translation of the Seraphic Guardian's personal transcript of the mortal's character, from flesh to Mota. The translation occurs independent of the resurrection chamber, however aspects of the resurrection process have prior preparation.

Preparation

For example, she is joined on Earth by others of her kind including at least one significant Seraphic resurrection hall coordinator and several workers (and observers) who undertake the duplication process of the mortal's mind transcript. She herself also enters a moment of "embrace with divinity" apparently. This is a divinely worshipful moment for her, which is recorded as a fact of her own experience, a qualification. During this time, the record of the mortal which is located in her own "superconsciousness" is conveyed to certain records keepers in Superuniverse liaison with the Orvonton Ancients of Days.

Subsequently, there is some form of liaison that occurs wherein the Seraphic record is perfectly adopted by the Adjuster such that, by the time of departure from the native planet, the Adjuster is in full possession of both records: that of the Seraphim of Destiny and that of his own.

Translation

Actual translation of the mortal, from flesh to Morontia and Mota, via the Adjuster's circuit, involving the two transcripts of the mortal's character, commences immediately the mortal agrees to depart with the Adjuster. By the time the mortal is able to experience the world fading away from view, and Mansonia coming into view, with all of its apparent increase in divinity and its light-based reality, the mortal is fully awake in Mota. The remainder of the journey, without loss of consciousness in the least, is devoted to conditioning the now translated Morontia being to feel at home and a part of the wider universe.

This is achieved in a number of ways as the person increasingly makes contact with Mansonian properties, such as: the person first recognises and feels that they are an heir of heaven, a citizen. They have a full and total right to being in heaven in every sense of the term "right"—that authority comes from God and is unquestioned, righteousness has decreed it so; the person feels no separation between heaven and Earth, they are acutely aware of how dimly lit is consciousness on Earth, but now they understand it from a Mansonian's view: Earth is recognised in a sense to be inseparable from heaven and the heaven of heavens; with a "whole body response" they recognise certain core features about Michael: his fatherhood; his creatorship; his place of being God (that's why Christians recognise that to be out of the body—dead—is to be with God, the God is who is Jesus); his absolute sovereignty over all his universe as far as the eye can see; the immaculate love with which he effortlessly commands from all his universe children and visitors; and his personal interest in the lives and careers of every single individual being within Nebadon, and to certain of his children who have passed beyond Nebadon's shores.

The translation makes the person a warrior for Christ Michael—fearless and adventurous for having partaken of the living bread of life himself. The person's sense of Michael being the life force in the universe in which s/he now lives, is central to all his/her learning, actions, thoughts, desires, plans and destiny. He or she perceives that all life is lived through Michael, his/her own father, and every other being solidly pulsates this same truth. All the person's beliefs about God and matters spiritual dissolve and are replaced with the facts about self, others, the meaning of life and the geography of existence, which have their origin in Michael, in Mother Spirit, and in the Paradise Father. Beyond these sources, these persons of Paradise origin and perfection, nothing can exist and nothing does exist in the mind of the translated Morontian child.

The glory of God

The full sense of the term the *glory* of God, God's *glory*, is suddenly perceived by the person as being his or her own life blood deep within his or her new translated form. The journey which is called Adjuster fusion, is both a translation from one world to the next without passing through the lapse of consciousness caused by death of the mind, and the person's becoming a glorified being—a being who's life force is literally the Glory of God.

At this time, the one time mortal is face to face with the fact that glory is a living force. Glory is the life of the Father himself, the life which is in the Son, his Creator Michael and in his daughter, the Creative Holy Spirit. The act of Adjuster fusion is a direct expression of the Glory of God, in which God is also glorified immensely. Glory *is* worship.

The translated mortal is now made out of the substance of worship: Father and Son are one. And that "one-ness" is glory. Now, honouring the Father, worshipping the Father, is as natural as breathing is to a little baby in a crib. This is why the fused mortal can never descend, can never unfuse...the substance of his or her very existence is the same glory that pervades the whole universe of light and life's perfection. The spirit of the Father, the Thought Adjuster, has gone through a transformation also and it enables him to bond to the evolving human mind. He or she perfectly knows the Father. In his or her own station in the universe, he or she is literally a perfect presence of the Father in that his or her character and substance is of the Father.[1] The glorified one-time mortal will now weigh all things against the truth, which is in Michael and the Glory, which is in the Father. He or she will ask, "Is it of Michael, then it is true. Is it of God my father, then it is Glorious."

This then is a portion of the kind of teaching about universe citizenship that one would expect to meet and understand on the lower mansion worlds which is fulfilled in the course of the Adjuster fusion journey.

❧

Notes

1. John 14:20

Chapter 26

A revelation of Adjuster fusion

When the child of the Divine Father indwelling is considered fit to receive information about the Adjuster fusion experience, the Father will endeavour to communicate the promise and the details of that experience to his mortal child.

It was on just such an occasion that I had the good fortune to receive such a communication from my own Father. With great devotion, he supported me in such a way that I could behold the revelation he had for me, probably in a way not dissimilar to the way Jesus' personalised Adjuster showed him the vision of his heavenly station on the day of his baptism.

"When the returned and now exalted Personalised Adjuster had thus spoken, all was silence. And while the four of them tarried in the water, Jesus, looking up to the near-by Adjuster, prayed: 'My Father who reigns in heaven, hallowed be your name. Your kingdom come! Your will be done on Earth, even as it is in heaven.' When he had prayed, the 'heavens were opened,' and the Son of Man saw the vision, presented by the now Personalised Adjuster, of himself as a Son of God as he was before he came to Earth in the likeness of mortal flesh, and as he would be when the incarnated life should be finished. This heavenly vision was seen only by Jesus.

"It was the voice of the Personalised Adjuster that John and Jesus heard, speaking in behalf of the Universal Father, for the Adjuster is of, and as, the Paradise Father. Throughout the remainder of Jesus' Earth life this Personalised Adjuster was associated with him in all his labours; Jesus was in constant communion with this exalted Adjuster."[1]

There is an aspect of the mind of our Thought Adjuster that enables him to be conscious of all history, past or future, across all dimensions, such that he is able to reveal to us his view of events as they are true and real for us in another time and another place. My father took me through the process of my Adjuster fusion with him. It was glorious. The vision was the reality of an event given into one's spirit and mind from the Thought Adjuster, God the Father. I asked him about this event at the time of writing this book, and he offered the following words to the reader:

"When I lifted up my son, for me it was the real thing. It was an event, which I reckoned as a fact. Since that day, the fact has not changed; the event in time has only drawn closer to materialising. My son does not see it as significant in his life. He thereby affords me optimum liberty to pursue matters as I see fit. He has no anxiety concerning his impending fusion. He does not rush about hither and thither in search of it. If anything, he is apparently so accustomed to the fact of Adjuster fusion since receiving this vision, that he has slowed down his interest in it in order to gain wider experience on his native planet. He will turn quickly, however, when the event can be delayed no more, and we shall in a instant secure our living vow of allegiance to the omniscient will of all light and all life."

Midwayer support

It was in 1991, I was forty-one years old, when I had this vision of my Adjuster fusion experience.

The vision included two Midwayer type people.[2] Now, I've never seen a Midwayer in the flesh; I wouldn't know one if he or she came walking down the street with a red hat on. I call them Midwayer type people because they seemed to be half way between humans and angels just like the Urantia papers described. In the vision, there were two of them. They were not human beings, yet neither were they from off the planet. They were local to the planet. The only characters I know of, who are as material as these people were, are the characters identified in the Urantia papers as Midwayers.

One was an older rather tubby woman. The other was a younger man around mid twenties. They both had something of a distinctly ancient air about them. In spirit, they were young, vibrant and dynamically alive, yet they both had a certain sense of antiquity. It did make me think that they might have been on the Earth 37,000 years ago with Adam and Eve,[3] and 500,000 years ago with Caligastia and the one hundred.[4] Both glowed with some kind of non-human inner radiance in their bodies. Both spoke in another tongue. Both could speak with the Seraphim who would fade in and out of the scene. I could only understand them when they spoke to me in my language.

Whenever they spoke to the Seraphim, or to themselves in their own tongue, I did not understand their speech.

The Seraphim looked like light. When the Adjuster is coming back from Paradise, the Seraphim announce his pending arrival. The Midwayers would converse with the Seraphim, and then translate the information on to me.

I went to the scene in the early evening, it was around 8 p.m. It was springtime, just dusk, and the Seraphim didn't start talking to the Midwayers till about 11pm. They showed themselves only briefly at that time, and the Midwayers communicated that this was the event, that fusion was to take place.

I did not know what they were talking about at first, and thought that they were talking about the older woman in the room. But the younger one pointed out that while the older woman had some benefit to gain from the event, the coming visitor was in fact my own Adjuster and that the event was primarily for me.

I didn't know what her relationship was. She was about to get something, some kind of upliftment. I didn't know it was my fusion as such...not at first.

Heavenly preparations

As the evening wore on, power managers started to arrive and influence the area. Around 3am, it all suddenly kicked into life. The whole place lit up. It was in the countryside near Melbourne, and the sky became very bright. The whole house lit up, inside, brighter than daylight!

Then the Midwayers said it was time to go outside. They instructed me to move away from the house, and we did that.

Then the light grew brighter and brighter. With it came an intensity of wind, and a strange kind of crackling, like the whole reality around the place was suddenly super charged with electricity. The crackling and the wind made a huge roar. Yet, within it all, in the mist of this tremendous cacophony, there was an absolute tranquillity as if the crackling and the wind were of this world, but the peace was of another world—or perhaps the crackling and the wind were of another world, but the peace was of this world. It was most strange yet very reassuring. This went on for twenty minutes or so.

Who was around at the time? The two Midwayers were thirty feet away. No other people were near. The Seraphim and the energy manipulators sort of appeared and disappeared whilst staying in the same place, as if they became slightly more and less materially visible whilst undertaking their duties. The place was totally awesome. It was filled with power; and you knew that God Almighty was coming to Earth!

Father arrives for his child

Then the Midwayers called out that the Father was descending. Suddenly the brilliant white light changed and became saturated with pink. The atmosphere changed from totally awesome power, to absolute love.

The Adjuster descended from about 1000 feet, visible to the human eye. But I think the energy manipulators changed the ability to see, and changed the whole reality around and about to make the fusion experience a mixture of matter and spirit.

Slowly the Adjuster, huge as huge, bigger than a ten story building, gently and with magnificent control, descended for all to see. He embraced their worship, absorbing their love. In return, he beamed his own love, the love of the Paradise Father, out to every heart.

In the midst of this amazing vista, with the incredible roar of the wind and the crackling, and the air so thick with the love of the infinite Father that your body simply became it, you could look up into his glowing face and see the face of God your own father.

The Adjuster looked magnificent. Truly magnificent.

The meaning of life suddenly becomes truly evident in the presence of God. The atheist and the sinner have not a leg to stand on in the presence of such majesty! Their shadowy lives of philosophical ramblings disappear in an instant under the light of God. Their weary souls caught up in the relief of his mighty forgiveness.

Gradually, still descending, he entered my personal space, whilst remaining several metres off the ground. As he descended his enormous size reduced somewhat until he stood before me perhaps ten to twelve feet tall. Here before me was one like he who descended like a dove upon Jesus.[5]

The Midwayers saw the dove-like descension and fell on their faces in adoration for a time. Perfect worship followed.

Paradise and Earth in unison

The link between Paradise and the Adjuster was fully open. The Adjuster was as if in Paradise. Through him I could see the headquarters of the way stations between here and Paradise itself—Edentia; Salvington; Uversa; Ascendington; Divinington; Paradise itself. The Father and huge numbers of the available Adjusters were applauding, through worship, this Adjuster's action of fusing.

Amazingly, the Adjuster was still in touch with Divinington himself. He had no interval in experience between Divinington and his actions on Earth that would bring about the Adjuster fusion with his child. He was fully conscious about being in Divinington and on Earth simultaneously. His joy was magnificent! His joy was unparalleled in all his experience!

Shortly, he stood before me and spoke with me, preparing me for the fusion, the lift off, the transportation process and the arrival in Mansonia, heaven. It was a full briefing, covered in mere moments.

He asked about my own needs: did I want others to see my departure? Was I satisfied? Was my life complete? Was I finished communing with the Midwayers?

When I told him I wanted some friends to see, he arranged for their linkage. It seemed that they would somehow be given a spiritual transcript of these events where they were, so that in spirit they would perceive it all.

I had been pretty rattled with the events so far. They were so thoroughly awesome for me. They were so far beyond my wildest imaginings that I had no adequate human responses to deal with the degree of sheer glory in the atmosphere. I was not scared, just moved to the core of my being—but the core of my being was being contacted with forces that were changing it somehow, obviously in preparation for the fusion.

Ascension

When, I was settled, my Father moved behind me and kind of enclosed me in himself. He just folded me into himself, like a big pink blanket gently wrapping itself around me and drawing me back into its inner depths. Somewhere in the midst of all of this, we two must have become the same substance so to speak; but I had never noticed. He absorbed me into himself and began to dissolve me just a little. He held me firmly, but without pressure, by sheer will. Then, we became more of the same substance. I took on his pinkness and his love. I still had the fleshiness of my human body and my humanness about me, but change was upon us both.

So much was going on. The Midwayers were standing up and gazing at us spellbound almost. The Seraphim were just about jumping out of their skin! (or should I say their light?) The energy manipulators seemed to be totally focussed on a million and one tasks. The whole scene was just not at all like doing meditation with the Dalai Lama! The joint was jumpin' if you know what I mean! It was an exciting time!

Then the lift off occurred.

In an instant we were rising above the Earth. In seconds I could see the lights of Melbourne some thirty miles away, and I felt my materiality dissolve into my Father's Adjusterness. In thirty seconds we were about two or three hundred feet above the Earth. At that point I felt somehow, he plugged in a circuit to my four or five friends and reflected to their Adjusters minds the event as I was experiencing it, from my own view. It seemed that they could have looked out over Melbourne like I was doing.

After that, we moved higher and higher off the Earth, like a red ball of flame, oblivious to the deafening roar of the wind below. Gradually the crackling began subsiding. In a short while the scene below turned dark, the light went out. The wind subsided, the crackling stopped, the scene was as if nothing had happened. I saw the Midwayer-type people for the last time.

Seeing heaven within and above

Then my Father asked me to look up and inward. I did so and I saw a curtain of reality that divided the mortal from the heavenly draw apart. Beyond it I could see Mansonia. At that instant, I could look down and see the Earth, my native planet, and I could look up and inward and see my Mansion World heaven.

Then the level of spirituality increased. I felt my customary physical form for the last time. My view of my native world disappeared, and the Mansion world became brighter, nearer, closer, more real. I had left my home and the grassy fields of my childhood in New Zealand, my young adulthood in Asia and my mature years in Australia. My new home lay before me. There was a moment, as we crossed a gulf between two worlds, when my Father and I were all we had together in the whole universe of universes.

The arrival

When arriving there was a welcome; a huge welcome. The welcome comprised a huge number of people and beings, but the most precious was the welcome from those people who had themselves attained Adjuster fusion on their own native worlds. It seemed that most were not from Urantia but from older and more settled worlds. They were welcoming one of their own kind, so to speak, into a rather unusual group. The fusion graduates of native planets, had something in common with each other. They had all, without exception, participated in the experience of lift off and arrival via their Father's circuit. They had all remained fully conscious during their transition from one world to the next. They had all not participated in death. Perfection had beaten the grave, quite literally. They knew it, and they loved it!

Then there was a welcome from Michael, Gabriel and Mother Spirit.

Michael's absolute and love-filled universe sovereignty and parenthood was perfectly made clear. Together, the Divine Father and Mother of an entire universe stood hand in hand with one of their mortal sons before the welcoming throngs. It was a tremendous celebration. It was like the opening day of the Olympics, times a million!

And oh! The glory of God! That wonderful truthfulness which is God's goodness and magnificence. It filled the place. Worship itself filled the place. The arrival on Mansonia was a glorious event. It was glorious for Michael and Mother Spirit, having raised up a perfect son. It was glorious for my Adjuster and Father, having the reward of his perfect works. It was glorious for me, having attained a level of perfection that was given universe recognition. It was glorious for the fusion group, for they had another who now joined their ranks. It was glorious for the Seraphim, I don't know but they probably had their own kind of celebration going on among their own kind with Mother Spirit.[6] It was glorious for the whole gathering.

Above all this, Michael's wonderfulness shone out. He was a proud father; a glad friend; a loving sovereign; a perfect guide; a loyal and true representation of the Paradise Father and the Eternal Son; It was, in a sense, as much his day as it was my Adjuster's and my day.

What a wonderful event this Adjuster Fusion is.

This ends my narrative. The vision of those events back in 1991, plus the words spoken to me on Israel's Mount Hermon in 1996, plus considerable other experiences with my Father have long confirmed my potential fusion, and I have never had a doubt about it since. With all my love, dear reader, I wish you well in your own journey into the perfection that is Adjuster fusion.

❦

Notes

1. 136:2.4-5 {When the returned ...}
2. 77:9.19 {Midwayers are the ...}
3. 74:2.5 {Soon after their...}
4. 77:0.2 {On Urantia there...}
5. 136:2.3 {Ordinarily, when a...}
6. 26:1.4 {3. The Ministering Spirits...}

❦

Chapter 27

Living with Adjuster fusion

In my view, we people in the world are far from the stage of Adjuster fusion where the Father will whisk us off the planet like he did with Elijah.[1]

The rapture isn't going to happen

An aside here is that I don't believe the Christian idea of the rapture of the Church, which is like the Adjuster fusion of every Christian simultaneously, regardless of their fusion capacity. The rapture is a mistaken idea based upon speculations about the manner of Jesus Christ's Second Coming to Earth and the fact that Adjuster fusion can transport a person to heaven bi-passing physical death.

Raising up fusion candidates

As we turn from the 1900's into the year 2000, it appears to me that there is considerable support being given to the readers of the Urantia papers. The bulk of the superhuman effort which is at present directed toward this goal of Adjuster fusion among Urantia papers readers, aims to raise up individuals who will qualify as fusion candidates.

These individuals will have sufficient grasp of the spirituality within the Urantia papers, in that they will have a living relationship with the universe and infinite Parents.

They will also have sufficient intellectual capacity as leaders, to translate and downstep that spirituality to a place where it becomes reachable by those with less spiritual grasp of things and less intellectual ability. In this way that there can become a living Jacob's ladder[2] from the least of us to the greatest of us— heaven touching Earth and Earth touching heaven.

Despite the increased attention given to the topic on the internet mail lists as readers increasingly distil the Urantia papers for their ultimate value in human life, I don't think the world is rushing headlong like a parade of lemmings over the cliff of fusion with one's Adjuster.

Adjuster fusion is simple enough in theory, but there is the practicum of the endless repetitious practice of doing solely God's will in ever increasingly complex decision-making and political situations, on levels in which the highest global ideals of spiritual expertise are involved out there in the market place where God's will is fully tested.

Fusion capability

When one approaches the fusion capability, long after much practice has ensued and one's "candidacy" has been announced and recorded in the universe records, the Father's will is found to reside within one's own will. So great is the organic transformation of mind that the practice of relating to the human and the Adjuster as two separate beings loses all value except in concept alone. Within this will, now made one, neither the mortal nor the Father is dominant, and still free will remains.

This is important to notice in one's speculation on these matters. The condition is no longer one of a mortal subservient to the dominant Father. No. Quite the opposite. The son of God has been so intensely practised in such a diversity of complex and critical situations that in a sense "all power in heaven and Earth" is given over to him or her.

Decision making

The individual mortal who is close to fusion can easily come to a decision that is fully within the Father's will. That decision can come about by simply making a perfect decision.

Are you familiar with making the perfect decision? If not, let it be your study. It is delightful to make perfect decisions...all the clamber of right and wrong, mortal and divine, winner or loser disappears under the sovereignty of perfection.

Such decisions are not hard to make. No consultation is required in the sense that one divides oneself into mortal mind and Father's mind to carry out some kind of a debate over the matter in question. It is simply a matter that a decision is made when the mind is unified in its human and divine nature.

A lesser way of stating this kind of decision making process, is that one seeks out and finds the Father's will within his or her own will and decides on that. But this is not as "fusion-based" as the former process.

It's OK to stick around a while

It is nothing at all, the simplest thing, to recognise that the

Father has no objection to staying around on the planet and foregoing fusion. I know from experience that it makes no difference whether one achieves Adjuster fusion here or somewhere else...it's always going to be right here within the Father's will which is within my own will, one will. Perfection doesn't choose to rush off anywhere, it absolutely cherishes to worship and exercise the existing perfection wherever it is here and now. Adjuster fusion is not an escape technique.

It is my hope, and I have seen it be so to some extent in the forecasts for the next few hundred years on Earth, that an increasing number of people will be prompted to consider sticking around to help the planet, and will vote "Yes" on that prompt. It is not far off to reckon that the mighty men and women of old who came from Jerusem and set up camp in Dalamatia with the Planetary Prince[3] were little different from the Urantia mortals of our generation who can exercise fusion mindedness. Oh sure, they had the mansion world experience of heavenly vistas and super human personalities, but we still have our Thought Adjusters.[4]

But nothing that is on the mansion worlds up to fusion level, cannot be delivered into the willing mortal here on Earth. As we approach the age of Light and Life, there will be little difference between the mortals of Urantia and the mortals of Mansonia. Michael's circuit will pervade us all, enhancing us in a glorious fashion to become fusion minded all the more easily.

This planet doesn't need more sages and gurus and martyrs. This planet is desperately in need of spiritually robust and qualified managers. These are people who have the capacity to come to fusion-minded conclusions, to lay plans for executives who can execute decisions with fusion-minded integrity. We don't need our spiritual experts to vacate the planet, we need the spirit drain to stop and the planet's spiritual pool to be replenished, sustained, nurtured, magnified, lifted up, multiplied and enriched.

Global fostering of Adjuster fusion candidates

One way of approaching this obvious need is to imagine, if you will, that every country in the world—what are there

190?—has 6 fusion minded people who each know each other. Let your spirit savour for a moment what those men and women might be able to create: surely their fruit would be extraordinary things for God!

Now imagine yourself taking on the mission of establishing those 6 persons in the country of your choice. What would they need? What would you need to achieve that mission? They're there all right, right now, waiting for someone like you to raise them up and connect them. You are the answer to someone's prayer, right now, today, somewhere on this Earth. Imagine what the world would be like in twenty years time, 2020, having raised up 190x6 fusion minded people who are Urantia papers literate and responsive. What a wonderful mission you could take on.

Say yes

The hope in the mortal heart, to vacate the planet as early as possible, is the signal of a heart and soul that is defeated by the planet. Adjuster fusion mindedness, however, is the heart and mind and soul who lives in a planet-overcoming reality for whom living in this their native world or living in the mansion worlds is little different.

I believe that it would certainly be Andon and Fonta's wish, the wish of Van and Amadon, the wish of Adamson and Ratta, the wish of Machiventa Melchizedek, the wishes of Paul and John and James and Matthew and Mark and the wish of the 24 Counselors, that Urantia be populated with a mighty team of fusion-minded mortals who live in such divine victory and such compassion and mercy for their fellows that they will make vows to prolong their care for this world's development under Michael's authority for as long as they possibly can.

I ask you to say yes, be among them, and continue the magnificent works of these wonderful predecessors here on our native planet. And do all this to the glory of Michael and our Mother Spirit and our Paradise Father and the ascension scheme, and to the eternal condemnation of the rebellion that has torn our world apart like an infant from its mother's breast.

I ask you to say yes to being among those who will be raised up to restore the wrongs done in the world; to being a part of the growth and atonement team, just as Michael atones through the power of his Spirit of Truth.[5]

I ask you to say yes to speedily being brought into alignment for fusion mindedness so that you can join the ranks of Van the Steadfast and Amadon and work for the victory of Christ Michael over this world and his children.

I ask you to say yes to giving yourself a universe destiny that begins right here on your native planet, the magnificent mortal home world of the Michael of this local universe.

And, of putting in place a legacy for your children's children[6] so that they will prosper in their own destiny of Adjuster fusion and also their contribution to uplifting the world through the plans of the Most Highs.[7]

❦

Notes

1. 2 Kings 2:11
2. Genesis 28:12
3. 77:3.1
4. 66:4.5
5. 120:2.3 {3. When you have...}
6. Deuteronomy 6:1-2
7. 114:7.6 {On many worlds...}; 134:5.4 {This rule of...}

❦

Chapter 28

Death and resurrection

This is the story of how God my Father foresaw my mortal father's death, and in his great compassion for me, arranged for me to go to him before his last breath.

The musician

Jack Lindley Crickett was a great musician. He began playing Dixieland and Swing when he was just fourteen years old. His three brothers had a band. One Wednesday, Ivan, the eldest, came into the family piano room where he was playing, plonked some music in front of young Jack and asked:

"Can you play that?"

Jack told me years later that looked it over, banged out a couple of notes, then went through a few bars, looked up smilingly and said, "Yes," and he got the job. Apparently the piano player was sick and they needed someone to fill in at the dance on Saturday night, way back in 1932.

His brothers were all much older than he was. They'd played Dixieland for almost as long as he could recall and they were pretty good. His brothers Harold and Guy had been asked to join the Benny Goodman band on a world tour.

Jack loved playing music. He loved that as much as he loved Betty, his childhood sweetheart. He was a simple country kid, with a whole lot of talent and a heart full of that quiet country kind of love. I loved him dearly, although I grew up with the firm conviction that he never should have married my Mum, Alison, after Betty's death when he came back from the war. He led an estranged life in our house, much of the time being spent either at work or out in the back shed with his ham radio set, talking to friends he'd met during the war who'd gone on home to their own lands. I never really knew the man. I felt befriended but I never felt loved by him. I only ever twice received his acknowledgement. I only ever hugged him once, late in his life, and that was like embracing a power pole—he just wasn't a touchy feely kind of fellow. I grew up wondering what it was that he hung around the marriage for, and I asked him that question one-day. His answer was, "Oh, I dunno, you just do." These days of course, you just don't. But then, growing up in the fifties, it was not the done thing to divorce. Their divorce didn't happen until the seventies, when it was more acceptable, in the days of single parenthood, when Thought Adjusters were given only half the resources to work with their little mortal wards. This story starts when Jack had a stroke.

The stroke

The phone rang while I was at work in the heroin detox in Melbourne. It was Jack's wife Jean, a woman with whom I didn't have a whole lot in common. She needed urgent help. Jack had had a stroke. Yes he was alive, but he was in hospital twenty miles from home and the doctors wanted to keep him there for two years. He would die there if left to their resources, she felt. Could I come over and help, was her plea.

On the next day I flew over from Australia to Auckland. I stayed with my brother David, who was then studying to be an anaesthetist in Auckland. He advised me that the prognosis was dreadful, and that Dad will be hospitalised for at least two years before they'll see any hope of recovery. I didn't want to accept that kind of a statement, so I just deflected it and kept my attention on God's version of the situation.

On the next day I went to Dad's home, spoke with his wife and then visited him in hospital. David was right in a way, he did look dreadful. Here was this little old man, curled up in a hospital bed, the mere shadow of everything he had ever been, and the medical people around him had little to offer by way of remedy. It was pretty hopeless.

Jack communicated to me that he really wanted to be at home. He figured that if he was going to be miserable and neglected, he could do that in the comfort of his own bed, with his cat. I went in advocating for him. Negotiations with the medical authorities of that hospital were predictably horrible and argumentative, but eventually they agreed to release him into my care. I swiftly bundled him up and dumped in the front seat of his car, rolled him a smoke and scooted off down the road for Raglan with a feeling of escape from the "cuckoo's nest".

When we arrived home, he went to bed, his cat joined him, and his wife fluffed around in her own way as she dealt with the fact of his being an invalid now. I let God lead me into his quietness, to pray, to appeal for Jack's healing. And so, when the time came, I prayed.

Prayer for recovery

The next day, on my fourth day in New Zealand, at a certain moment I had the distinct impression that angels were telling me that it was going to be all right, that Jack would recover.

On the sixth day, he awoke in the morning, called us into his room and proceeded to speak normally and wave his arms and legs around to show us that the paralysis had gone and that he was well. We all really were relieved and thrilled for him. I took time away from them to thank my God and those angels.

That same morning, my brother phoned from Auckland, inquiring as to Dad's welfare. The conversation was pretty unusual:

"How's your father Robert, pretty grim isn't it?"

"No, he's fine now. He's at home and doing much better."

"What do you mean he's at home. Did you bring him home?" I could feel David's irritation welling up, after all, he *is* the doctor isn't he?

"Yes he is at home. I persuaded the hospital to release him into my care."

"Well, how is he? He'd be pretty bloody useless at home wouldn't he? He's paralysed from head to foot, and way too much trouble for that wife of his to manage."

"Hang on, I'll get him for you David."

"What do you mean by 'get him'…have you hooked up the phone to his bedside?"

"No. He'll come to the phone. Hang on, I'll call him."

"What do you mean 'call him'? Can he walk? Can he talk? What's going on?" His being out of the loop was starting to raise his heckles I thought.

"Yeah, he's doing fine. I prayed. God's working on him. He's doing fine. Hang on David, I'll get him…Hey Dad…David's on the line from Auckland."

And Dad called back, "OK Rob, tell him I'll be right there," and he slipped on his dressing gown and slippers, came on down the hall to the only phone in the house and took over the conversation.

David was speechless. This healing defied everything he stood for.

A few days later, I went back up to Auckland to fly back to Melbourne. I stayed with David. We barely spoke about the matter, but Dad went on to live very well.

Jack had died and came back

Jack shared with me that when he had had this stroke, he had died and that the ambulance men had brought him back from death. He looked at me very tenderly and said, "You know Rob, death's nothing. It's not painful. It's very pleasurable in fact. And when you're there, it's just nothing, you're just there. There isn't any place you go to, like another world, you're just somewhere that isn't here. It's all very nice really. I have no more fear of death. It is like I have conquered the world and all its ways."

I smiled, nodded, and let him enjoy his discovery. I didn't say anything to him, but what he described sounded more to me like the kind of death Lazarus would have had. It wasn't a real death. Oh Lazarus was dead all right, the Bible tells us that Lazarus "stinketh."[1] But the Urantia papers tell us that Jesus' Personalised Thought Adjuster ordered the Thought Adjuster of Lazarus to not vacate the planet, to wait.[2] Then, on the fourth day after Lazarus' death, Jesus called that man out of death and he arose from the tomb.[3] Lazarus, like Dad, hadn't been anywhere but dead. They hadn't crossed to the Mansion worlds and the resurrection chambers of the Seraphim. Their Thought Adjusters hadn't departed for Paradise. Dad's Thought Adjuster had not left this world. There was a glory to be had, and he claimed it in Jack's healing. Dad might thank the ambulance fellows for his life, but he couldn't but give God the glory for his healing. Dad's actual death was some years away.

The will of God

As I said, Dad and I lived pretty estranged kinds of lives. Occasionally I'd phone him, I'd never write. One Saturday morning in Melbourne I was sitting out on the patio of my home and my Father's presence came over me. He didn't say a word to me. My attention went to New Zealand and onto my mortal father. I felt my Father's will pressing in on me to make a statement, to enact a decree of divine will.

As I thought about my mortal father, I realised that at some stage he would die. I thought about that and it was a problem for me. I didn't want to go to his funeral, but I did want to say good bye to him. How could I achieve that? If he had a stroke, he'd be dead and gone before you could say boo. Then, in an instant, I had it.

The will of your Father lets you focus onto an object or a person or an event in time and it gives you command over that thing. Look around you right now, do you see something, a cup perhaps. To make a decree in the will of God is like looking at that cup whilst you are filled with a force that is deeper than the cup's very Earthly foundations, and then you tell that cup what is going to happen.

As I looked on Jack, in Spirit, I said my words aloud:

"Jack you will not die until I kiss you on the cheek and say my farewell. At that time, you are released to die and not before."

I have never given it much thought, but I think that this command was made possible for me after a liaison between Jack's and my Thought Adjusters. Perhaps his Adjuster thought it was a nice gift to me to end Dad's life. Perhaps Dad had one day been told by his Adjuster that he would die soon, and Dad gave rise to the thought that he would have liked to see me before going. Whatever it was, I know it was a gift, and I appreciated it.

The last stroke

More than a year later I received the phone call to tell me that Jack had had a stroke and he was in hospital and that it was highly likely that he would die any hour now. I went to prayer, as is my custom, and my Father reminded me of the decree we had established before, involving the kiss on the cheek and Dad's detention on this world before I farewelled him.

"What of his Adjuster?" I asked my Father.

"He has already left your father's mind," came the gentle reply. "Whilst he has not yet left the precincts of this world, he is ready for his Paradise journey."

"What is there of my father then Father?"

"What remains is the physical organism, maintained under the biological mechanisms of life support, awaiting the complete release of physical death."

"Is my farewell holding him here?"

"Mostly," he replied.

It was a strange thing for me. I had never been in this kind of situation before. This was an unusual kind of thing to be doing with one's God, and yet it was so very right and authoritative: God's hand was definitely upon it.

So it was that I flew over to New Zealand. To another town and another hospital this time, for he and his wife had moved to the town in which my sister Mary lived with her husband and two boys—before they too later separated.

In Dannevirke

I immediately went to his room. There he lay with an oxygen tube in his nose, this old, old man. Thin; frail; exhausted. The most obvious feature about Jack was his breathing. He couldn't catch his breath. He would laboriously breath in and out with not a single break in between. Sitting with him in vigil all through that night meant nothing. My Father was right; there was no spirit in his mind. As I sat looking at him all night, it was like sitting out on an open field in Oklahoma under the full moon, peacefully gazing on one of those oil pumps rocking back and forward in its mindless action.

I tried speaking to his Thought Adjuster, but all I noticed was that my plea was diverted out to some where in the Mansion worlds and then back to my own Father.

Everything in my spirit told me that there was no recovery for Jack. His death was his only next step. I realised that, given the purely mechanical way he was breathing, his death could be weeks if not months away. I appealed to my Father, saying that I had decided to bid my farewell and that he could arrange the circumstances when it suited him.

The next day I spent at Mary's house. I napped a bit, met the kids and her husband for the first time, and briefly got to know their lifestyle. By evening, I knew that I would farewell my mortal father on the next day.

That evening was spent light heartedly. I shared with Mary my convictions that Dad's death was immanent, but unable to be timed, and that seeing as how she and Jack's wife seemed to have things pretty much under control, I would go back to Auckland and then Melbourne the next day. That was fine with her.

Goodbye Dad

On the next day, around 1pm, I visited the hospital. Dad was exactly as he had been on the day I arrived, still mechanically sucking air in and blowing it out with tedious monotony, still unable to catch his breath, never moving, never flinching, never blinking, just lying on his side puffing.

After a few minutes, I disengaged conversation from my sister and Jack's wife, and let my Father's anointed presence mingle with my mind. In a moment it was there, that deeply personal affection which has a sincerity to it that is as deep as space itself.

Once I was consciously sharing my Father's mind, I was identified with his will. Suddenly it was as if Jack and I were the only mortals on Earth. For some unknown reason, as I stepped forward to be with my Dad, the others present hastily vacated the room and fussed over some flowers or vases or such like in the corridor. I was alone in the room with him.

Tears trickled down my cheek. Not out of grief. I was not grieving, for his death was a thing already settled within me. No, I was sad that we had never had more of each other. I was sad for him, and his lost love Betty, and his stifled life with my mum, Alison.

I looked into the face of this man that I loved the most and the longest. I recalled the days of my youth, the sights and sounds of his music, the things we had done together, the only two conversations we had ever had that resembled anything to do with the meaning of life. I felt proud for him as I recalled how he was the first person in New Zealand to own a television set. He'd built it himself, and we used to watch the first broadcasts that wafted across the Tasman Sea from Sydney in the fifties before New Zealand had its own channels. He had remarkable talent.

Then a peaceful satisfaction welled up within me. It was complete. I was farewelling my own Dad. I ran my fingers through his soft grey hair. There was nothing left to do. We had time, but nothing to do in it. As absent as he had been throughout most of my life, he was in his death also.

I leaned over and kissed him on his right cheek. "Goodbye

Dad," I said. And with those words, he suddenly made as if to rise up from the bed. He mumbled and blinked a lot. Then he settled back down and continued his robotic out-of-breath puffing just like before.

What was it that rose up? I have no idea. I received it as his goodbye.

Jack died

I was in Auckland when my sister Mary rang. "He died about four hours after you left," she said. "I just wanted you to know that I tried calling you yesterday but I couldn't track you down. We'll look after the funeral and everything." I knew there wasn't going to be a will. There was only his piano, and he'd willed it to me. Some years later when his wife finally let go of it, I gave the piano to the grand daughter of Jack's favourite cousin, Joyce McKee, so that his love would live on his family.

And went to heaven

It was while I waited for my flight in the lounge of the Auckland Airport to return to Melbourne that the glory of God would show itself in all this. My Father made his presence feel very close to me. "I have a surprise for you," were his words. He conveyed them with a velvet-like expression that appeared to be a mix of both comfort for the bereaved and like a cat on a hot tin roof jumping out of his skin with excitement.

"You can keep it open for as long as you wish. You can close it any time you wish. You can focus in and out as much as you like. It is my gift to you Rob."

Then he literally peeled back the airport scene in front of me and showed me a vision of the mansion world resurrection halls. He brought my attention to a cluster of angelic looking forms, hovering around a kind of operating table. "This one is your father," he serenely said. "This is his day of resurrection in Mansonia. Enjoy, even for the days to come, for the process will take three of our days."

Then he fell into silence as my entire spirit came alive with the astonishment and sheer exhilaration of watching this, my very own father, being literally reconstructed in heaven. Here before my eyes was the resurrection process itself, as it occurs for everyone who journeys to that heavenly shore.

The bearer of amazing gifts

What a gift!

What an amazing Father I have! To do this for me. Wow! I was truly staggered at his generosity. Over the next couple of days, my mind would from time to time imagine all the red tape he would have gone through to set this up for me, and how precious the giving of this gift was for him.

Can you imagine dear reader, the amazing depth of love he had for us in giving his Son Jesus? Can you, dear one, appreciate such a love? Can you imagine what kind of a gift your own Father would like to give you right now, dear one?

I wandered onto the plane in a daze. I have almost no memory of the flight; my attention was fixed on the extraordinary events going on in heaven.

Resurrection

I watched these angels working. After some time they had a cocoon-like form made out of something like luminous white living fibres. It was about the size of a football. As they worked it gradually became longer and wider and much more complicated. Every now and then, it would be as if a whole new dimension of his personality and character would be added, like a ball of different wool being wrapped around the elliptical cocoon of this emerging life form. This process went on for hours. All around these angels were other groups, as far as the eye could see through the building, doing exactly the same kinds of thing. Hundreds of cocoons were being woven into shape, as the dead of one world were being resurrected in another and eternal one.

The vision was in full living colour, the kind that has a heavenly life to it. I was not permitted to speak to anyone that I could see, nor to send a message, nor to seek to receive a message. Early on in the procedure, I was addressed briefly by one of the angels who simply acknowledged, by looking directly at me, the fact that I was witnessing her team's work and that it was my mortal father.

The Seraphim who contained my father's character records,[4] and whose blueprint for his on going life was being slowly transferred into this new Morontian form, stood out from among the two or three other workers present. What was pronounced about her was that she seemed to be filled with life far exceeding her counterparts, and that she was clearly not wholly present in the room. She was in communion with something or someone else all the time. I could sense that her consciousness was extremely elevated.

From time to time, other angels would literally appear beside the table. Occasionally, those present would simply dissolve out of the scene. There was a regular coming and going of all but about three of them, the Seraphim of Destiny from whose being Dad's life was being restored, a primary maker of the fibre-like embryonic form, and an assistant.

By the end of the first day, as I sat out in the garden of my home in Melbourne, still continuing to watch this unbroken transmission of heavenly vision, the football sized cocoon had been increased to about the height of a twelve-year-old child. Still, though, there was no self-consciousness within it. I was amazed at the intricacy with which this process was undertaken.

The awakening

All through the night the process continued. I awoke about four or five times and looked straight into the scene again. The form was becoming bigger and bigger. It was around five the next morning that my Father alerted me.

"Watch," he said. "The awakening."

In a few moments I saw the first flickerings of intelligence within this fibrous cocoon. A flood of joyous tears just leapt out of my eyes. My heart exploded in a sea of feelings. I could hardly contain myself. I dashed into my bedroom to awaken Mary and tell her that I had just seen Dad's first signs of Morontian consciousness, but I had a moment of second thoughts for which she later thanked me, and I returned to my solitude to savour the events alone.

Over the next few hours the consciousness grew. I could identify a person now. The fibrous form was alive in the Holy Spirit, assuredly, but now deep within it there was a person. All through this second day, the cocoon was added to, and the personality consciousness within it became larger and brighter.

By the end of day, Dad was like a newborn baby. I could identify that he was conscious of others, but it was as if he was a baby. He had no memory. No history. No future. No bearings. He simply was. And still, the weaving of these extraordinary fibres of life continued, ever deeper, broader higher and vital.

As I watched the events from time to time throughout the night of the second day, his changes were continuing in the same vein as for the day. He grew in consciousness.

Around midnight, I saw a new group of angels appear. They began communicating to him, by moving in and out of him. They would metamorphose themselves to become like the fibrous material forming his cocoon like form, and they would enter into it, their attention going deeply into his emerging consciousness, awakening him, perhaps seeding what was already his, perhaps planting what was Morontian for him, language and perceptual keys perhaps. Within a few hours, Dad could perceive enough of what was in his environment. The angels then gently coaxed him off the table and into an upright position.

They continued working, adding different kinds of fibres, linking him to the consciousness of other kinds of angels and teaching sons of various forms who would barely make themselves visible during the connecting process. One such character stood out. He seemed like a supervisor or some kind. It was as if Dad was being connected in to the personalities of Mansonia's administration through these beings.

The majestic return

Around seven in the morning of the third day, Dad's consciousness seemed to be fully installed and prepared. The most spectacular event occurred.

It was as if the lights came on, in what was already a brilliantly illuminated sphere of operation. There was an echo from some distant and much greater dimension of spirituality. I could barely make out what was in the atmosphere, but it was like millions of heralds were hovering in the sky all around the resurrection halls. They were only partly visible to me, as if they were part way into the Morontian sphere and part way in some other and non-Morontian spirit domain. The place filled with celestial music, and I was filled with a sense of awe, of impending arrival, and an arrival of utmost majesty.

Suddenly, there burst onto the scene brilliant rosy glows of hundreds of Thought Adjusters as they descended out of thin air so to speak. They just burst into reality, like fireworks a million fold grander and brighter and bolder. The scene was simply magnificent to behold. To see these magnificent beings, the Paradise Father in fragments, come to claim his mortal child. Oh what a glory! Everywhere I looked, they were bursting forth between these partly visible Heralds. What can I say about such beings? Their glory is so profound! Their purpose is so unstoppable! Their aim is so direct! They have but a single thought, "I will that my son lives!" And all who are in the heaven of heavens turn and obey, rejoicing with great celebration to be a part of the Father's will.

In an instant they are with their child, gazing upon them with a love of such magnificence that mortal hearts could not sustain it and live almost.

I looked at my one time mortal father, now barely recognisable to me as he is bathed in the glory of his Divine Father. They were speaking the one to the other, an eternal Father and his little baby son, Jack, my Dad.

Given such contact with both this world and the next, Paul's words are given even added power:

> "When this perishable body puts on imperishability, and this mortal body puts on immortality, then the saying that is written will be fulfilled: 'Death has been swallowed up in victory.' Where, O death, is your victory? Where, O death, is your sting?"[5]

Dad's Adjuster didn't look at me, or any one else for that matter. His entire attention was on his son, with a devotion that was absolute. Nothing intruded upon his time with his son.

After a while, the glorious Heralds ceased to be so visible in the Morontian skies and they twinkled back to from wherever they came.

Re-indwelling

One by one, the Thought Adjusters were entering into the very minds and beings of their sons, again to occupy the position of God in man,[6] so to speak. I watched as, in a matter of a minute, Dad's Thought Adjuster entered into the Morontia form of my one time Earthly father. It was a poignant moment. Here was the very being who had been God to the father of my boyhood, who had doubtless helped my own Father and me throughout my life. Now he was disappearing from view into the upper levels of the backroom thinking of this newly emerged Morontian being who was once Jack Lindley Crickett, the best darn Dixieland musician you'd ever want to meet. And the resurrection of my father was all but complete. Goodbye Dad. So long ZL1DY, as he was on the ham radio—and the television whiz-kid of New Zealand.

I popped a look in from time to time over the next day or so. Somewhere in the fifth day, my Dad's second day in heaven, I told my Father that he could turn it off now. He did. Mary, my little sister, rang from New Zealand to tell me that he'd been cremated, and that they'd bought a rose bush for the Dannevirke Hospital and scattered his ashes around it, as he would have wanted. Jack just adored roses. She had a little cry, and I told her, "It's all right, he's in heaven." And she said, "Yeah, I know. I hope so." And I replied again, "Trust me, I know. He's in heaven."

The assurance of Adjuster communion

After living with your Thought Adjuster for a while, you stop dreaming about the things of heaven and worrying whether or not you're going to get there. You stop doing meditation practices to quieten your mind, and your interest in resolving complex relationship issues just fizzles out.

After an experience like this, where you witness your Dad getting reborn in heaven, you find yourself living in two worlds that have no barrier. You live with facts that are not common to the average person's perspective on life. You know that heaven and Earth are not different, not really, not to the God-knowing son of God.

Your spiritual life becomes no longer a matter of practices and rituals, beliefs and theories. The son of God has a spiritual life in which he or she is observing the goings on in heaven, and participating in them in some deeply personal way.

Such, inevitably, is the will of God.[7] When once you participate in the things of heaven, your entire religious outlook changes. The theologies of the men and women of the world's religions, who have never touched heaven personally, are little more than children's chalk drawings on the footpath—and the rains are coming very soon.

One day when I was a monk, about ten years previously, my Father said to me:

"My son, would you be a monk if you were dead?"

I thought deeply about his question and replied:

"No Father, I would not."

"Why not?" came his reply.

"Well my Father, I would not need to be a monk, for I would have found you."

"What would you do?" he said.

My vision spread out across all the worlds that I had read about in the Urantia papers and I replied:

"Why, I would go around all the worlds to help out their peoples, bringing them your grace and mercies, helping them to know you and to grow up in you."

That was all he needed to know, and four days later my entire life changed. I arrived in Melbourne Australia, standing in my floppy grey Chinese Buddhist robes, clutching my copy of the Urantia papers and less than a dollar. I was fully caught up in the inevitability of the will of God that I chose to do.

Fathers

Most people on Earth do not live across these two worlds, they are isolated in one—if only because they believe themselves so to be. So much of the world's fear is driven by the lack of knowledge about what lies beyond mortal death. As I look around the world at the fathers in this world of ours, I am gently reminded that just such a divine Father dwells in the mind of each of them.[8]

Some fathers are good. Some a bad. Some kill their children. Some have sex with their children. Some are violent drunks and drug addicts and they bash and neglect their children. Some betray their children's mothers. Some love God and some detest all things good. Some bury themselves in their concerns over money, as if to disguise their wretched poverty. Some father's are absolutely magnificent. In each of them, there resides the Father that came from Paradise to lead him home.

What was your father like? Were you hurt by him? Do you bear the scars of his difficulties and burdens in your heart and on your body?

One day, each father will face the judgement of the Ancients of Days[9] and may pass on to the Mansion World resurrection halls, as did Jack Lindley Crickett.

In the light of the presence of such a glorious Divine Father who dwells inside your own mortal father, there is great hope that one day you will behold him in a different light from the one in which you were wounded. Given time under the Father's influence, your father will take on the glory befitting a true son of God.

The hope of sonship is in the life and the words of Jesus. On the night that he was betrayed, he instructed his disciples. He spoke of a time when he would not be physically present with them on Earth, but present in spirit within their hearts and minds. He said:

"I am telling you these things while I am still with you that you may be the better prepared to endure those trials which are even now right upon us. And when this new day comes, you will be indwelt by the Son as well as by the Father. And these gifts of heaven will ever work the one with the other even as the Father and I have wrought on Earth and before your very eyes as one person, the Son of Man. And this spirit friend will bring to your remembrance everything I have taught you."[10]

Look upon your own mortal father, dear reader, with the knowledge that in him resides one of those mighty Thought Adjusters, and even the Spirit of Jesus Christ himself. Let the Father's forgiveness be in your heart, and as your heart, and let that forgiveness create a bridge of divine optimism between you and your own mortal father. One day, you each shall journey where my own father has journeyed, free of the burdens of this world. What a great and powerful hope there is in these magnificent Thought Adjusters who seek our sonship and enduring loyalty.

Loving the unlovable

The question does come up for us, how to love a person, like the parent who has abused us, and love them in a way that really makes a difference. Sonship has taught me how to love like Jesus loved.

How I dealt with the problem of bringing love to someone I'd rather have seen "fry in hell" so to speak, was several fold. My manner was to:

- ❏ love the God who loves that person;
- ❏ love the possibility of their opening up to God at some stage, even if that might occur in the mansion worlds long after they're dead and gone from here;
- ❏ love the effort their Thought Adjuster puts into their survival;
- ❏ love the endless service of their supervising seraphim;
- ❏ love Michael for his heart break over all the children who struggle with their mortal limitations;
- ❏ love Michael and Mother Spirit for their experience of all their millions of children who fail to survive;
- ❏ love the Father in Paradise for his experience of suffering the failure to survive of so very many of his personality wards.

When I do this, I find that my love for the person was anchored in those divine beings I loved the most, and it helped me immensely. By anchoring my own love, tethering it to the unshakeable rock, it freed me up to all the better be there for the person I sought to love.

It may surprise you to know that Jesus put the kingdom's kind of love before all else—before family, friends, business, even his life.[11] He also walked past those people who were not responsive to the kingdom's kind of love.[12] Sometimes, regrettably, we must walk on by.

To you, dear reader, if you are a parent, remember the great Father who resides in you, and be courteous and courageous to the young children you have in your care, for they are indwelt by magnificent beings who are so very worthy of our respect, even our worship.

Move on, in our Parent's love

I invite you to lay your troubles and burdens down at the feet of your own Father. Receive his forgiveness with a willing and an eager heart, and bring your children into the knowledge of him. Seek from him his wisdom for your situation with your children. One day, they too will say, "Goodbye Dad" or "Goodbye Mum", as have I.

One day, regardless of what you have attained in the world

here on Earth, you will be that little bundle of sparkling fibres in a resurrection chamber of Mansion World number one. A little bundle who has been immaculately saved by grace and who is now being brought into newness of life by the angels of the Holy Spirit and Christ Michael, through the perfect will of the infinite Paradise Father.

One day, you will be standing somewhere completely new to you, basking in the radiance of the angels' tender care for you. Totally unannounced, the Superangelic Heralds will sound their gorgeous call, the heavens will burst apart as your own Paradise Father hurtles into your presence from some far off land of perfection, and you will behold your Father as did Jesus Christ on the day of his baptism in the Jordan.

Oh how preciously you are loved. Oh how perfectly your Michael has prepared the heavenly home for you:

> "In my Father's house there are many dwelling places. If it were not so, would I have told you that I go to prepare a place for you? And if I go and prepare a place for you, I will come again and will take you to myself, so that where I am, there you may be also. And you know the way to the place where I am going."[13]

One of my best friends, Bill, lost his son unexpectedly to a heroin overdose at the age of 21. I heard Steve Brock tell Benny Hinn once, that losing one's child is surely the greatest loss the human can ever experience. All that I have said regarding one's father, obviously applies to one's child too.

If we give our pain and confusion and anger and guilt over to our Father, he *will* move us beyond it and bring us to a place where we can live with it and have it not crush us but strengthen and purify us, "so that where I am, there you may be also."

This was certainly true for my friend Bill too. Last year in the Church of Christ Michael, we held a memorial service for his son Brad who had died suddenly and expectedly. Many months later, on the very day that he buried this son's ashes, his first son phoned and introduced himself to Bill. These two had never met, because the boy's mother had separated from Bill while they were still courting. She went her own way while she was pregnant with the boy who now, at thirty-five, and with a ten year-old son of his own, following the death of his mother, wanted to meet his father.

New life dawns in the most remarkable and unexpected ways. The seed must have been sown, of course: but its flowering can be most extraordinary.

❧

Notes

1. John 11:39 KJV
2. 168:1.3 {And now we...}
3. John 11:43
4. 49:6.4 {1. Mortals of the...}
5. 1 Corinthians 15:54-55
6. John 13:31
7. 181:1.8 {A certain amount...}
8. 1:2.5 {Those who know...}; 1:3.6 {In the universes...}; 107:0.3 {God, having commanded...}
9. 110:7.10 {During the making...}; 18:3.7 {In power, cope...}
10. 180:4.3 {I am telling...}
11. 140:8.4 {The family occupied...}
12. 130:8.4 {At last they...}
13. John 14:2-4

❧

Chapter 29

Sonship with God knows no reincarnation

According to my own experience, I find than when a person is in the presence of their Michael—in our case Michael of Nebadon—all questions about reincarnation become obsolete. They are like questions about shadows in the cellar when once the lights of the house are turned on. Similarly, in the presence of Michael, matters of mind and its operations and contents become increasingly disciplined, organised, understood and manipulated according to one's desire for loyalty, discernment and obedience to very real forces in him, which are identified as Michael's will and the will of the Father.

I am convinced by the extraordinarily personal nature of his sovereignty in Nebadon that Michael personally experiences all of his children's minds as an everyday and integral part of his own consciousness. He certainly experiences mine. And when I ask him to disclose the workings of another's mind, in instances of prayer, healing, caring and so forth, he does so with utmost familiarity. And in those instances where I appear to have been elevated to his domain, I have found his sovereignty to be absolute, thorough, and in perfect contact with every being in Nebadon.

I find that the Urantia papers invite us to forsake our own beliefs and concepts and mindal experiences and to join with Michael and his universe mindedness. Trusting in him, the believer in these papers is courted eventually into his presence and sonship is birthed as a universal reality rather than a localised fact of faith. That has been my experience any way. Sonship dispels any doubts about the primary forces in existence, and those forces do not engender reincarnation. The experience of sonship reveals reincarnation to be merely a description for sense-based conceptualisation, and not much related to actual spirituality.

It has been my experience that our lovely Michael invites his believing son into a completely different kind of spiritual experience than that which is prescribed by any other religion on Earth. Sonship is driven by far more sophisticated and powerful forces than reincarnation ever could be. The central difference is that the absolute head of this universe, the core gravity that holds the whole show together, is a person and not a system of cause and effect and recycling.[1]

Whilst the pursuit of reincarnation, its mechanisms, it's phenomena, it's end, may occupy the interests of a great number of people on Earth, my writing obviously indicates that I believe it is a lesser vehicle for the perfection of mind than is sonship with God. To this end I invite people to meet their Michael, and then to ask the questions that have always held great interest to them. Sonship enhances one's mind with the mind of Michael— as loving another individual enhances one's mind with their mind and way of thinking. Making spiritual inquiries is far better determined from within sonship mindedness than within reincarnation mindedness. Reincarnation mindedness offers no support for its own transcendence whatsoever. Reincarnation mindedness is a conceptualised mind system which is indulging itself, and the only escape from it is by the intrusion of a completely foreign mind...which is why the enlightenment experience is so astonishing...one experiences the action of a completely foreign/unfamiliar mind which dissolves the previously held conceptual mind.

But Michael! Oh what a splendid patron of our efforts he is. He is so powerfully present to the willing heart. He is so eager to explain, to uplift, to liberate the willing heart, the friendly mind, the spiritual "child". He is the lover of our well being: reincarnation has no consideration for our well being. He is the liberator of mind: reincarnation is the enslaver of mind. Michael's gospel is:

"If you could only enjoy the inspiring satisfaction of knowing God as your spiritual Father, then you might employ your powers of speech to liberate your fellows from the bondage of darkness and from the slavery of ignorance."[2] And;

"I am on Earth solely to comfort the minds, liberate the spirits, and save the souls of men."[3] "Go into all the world and preach the glad tidings of the kingdom. Liberate spiritual captives, comfort the oppressed, and minister to the afflicted."[4]

Ultimately, Michael's call in our hearts to sonship simply asks us if we believe what he once said as Jesus, and what he continues to say as Michael:

"I have taught you much by word of mouth, and I have lived my life among you. I have done all that can be done to enlighten your minds and liberate your souls, and what you have not been able to get from my teachings and my life, you must now prepare to acquire at the hand of that master of all teachers-actual experience. And in all of this new experience which now awaits you, I will go before you and the Spirit of Truth shall be with you. Fear not; that which you now fail to comprehend, the new teacher, when he has come, will reveal to you throughout the remainder of your life on Earth and on through your training in the eternal ages."[5]

He eternally echoes his gospel within us that: God is our Father; he himself, Michael, is our Father; we are God's sons and Michael's sons, literally; and that, in the father-son relationship, our entire destiny in him rests like a mustard seed waiting for planting.

Have you a question?

Take it to him.

Have you a hope?

Take it to him.

Have you a need?

Take it to him.

Are you weary, lonely, ill, impoverished, too complicated, addicted, dying, afraid, angry, ignorant, insincere, callous—take it to him and he will give you a new heart and a new way that is secure because it is in him. And he has overcome the world because he is both a man who overcame the world by means of the will of the Father as well as by means of being the world's Creator Michael.

It seems so very hard sometimes for so many on Earth to hear this simple reality in their heart. The next story is about a little girl whose problem we took to Michael.

❧

Notes

94:2.3 {The undue concentration...}

132:4.7 {To the speaker...}

140:6.6 {Jesus was minded...}

140:9.2 {Jesus reviewed many…}
181:2.24 {I have taught you…}

❦

Chapter 30

The twin that died and the twin that lived

Claudine came to see me in the garden. She was troubled about the twins she was carrying. Doctors had told her that she had lost one of them and needed to let it go. We worked together and prayed and came to new understandings about the babies inside her body and she delivered the dead child the following day.

Around seven years later I had a phone call from her.

"Rob, Rebecca is now seven years old. She has been plagued about her twin sister for some years. Now she isn't sleeping. She's restless. There's something wrong. Around eighteen months ago, I mentioned your name, and how you had helped me before she was born. Straight away she said that she wanted to see you, and that you could help her with her problem about Christine, as she calls her baby twin. I have no idea where she got that thought, but could you help us please?"

Visiting the family

So of course I went to see Claudine and her kids. We spoke for a while about her pregnancy, the loss of one baby and the grief associated with that event. Mary and I had lost twins too, so there was room for empathy.

Eventually the topic came around to Rebecca and I asked Claudine what she had explained about the dead twin.

"Well, I said maybe she was reincarnated into another little girl." Then she looked at me with wide open eyes and said, "But Rob, I don't really know where she is. I don't even know if reincarnation is real. I don't know anything about it all."

I explained my experience with the Urantia papers, and with my final question about the reality of reincarnation and how I had come to recognise that there was no such a thing as it is popularly understood.

Bean

I explained an experience I had when Mary gave birth to Bean, as we called her—because when the gynaecologist confirmed that Mary was pregnant, the child was the size of a broad bean—whom she had as a dead baby carried for two weeks.

"Mary was induced and delivered Bean around 2.30 in the morning. Around 3.30, as she was drifting off to sleep, I drove home for a bit of space from the whole ordeal. We lived only five or six minutes from the hospital. When I arrived home I sat in the recliner chair I had bought her to nurse the twins that had now died—we would not get to raise them here on Earth. As I sat in the chair, after about ten minutes, my Guardian Seraphim drew close to me and quietly said: 'Rob, you are about to have a visitor.' About a minute later, my vision was opened up and I saw an Angel descend from heaven carrying a tiny little bundle. Within seconds she arrived in my lounge room where I was sitting and stood to my left. She looked at me with the most sympathetic and comforting look imaginable. Without saying a single word, she passed this little bundle to me to hold. I knew it was Bean. My heart choked up. I cried and cried. I held this little bundle ever so close to me. I looked across at the Angel who had brought her to me to hold and I saw in her the epitome of motherliness. She was Bean's guardian. She was the Angel who would hold Bean in trust until either Mary or I died and were resurrected in the mansion worlds. Whenever that would be, she would proceed to release Bean for resurrection too, and one of us would commence the parenting process in heaven with our little Bean."[1]

"Well," I continued, "the Angel let me hold Bean for about ten minutes I suppose, until there came within me a sense of spiritual satisfaction. The grief in my spirit left me. My own Guardian Angel drew close and softly said, 'It's time now Rob.' I passed the bundle back to the heavenly visitor. She received Bean, held her close to her own heart, turned and in an instant ascended back into heaven, and my vision closed over."

She's with an angel in heaven

Claudine sat on the lounge suite a couple of feet from me, and I looked up to catch her face. She was wide eyed. Her glow spoke much about her being fully able to relate to what I had spoken of. I continued speaking,

"So Claudine, what with the experiences around reincarnation, enlightenment, Bean's death, and communion with God my Father, I am of the opinion that Christine is held within a similar Angel in heaven, awaiting either your or her father's death and resurrection to be raised up from this transitional sleep. At which point, you will continue your parenting of her to the age of consent, adulthood, which here on Earth is puberty, that is, when the person can reproduce the species and when they can make a spiritual decision for herself."

Satisfied that there was some kind of explanation that her young daughter would hear, she called her in.

Meeting the girl that lived

Into the room sprang the liveliest little girls you'd ever want to meet. They were just gorgeous. One was seven years old, that was Rebecca, the twin that lived, and the other was Janice her five year old sister. Janice immediately handed me a picture, saying, "I have drawn this for you Rob. This is you. And this is the garden. And this is a Christmas tree. I'm singing in the school Christmas play. It's great!"

On and on we chatted. For some reason it was like meeting my own relatives. There was an immediate and an easy connection to these kids.

Rebecca jumped up on the lounge suite by her Mum. I sensed she wanted to touch me and so I put my hand close to hers and quickly we held hands. In an instant she was sprawled all over the couch, her Mum's legs, the pillows, as kids do, and still she held on to my hand very firmly. We had met.

Casually, with no effort, we started talking about a whole range of topics. With impromptu abandonment, Janice and I sang "Away in a manger," and I complimented her fine singing.

The family's spiritual foundations

I wanted to find out about the spiritual basis of the family. Did Jesus have a place in the hearts of this family? Was the occult present? Was new age personal growth "stuff" the centre of the family? Where exactly did this family come from? I asked a single question in order to find out.

"Claudine, if I asked you to have God bless your home, the children and your finances, how would you do that?"

We spoke for a while around what that meant to me, and to her, and then she replied.

"Oh I would write a script. I would put down on paper the needs I wanted to have God bless in each of those three areas. You know, what I wanted God to bless in the home. What I wanted God to bless in the kids. What I wanted God to bless in my finances."

"And how would you go about linking God's blessing to that script?" I asked.

"Well Rob, I would sort of meditate on that script; I guess; kinda."

Then she thought some more on the topic.

"Actually, yes, that's what I'd do." Then she seemed to see a certain futility in her own methods and added quizzically, "Not very good huh?"

"Do you mean to say that you would think about it all, then hope that God would just some how know that that's what you wanted and that he would then go about blessing it?"

"Yes, sort of like that, I guess. But, I don't really know."

"Do you believe they would get blessed that way?" I asked.

She thought for a while then she looked into my eyes and said, "No Rob, not really." And her hope faded.

"There are people who use prayer instead of meditation Claudine," I said. "People call upon Jesus who will answer their prayer, and give them the evidence of their prayer being answered even before it manifests in the world. Let me teach you how to meditate in a way that brings you into that kind of prayerfulness. Would you like that?"

"Yeah, sure I would. But I've never been any good at this sort of stuff. It's all so foreign and there's so much to learn," she said.

"Yeah I know," I replied. "It's really silly but it's a fact all around the world. People in the west and the east teach this really complicated stuff that ultimately takes you away from the God who is so very close to you. And people fall for it, as if all the techniques and formulas are better than their own simple understanding. Let me show you something, it's really simple."

A simple meditation to do

Janice was out of the room at this stage but I wanted to include Rebecca because I sensed that she had a troubled spirit about her: all was not well inside her heart.

"You both can do this. It's really simple. And when you do this, God will visit you," I explained.

"Firstly, think of something that is a spiritual statement, some words, that for you are spiritual."

"What do you mean Rob? What sort of words," Claudine asked.

"Well, the phrase could be "Our Father who art in heaven." Or it could be "Silent night, holy night." I let go Rebecca's hand and let her place it on her lap.

"Oh, OK," Claudine said, and off they both went into their own thoughts.

After a short while, Rebecca looked up at me with a big smile, "I've got my one Rob."

"Yes, I've got my one too thanks Rob," Claudine followed.

"Alright then. This is what you will do next. For about fifteen or twenty breaths, you're going to say that phrase in your thoughts, not out loud, just in your own thoughts, every time that you breath out." Then I showed them.

"See how I am breathing out, just naturally, not hurried, not special, just normally. Now every time I breathe out, I say in my own thoughts, that little phrase. Do you both understand that?"

"Yes."

"OK. Start now, and I'll tell you when to stop."

The room fell into a hush and I began counting Claudine's exhalations, waiting for the moment when the mortal mind would meet the mind of God, which so easily happens during these types of meditative moments. From time to time I looked at young Rebecca's breathing. I was glad that she participated so willingly, but even when the mind of God met her own human mind, there was still evidence that she was troubled about something quite disturbing. A Pentecostal worker more than likely would have said that she had an evil spirit attached to her, but I didn't really want to go down that path.

Suddenly, it was there. The presence of God came upon both of them within seconds of each other. I waited for a few more of their breaths, observing the settling of their human minds. Both Rebecca and Claudine had found the presence of God, and it reflected in their postures and the glow in their faces.

"There it is," I said. "Do you feel God's presence in you now?" I asked.

"Yes, I do," said Rebecca.

"Most certainly, I do," said Claudine with a sense of utmost astonishment that showed me she had never before encountered God so tangibly and easily.

Praying in the meditative atmosphere

We celebrated God's presence with a little discussion and much joy. Claudine expressed how easy it was to be with God, compared with the things she'd been taught in all the personal growth type groups and seminars she'd attended. Then I brought the topic back to its focus and I asked the question again:

"Claudine, you'll remember that I asked you about how you would go about arranging for God to bless your home, the children and your finances. Now that your mind and the mind of God have kind of merged," and I looked at her for her consent, "I'd like to direct you toward prayerfulness."

"Pray to Jesus," I said. "Say this: 'Dear Jesus, please bless my home and make it a good place for God to live." She said what I said. Then I said, "Now wait Claudine. Just wait on Jesus. He will come into your mind shortly with his confirmation."

We waited for around ten to fifteen seconds. Suddenly, there it was. I could detect it in her mind, so I commented.

"Do you feel that change?" I asked.

"Yes," she replied somewhat astonished. "It's Jesus. He's confirming my prayer. I can feel him Ok-ing his blessing on all the house. That's amazing!"

"Ok Claudine," I continued after a while of letting her bask in that blessing which would cleanse and sanctify her home; "Now ask Jesus to bless your three children: Ellen, Rebecca and Janice."

"Dear Jesus," Claudine began, "please bless all my girls."

Again we waited.

Suddenly the room about us filled with the presence of God. It was like a thick blanket enfolding Claudine and Rebecca who was right beside her, and it spread across to Janice who had come back into the room and was standing beside me on my left, sort of hanging off the arm of the sofa.

I recognised Mother Spirit immediately and I said, "Do you feel how feminine that provision is for your children?"

"Yes I do," Claudine replied immediately. "Yes I do. It's

amazing. How come it's so female? So motherly?"

"Why, that's Mother Spirit, Claudine. The kind of ministry that you have received to watch over and nourish your three girls is coming through Jesus Christ directly from Mother Spirit. The Urantia papers will tell you more about her if you ever want to read about her.

"Wow, that's just amazing," she continued, and her sense of relief over the direct connection to the Holy Spirit and the magnitude of her presence and care was truly amazing to her.

"Now, let's do the third prayer. Ask Jesus to enrichen your finances. You've told me that you are in financial difficulty so now, say to him, "Dear Jesus, please uplift my finances."

"Dear Jesus," she said, "please uplift my finances."

"OK, now let's wait until he gives you confirmation of his will to do that."

We waited. We waited some more. We kept waiting, like somehow it wasn't going to happen, but on we kept.

Then all of a sudden, Jesus' presence and his joy broke through into her somewhat stuck and muddy human mind. Obviously, finances were a sticking point in her life-a sole Mum whose husband had gone, three kids aged eleven, seven and five, home in a good suburb but costs were high, and a livelihood that simply wasn't working enough for her.

"Jesus is here!" I said.

"Yes he is!" she replied. "I can feel his joy. I have his confirmation of success. He is going to change things in me and for me. Fantastic!"

Claudine was elated. The burden lifted off her immediately. Jesus breaks burdens, destroys the things to which we are yoked, and restores God's provision for us. That's how the Christian describes it, and that's exactly what Jesus does.

"Wow, I've got to say Rob, I feel a whole light lighter now," Claudine said.

"Jesus lifts the burden, doesn't he? His word is true when he says 'Come to me all you who are heavy laden and I will give you rest.'"[2]

"Oh he sure does," she said.

"So now, looking back into this process of prayer Claudine, I want you to see that you have asked for three blessings and Jesus has provided the confirmation that all three blessings are now in place. Isn't that wonderful?"

"Yes. Yes! Truly wonderful. Thank you Jesus," she said.

"So that's meditation and that's prayer," I said by way of summary.

"Just wonderful Rob," Claudine replied.

The twin that died

After a while and a bit of chitchat, Rebecca asked me about "Christine, my dead twin," as she called her.

"Rob, is she reincarnated some where?"

"God is my Father, why don't I ask him?" I replied.

"Is God your Daddy?" asked now wide-eyed Janice.

"Oh sure he is, Claudine said. And he's your Father and he's my Father too."

"What do you mean?" asked Rebecca.

"Well," I started in, "you know when you see a lady with a big tummy and she's got a baby or two inside her?"

"Yeah," the kids answered.

"Well, how the babies get there is because the Mum and Dad make the life of the body happen," and I touched them on their skin, "but God brings in the life that lasts for ever, the spirit."

They looked at me like they understood what I was talking about, but I continued anyway. "You know when you see a little bird out in the road, and he's died."

"Yes, " they replied, as they talked about one they had seen only the other day.

"Well, you can see that the body is dead. It's just lying there. There's no life left in it, right?"

"Oh sure," Rebecca replied.

"Well the life that goes on forever is different from the life that was in the body."

"Yeah, OK. I understand that," said Rebecca.

"So when I say that God is my Father I mean that God has given me the life that goes on forever. He's given that life to you too."

"OK. Neat," Rebecca added. "So has Christine reincarnated?" she asked.

"Well, why don't I ask my Father. He's right here, I'll ask him."

Let's ask God

My Father was indeed nearby and I asked him. He didn't want to talk to me. He wanted to speak directly to Rebecca; such was his profound love for this little girl of seven years. He said, "Christine is here with me in heaven," and I started to retell his words to Rebecca. She is being held within an Angel who is keeping good care of her until your Mum or your Dad comes to heaven. And then she'll grow up with your Mum or your Dad, whoever comes first.

"She's not the same age as you Rebecca. She's still a baby waiting to be born. She is sleeping like that until your Mum or your Dad comes to heaven. That's why you haven't been able to locate her anywhere...'cos you've been searching for her with your soul haven't you?" Then he waited while Rebecca took that in.

I could sense that these words made a profound shift in Rebecca. It shattered her beliefs about her missing sister. It raised up newfound hope and opportunity. She was found. She was no longer a twin, so to speak, because Rebecca was seven years old and Christine was yet to be born. She was safe. She was not reincarnating. She was in God's care. There was another dimension to the sisterly relationship now.

Is hell real?

The conversation went on around that topic for a little while and then little five-year-old Janice asked me, "Is hell real?"

"Well, why don't I ask my Father and hear what he has to say on the matter?"

"OK," she said.

"Father," I asked, "is hell real?"

"No it isn't real," he said to both Janice and Rebecca through my retelling of his words. "It's a story that some people made up a long, long time ago. As a result, some people believe it to be true; but it's not really true.

"You see sweethearts, there was this group of people once, and they were very bad people. They did all sorts of nasty things to each other. They were horrible people. Have you met any bad people?"

"Oh yes," Rebecca exclaimed. "At school, there's this

Penelope. She's horrible." And then followed a discussion that perhaps her parents were bad and she just brought that trouble to school with her.

"Well actually, her Mum's really nice," said Janice.

"Yeah, her Mum's nice," said Rebecca. "But her Dad's horrible."

So we settled that point.

"Well," continued my Adjuster, "these bad people had a few good people in amongst them. The good people really wanted the bad people to become good. The way they did it was that they pointed out to all the bad people how bad they were and they said that if they didn't become good people that when they died they'd spend forever in a bad place where there was never any escape from other bad people, even people badder than they were.

"Well, it seemed to work. I didn't tell them to say that. There isn't really any such a place. But the good people made up the story to help out the bad people. And it worked too, on a lot of the bad people. They became good. They saw that they were bad and they didn't want to stay bad forever and so they became good. And I helped them to become good too. So that's the story of about hell came to be invented.

"Later on, some of the bad people who had become good people moved to other places. When they saw bad people they told them the same story. In this way, some of the bad people who became good people helped other bad people to become good people. As they did this, the story about hell became more and more popular. People believed it was true, because it helped bad people to become good people they thought that it had to be true. But it isn't really true. There is no hell. When you die you come to heaven with me."

It didn't dawn on me until the following day that, whilst this was enlightening information for seven year old Rebecca, young five year old Janice might have be preparing to make her first moral decision, the one that would bring to her a Thought Adjuster, God indwelling.[3] Oh dear reader: what a precious decision that is!

I wanna see my sister

I reflected on Rebecca and looked into the depths of her mind, as my Michael had taught me to do so long ago.

"Do you have any other questions?" I asked the girls. "I will be leaving soon." I had already been there about an hour and a half and they had not yet had their supper.

"I wanna see my sister Rob. Can God show me my sister?" Rebecca asked.

"Sure he can sweetie. Come over here and sit on my lap," I said, and she jumped up and came and sat on my lap.

"I'm going to place one hand on your back like this, and one hand on your chest like this, and now we're going to ask Jesus to show us your sister. OK?"

"Yes," she said quietly. This was a very special moment for Rebecca. She had such a love for Christine, as she called the twin who had died during pregnancy. Rebecca was very sincere in her quest to resolve her problem over being a living twin.

"Jesus," I said.

"Jesus," Rebecca echoed.

"Please come and be with us now," I continued.

"Please come and be with us now," Rebecca echoed.

"Please show us one picture of Christine, wherever she is now," I asked.

"Please show us one picture of Christine, wherever she is now," Rebecca echoed.

Then I heard Michael speaking to me about the necessity for this to be a one off event, and to establish in Rebecca the understanding that it is good and right for her to keep on living here and to be comfortable about meeting up with Christine after she, Rebecca, had lived a long and full life on Earth. This was to avoid any kind of obsession that might develop in Rebecca to lead her into unusual spiritual demands on herself.

"Jesus just told me that this is a special request and that you have to promise to him that you'll only ask it once," I said to Rebecca.

"OK Rob, I promise," she said.

"No, you have to promise to Jesus. Say this, Rebecca. Jesus."

"Jesus," she echoed.

"Thank you for helping me to see a picture of my sister Christine."

"Thank you for helping me to see a picture of my sister Christine," she continued.

"And Jesus, I promise that I will never ask for this again," I said.

"Jesus, I promise that I will never ask for this again," she echoed after me.

"With all my heart, I promise this," I said.

"With all my heart I promise this," she said.

"And Jesus I pray like this in your name. Amen"

"And Jesus I pray like this in your name. Amen," Rebecca finished off.

"Now, Rebecca, we have asked together. Jesus will do it, he told me he would. Now we'll wait," I told her.

Our faces were just inches apart as she sat on my lap. My hands on her back and her chest seemed to form a current running through her. Like this, prayerfully, with our eyes closed, her Mum sitting just a foot away, her little sister Janice standing only a foot away nearby, we waited. Longer and longer we waited. A few minutes went by, and still we waited. Our waiting was expectant, hopeful, faithful, deliberate; like being a body of water that is placed on a fire, waiting for the first bubbles to announce the expected boiling going on within our depths.

The twin that lived sees the twin that died

Suddenly the atmosphere changed. Into our minds there came a wonderful and fresh sense of Jesus' presence. An image was forming in us. Then, in an instant, suddenly there it was. As if suspended in some golden universe of living love, we could see this little baby nestled in a bundle of heavenly clothes.

Christine was not portrayed as a living, moving, wriggling baby as one would imagine her to be, but neither was she dead. She was somehow completely personal; she had personality to her. When I quizzed Rebecca moments after, both she and I knew that it was her sister. She was suspended, just as Father had said earlier in the meeting, within the person of an Angel. Jesus, in his great mercy for this believing little girl, brought about an image that would truly satisfy her and lift her burden.

After a few moments of seeing this image, I spoke to Rebecca, saying, "Do you see that Rebecca? Do you see Christine? Wow! Isn't that amazing?"

"Yes, I do see her Rob," this little girl replied.

Her reply just thrilled me. I had great hope that when she was contacted by God in this way, the burdens of her heart would be completely lifted.

After a minute or so, when the vision had passed, we started chatting about it. What was uppermost in my mind was, not the fact that it happened for her, for I do expect prayer to be answered, but the degree to which she was lifted out of her burden through Jesus' kindness.

A little while later little seven-year-old Rebecca went out of the room. Claudine and I had been chatting for a while and then Rebecca came running back in. She ran up to me and hugged my neck. I held her, and held her, and held her. It was like she was my own little girl; such was the love of the Father in me for this child of his.

"Thanks Rob," she said.

I could feel that she was deeply moved by her experience with God's image of her twin sister. It seemed to add a certainty of her sonship with God at the deepest level of her inner person.

"Are you feeling better now Rebecca? Is all this trouble over Christine cleared up now?" I asked.

"Yes it is, thanks to God."

We spent more time together. Slowly and gently I began to close our visit and after a little while, I left their home.

Dealing with the death of a young one

This, then, is the story of the twin that lived and the twin that died. Of course, both of them are really living, it's just that one is living in the embrace of a Nursery Angel. One day she will awaken on the Finaliters' nursery world,[4] as a little baby, joined by her actual Mum or Dad.

What a great burden it is not to know what happens to our little ones who die prematurely. Only in the Urantia papers is there such a revelation that gives us such a complete and dynamic hope, through Christ Michael, that heals the wounded hearts of this world. What a great hope we have in our Michael and the provision he has for us in all things, even for the little ones who leave our world by the millions each year. The Urantia papers give such a hope and such a relief to all the countless mothers and fathers of this world. What an extraordinary miracle of hope it is, that our own child remains ours to nurture, even in heaven.

What an extraordinary respect God has for the links between a parent and child. I pray mercy on the parent who has abused and killed their child, that you may receive all of the Father's forgiveness you need because, if not here, then in heaven, you shall retrieve that little one and continue parenting in an atmosphere that will bring out the very best in you. Given his forgiveness and divine love, and the abundance of our Mother Spirit's ever-supportive motherly care, you will be so proud of yourself and of your child. You will be so glad to have so much love for another human being. Your child will be so glad to have had the opportunity of the life you and Michael provided.

If you, dear reader, are a parent or sibling who has lost a little one, please join with me in an invocation to dear Michael and Mother Spirit, our own Father and Mother. Let us receive from them relief from the burden and the pain, right now, even as you read this and as you reflect on your own life. They hear your prayer. They *will* come to your support—this story of the two twins is a witness of that fact. If they will come to me, and to little Rebecca, and to Claudine, then they will come to you, for we are not more special than you. And don't be fooled by thinking, "Oh they will never come to me, I am unworthy. You don't know what I've done wrong. They'll never come to me." I tell you, yes they will. They are your Parents, and their love for you is true and pure. Trust what I say on this, for I say to trust what Jesus himself said:

"Come to me, all you that are weary and are carrying heavy burdens, and I will give you rest. Take my yoke upon you, and learn from me; for I am gentle and humble in heart, and you will find rest for your souls. For my yoke is easy, and my burden is light."[5]

When he said "all you," that includes you dear reader, for you are a part of the "all" that Jesus was inviting. You are a part of the all that Jesus invites right now. So please do not think you are unworthy to be received by God. Do not deny God the opportunity to come to you. Come now; be a part of the invocation to Jesus to receive from him, just as little Rebecca received the fulfilment of her healing needs from him.

Say with me now:

"Jesus. Please reveal to me the kinds of love filled healing and care you have for me, that will release the burden of this birth event in my life."

And now wait. Wait as I waited, in anticipation. Wait an hour if you have to, but wait, poised to receive your Father's own blessing for you.

Once you have this revelation, simply claim it, and let it claim you, saying:

"Thank you Jesus, I claim this healing that you have for me now." And it shall be yours.

This might not sound like you're doing much, but it does open the door to God's provision for you. Most of all, it opens the door to you being able to receive the Father's forgiveness. Once the spirit of his forgiveness resides with you, all else is forth coming.[6]

His forgiveness is a big part of the events around the twin that lived and the twin that died. For, once Rebecca was touched by Jesus, she was touched by his forgiveness. All her hurt and disappointment vanished. She could move on with her life.

Forgiveness is not just saying you're sorry. Rebecca's little baby sister Christine was made able to say sorry to Rebecca as well. It wasn't with any words. But you can understand that by means of Jesus' own revelation of her to Rebecca, Christine was shown to be communicating too.

When Rebecca saw Christine, she suddenly knew that everything was well between the two of them. And more than that: between the two sisters and God too. And that kind of an answer is always final as concerns our victory.

Consider for a moment how different it is for the person who believes that their little child is reincarnating as an animal, or a spirit, or another person—if they're unbelievably fortunate—or a ghost, or lost in any one of several hells. How tragic for that parent, or that brother or sister. They live through all manner of grief and heartache and hopelessness because they are convinced that they will never again meet up with their loved one.

This was never more apparent at the funerals conducted in my monastery in Singapore. Buddhists and Hindus, sadly, can experience dreadful grief at times of death. Many are convinced that the birth of a child is not a happy event, simply the beginningless and endless continuation of the round of suffering for some poor lost soul.

What a joy then, to bring this story to you of the actual way things are in the heavens, so aptly revealed by these two little girls, the twin that died and the twin that lived. How wonderful it is that we are born into a universe in which our Michael and Mother Spirit care for every single one of us, regardless of the tragedy of our material life.

❧

Notes

1. 49:6.6 {3. Mortals of the...}
2. Matthew 11:28
3. 108:2.1
4. 45:6.7 {This probation nursery...}
5. Matthew 11:28-30
6. 133.3.7 {As they stood...}

❧

Chapter 31

There is no reincarnation

Reincarnation is a fact of life held by millions of people the world over. The people largely responsible for this philosophy's dissemination, and held in high regard for their knowledge on the subject, are Tibetan and Chinese Mahayana Buddhists, Thai, Burmese, and Sri Lankan Hinayana Buddhists, Chinese Taoists, Indian Hindus, and a seemingly endless array of homegrown pantheistic Asian offshoots which vary from town to town. It is from these Asian sources that the idea of reincarnation filtered into Western religious arenas of thought. Some of the theory came to us in complete systems, such as with the growing-in-popularity Tibetan Buddhist approach, while some of it came in dribs and drabs, snippets from mainstream religions neatly edited by the evangelist to suit the social climate and his or her spiritual capacity and conditioning.

During time as a monk in Asia I was led through the training steps provided to such a person who is clearly devoted to experientially exploring spiritual realities for the sake of enlightenment and its freedom from the whole reincarnation package, as well as for the sake of awakening others to the fact of reincarnation, its consequences, philosophy and transcendence.

Popular reading

Like thousands of Westerners, my first serving of the reincarnation idea came to me from the author of a number of books on Tibetan Buddhism, one Lobsang Rampa. He claims to have been a Tibetan Buddhist Lama early this century. He claims to have died and transferred himself into the body of a Canadian man who was himself about to die. Lobsang still is alive and well in Canada apparently.

His books captivated a large Western audience and set many people on the path to believing in reincarnation. His was a case of the delivery to us of a dribs and drabs package and in the light of what "real" Tibetan Lamas teach on reincarnation, Lobsang didn't really do such a terrific job in his presentation of the subject. As a result of exposure to his writings however, large numbers of Westerners took up the belief, never researching the idea any further, nor even seriously questioning it.

Rejection of one and adoption of another

The common scenario I came across was people who had rejected Christianity due to their feelings toward the Church's dogmatic approach and its stifling effect upon a virginal spiritual urge eager for the dynamic exploration of new horizons rich in love and nourishment, who had a vacuum to fill. There seemed to be many from the Jewish faith as well, for similar reasons that they wanted a lot more than what they were getting. Along came reincarnation, the mystical, the spiritually appealing, the romantic, and, quite naturally, folks grabbed onto it. Most of us want to fill the vacuum created by a negative with something we construe to be a positive, and many more of us want to believe in anything at all, just so long as it doesn't accord with whatever we've previously rejected.

Lobsang's teachings certainly appealed to me at that time. Reincarnation was innocuous enough, sufficiently radical, and it was buried deep in the bosom of romance itself...the aloof and mystical community of Tibetan sages, renowned for their loving kindness and spiritual expertise. It could be said that when I did trek off to be with these kindly people, my thirst was for spiritual experience in the company of loving companions and reincarnation just happened to be a part of the deal.

Reincarnation is a philosophical hub for many faiths

I arrived into their midst with ideas about life, death and reincarnation, being largely undeveloped at all. I was open to suggestion, being biased neither one way nor the other very much. I had, however, developed a psychic ability which enabled me to do "Past-life readings' for people...and seemed to be pretty good at it. I harboured a belief in reincarnation which provided access to the Tibetan community, exposed me to people's inner world and behavioural tendencies, yet it wasn't a belief I would fervently defend. In past-life readings I had no explanation for the flood of information accredited to past lives. The idea of that information having its origins in actual past-lives seemed good enough at the time, until I could verify it or find a better explanation for it at some later stage of spiritual development.

My training, and a monk is afforded far greater access to teachings and initiations than laypersons, consisted of firstly learning the principles by which reincarnation operates.

Without reincarnation Buddhism, Hinduism, Taoism, Western mystery schools, and the many pantheistic cults of the world are without their "raison-d'être". Without reincarnation there is no philosophical foundation for religious experience, or for explanation of the human condition. Without reincarnation these religious approaches would be reduced to evangelising spirituality for its own sake alone—and so very much of the potency of such an approach depends upon well developed faith, an attribute few of us enjoy until we have survived a great deal of soul-searching and experiential trauma.

If you want to question this, notice how you, yourself appeal to someone as you evangelise. Find out what you use as leverage to convince the person to begin to draw on God in daily life. Somewhere along the line you'll use reasons such as: "Jesus died for you", "What will happen to you after you die?" "How do you account for synchronous events: karma?" and so on. You use your philosophy to convert people to the God you believe in, as if the direct experience of God isn't sufficient reason alone. The kids' reply to "Why do you believe in God?" "Because." "Because why?" "Just because;" is God for God's sake rather than God for reincarnation's sake or the sake of some other philosophical argument.

The principles of reincarnation

And so I was taught the foundation of Buddhism, the very reason for being faithful and clearing my way for the enlightenment event and its overturning of the self-identity whenever Self Mind generated Nirvana. I was taught the foundation of reincarnation—that the human condition is one of never beginning, endless recycling of birth, decay, death, birth again, all across an horrific array of possible environments: endless suffering.

The principles I was taught agree totally with those found in all the various sects of Buddhism, Hinduism, Taoism, Western mystery schools and those presented to people through mediums and psychics in general here in the West.

The principles, surprisingly largely ill defined or unknown to most Westerners who believe in reincarnation, are as follows:

1. SELF (Buddha Nature mind) is real and self-generating. Everything else is unreal and not self-generating, they are selfless: the universes filled with life forms, the cities filled with people, the landscape filled with trees and plants and lakes and seas, your body and feelings and mind and its thoughts, what you see and hear and feel and taste and smell. Our feeling of selfhood and even our life and death itself is recognised by the enlightened mind, the Buddha Nature mind, to be nothing more than names and appearances, the substance of which remains in Self, the appearance of which however at no time results in actually self-existent things. It's a bit like peeling away the leaves of an onion in search of the core being of the onion and of course finding no such thing. When someone asks you "where is the onion", you look and in fact only find a mere suggestion that the onion exists. As you read these words and think "I," it's exactly that "I" that is an illusion. When one awakens from that sense of self, it can be like literally waking up even though one is absolutely convinced that one is fully awake in the first place.

2. TRUE REALITY is said to be a condition in which you, as Self, are like an immense mirror which has no individual sense of self that can be set apart from anything. And that ALL phenomena that make up life are empty reflections, which appear and disappear in the mirror of Self. As Self you know you are, as such; it's just that you are not bound by the limitations arising from behaving according to the understanding that you are your body or your mind or a feeling called "I." Instead, you encompass them; body and mind exist within you rather than the other way around.

3. MAN'S ERROR is the belief that he is a self-feeling called "I" and that he behaves according to the limitations and capacity for truth that his own particular "I" holds to be true. Enlightenment, the goal of all reincarnation theories, delivers man from his deluded notion and consequently that notion's limitations. The basis for these limitations is fear, greed, anger and ignorance of True Self—the enlightened or Buddha Nature mind.

4. KARMA, meaning cause and effect, is the act of generating

changes. It can be good karma, bad karma or neutral karma. The sage transforms his or her behavioural tendencies so as to generate good karma, that is, set in motion only those things that will return prosperity to himself and all others. The ignorant person is so completely driven by the delusion of believing in personal gain and loss that most karma is bad, that is, he sets in motion those things which result in his demise and the demise of others. Some reincarnation beliefs hold that over countless lifetimes man becomes ever-increasingly capable of generating good karma. Some, such as is commonly found within primitive Hindu and Buddhist theories, hold that man is no more likely to live one step up the ladder next time around than revert to being a plant or a bug. The belief holds that in fact the latter is more likely.

In reincarnation-based lives, great importance is placed upon generating good karma: support priests, because they can show you the way out; do kind things for others, so you'll get it back to you in return; make bountiful offerings to gods and your ancestors, just in case they have any sway over what happens to you in this lifetime or the next...and so on.

The heart of the belief in reincarnation, as it is experientially taught to monks, is that Self is uncreated (like the Thought Adjuster) and that what it is that incarnates over and over again is merely an "I" thought. Due to the belief in a self-existent "I" in one lifetime, those seeds sown are seeds designed to perpetuate the sense of "I." Self is responsible for generating and supporting these causes, it being utterly unmoved by any of the goings-on, which the "I" considers are real. Self has the perspective, blatantly obvious and blatantly correct once enlightenment occurs, that everything is OK and could never be anything but OK. Self doesn't acknowledge any perspective that the "I" has...so the "I" can be scared to death, craving personal survival, fearful of extinction and busy generating all the causes that reinforce the "I", and Self doesn't give a hoot! Self is to all intents and purposes an aloof God: God the creator; God the supporter; God the lover; God who is free from the clamour for mortal strivings; God who is fully aware of what is transient and fleeting and what is eternal and enduring—and who is quite OK about letting the transient, the "flash of lightning in the dark night", be true to its nature. And God who has no impulse to muster a neatly edited selection of some of the possible phenomena around and call it "I" and belief in it to the complete forgetfulness of the reality, security, enormousness and value in being Him Self. Only we, it seems, are that silly.

Reincarnation theories consider that we have been running the "I" trip forever since an eternal past. There was no beginning to our adoption of the "I" which is responsible for reincarnating time and time again.

Everyone has been your mother

One of the spiritual exercises designed to generate the loving kindness which will enable the "I" to loosen its grip and thus be more inclined to awaken to Self, is the "Truth" that since we have lived forever, and in every conceivable form imaginable, every single thing has at some stage been our mother, our father, our child, our friend, our enemy. We have deeply loved absolutely everyone at some stage, and at another stage hated them with a vile evil to the extent that we delighted in chopping them into little pieces.

If everyone has been our mother then, it's only right to love everyone now with the love we have for our mother, or at least with the love of a mother. Yet I've come across only a few monks who live like this and next to no lay people, Asian or Western, who strongly adhere to the belief in their own reincarnation. Most reincarnationists have the rather unnerving attitude that they can relax and take it easy during life because, when it's all said and done, Enlightenment is seemingly so impossible to attain, and life really isn't all that bad, and ultimately it's in the hands of something presumed to be spiritual and presumed to be leading the person gradually into greater proximity to the enlightenment—salvation—event, which according to the actual premise for reincarnation itself, is absolute nonsense. The person merely lives with a belief that is fashionable, or comfortable, or romantic, or sufficiently mystical to appease a part of the inner-life cravings. They live without ever seriously researching the belief itself; a belief that, when actually understood in its fullness, is horrific and sufficiently repulsive to make a person crave enlightenment with such an unwavering determination and such a spiritual ferocity as to bring about radical shifts in their self-identity.

One of the common traits that many Western reincarnationists share however, is the almost total lack of drive to exit the reincarnation cycle; they have no spiritual practise in their daily lives to speak of at all. Day after day, month after month, and year after year, they go on letting their precious time here slip away fruitlessly without ever coming to anything very substantial that is capable of *acting* on their firmly held belief in reincarnation; with the exception of perhaps a repertoire of other possible explanations they reject with a vehemence. Most Westerners I have met who harbour a belief in reincarnation pale into insignificance when compared to the true sages who share the same belief, yet who have turned their lives around and now veritably ooze the unfathomably rich self assurance, love, and faith of a True Spirit. And ironically, it is these ones, humble in their perfection, ordinary in their, by human standards, overwhelming spiritual self identity and potency who, behind the scenes, begin to doubt the whole reincarnation hypothesis.

The post enlightenment perspective

In a sense it is only their perspective gained subsequent to enlightenment that enables a person to draw on sufficiently spiritual resources to know reincarnation fully at all. And if you're enlightened, reincarnation is, as promised in the reincarnation teaching itself, the first thing to get tossed out! To the enlightened person it is blatantly obvious that no one was ever reincarnating, no one was ever born, no one could die. Life and death are merely empty names, names that have been ascribed to mirage-like goings-on possessing the substance of a dream or a fantasy. "I" never was real. "I" never did all those things that comprised daily life. "I" never did have all that suffering, all that confusion, and all that desperation. It all took place within Self—unmoving, eternal, self-generating, divinely wise and compassionate Self.

Ha! The joke of it all.

When your self-identity returns or awakens from "I" to Self, you can't help but laugh at yourself for having been so silly as to endorse your "I" as host of your life.

Once enlightened, when you behold your Self-Mind directly in front of you, then it is only a matter of conditioning that determines the type of explanations you use to teach others. Some individuals still employ the reincarnation-nirvana concepts, some use only the enlightened perspective (such as Zen Buddhism often does), some revert to "this is your first life," and so on. It's only a matter of conditioning and who it is you're teaching that determines your explanations, because when you're living from Self the daily life reality is so extraordinarily different from that lived with a conceptual "I" host that all the words and explanations are really beside the point and are seen to be more often than not a cause for greater confusion in the minds of those listening.

So, in a nutshell, that's pretty much what reincarnation is about as it's taught at the source, by those "in the know" whose spiritual lives depend on it utterly; and there is no truer origin to derive such teachings from here on this planet.

Teachings to liberate us from the I-concept

In the course of my journey with Buddhism then, I was taught all the above and more experientially; I experienced each exercise in the teachings. And I quite fancied it too. I was taken through the Bardo, the post death event. I was taught how to wilfully die and how to wilfully be born again. I was taught how to experience the "truth" that Self is host and "I" is just a fleeting guest in my mind which has no root. I was taught how my delusions about "I" wreaked unimaginable havoc in my life and the lives of everyone else; and I experienced it. I was taught the "truth" about reincarnation, the "truth" about our human condition; and I believed it. Well, I could prove it. I had experienced absolutely everything, except enlightenment, involved in reincarnation's premises. Reincarnation was an obvious fact of life to me because I could recount any of the infinite past lives I had already lived, as well as recount those in any other person for them—and that's pretty convincing. I could also testify that life is suffering, and that it has a cause: the foundation of Guatama Buddha's teaching.

The Urantia papers enter my life

But then along came the Urantia papers, a wordy, heady immensity that, I must admit, didn't grab me much at all. However, I saw a bit on Thought Adjusters (the presence of God indwelling the human mind)[1] and, although not reading that part in any coherent way for at least another two years, I had a mild interest in the book because I thought it might have something to say on "Buddha Nature"—the seemingly illusive Self which was central to the enlightenment experience.

A number of years passed before I could actually understand the terminology and concepts employed in the Urantia papers.

One day I found something written about how mind communications are made in mortals. The words held my attention because here was somebody writing on things about which I had become conscious since my experience of spiritual death on the cross. I knew that this was not something common to the average person, and so the author must have at least spiritually developed to my own stage. Yet when I read the words before me I saw that he was writing with such an expertise on the subject, something I could in no way achieve. My next deduction was that this author must have been writing the truth. If he can be so authoritative on such highly classified and secretive and spiritually demanding matters that I had become familiar with, and there's no conceivable way that I would or could knowingly lie or exaggerate to others on such matters, there's no possible way for him to lie either. And so I tentatively gave the Urantia papers an opportunity to teach me.

First life—no previous lives

All went well until I came across the First Life notion, no previous lives: ever! That was a bit disturbing. I knew these authors must be writing the truth simply because much of the content of the book was far too lofty for the average person to have such an in depth knowledge of. So I was in a position of having my foolproof, still enlightenment-less spiritual reality in a dilemma.

I have unquestionable faith and admiration for anyone who can prove their spiritual older brother-ness to me, their "one step or more further down the track than I am" qualities. These authors demonstrated this to me in no uncertain terms. But still I could not address the First Life issue satisfactorily. Out of a genuine thirst for Truth in my very being I scoured every possible avenue and resource inside me to resolve this dilemma, to no avail. I read and re-read the Urantia papers for some indication that they had meant First Life in some other context than no previous lives ever, to no avail. And all the while my spiritual reality was becoming more and more in line with the consciousness of and conscious communication with what I have come to call my Thought Adjuster. I began to experience wholly new and refreshing insights into the mortal condition and more impressively, my own spiritual identity in far more real ways than I had ever previously known.

I reach the end of my own ability

There came a day when, having already tried conscious communication with my Thought Adjuster and numerous personalities outlined in the Urantia papers, I addressed them saying: "I cannot resolve this dilemma of past-life: first-life. I have done my best. I need something more than what I have to work with in order to solve it. If you want me to believe what you are teaching me in this Urantia book then you come up with the goods that'll help me to resolve this dilemma so that I can progress in my spiritual journey; otherwise you and your book can take a hike!" And three days later the most extraordinary thing happened to me. The goods arrived.

A friendly helper

And so three days after I made my earnest request, I found my day interrupted. By my spirit faculties, I suddenly noticed the presence of a spiritual person. He was of a species I had never before encountered. He appeared to be a resident far from my home shores of Urantia and even far removed from Jerusem. He had a spiritual luminosity and consciousness so extraordinarily out of place here, like a physics professor turning up in the arithmetic class of 7 year olds, a person with resources far in excess of the immediate needs and in fact far in excess of the needs likely to be encountered in many, many years to come. And he addressed me.

Silently, wordlessly, we engaged a state of worship together. My whole being filled with an indescribable joy and dignity. We remained like this for quite some time until at length he, again wordlessly, communicated to me deep within my being that he knew of my request to understand this matter of reincarnation; and that he knew that I had exhausted all of my resources in this quest; and that he wished to enlarge my consciousness to a level compatible with his own; as it is for him, yet at the same time holding my mortal framework intact so that the new meanings I would discover might be meaningful to me in my mortal station rather than as one of his order, and he asked me if he had my permission to do this?

Oh boy! Did he ever! Let's go for it.

The outward, upward, inward journey to truth

Then we seemed to proceed on a lengthy journey through space together. It was an inward and an upward journey simultaneously, as if we were travelling through space and as we did we went deeper and into greater contact with divine consciousness.

I noticed that we seemed to go far beyond the spatial locations, the worlds. I noticed a certain feeling of entering an entirely new territory, one wherein who I was and how I behaved and thought was almost infantile in comparison. It was the light of this greater reality and consciousness my teacher was so at home in.

And then at length we came gently to a halt somewhere seemingly far out in space beyond both Urantia and the Morontian worlds and their levels of reality. It was as if he took me beyond the borders of Adjuster fusion so that I could perceive the nature of the human sense of self, and its destiny. Yet, where ever we were, it somehow seemed closer to the Centre of things than anything I had previously experienced; and all the while my physical senses and reality were no different from normal daily life here on Earth.

Then this wonderful Being, obviously a master at communicating with mortals when the occasion arises for him, asked me to turn around and face the direction wherein Urantia and my whole life lay. And shortly after doing this he asked me to pose my question to myself again, the one about if there was reincarnation or if my life on Urantia was indeed my first life.

The truth

I did this and instantly there came the unmistakable deeply known recognition that, and I cried it out aloud, "There is no possible way that reincarnation *can* exist!"

I saw the universe's incapability to sustain a link with the world for a person because following the cessation of mind the person was relocated to a whole other dimension never to return to the world. In the instances of death of the mind, the person simply became as though they had never been. Either way, the individuality of the person had no continuity with the world. It was so obvious, it was almost visible.

My guide just smiled and left me alone in my thoughts and deliberations as I clearly saw my world, far off as it was, in the light of this exalted reality of his. My thoughts, deeply moving my very essence, moved over extremely convincing perceptions and understandings. Things came to a completion within me in a way that was so exquisitely divinely coordinated. The mechanism of life does not have a reincarnation element within it on Urantia. It's not that reincarnation is a possible, or a likely; it simply is utterly absent.

How difficult it is to tell others

At the same time as I was bringing up my dilemma to completion I came to the unmistakable conclusion that in truth there is no possible way any of my fellow men and women on Urantia could ever be one hundred percent sure about the same question on reincarnation unless they asked the question in this or a similarly transcendent state of mind. They just simply didn't have the consciousness resource-pool to draw on which would enable them to come to a universally acceptable conclusion unless they could plug into something that could augment their Urantian and even perhaps their Morontian communication/perspective circuitry. So back home on Urantia centuries may pass and still the belief would persist in the minds of the mortals and we would have nothing much to work with that could "prove or disprove" reincarnation once and for all. Most people who would believe in First-Life would never have anything much to back that up with. And most people who would believe in Past-Life would equally never have anything much to back that up either, except a few rather flimsily wrought excuses created out of the very matrix that cannot survive the dynamics of eternally oriented energies and careers.

Both the belief in First-Life and Past-Life are constructed

from the same matrix on Earth; and life in its deepest, most eternally nourished, and most personally fulfilling is not a matter for belief systems and words and philosophies. Rather it is a concern of the inner depths, the wordless, the quiet, that reality within us that knows direct rapport with the First and only Source of everything in heaven and on Earth: that is, the domain of sharing the human mind with the mind of God—sonship.

What this means to us is that, because we function on many psychological levels, some more conscious and word based, some deeper and less word-based, we are capable of living from different capacities for meaning in our lives. The Urantia papers teach that the meaning we are capable of giving to our lives is directly related to level of God consciousness plus the level of universe citizenship consciousness we have attained; with more universal consciousness we are going to be able to create an entirely different scope of meaning than that which we could create from being only locally orientated.

The outcome of either perspective is that when we endeavour to research in ourselves any questions whose answers will provide the fabric of our beliefs, we can do so only within the parameters of the level of truth and intellectual grasp to which we have access; and our beliefs will reflect that fact.

Many of the realities we use as building blocks for more universally mature beliefs, beliefs which make us capable of eternal life, are in fact incapable of surviving our deaths or translation from the planet. In the same manner, many of the building blocks we use which are Morontian circuits will fizzle out when we have the need for circuits to enable us local universe reality values. As Paul said:

> "When I was a child, I spoke like a child, I thought like a child, I reasoned like a child; when I became an adult, I put an end to childish ways."[2]

It does make one wonder about the obvious immense universal comprehension and capacity for meaning used by the authors of The Urantia papers.

Why we believe in reincarnation

Turning our attention to those events and experiences here on Earth which contribute to our interest in developing faith in reincarnation, we find only a handful of such items: They are:

1. People who truly believe they have lived before because they visit a place or experience something which is a deja vu for them.

2. Past-Life regression sessions out of which we find data coming to mind which we identify with and attribute to "memories" of times past, times historically dated prior to our present birth.

3. Infants who display all the behavioural tendencies of known deceased predecessors, such as is most common in the Asian cultures and is *the* significant factor in the Tibetan practice of discovering reincarnated monks.

4. Clairvoyantly derived data, either personally obtained or given us by psychics/mediums who believe in reincarnation themselves.

5. Books on the subject by so-called authorities: Lobsang Rampa, Claire Prophet, Edgar Cayce, Alice Bailey, various Buddhist and Hindu authors and Gurus etc. etc. Theosophical bookshop shelves are abundant in authors expounding the virtues or logistics or reincarnation because it is central to the beliefs of that organisation.

All or some of the above we have experienced ourselves, or we believe that truly someone else has, and it is our firm conviction in this faith that enables us to believe in reincarnation. But the interesting thing is that the belief does not make it real, just as Cargo Cult belief that life can be more prosperous by praying for the Cargo planes of World War II who accidentally dropped a few tons of supplies into the isolated villages of primitive peoples, to return and deliver the people an abundance of goodies, is real. The planes are all scrapped. The pilots are ignorant of any of the natives' prayers. No one is supporting the system, which the natives are using as their "spiritual" foundation for life. The system doesn't exist. their intellectual model is incorrect, yet still they receive the blessings of the Father, son and Spirit as best they can.

Another, and probably prior criteria for us believing in reincarnation is *that we really want to*. And if we want to, we will look through those rose-tinted glasses and make sure we have sufficient support to back up our beliefs. One of the most supportive supports is numbers—if millions believe in it, it's easier to believe it must be true. However, there are probably only one or two people who believe in you, but that doesn't make you unreal or invalid. Most people believe for convenience sake and for emotional gratification; few believe for the love and liberty of truth. The biggest difficulty facing the person who believes in reincarnation and who wants to honestly check out whether or not it is our life condition, is the authority he has invested in his source of information. Is Edgar Cayce capable of really knowing about reincarnation, outside of the fact that he is obviously capable of believing in it? Just because the Tibetan spiritual program generates extraordinary personal power and psychic skills, does that mean that although they believe in reincarnation, and eagerly look for its existence in anything that crops up, that reincarnation itself exists? Or is reincarnation an inherited belief that is part and parcel of an explanation package no one dares or wishes to challenge because to do so, at first, appears to be more risky than believing in it? Yes, no one will answer their own "Reincarnation" question satisfactorily until they can act utterly free of all authorities on the subject.

Moving past the trend and tradition

When, if, you do ignore all of the world's numerous and difficult-not-to-believe-in authorities on reincarnation, you'll find that such a step alone will doubtless bankrupt your investigative resources. This stage then is the appropriate time to ask for a framework or some spiritually potent perceptual resources that are not generated by your own bias. It is only at such personally bankrupt levels of honesty and earnestness that truth can be revealed—whether on reincarnation or anything else. When we read and study The Urantia papers we have two choices in our approach:

1. hear what it says and test it out; or
2. hold on to our own possibly untested beliefs without allowing room for spiritual growth in regions beyond our already well defined parameters that the Urantia papers lessons might provide.

In 1985, I had an own enlightenment experience. "I" vanished and "Self" became the conscious host of my life. With this rather extraordinary awakening came a flood of realisations about the matters of reincarnation, God, religious practices and philosophies, etc.

There is no one to reincarnate

To the enlightened mind there is no reincarnation, there is no one to reincarnate: no one enlightened or unenlightened.

This view is held by all those who share enlightened minds' One-Mind perspective, however in order to communicate with people concerning their spiritual realities, many expedient measures are employed—reincarnation being one of them.

Judda Krishnamurti was probably one of the first, certainly one of the very few, ever to go against the tide of popular belief in reincarnation. Hosts of us here on this planet recognised that here was an exceptionally beautiful and enlightened human being who frequently openly decried the entire reincarnation hypothesis. He was the friend of all who elected spiritual freedom over the comfortable drowsiness of following traditional beliefs unquestionably. He was a thorough nuisance and embarrassment to all the teachers who taught their flocks the traditional and somewhat inert spiritual lessons most people preferred.

When the spiritual perspective is far-ranging enough, reincarnation theories are recognised to be merely expedient measures to stimulate people into some form of spiritual commitment. When the spiritual perspective is local, the reincarnation theories are the truth. Ironically though, truth seems more to be a matter of the capacity of the spirituality and morontia style of intellect to which we have access rather than the content we ascribe to our lives through their usage.

Nothing unusual

I have found nothing in the available proof presumed to validate reincarnation, which cannot be fully and satisfactorily ascribed to the nature of mind, faith and one's first-birth-ever occurring here on Earth. In the process of plumbing the very quiet and subtle depths of mind, all of the mechanisms involved in creating "Past-Life" readings is found. There are similar explanations for all the other phenomena which people ascribe to reincarnation. When once it is seen that the Adjuster of one individual can relay whole concepts and even a copy of the "I-concept" of his human subject to another individual's Adjuster, then the means of identifying the phenomena that is linked to reincarnation becomes plain and simple.

Most people, who believe in reincarnation here in the West, seem to hold the belief that they are embracing a belief that is larger, more generous, more truthful, more resourceful and more spiritual than any other belief presently held on the planet. But I say quite categorically that of all of the world views and beliefs into which we can invest our faith and our spiritual careers, reincarnation is *the* most crippling, *the* most stifling, *the* most confusing, *the* most evasive, and *the* most spiritually deprived of all—even if it may appear at first to be a little more psychically tantalising than the rest.

In saying this, I do not contest the enlightenment process of realising Self-Mind however. The experience of self-realisation is so utterly unique and precious to the various ways that we come to master the human mind, that I could not blaspheme that sacred ground. I am forever grateful to Ramana Maharshi, Lin Chi, Thubten Yeshe, Zong Rinpoche, Urgen Tulku and my own abbot Su Fu Hong Choon, without whose kindness I would never have progressed so well. In all this, I refer only to the philosophical premise of the reincarnation of the self—there is no reality to that concept whatsoever.

But these words are only one person's findings and opinion. If you are a student of the Urantia papers the odds are that if you also believe in reincarnation, you'll be having some difficulty accepting the papers' revelation in their entirety, and hence the fullness of your own faith's expression.

Perhaps you might consider asking, like I did. Perhaps you might be interested in challenging both The Urantia papers and your beliefs by laying them both on the line and letting someone more divine and more enlightened teach you the truth.

The universe, whether the model is portrayed by the Urantia papers, esotericism, Hinduism or Buddhism, is teeming with a host of our elders who are more than happy to help us develop our truth. For your own sake, and the sake of all of us who share your space and who doubtless will share your companionship for aeons to come, ask them.

The world *will* advance toward light and life without the plague of reincarnation among us. All of Buddhism and

Hinduism can, should its teachers so wish, keep everything about its enlightenment program and dispense with everything to do with its reincarnation philosophy and the liberation through self-realisation would go on unabated.

May God bless you and keep you spiritually hungry, and may your Adjuster fusion be swift and sure.

❧

Notes

1. 108:0.1 {The mission of the Thought Adjusters to the human races is to represent, to be, the Universal Father to the mortal creatures of time and space; that is the fundamental work of the divine gifts. Their mission is also that of elevating the mortal minds and of translating the immortal souls of men up to the divine heights and spiritual levels of Paradise perfection. And in the experience of thus transforming the human nature of the temporal creature into the divine nature of the eternal finaliter, the Adjusters bring into existence a unique type of being, a being consisting in the eternal union of the perfect Adjuster and the perfected creature which it would be impossible to duplicate by any other universe technique.}
2. 1 Corinthians 13:11

❧

Chapter 32

The Thought Adjuster's perspective on sonship with God

Chronology of growth

I first met God when I was five years old. I had dreams and visions of God and of monks and recluses between the ages of seven and twelve years. I gave my heart to Jesus at a Christian youth camp when I was twelve. I was baptised in water when I was thirteen. When I was sixteen, I had a dream in which Jesus asked me to take confirmation lessons so that we two could share communion with the bread and wine together.

At twenty, I left the Navy in search of a spiritual vocation and, at twenty-two, I had a revelation about the nature of causation and reality.

At twenty-three I went to India to be a wandering Sadhu and Yogi. In New Zealand at twenty-five I was baptised in the Holy Spirit during a spiritual death on the cross through Christ.

At twenty-nine, in Ladakh India, I experienced worshipful union with my Thought Adjuster. At thirty-three, I experienced the transcendence of reincarnation. At thirty-four I experienced the realisation of my Original Self-Mind, and commenced the study of Adjuster fusion.

At thirty-six I identified the Urantia papers as being more akin to the expression of my religious convictions than any other stream on Earth.

At forty-two I was given sonship with my Thought Adjuster; then the realisation of sonship with Michael and sonship with Mother Spirit; then given to the Paradise Father by Michael. At forty-five, at Flagstaff University Arizona, I first presented the fact of sonship with these divine Parents at an international conference for students of the Urantia papers.[1] At forty-seven I pastored the Church of Christ Michael in Melbourne for a year and at fifty I am writing this book on sonship and the Urantia papers.

All of these experiences represent my own search, encounters, ministry and growth in God. You too have your story and it is just as valid as mine or the next person's—they are all precious records of the extraordinary spawning of would-be Finaliters.[2] Notably, just about all of my own journey was difficult, as far from plain sailing as taking a three-master around Cape Horn, filled with doubt and uncertainty and riddled with awkward adjustments to all manner of conflicting emotions and beliefs. But that, as we all know, is what it is like to be human. It is a continuing challenge, across ever changing horizons, to "feast upon uncertainty, to fatten upon disappointment, to enthuse over apparent defeat, to invigorate in the presence of difficulties, to exhibit indomitable courage in the face of immensity, and to exercise unconquerable faith when confronted with the challenge of the inexplicable," and develop the battle cry that, "in liaison with God, nothing—absolutely nothing—is impossible."[3]

Copernicus' revolution

Copernicus is credited with the discovery that the world rotates around the sun and that even the sun is not the centre of the heavens. This discovery helped to shift the focus of man, and in particular occidental religious thinking, from previous primitive beliefs of the world being geographically and philosophically the heart of the universe. Similarly, there is a self-centred focus in spiritual life that is somewhat pre-Copernican, where one is the centre of one's own universe. This is broken apart when once we become conscious that, whilst we ourselves are all important, we owe life-bestowing allegiances to others than ourselves. The catalyst for this kind of Copernican revolution in ourselves is the awakening that God has a character, a mind, a will, and a life that we can share as an equal. It is at this point that we are enabled to safely and creatively move our thinking off ourselves and onto others and, inevitably, how God himself perceives our sonship with him. This is a part of the awakening to Adjuster fusion that we who are willing to traverse its waters encounter, as we come to know the mind of God from the inside.

Channelling and communion

With regard to the knowing of God, I feel it prudent to mention that none of what I have written about in this book involves the practice of channelling. Sonship with God is wholly different from channelling. The human mind is employed differently. One is the passage of information during which process the human will is largely or wholly suspended: the other is a communion with one's own divine Mother and Father with a wholly activated and dynamic human will. It is the mission of the Thought Adjuster to bring the human will into a consciousness of sonship with himself, and then to develop an eternal fusion of will with that son of God. Whilst, for some people, there may be a period of experimentation into channelling and associated types of extrapersonal communication in the very early stages of learning about the nature of mind, it should be noted that sonship with God which leads to Adjuster fusion involves processes which quickly try to conquer the passive will, along with all of its material lethargy, and focus on the active pursuit of Adjuster fusion—the union of the human will and God's will.

God's will is always active and never passive. For the human will and the will of God to become one will, obviously the passive-willed channeller is going to have to change if they want to progress into God's will.

Before I was born, God cared

My Father planted the seed of his presence in me before I was born. At the time of the transmission of information from the mother to the baby in the womb, there is a liaison between the generic mindedness of the Thought Adjuster and the embryonic mind of the foetus. From that time on until the arrival of the appointed and voluntary Thought Adjuster when the child is some five years ten months old, the seed presence develops in the human mind until it reaches the point of being accessible to the Thought Adjuster. At that stage in the development of mind, this is evidenced by the child making his or her all-important first moral choice and decision. Such a decision sparks the call for the Adjuster who arrives into a fully prepared mind. I have written about that experience in the chapter titled, "Thought Adjuster Arrival: how I got 'saved.'"

From the point of arrival to indwell the mind of the human child, the Thought Adjuster works diligently to develop his kinds of solutions for the human child's kind of problems. He is actively involved in developing ways to communicate those values to the human mind in such ways that the child can fully believe in them and build personal meanings around them, without the child necessarily believing or experiencing God's presence.

Finaliters

As great as is the Thought Adjuster's ability to fully be God for the child, so too is the greatness of the Finaliters who assist them.[4] "Many times in our own sojourn," said my Father to me, "have I turned to one of these great and mighty personalities who were once like you are now. Their journey from a world of nativity like Earth, all the way to Paradise and into the Corps of the Finality, is absolutely vital to the success of the mission of Thought Adjusters on Earth. Many times have I consulted with them, seeking their map, their way. From within their vast experience I have found the ways that were discovered by others of my own kind who once traversed similar problems as I am encountering.

"Though the mortals of Urantia may not now think very highly of returning from Paradise to some nativity world in service, I hope this revelation of their importance will boost respect and enthusiasm for this aspect of their loving service to the universes of time and space.

"Without them, my own efforts," he continued, "would be so immensely handicapped that, whilst an Adjuster fusion as occurred with Elijah could from time to time be achieved with the extraordinary individual, most fusion endowments could not be completed until the human subject reached the upper mansion worlds. Pentecost brought with it the new order for Adjuster indwelling, and we arrive daily in the thousands. It also heralded the invitation to large numbers of these one-time humans who are now thoroughly perfected through the ascent to Paradise. Large numbers of these Finaliters responded gloriously and now serve on Earth.[5] What should be considered well is that each one, whilst fully respectful of the sovereignty of Michael of Nebadon,[6] is literally God perfected through the human struggle for divine love, present on Earth.

"What a mighty and incomparable asset they are to us; to me!" he conveys to you the reader today as you read these lines. "You dear child, one day, may be one of them. It is not only possible for you, but the path has been well prepared for you."

The Urantia papers tell us that, "Every mortal craves to be a Finaliter."[7] This is not difficult to recognise while we are reading about the Corps of the Finality, but it was a very distant and foreign notion for me even after many years of reading the Urantia papers. Actually locating that feeling inside me took a long time—that I firstly actually had the desire to be perfect, and secondly, that I wanted to attain the Father in Paradise. I had other goals, and other more worldly feelings. That kind of a feeling required me to have a much larger sense of destiny than the one I developed through my ordinary life. School didn't teach me about after life matters. The Church didn't tell me what would become of me after I attained heaven. Uncle Hal, God love him, couldn't tell me about these things. Nothing in this world described the kind of destiny that is represented in the Corps of the Finality. Only the Urantia papers could tell me about that kind of a destiny.

Write a book for us

I remember yelling out to God when I was about nine years old, from our back yard in Morrinsville, saying, "Why don't you just write a book and explain what the whole show is all about so that everyone can read it and have a single source of information about heaven and death and clear up the confusion on this planet." That was a pretty naive idea, but only two or three years earlier, the Urantia papers had been published, and to some extent they answer that kind of a prayer fairly well.

Because of my association with the Urantia papers, my Thought Adjuster is enabled to communicate the earliest beginnings of Finaliter type values to me. By reading the word in the Urantia papers, then by the efforts of the Thought Adjuster to link me to universe realities, such a reality becomes mine. Many other readers share this vision: that they began their life on Earth and their destiny is the Corps of the Finality on Paradise. This goal then, attaining the Corps of the Finality on Paradise, represents the Thought Adjuster's overall view of sonship with God.

Thought Adjusters learn too

That conversation with the Thought Adjuster who attends my life with the view to fusion, enlarged my view on the simple

380

concept that, "with God all things are possible."[8] I came to realise that the Thought Adjuster doesn't come with all the answers to our own problems of living, or the problems he will face in living with us. He arrives with the idealistic goal and his abilities to draw from his own experience and considerable resources, not the least of which are our Seraphim of Destiny. The journey from each problem to its solution, all the way from human conception to birth and from Thought Adjuster arrival and Adjuster fusion on up to entrance into the Corps of the Finality, is an extraordinary adventure for God just as it is for a man or a woman.

The biggest handicap

Doubt

The handicap most affecting the Thought Adjuster is doubt. Even the limited ability for the primitive, pre-Pentecost man to be contacted and led by an Adjuster is successful if the heart is stable and pure. Doubt, with its associate fear, which then breeds hate, which manifests as anger and depression, severs the ropes on the swing bridge between the worldly and the divine and leaves man dangling, knife in hand, shackled to the Godless forces of the world. If there is one negative force to reckon with, it is doubt.[9]

The Thought Adjuster perceives the human heart in his child as being willing, cooperative, sinless, free to discover, excited by the romance and adventure of knowing God. Doubt can easily be learned and is often inherited. Doubt is taught, practised, tried and proven true. Doubt can grow into the folly of insincerity, the pride of argumentativeness, the shame of impurity, the insatiable hunger of tasting only that which is unreal and immature. Doubt can corrupt the once fragrant, sinless mind so that it comes to worship evil and the will of the created one instead of the will of the creator. If the Thought Adjuster has an enemy to his mission, it is mortal doubt springing up in his child's beautiful mind—the mind that was so exquisitely created by the Mother Spirit of Nebadon, now engulfed in shadow, enslaved, impoverished, crushed by unbelief, isolated in mortal orphanhood by doubt and its accomplice guilt.

Doubt is not questioning. John the Baptist was many times tempted to doubt even the genuineness of his own mission and experience.[10] During the forty days of "momentous dialog of Jesus' communing with himself, there was present the human element of questioning and near-doubting, for Jesus was man as well as God."[11]

To question, frequently means to lay aside all given knowledge and to wait on revelation about the true nature of some issue or detail. Doubt, on the contrary, is to sever oneself from the revelatory process itself. To doubt is to cut off the life that exists in questioning.

Jesus monitored the progress of his disciples by their "ability to triumph over doubt and courageously to assert their full-fledged faith in the gospel of the kingdom."[12] Those who were not achieving such spiritual victory he perceived to be "slowly but surely preparing their minds finally to reject him."[13] He instructed on the kinds of things that induce doubt, and how to overcome them:

"Be not deceived by their show of much learning and by their profound loyalty to the forms of religion. Be only concerned with the spirit of living truth and the power of true religion. It is not the fear of a dead religion that will save you but rather your faith in a living experience in the spiritual realities of the kingdom. Do not allow yourselves to become blinded by prejudice and paralysed by fear. Neither permit reverence for the traditions so to pervert your understanding that your eyes see not and your ears hear not. It is not the purpose of true religion merely to bring peace but rather to insure progress. And there can be no peace in the heart or progress in the mind unless you fall wholeheartedly in love with truth, the ideals of eternal realities. The issues of life and death are being set before you—the sinful pleasures of time against the righteous realities of eternity. Even now you should begin to find deliverance from the bondage of fear and doubt as you enter upon the living of the new life of faith and hope. And when the feelings of service for your fellow men arise within your soul, do not stifle them; when the emotions of love for your neighbour well up within your heart, give expression to such urges of affection in intelligent ministry

382

to the real needs of your fellows."[14]

And, again:

"I will not forsake you; my spirit will not desert you. Be patient! doubt not that this gospel of the kingdom will triumph over all enemies and, eventually, be proclaimed to all nations."[15]

Mastering doubt

Doubt comes through our attempts to receive the favour of God. We doubt our faith. We doubt our prayers. We doubt our luck. We doubt our chances. When we pray though, our little human mind is reaching out to contact the infinite mind of God. We are limited by our knowledge of God and our wisdom concerning prayer. The answer to our prayer is always shaped by God's view of our needs. Often, it can seem, it appears that he is too slow, too miserly, too distant, too concerned with the larger issues in life, too concerned for the good and the holy and not enough with the grubby and the forsaken. Our prayer, it seems, goes unheard: wasted wishes on a wasted Adjuster. We all know the barren, impoverishing, bone-drying misery of wanting deeply needed prayers fulfilled, and not a whisper, not so much as a murmur from the heavens comes our way. The Urantia papers tell us that, "there never can be observed an unbroken continuity of material phenomena between the making of a prayer and the reception of the full spiritual answer thereto."[16] For the person who is trying to establish himself or herself in God by faith, as much as for the person who is already so established, it is during this period of the apparent lack of connection to God, between the time of asking and the time of receiving, that the tendency to doubt emerges. The significance of the doubt is different to each person, but the tendency to give rise to it exists in the same place.

Jesus had fully mastered doubt, and he eternally welcomes us into the same victory. When David Zebedee came to know the certainty of the threat to Jesus' life, Jesus confidently invited him into the assurance that exists beyond doubt and fear, saying:

"Only doubt not in your own heart that the will of God will prevail in the end."[17]

What a great assurance that is. On the next occasion that you are trusting in God and doubt starts to raise its evil head, position yourself in the close proximity to Jesus as was David that day, and hear Jesus' words spoken to you:

"Only doubt not in your own heart —your name— that the will of God will prevail in the end."

Both the Bible and the Urantia papers instruct us to pray in faith and to expect a certainty of answer. "Do not hesitate to pray the prayers of spirit longing; doubt not that you shall receive the answer to your petitions." And, "All genuine spirit-born petitions are certain of an answer. Ask and you shall receive."[18]

Doubt is overcome by faith that is steadfast. Paul wrote of his practice of having done all, standing firm in faith until the victory emerges.[19] That kind of faith is one that asks for a result, then waits knowing that the emergence of the result is still just as much in process as it was the moment it was asked for. Doubt creeps in when we lose sight of the momentum of our prayer and, considering it to have withered away in time, we count it as lost and give up on faith and our own Father.

Doubting your own spiritual life

The biggest problem that faces people who come to the Urantia papers is often the doubt that sets up in their minds concerning the genuineness of their own spiritual lives. They may have believed that they had full, rich lives in some other religion. When they encounter the Urantia papers, they have no idea about the names and places and personalities. They are easily swamped by the enormity of the universes and the destinies in that revelation. It takes a long time to get acquainted with enough of the details to settle down and find that your faith works on the new footing you are building. People who once knew that God was with them can become quite disoriented, doubting their spiritual growth and even the closeness of their Thought Adjuster. The familiarities of their favourite hymns, or style of worship service, or method of prayer sometimes are lost as the searching soul is caught between two worlds—the old and familiar faith practices, and the new and as yet formless world of a new horizon with new players and new realities.

Do you know how many Thought Adjusters there are in the universe right now though, that in the twinkling of an eye, would rush to your side and confirm just how well you are progressing in your journey toward Adjuster fusion? That's right: every single one of them! Never forget that fact dear one. Never forget that it doesn't matter what stage of growth you are living, or how many successes you have had, or how many troubles and errors you have found. Even if you are standing in the muck up to your ears right now, today, there's always an Adjuster somewhere who believes in you, and who can see past the conditions of your life, who will confirm the worth of your possibilities and your past. Ever do they confirm you by who you are becoming, according to their own vision for you, rather than by your own limited view of yourself. Adjuster fusion has many stages, many milestones. In the mind of God your Father, all of them are credited to you as a victory. That you are reading this book, is a significant victory in itself.

Jesus' kind of faith

The kind of faith that Jesus demonstrated began to be a beacon for me around the time I was approaching thirty years of age. I had read in the Urantia papers how Jesus raised Lazarus from the dead, and I was deeply impressed by a couple of the features in what he had said to Martha:

"Did I not tell you at the first that this sickness was not to the death? Have I not come to fulfil my promise? And after I came to you, did I not say that, if you would only believe, you should see the glory of God? Wherefore do you doubt? How long before you will believe and obey?"[20]

I had no idea how one could have a spiritual relationship with God in such a way that the dead could be raised back to life by a simple command or prayer—nor was I particularly looking for one. I was, however, lured on by the fact that he knew that a condition was not to the death; and that believing was the key to participating with the glory of God and doubting was the way to be excluded from it.

Seeing the problem and the solution

A lady once came to see me, bringing her adult daughter for acupuncture treatment. At the end of the session, she casually asked me, "Can you tell me what's wrong with me?"

I was tying up my shoelace with my back to her. Immediately, without hesitation, my attention went to her chest and I told her about an operation she had had regarding a breast tumour: she was still anxious that the cancer might return. Then my attention went to her right arm and shoulder, she had once had an injury that had left her arm paralysed for some time: she still had pins and needles in it from time to time. Then my attention went to her back: she had had an injury to her thoracic vertebrae, leaving her with migraines that came and went, and broken sleep. Then, lastly, my attention went to her womb: she had had several miscarriages, two abortions and had finally had a hysterectomy around eighteen months earlier that still seemed to leave her weak and fatigued.

All of my perceptions were correct, apparently.

That was the first time I found that God's mind, in liaison with my own mind, could effectively identify certain pathological conditions in the context of Chinese Medical physiology. It was an experience that took me beyond the borders of a certain kind of doubt. It wasn't long after that however that I became deeply hungry to know God beyond spiritual doubt. This gift of discernment that I had begun to use in my acupuncture practice was insufficient to satisfy my spiritual doubt that wanted almost skin-to-skin contact with God, a union of mind. After praying, I was invited to journey to Ladakh in North East India, in order to engage my Thought Adjuster in just such an experience of worship—a transformation, I was assured, that would overturn the doubt in me.

Ladakh pilgrimage

And so, faithfully, I packed up and went to Ladakh. On the fifth day after I settled in Leh, a week after I had left Srinagar in Kashmir, I met my Father and for the following two months we journeyed together into our worshipful liaison. I have always considered the culmination of that episode in our life together to be represented by a single event which involved the evidence of our unified minds. Here is that story.

The time was 1980-81. India was speckled with people who were spilling out of the ashram of Bhagwan Rajneesh, just south of Bombay, which had deflated after his departure to America. A number of these red-clothed "sanyassins" as they called themselves, mainly westerners, had journeyed to Kashmir and on to Ladakh. I had met a number of them, treated a few with acupuncture, and with some had discussed the Urantia papers, meditation and the Chinese Buddhist order whose robes I was wearing at the time.

Among these people was an American lady, Shavda, 43 years old and from Santa Monica California, who brought another sanyassin to my attention—a German; aged twenty-one years; she made her living by prostitution apparently; according to Shavda, she was very ill with a mixture of altitude sickness, dehydration, dysentery, vomiting and some kind of vaginal infection. I never knew her name.

The German with a lung infection

On that day, a very panicky German fellow stopped me in the market place. His breathing was dreadful and he seemed to be in pain, wincing as he asked in very broken English whether I was the acupuncturist that was working with the head Umchi in town—the chief doctor of traditional Tibetan medicine. Eventually we found a translator and I was able to tell him that he needed to go to Leh Hospital immediately, and to get whatever help he could to treat what appeared to be a respiratory infection. Such things quickly kill people at Leh's very high altitude. I had given a lecture and demonstration of acupuncture to all of the doctors of Leh hospital and, despite their incredible lack of facilities and provisions, I had every confidence in their ability to help this fellow. Sure enough, I found him in the market place a few days later, well recovered, thankful that I had been able to find a cab for him without delay—a miracle in itself—and given him the referral to Leh hospital.

Shavda met me on that day, asking me if this particular German tourist had tracked me down and if I had been able to help him. I replied that he had, and that I had.

The young woman who was dying

She then mentioned this other German woman. I must confess that I questioned the integrity of her spiritual pursuits when it was mentioned that she earned her livelihood as a prostitute. I said something about her problems being the result of her sin and that, before anything could happen for her she would need to take her soul to God. Shavda replied, "Yeah, right. Like she's going to do that! Just go and see her. I know you can help her. Pray for her, if you have to. Do something. They think she's dying."

"I haven't come here to get involved in everybody's illness, Shavda," I replied. "I am here on a mission to achieve spiritual union with God in worship."

She nodded her understanding.

"What has this person got to do with me? She's not my business," I continued, indicating that I felt in my spirit that whatever her fate was, it didn't really involve me. And I walked off.

The following day, Shavda found me.

"That German woman has moved into the same Ladakhee family home where you are staying. Have you seen her?"

"No," I replied politely.

"Do you want to see her? I think God's bringing her closer to you so you can help her?"

"I have no word on that," I protested.

"It really seems that she is too sick to travel—she went to the Leh Hospital but the doctors said they can't do anything for her," Shavda said. "They can't fly her out because the sudden change in altitude will kill her, and she is in so much pain that she can't be moved by bus down to Kashmir."

She could see that I was still unmoved.

"What do I have to do to get you to do something for her?" Shavda asked. "She's only a kid. What does she know?"

I thought for a moment. I had already looked into the will of God and could see that my acupuncture would do nothing for her. She needed allopathic medical care, or else a miracle from God.

"Shavda, this girl is not in God's will as it concerns what God is doing in my life."

"What? And the other German fellow was?"

"Yes he was. He sought me out, and he found me by God's will," I replied.

"But this girl can't seek you out! She's flat out on her back on the bed dying. How's she going to seek you out?"

"I'll tell you what Shavda," I said. "The best I'll do is this. I'll pass this matter over to my Father. If he wants to do anything with this, then I'll do it. If he doesn't, then I won't. OK?"

She looked at me with a faint flicker of hope as if to say, "Yeah, but if he doesn't do anything, you'll still do something won't you?"

I then dropped the matter, asking her not to raise it again.

The Snow Lion

On the next day, I ate my evening meal at the Snow Lion restaurant up on main street—famed throughout all Ladakh as the hottest joint in town because it had a jukebox. None of us patrons seemed overly disappointed that on the occasion of our meal the thing wasn't working.

By seven o'clock, I was heading back to my room, all rugged up in the autumn cold of October. The nights in Leh were falling into their starlit blackness earlier each day. The winter snows were starting. The air that was always cold in the shade at that altitude was now also cold in the sunshine. Tea that was poured boiling hot one minute was as cold as the chiselled stones on the prayer walls within five minutes.

At around seven thirty on that Saturday evening, I closed the wooden shutters on my windows and I made myself one of those teas in my little room. I lit a stick of local Tibetan incense and a couple of butter lamps—there was no power in most of Ladakh, and in Leh it closed down at 6pm on weekdays and all weekend, like clockwork. I sat down cross-legged on a cushion on the floor, and leaned back against the wall. Ordinarily when I sat here in the day time with the easterly windows open, I could see the mountains that rose up to the east of Leh, towering a thousand feet above the main road into the township. That night my room, with its little green shutters tightly wedged against the glass panes, was very small, very close around me, bitterly cold and coming to an end. I sipped my tea, finishing it when it had all but turned to ice, and I let the peace of the day's end settle on me.

My Father's will for her healing

After about twenty minutes of just sitting there being myself, without hurry or intention, my Thought Adjuster became apparent to me as a mind who was in my room with me.

I was so relaxed. He seemed almost excited that our communication was so crystal clear and easy. Without much delay, he said to me:

"Do you see that woman in the room next door?"

I looked through the wall and saw in my spirit this German girl lying on her bed. I had been told that she had only two days to live: she would be dead by Tuesday. I still had no real interest in her or her welfare.

"Yes," I replied to this Thought Adjuster.

"Say, 'You are well' to her," he continued.

I looked at her, as she was in the room next door, and with absolutely no effort, and little personal interest in the outcome, said those words:

"You are well."

Then I waited.

I must have waited for about two minutes, waiting for him to say something to me. Finally, I broke the silence because the whole exercise seemed somewhat futile to me:

"What's the deal Father?" I said. "You tell me to say 'You are well.' But, so what? This woman's apparently dying. Nobody's treating her. She can't be moved and she can't move herself. What on Earth has my saying 'You are well' got to do with making her well...you know, like, really making her well? It's one thing to say it and it's a whole other thing for her to get well."

Then he said the words I'll never forget:

"Tomorrow night, she will dine and sing and dance at the same restaurant you yourself ate at tonight."

I couldn't believe what he was saying. It was just too way out. I had never experienced anything like this before. This girl was as good as dead. Folks had been talking about giving her one of those Tibetan funerals where they lay her out for the buzzards. It's a kind of ghoulish thing, but twelve thousand feet up in the Himalayas, in Ladakh, it wasn't all that unusual really. Nobody expected her to live. Now, here was my Thought Adjuster—and in those days I didn't know much at all about Thought Adjusters—telling me that by my saying, "You are well," she was going to be raised up.

All I could do was accept it and run with whatever happened: it was well over my ability to fathom.

Some fifteen minutes after saying this statement, this command of God's will, his mind had still not subsided and we entered into a union of mind that was absolutely magnificent. This great being, and me a tiny little mortal, merged the one into the other and stayed there at rest. With that one experience, my hunger for worshipful union of mind and being with my Father was fully satisfied. Mission complete.

Prophesying the healing

It was around nine-thirty that I felt feet coming up the stairs inside the house and along the hallway to my room. There was a hefty knock on my door, a jiggle of the handle, and Shavda stood in the doorway with a big lantern lighting up her face.

"I thought I'd find you here. We're all dancing up at the Snow Lion; the guy finally got the jukebox working. They've only got about twenty records, and they're all Bobby Vinton I think, but the dancing's great. Wanna join us? People have been asking after you."

"No, I'm fine Shavda," I replied, still in the union mind with my Father.

"What about the girl next door?" she asked.

"She will be dancing and singing and dining at that restaurant tomorrow evening," I said, repeating what had been said before by the will of God.

Shavda looked at me like I was a complete lunatic.

"What?" she blurted out contemptuously. "That girl next door is going to be dead not dancing. And as for eating, she hasn't eaten in days 'cos she throws up everything. She can't get off the bed she's that exhausted. I went in and saw her just this afternoon—she's dreadful."

She looked at me to see that I was nonplussed. Then, in an explosive gesture, she stepped back out into the hallway, slammed my door shut, yelled something about me being full of something, and stomped on down the hall and down the stairs and out of the house. I was so intrigued with the fact that I had total faith in what my Father had asked me to say that I completely forgot to get offended with her!

The head Umchi of Ladakh

I spent the next day visiting some Ladakhee friends in one of the handicraft centres where they make the most beautiful rugs with Tibetan motifs. Then I visited the head Umchi and gave him some more acupuncture for his lower back pain. He said how pleased he was with the previous treatments and that, although he had never used acupuncture himself, how well it fitted into Tibetan Medical applications. He had been developing beautifully detailed medical charts for the Indian Government, as a way of validating and systematising the practices of Tibetan traditional medicine. Over the previous couple of months, we had talked much about them and now I gave him a couple of acupuncture charts, some needles and some sticks of moxa. Then we went upstairs and onto the flat roof of his home. We wrapped ourselves in our robes and hats and scarves and sat near the edge of the roof, overlooking the gardens of some key tourist hotel where often traditional dancers would be seen performing in the gardens for the tourists. Shortly after, his servant popped up out of the rooftop hatch with some wonderful little sweet cakes and some beautifully prepared hot butter tea.

We talked about many things, not the least of which was the coming winter. We really were saying our farewells. It was a romantic time. It reminded me of everything I had ever read in Lobsang Rampa's books in my late teens. Before me, spread out like a great fortress wall, were the Himalayas, all snow clad and glistening with icy white brilliance. All about me were the tall poplars, now losing their yellow leaves. Below was the sound of the children playing around at the nearby school. It was a wonderful afternoon. I felt deeply honoured, immensely privileged that God should enable me to travel to this part of the world and to spend such quality time with such noble company as this fellow.

The bus driver

At length, we parted and I walked down the hill to the main market place where I met a Kashmiri bus driver, the driver of the first bus ever to make it up the new road from Srinagar to Leh, with all its 64,000 curves.

I had treated this fellow, and many of his friends, for the sore shoulders the drivers get when they haul their trucks and buses around those 64,000 curves twice each week. The treatment worked well and we had become good friends. He had the most amazing twinkle in his eye, the sparkle of an adventurous go-getter. I had never accepted money for my acupuncture services and now he offered me a free ride down to Kashmir in his empty bus.

"The winter is coming don't you know? The last bus leaves Leh next week. You had better be on it or else you'll have to stay here all winter until May when the roads open again. Do you want that?" he asked.

"No, not really," I replied. "I think my time here is done."

He looked at me with eyes like a hawk, then he said:

"God has been with you, I can tell," he said in his rolling Kashmiri English. "I have seen you many times now and I can tell that you have come here for God and God has met you here in this high wilderness. It has been a very good thing to meet you, and I hope you will accept the offer of my free ride back to Srinagar. My house is your house there. I have told all my friends and family about you and you are most welcome to come and live with us for as long as you want, all completely free. I am not a wealthy man but I can give you anything I have. Please come down the Himalayas with me. I am leaving on Tuesday morning at 5.30."

I told him I would confirm it with him on Monday and we parted company.

Vision of the bus accident

Then I saw Shavda. I told her to get my copy of the Urantia papers back from a friend of hers, one Fleur, who had borrowed them from her.

"How come?" she asked.

"I think I am leaving on Tuesday with Roul on his bus."

"Oh, can I come too?" she asked. "I know that Fleur is going on that bus too, with her friend. Roul invited her too."

Suddenly, I saw a vision of the bus having an accident, of rolling off the road and down a hill. When it reached the bottom, Fleur was lying on the ground as if she was dead.

"Please be sure and get the book from Fleur," I repeated.

"But she's going on the same bus as you, get it off her on the bus."

"No. Be loyal to your arrangement Shavda," I said. "You

asked me if she could borrow it for a few days and then you'd make sure she returned it. Go now and get the book back for me."

Later that afternoon she brought me the book, still not happy with my insistence. I then told her that I thought there would be an accident on that bus and that Fleur could be seriously hurt and that if she were to be removed from the bus the book might go with her and I didn't want that to happen.

Shavda was alarmed at the prospect of the accident, understanding that I wanted the book returned, and curious whether she should say anything to Fleur.

"No, don't bother. What's hers is hers," I said.

"Are we going to be alright if we go on the trip?" she asked.

"Yes, it seems so."

"Can't you just pray or do something to help her. She seemed to have a really good spirituality about her. Surely there's something you can do to help her."

"OK," I said, "I'll see," I replied.

I ate alone that evening, cooking something simple on my gas cooker and eating it out of the pot while it was still on the stove, before it went cold. I sat fully dressed in whatever warm clothes I had left, quietly enjoying my Father's company in the glow of the butter lamps and the little flame of the kerosene cooker. Then, from outside, I heard my name being called. I heard the patter of feet running down the road from Leh to this house, the Green House, where I had lived those past two months.

The miracle

"Un. Un,"[21] she called out, for she only knew me by my monk name. "Un, Un, you'll never guess what!" And in a few moments she was charging up the stairs and along the hall and bursting into my room.

"She's up there in the restaurant just like you said she would be!"

Shavda was breathless—you don't run in Ladakh at the best of times.

"She's been eating and singing and dancing. It's like she was never sick. She said that around two-thirty she suddenly felt healed. By four-thirty she got up out of her room and went for a walk up to the market place. When we all went and had dinner

394

up at the Yak, there she was, already eating, as hungry as an ox and with no signs of illness whatsoever.

"It's a miracle Un. A miracle. I don't know what else to call it. What did you do? I know for a fact that no one else did anything to help her, so what did *you* do?"

"Nothing. My Father healed her with his words. He asked me to say, 'You are well,' and I did. And she is well. That's all there is to it Shavda. I am very happy for her."

"Oh I told her all about you. She really wants to meet you. Do you want to come up to the restaurant and see for yourself and meet her?"

"No, we won't meet. Just wish her well from me and tell her to thank God and change her life," I replied.

"Oh. OK." Shavda said. "Well, anyway, isn't it great?"

"Oh and bye the way," she continued, "did you do anything to help Fleur? Now that I've seen what you've done for the German girl, I kind of don't know what to expect out of you. Whatever you've got is way too special and not in my league at all. What about Fleur. I asked her if she had to go on that particular bus and she is adamant about going."

"I said something. She won't die," I said.

"But she'll still get injured?" she asked.

"Yes. The injury's unavoidable. She hasn't got whatever it takes to get out of that one. If she could loosen her grip and take a different bus perhaps it would all work out differently; but she is moved by the flesh and she won't budge. Maybe she and Roul have a thing going on. I don't know. But I believe the injuries will be lessened immensely. We'll see."

Shavda thought about that for a moment, then reflected on the events of the last twenty-four hours, and put aside her doubts, even if she couldn't quite grasp the assurances of faith in God.

The bus trip from Leh

On Tuesday morning we all met at the bus depot. It was freezing cold. There was not a breath of wind. The stars were so close because of the lack of air at that altitude, it made me dizzy looking up at them.

By six o'clock we were on the bus, five of us, and by first light we moved off down the road towards Srinagar.

After we had driven for about an hour, Roul began pumping

the brakes to test them. This was common practice. Then he pulled the hand brake on a few times. Throughout both tests, the bus seemed to slow up appropriately. After another half an hour however, he tried them again and this time he was disturbed.

"We've got to go back," he said as he slowed and wheeled the bus off the road and around into the early morning sunrise. "There's a small problem and I want to get it one hundred percent checked out. We won't take long. Maybe you can have breakfast while you're waiting."

The accident

We arrived back at Leh and he parked the bus up on a hill, right behind two other buses and alongside one of the big mechanic workshops that service these long haul vehicles. We all got out and eventually went for a stroll.

After about an hour, Shavda and I heard a scream and a big crash and saw a lot of people running down the road. Something big had happened. I was of a mind to ignore it but then a shopkeeper who knew that I had practised acupuncture and considered me to be another Umchi said to me:

"Doctor, you'd better go down and see. A bus has run away and I think there's somebody been injured."

Immediately I thought of Fleur.

We ran down the hundred yards or so to see that our own bus was the cause of the commotion. The most amazing thing had happened. It had somehow lost its brakes, steered itself out of its parked position behind two other buses, run on down the hill some fifty yards until it came to the end of the street and banged into a big solid mani wall—the kind of wall that is made out of little rocks that have had Tibetan Buddhist prayers carved into them. What was most peculiar is that we all knew that Roul had locked the bus when we left it, and that it was simply bizarre that it should steer itself around two other buses to head on straight into the wall.

As we drew near, somebody rushed up to me saying:

"Umchi lama! Umchi lama! Come see. Your friend. Your friend hurt!"

I made my way through the people and there was Fleur lying on the ground. She had bus tyre marks across her abdomen and chest. I was astonished. I was also relieved that the accident had not occurred on one of the many precipitous cliffs on the Zoji-la road to Srinagar. Somebody said that she had been in the path of the bus and knocked down by it and then literally run over by it with both the front and rear wheels as it headed for the Mani wall.

The prophecy in my Father's mind was fulfilled.

Did God cause the accident?

No, of course not. He did see it coming though. Doubtless, he would have given Fleur communication which she ignored or didn't translate effectively.

While the bus was being repaired, we took Fleur off to Leh Hospital for a checkup. She was in deep shock of course, but she seemed to have no broken bones, no spinal damage and no immediate signs of internal bleeding. The doctor wanted to hold her over for a day or two, to verify that she had no internal damage, but Fleur vigorously refused. By one o'clock that afternoon, we were all loaded back on the bus, the locals had been thanked for their immeasurable kindness—Ladakhees and Tibetans are patently the most friendly people on the face of this Earth—and off we headed. Shavda looked at me, convinced that she needed to get a copy of the Urantia papers for herself, and discover who this Thought Adjuster thing was—which, the following year in Penang, she did.

And that's the story of the first time I encountered my Father's will through his word. It was the first time I experienced a union of mind with him that I counted as worship. It was an experience in which I grew over a two month period, that enabled me to conquer human doubt by means of the divine assurance that he gave me, and which I made my own.

If ever these was a single enemy to the Thought Adjuster's mission of creating in you sonship with God and then Adjuster fusion, it is doubt. I believe that every Thought Adjuster loves to bring their human child through that barrier of doubt into the green pastures of divine assurance as quickly and as effectively as possible. Believe with me also dear one.

"Did I not tell you at the first that this sickness was not to the death? Have I not come to fulfil my promise? And after I came to you, did I not say that, if you would only believe, you should see the glory of God? Wherefore do you doubt? How long before you will believe and obey?"[22]

The biggest door-opener

If there is one thing that is helpful to the Thought Adjuster in his mission of developing a sense of sonship and the immediate goal of Adjuster fusion, it is the combination of believing and obeying him.

Believing and obeying

Believing means finding your foundation in your Thought Adjuster's intention; and obeying means carrying out his wish or participating fully in its outworking with him. Believing is faith; obeying is action—you can't obey unless you're actually doing something, and you can't do something unless you understand what to do and have the faith to do it. To believe God is to take God's ways into your daily life and to see the results of God's will in your everyday affairs—be it for your own benefit, or the benefit of others, or both. It may also simply be for your Adjuster's benefit.

If action doesn't spontaneously arise out of believing, then one is confused over what to believe. The problems of believing are usually limited to a person not knowing what to believe, how to believe, who to believe, when to believe or why to believe. But the problems of obeying are limited to the fact that one doesn't understand what to obey—what to do—or else, in the case of sin and iniquity, one does indeed know what to obey—what to do—but one chooses to disobey by refusing to do what is known in God's heart or by deliberately doing something contrary.

Most people are fearful of issues around obeying when in fact they're struggling with issues around believing.

Believing has levels of risk to it, whereas obeying that which is known to be God's will has little risk in it at all. The more you risk and dare to believe about God, the more you will draw of him into your life.

Believing with God's faith

One of the earliest encounters of believing at a level well over my head was an experience of believing my Father for the healing of cancer.

I had been detoxing heroin users for around four years and I was becoming very hungry to see my Thought Adjuster in action in the healing arena.

When you stand in front of a person who has cancer and who has been told she has three days to live, and she has, and you think about healing her, you'd better know that God is with you because I can tell you that your faith drains right out your feet. You feel absolutely disconnected, alone, useless, powerless and overwhelmed by the enormity of death and its closeness, the seemingly infinite roots of the disease, the obvious decay of the person's hope and the inevitability of failure to help.

My wife Mary told me of Shirley, and that she ran a cancer support group. I visited Shirley and talked with her about how I worked with people. The following day she called me, saying that she had spoken with two people who were really difficult cases who would both like me to come and visit them in their own homes. We arranged a visit for the following day.

It was later that evening when the doubt set in! What had looked good in principle, suddenly loomed larger than life and looked utterly impossible to me. All manner of doubts ran through my mind. I didn't know what to believe about my own expertise in this field. I didn't know how to believe in God for his involvement. I didn't know who to believe—God, Jesus, Chinese Medicine, Holy Spirit, Spiritual Energetics. I didn't know when to believe. Should I be more prayed up than I am? Do I believe for her healing now or tomorrow? And I didn't know why to believe. What exactly did I want out of this deal? Was I going for healing or help or cure? What, exactly?

I sat outside on the patio and looked into the garden. I tried really hard to focus and calm myself, to get a grip on the aspect of believing. My problem was that, essentially, I had for some time wanted to move out of all of the medical and psychotherapeutic strategies I had been using. I wanted to work exclusively with the will of God. And the bottom line was that it was a whole new thing for me. I had to believe well over my customary level of believing.

Christians with healing ministries, such as Charles and Frances Hunter, Oral Roberts, Tommy and Daisy Osborne, the late William Branham and the late Smith Wigglesworth[23]— they all believed at a level that was way out in the deep water, well over their heads, in that place of believing where it's God's believing that sustains things and not one's own believing.

Now that's a strange concept, "God's believing," but your own faith will only carry you so far and then you have to rely on God's faith. For example, who has the faith to bring us to Adjuster fusion, us or God? God does—why, we barely know what the term means. God is bringing us to Adjuster fusion on his own belief; we are being ferried into fusion and even on up to Paradise by God's own grace and efforts. All we have to do is believe and agree. That's it, everyday, just believe and agree, believe and obey, day after day.

At a certain point, my Father said to me:

"Just be yourself and do whatever you feel like doing."

I accepted that counsel as a prophecy of success, even though I had no confirmation of a promise of complete healing like I had had in Ladakh with the words "you are well."

Jenny, with cancer

When Shirley and I arrived at Jenny's house, we were quickly ushered into her bedroom. Before me was a lovely lady, in her mid thirties, all skin and bone with huge cancerous growths all over her body.

I quickly adapted myself to hide my shock and to check the faith that would have run out my feet were it not for the confidence I had received from my Father the night before.

We talked for a while. She told me some of her history and then told me that she had returned home from hospital the day before, and that the doctor had visited her this morning to take back the hospital's equipment. She had three days to live and wouldn't need the equipment any more.

At a certain point in our visit, I saw a cloud like presence of the Holy Spirit resting above her head.

"Jenny, the Holy Spirit is nearby you. Ready to bring healing to you. If you are willing, I will pray now and ask Jesus to send this Holy Spirit into you for your healing. Would you like that?" I asked her.

"Yes I would, Rob. Very much," she replied.

"Very well then, I'll do that."

This was before the days in 1993 when I had received sonship from my Father, Michael and Mother Spirit. I was still not well connected, and more than a little in the dark about how these things ought to or could happen. So I just worked with what I did know.

"Jesus," I prayed out loud so she could hear me, "please bring your Holy Spirit into Jenny now for her healing."

Then I waited to see what that cloud of anointing would do.

After a few seconds, it seemed to me that it wanted to go deep inside her and so I said:

"Jenny, breathe that Holy Spirit inside you now. Take one big deep breath, and the Holy Spirit will enter into you with healing."

She immediately did just that, opening her mouth wide and sucking in the air.

As she did so, I watched the Holy Spirit anointing that was above her head just get drawn into her body, through her head and face, as if it was responding to her will for it to be in her.

After this huge inhalation, she closed her eyes and seemed to be feeling around inside herself, perhaps looking for the impact of this "Holy Spirit". Then, suddenly, she rose up out of her prone position as if to sit up in bed, grinning from ear to ear with great joy, and she began shouting:

"I'm healed! I'm healed! I'm healed!"

I was more flabbergasted than she was, I'm sure. I had no idea what was going to happen. Her outburst had little credibility with me: whilst I thought it would be wonderful for the Holy Spirit to heal her, I had serious reservations because of lack of experience in being out so far in the deep with God in these kinds of matters. I did find myself immensely empowered and filled with the power of God however, and I wasn't expecting that at all. Maybe, after all, she was healed like she said.

After a few minutes, when I discretely turned my attention onto her and within her to see if any of the cancer was still active, it appeared to me that a considerable amount had indeed disappeared—but not all. I made up my mind to be quiet and simply see what worked out. It was clearly in God's hands.

The following day I had a call from Shirley. Apparently that doctor had been around to see Jenny that morning and had said:

"I don't know what's happened Jenny, but you certainly aren't dying. You have every sign of being in remission."

And she was.

Now that's a strange thing dear reader, isn't it? A lady is one day dying of cancer with three days left to live, and the next day she is recovering and her cancer lumps are deflating like slow leaking balloons. The only thing that has happened is that someone prayed, asking the Holy Spirit to enter into her, and it did.

She lived for several more months with all the signs of complete recovery. She had vitality and life again. The kind of miracle you only read about or see at spiritual healing meetings. Shirley was out of bed, doing the gardening, getting the kids off to school, loving her wonderful husband and going shopping at the supermarket with her Mum.

Jenny dies

Months went by, and then one day she became weak and went back to bed. She called me over and we talked. Finally she admitted that, until her healing, which she had so fervently prayed for, she had lain so close to death, and for so long with God as her only real companion, that she couldn't relate to being alive and well again. She told me about the minister in whom she had placed her confidence, who subsequently tried to have sex with her, and shattered her faith in religious organisations. When she complained, the Church simply covered it up and moved him. It was around that time that the cancer first showed up in her life.

For Jenny, actual recovery was too much the new thing. Perhaps she didn't want to travel back into that experience with the minister and the Church. She now opted to go with the familiar thing, and depart. Whether she had cancer or not, Jenny's new agenda was to depart, and within the week she died.

Such determination is not all that uncommon. Perhaps you know someone like that. My own mother was like that. Within a month of the diagnosis, she died.

I once heard Kenneth Hagin say, "Die if you want to, but don't die sick!" Now that's an interesting 'fusion mind' type of statement, isn't it?

A vision for cantankerous Kevin

The other person that Shirley had lined up for me was Kevin. He was a cantankerous old coot who had chased off many a well-wishing comforter in the last months of his illness. Actually he was probably only in his fifties, and he had all the fire of his Irish miner's gall boiling away in his blood just looking for a victim. He didn't particularly want to get healed. He seemed to have well and truly had enough of living, being a father and husband and of working. All he wanted was spiritual peace, and the cancer volunteers and healers and prayer warriors just hadn't delivered. Kevin was an argument looking for a place to happen.

As Shirley and I walked out of Jenny's place on the first day that we visited her, when she still had only three days to live, Shirley mentioned Kevin to me. I turned my attention toward my Paradise Father and observed the outplaying of His will for this man. He revealed all of the information I needed.

I consented to go with the Shirley and visit him. She warned me about his attitude. I again consented.

"You seem pretty confident. What will you do?" she asked me as we drove off.

"I'll give him peace. Maybe I'll check out if he will be healed as well" I replied.

"It's OK," I continued. "I don't mind where he's coming from. He'll do OK. But he might go through the mill for a day first, while God brings him into the spiritual desert. But he'll do OK. He'll have the peace he wants."

She looked at me like I had just stepped in from some other world. But then, she didn't know Jesus. She didn't speak with her Paradise Father. She wasn't born again. She wasn't baptized in the Holy Ghost. She didn't walk the faith walk in utter simplicity. And I did. It makes a world of difference when you're available for the Holy Spirit to work in you for the sake of God's efforts in raising up his sons—even if you are operating out in the deep, well beyond your own level of faith.

Meeting cantankerous Kevin

We stepped into Kevin's room and I caught both barrels in one blast. The old bloke's wife was sitting off to one side of the bed, resigned to the fact that if I couldn't handle her husband's manner, then I wasn't much use to her either.

After a few minutes of Kevin's verbal abuse and grumbling, I felt the power of the united human and divine mind come upon me and I felt like getting right to the meat on the bone.

"What is it exactly that you want Kevin?" I quietly asked.

"Peace mate! Spiritual bloody peace. Can you give me that?" And he looked at me with complete contempt. "No I don't think you can. No one's got any peace these days," he bitterly snapped.

On and on he prattled until I'd had enough, and then I said:

"Chill out Kevin. I know you're in pain. I know you're hurting. I know you want peace. And I can give you that peace Kevin. But you're going to have to pay for it." And he looked at me. I had his undivided attention. Even his wife seemed to prick up her ears.

"What do you want?" he demanded.

"We haven't got any money left," his wife quietly proffered from the other side of the bed.

I had to laugh at that.

"Hey I don't want your money Kevin. You have to understand something. I'm in control here. I have the controls here. Not you. Not cancer. Not money. You wanted spiritual peace and I came here to give it to you. I only go to places that my Father agrees to. I'm here. You want peace? You can have it. But you're going to pay a real high price for it Kevin."

I could see these words had this man glued to his bed. I think his wife was ever so thankful to find someone who wasn't going to back away from him, as she had more than likely done all their married life.

"Kevin. Today's Wednesday. I want you to think very seriously about this. I want you to take all the time you need to get an answer together for me. Here's the deal. If you'll agree with God to have one day in which you'll have the worst day of your life, you'll have your peace," I said.

He looked at me with utter disbelief. Then he let fly.

"Don't talk to me about pain mate! I've had so much pain I've been rolling around the floor screaming at the top of my lungs for days on end. I've had so much pain I thought I was insane with pain. I've had so much pain that I've..."

But I quietly cut him off. My Father and I looked deeply into his tired grey eyes and into his unbelieving soul.

Taking control

"Kevin," I said. "I'm not talking about physical pain my friend. I know you've had enough of that. I'm talking about spiritual pain."

There was a stunned silence. The whole room fell into a hush. His wife glanced at him nervously, not sure how he would respond. He looked up at me with that look of innocence one has, that fresh mind that comes to us when we know we're facing a wholly new thing.

"I'm talking about pain that is so deep Kevin, it's deeper than physical pain. It's pain that's in the core of your whole being my brother. It's pain that stands between you and God, Kevin. You have never met this kind of pain mate, ever!

"I know that," I continued. "When I look back into your life, I see a young Irish lad growing up in the Catholic Church back in the old country. You had ideas about God. And you didn't get on all that well with the priests. And you didn't like religion all that much. And you couldn't fathom nuns. But you loved Our Lady. Even though you didn't know why, you still thought she would always hear your prayers.

"But you never prayed," I said. "Life was for the living; and it was hard; and poor; and you had to fight for everything you had. And then you got the migrant boat out to Australia and it all continued out here for you. You've been a grumpy old bugger from start to finish, and Lord knows what your family has had to put up with all these years.

"And if you want spiritual peace my friend," I said by way of summary, "then I'll give you the peace of Jesus Christ but by God you're going to pay for it. Have we got a deal? Do you want to promise God and me, that you'll give him the one day he needs?"

The deal is struck

Without any hesitation, and with a quiet and solemn conviction, Kevin looked out of those tired grey eyes with what was more than likely the first glimmer of hope he'd felt in months.

"Yes," he replied

With that agreement, I drew my attention to my Paradise Father and said:

"He's all yours Father. You have your one day." Then I stepped forward and shook hands with him. As I did so, I looked at Kevin and, with a view to monitoring his inner progress over the next few days through the gift of the Spirit, I said:

"I'll keep my eye on you Kevin; you'll do OK. I'll be back on Friday evening. See you then."

I gently nodded my farewell to his wife, turned and left the room, got out to my car and drove off, and about a mile down the road had to get out of the car and run down the beach near his house just to release the Holy Ghost energy and scream out:

"YES! YES! YES! Thank you Father!"

You Holy Ghost preachers who are reading this know what I mean.

I didn't really think that God would put Kevin through a day of spiritual pain. He simply doesn't work like that. In the face of someone who was so totally right, however, in that he knew for a fact that there was no hope for him, I needed an edge to give his Thought Adjuster one last shot at getting through to him. I had gambled on the fact that he didn't know spiritual realities and the actual way to achieve spiritual peace. I didn't want to explain to him that he could have all the peace he wanted if only he would receive his Father's forgiveness. So I went about securing his attainment of that forgiveness by the means God's will offered me: he's tough, but God's tougher. He could relate to that, being Irish. And it worked!

Giving him peace

On the Friday evening when I arrived, Kevin was little improved.

"I thought you said I'd get my peace today," he said.

I noticed that his grumbling snappiness had simmered right down. I looked into his spirit and saw his Father's will for him, then I spoke about it:

"Kevin, I said I'd bring you your peace. I said that God wanted one day out of you—yesterday—and I think that day passed pretty well, considering." And I looked at him to see him acknowledging the truth of my words.

"We've come to a new day now Kevin. I think you're ready to receive your peace."

As he looked at me, his confidence in me lingered. Then I looked into his Saturday and his Sunday.

"Tomorrow, Kevin," I continued, "your pain will completely vanish. Then on Sunday you will have your peace."

He looked at me like a believing little boy, saying:

"What: all my pain?"

"All of it Kevin," I replied.

"Thank you," he said.

"And then Shirley will call me on Sunday evening to confirm with me the working of these things." Then I left his home, saying my farewell to his wife and two teenage girls. They all thanked me, expressing how their Dad had changed somewhat over the last two days since I came on Wednesday.

Shirley called me on Sunday evening. Sure enough, the pain disappeared on Saturday and he got his spiritual peace on Sunday as promised.

His new found spiritual peace brought with it the love of its Parents—Christ Michael, the Indwelling Paradise Father, and the great power from on high that is within our Mother Spirit, Our Lady as he knew her. This peace is so very unifying. He made peace with his family over the next couple of days, and they later expressed their great indebtedness for my intervention. On the following Wednesday, surrounded by his love-filled and forgiven family, Kevin died—in peace.

Victory doesn't exclude dying

That was the story of Jenny and Kevin. It is the story of stepping out into the deep, trusting God beyond the limits of our own faith and believing, and trusting his believing.

What kind of new thing do you want for yourself in your life right now?

Do want to go all out and reach for the stars?

Do you want to go right out on a limb for a new thing that's loaded with high risk but high impact?

Do you want Kevin's one-day-with-God kind of a new thing? Or would you prefer a medium impact, or even a low impact kind of new thing?

The level of believing you have is exactly the level of contact with God you will enjoy.

Both Jenny and Kevin believed and obeyed. They believed in their spirit that the Holy Spirit had the power to make a difference in their life. They believed in God's contact with their inner person, confirming his will for them if they so chose to receive and obey it. They obeyed the command that would initiate the empowering action of God, and they received their desired result.

And then they both died!

But let us not forget the glorious process of resurrection in the mansion worlds, just such as my Father showed me that great event as it was for my own human father, Jack.[24]

The plan most used

Without doubt, the rescue plan that the Thought Adjuster displays in the life of his child, is the most frequently activated plan of all.

Little does the human child realise just how precariously life is perched on the abyss of default and dissolution. And yet the Thought Adjuster valiantly wages against the odds and the predisposition for the brutality and the incidental forces of the world to rob him of his human infant. The Christian Church has made a main theme out of this aspect of the Thought Adjuster's loving involvement with his child. Many a person thinks that salvation is a silly thing, a sissy thing, a nonsense thing, a religious thing. But I will tell you of three incidents of rescue that will show you just how the Thought Adjuster rescues and saves.

The rescue plan

It was on New Year's Eve one year when I was looking after three heroin users who were completing their drug withdrawal program. They had all been in the program for about two weeks, and they were feeling excited about going out for a stroll in the New Year's Eve celebrations down town. This was denied them. It was my job to be with them overnight, and to somehow nurse them gently and lovingly through this disappointment; to somehow compensate them for their imagined loss of not being able to go out that night on a supervised outing.

As I drove to work, I spoke with my Father.

"What shall I do with them tonight Father? Is there anything you would like me to do? You know they will be restless and then more than a little disappointed."

After a moment, as if he was consulting their Thought Adjusters, he replied saying:

"It would be a good thing to run a spiritual group that will enable these three people to experience God's salvation."

"OK," I replied. "I'd love to do that with you."

After a few minutes of thinking that idea through, and realising that I didn't really know too much about doing a "salvation" group, I added,"

"You'll be there and help it through, right?"

"I will. It is an important event," he gently replied.

When I arrived at the house, the staff warned me that everyone was restless and wanting to go out. After the hand over, I gathered the three and sat them down around a table and calmly pointed out that we weren't going out and that we were going to do a spiritual group instead.

That recommendation was greeted with predicable jeers and hoots and whistles but then I said, "I know it's very dear to your hearts to go out. But I want to look after you. I know that when we go down the street, someone will slip you a loaded syringe and you'll relapse in an instant, and then where will we be. You have all done so well. Don't let this night undo everything for you."

They heard my words, and even though they knew they were forfeiting some fun by not going out, and the possibility as I described, of quickly injecting some heroin as they passed by known friends and dealers, and they agreed to stay in.

"So what's the spiritual group you're going to run Rob?"

"Well, just God stuff. I want to let you all have the opportunity to meet with God in a way that can settle your doubts and fears and maybe help you to receive something from him that will take away the most disrupting feature in your life: you know, something that will help you to deal with the drugs and kick on and get a life for yourself."

"Great," they all said. "We all sure can use something like that."

So off we went. And for the next couple of hours they had a most wonderful experience together, doing exercises and bodywork that brought God's will into their lives.

The upshot of the group was that all three of them spoke about it for the next few days, telling others how it had helped them to somehow find missing pieces in themselves. Each had a different outcome, and it was delightful to see them changing and adapting to newfound strengths and convictions.

Changes

A couple of days after the event, when I spoke with my Father about the group, asking him if it went alright from his perspective, he said that it had, and that he wanted to pass on the gratitude and approval of the other Adjusters.

But events took a sour turn, as they so often do in the lives of people who are caught up with drugs.

The young lady in the group left the program but two weeks later she was murdered. Sadly, the little baby she was carrying died with her. She was deeply mourned by her parents who conveyed to us that she had been drug free since leaving the program and was so enthusiastically looking forward to making good healthy progress in her life. It seemed that the baby's father had been involved in transactions over drugs that led to people entering their home and killing him. She was at home at the time and a witness and simply got sucked into the event.

When I heard the news, I felt deeply within me that her Thought Adjuster had made one last valiant attempt to win her heart toward his own destiny for her on that New Year's Eve night. And that he had been very successful.

That understanding softened the impact in my spirit, of the dismay over her death. It also afforded me a new vision of the way that the Thought Adjuster is relentless in his efforts to convey to his human child, in this case in the light of the urgency of the certainty of impending death, whatever it takes to rescue that child from hopelessness and bring into the course of events the assurance that, even in death, he is sovereign and Parental.

One of the fellows in the group was so profoundly moved by what he had come to realise about life and about himself that, overnight, he went through the most amazing transformation. He had been through the program a few times and had always been like a dyslexic who was unable to learn. He never had any energy and as a result he slept all the time. Everything was always way too complicated for him, too much effort for him, unrelated to him. It was like he ran on perennial burnout, but he'd never exerted any effort to get that way.

His change was so profound and dramatic that everyone noticed it. More than anything, he noticed it. He came alive. Suddenly he was fully at home in his body. He had enthusiasm and energy just bounding out of him. He was doing the dishes and mopping the floor, helping people out with the laundry and digging the vegetable garden. He was absolutely convinced that he would never again touch drugs: some kind of awakening and newfound sincerity simply flooded out of his inner being. Clearly, the guy had been rescued from what he had always been! The rope had been lowered down, and he had managed to scramble up it and out of the pit.

About nine months later, he visited one of his old using buddies up in New South Wales, and agreed to having a taste of heroin for old times sake, just for fun, and he dropped dead. Even the half measure of heroin he injected was too powerful for his drug free body's sensitivities.

The other guy in the group lived on. I heard about him three years later as being "intensely into Jesus," as clean as a whistle, and doing fine.

Working for the cause of Thought Adjusters

You can never underestimate the work you do for your own Adjuster or the Adjusters of others. And through them, the work you do for your brothers and sisters for whom you have Christ's love. What might seem like a silly concept—salvation—is deadly serious business to God.

It may not be a work that is open to too many people who seek sonship with God, to work on a one to one basis with the Thought Adjuster, or the Thought Adjuster of others, but the work is there and available if you so choose. Most people will do things according to the love of God within them, with little or no consciousness of the Thought Adjusters involved, and will do well with the people they serve and help. Since the earliest days of my adult spiritual life, I have valued the knowledge that there resides within the mind of every person, one with whom I can negotiate; one with whom I can serve; one from whom I can seek advice concerning the person; one who can serve my Father's interests as well as his own; one who will form a liaison with other Adjusters in order to achieve some kind of group task among several people; one in whom the full glory of God and the full wisdom of God is able to be drawn into any human situation, through his mortal child, or through myself, for his child's benefit.

I love how Psalm 107:28-31 speaks of the way that God rescues people. It speaks to me of several stages in the rescue process, including: the calming of one's distress; the calming of the problem itself; the joy and hope that returns to one's heart after God's assurances are recognised and claimed; the fact that God brings one to the desired shelter and victory; and the giving of joyful thanks to God for helping us to get through it all. Perhaps you can identify times in your own life, when this exact same sequence has occurred for you.

> "Then they cried to the Lord in their trouble, and he brought them out from their distress;
> "he made the storm be still, and the waves of the sea were hushed.
> "Then they were glad because they had quiet, and he brought them to their desired haven.
> "Let them thank the Lord for his steadfast love, for his wonderful works to humankind."

The Adjuster's saving plan has being going on longer than that twenty five hundred year old Psalm. It has been active in your own too. If you think that God has never rescued you, consider again the words of my Father and reflect upon your own history.

> "Without doubt, the rescue plan that the Thought Adjuster displays in the life of his child, is the most frequently activated plan of all."

That statement tells me that there are several plans he employs. There is the plan of planting seed values in the human mind in such a way that we adopt them, aspire to be like them, and thereby grow to be like God. There is the plan of social continuance, whereby we participate in continuity of our species. There is the plan of fostering obedience to, allegiance to, and creativity within social constructs, organisations and missions, business and commerce, wealth creation and distribution, ideologies and vehicles for change on a local or a planetary scale. There is the plan of light and illumination, revelation and integration into the wider universe. There is the plan of parenting, of fostering his own Fatherly loving concern for others in the experiences of raising children in his image of parenting. There is the plan for developing values up to the time that survival is pretty much assured when one becomes a candidate for Adjuster fusion, and a plan for the years ahead after that assurance is in place, when, for example, he might steer his child into any number of worthwhile pursuits for the sake of enhancing life on the planet. And there is the plan for Adjuster fusion itself which also includes a composite of the above.

The plan to rescue people, to save us from ourselves and from our surroundings, is necessary. Some of us are too busy to grow.[25] The Urantia papers also tell us that so many of us spend so much time and thought on the mere trifles of living, while almost wholly overlooking the more essential realities of everlasting import, those very accomplishments which are concerned with the development of a more harmonious working agreement between ourselves and our Adjusters.[26] The angels, who "develop an abiding affection for their human associates" really find it hard to understand why we so persistently allow our higher intellectual powers, even our religious faith, to be so dominated by fear, so thoroughly demoralised by the thoughtless panic of dread and anxiety.[27] In our worldliness, we occupy ourselves with worldly pursuits. In our adventurousness and our foolhardiness, we often disregard the warnings our sincerity could have given us were it not weighed down with our worldliness. But sometimes our situations are just plain hell on Earth. They are so entangled; so bereft of progress; so incapable of sustaining life; so suffocating; so debasing; so enslaving; so violent, so horrific, so overwhelming, so corrupting, so damaging, so isolating us from God and his goodness and truth; so evil. Jesus appropriated the truth in the Father's words to the prophet Isaiah:

"The spirit of the Lord God is upon me, because the Lord has anointed me; he has sent me to bring good news to the oppressed, to bind up the brokenhearted, to proclaim liberty to the captives, and release to the prisoners; to proclaim the year of the Lord's favour, and the day of vengeance of our God; to comfort all who mourn."[28]

What a magnificent rescue plan that is!

The spirit of the Lord God is of course your own Thought Adjuster. He can anoint you—empower you with the power of his own mind—for the purposes of equipping you to assist him in his rescue plan. He can send you on mission to help raise up sons of God in health and prosperity and blessing. He can assist you in teaching spiritually oppressed people, to awaken them to the joys and liberties of sonship with God. He can help you to help brokenhearted people who are weighed down because of a separation from God, to move beyond their wounds and to continue growing in sonship with God.

The proof of him being able to do this with you in your own life is found in the fact that he did this in Jesus' life. Consequently, Jesus himself said that if you believe in him and will walk with the Father in sonship with God, then it will be guaranteed to you that the same power that is on him will come upon you and you will do even greater works than Jesus.

"Very truly, I tell you, the one who believes in me will also do the works that I do and, in fact, will do greater works than these, because I am going to the Father."[29]

Of course, you won't do the works that Jesus did if you remain isolated in your own world. The works of Jesus, the works of the Father, the fruits of the Spirit, are done in the world of others. You go into their world with your world. Or, you invite them, into your world. However you manage your affairs, you will find that wishing and hoping is not counted in spiritual life. What is counted, is actual contact with other people and their needs, and contact in which you are equipped and being moved by the desire for victory that is in your Father's mind, and the power that he has over the person's needs.

Equal in power to the act of receiving the Father's forgiveness, then, is the act of receiving the Father's rescue— the two are not separate in the love filled mind of our own Thought Adjuster. We simply cannot meet God except we first receive his forgiveness and become forgivers in his way of forgiving. That is the dawning of our spirituality. Similarly, we cannot forgive someone without the element of rescue, salvage, coming into it. Sometimes the rescue does involve literally rescuing someone, but when we exercise God's type of forgiveness, it mostly salvages us from some kind of untenable situation, relationship or injury. God's forgiveness rescues us and delivers us into the safe haven of our own sonship's favour with God.

We cannot grow into the likeness of our divine Father, or our local universe Father and Mother for that matter, without at some stage being like an oil-soaked penguin in need of rescue and cleansing and literally being plucked up and gently redirected because the problems of living simply overpowered us.

We experience acute conflicts between the spirit and the flesh.[30] Oh how the hurting soul aches to be with an authentic son of God so that the favour of God, which is on him or her, might fall upon it. The happy-go-lucky, careless, insincere or ignorant soul doesn't bother with such things. But the hurts that are too deep to reach, too lost to be found, too ugly to be brought into the light, too shameful to be pronounced, too big to embrace, too savage to pardon—it is for these that the Thought Adjuster looks upon his son with unsparing love and engages the plan of rescue. Just as would you, if you could, for your own child. And, if we will release ourself to him, running to him like a little child who is so very grateful to be held by him. Running, not caring to check if our make-up is in place; not caring what our friends say about us; not letting the worldly customs of reserve and intellection hold us back; running as if we were running from death into the arms life; then we will let this divine Thought Adjuster have his way in us and we will be made whole by his rescue plan for us.

The plan most cherished

The plan that is most cherished in the mind of the Thought Adjuster is the one that enables us to love with his kind of love.

Loving with his kind of love

This is more at the heart of his heart than any plan to foster our expertise in prayer, meditation, gifts of the Spirit, healing, performing miracles, communication, finance, politics, government, parenting, education, renunciation, asceticism and religious practices. To love as God loves, stands side by side with sincere contemplation, and freely giving of oneself. Realistically speaking of course, to love as God loves involves loving as he loves within all of these fields and pursuits I have mentioned, and more. His love is able to be found in everything but sin and evil. His love is available for us to bring to bear as a formidable force for good in all things. Before he arrives into our mind, the Thought Adjuster who will give us the opportunity to become a Finaliter in Paradise—a one-time human who is now perfected in his love and the way that his love finds solutions in the challenges and pursuits of entire universes—he first loves us implicitly, without reserve, with a life-giving love that is filled with destiny.[31]

He loves us before we have accepted into our own heart, his forgiveness. He loves us while we are still of the world, and able to get into many a worldly situation from which we need rescue. The Thought Adjusters who loved Andon and Fonta were fully apprised of their natures—everything they thought, did, said and dreamed of becoming—before they ever received the Father's forgiveness into their hearts, and exercised it.[32] If so for them, then so too for you.

One author in the Urantia papers wrote of the Thought Adjuster's love:

"As far as I am conversant with the affairs of a universe, I regard the love and devotion of a Thought Adjuster as the most truly divine affection in all creation. The love of the Sons in their ministry to the races is superb, but the devotion of an Adjuster to the individual is touchingly sublime, divinely Fatherlike."[33]

However well you can receive this news, I would love you to appreciate that you are loved completely by God and he brings you his unswerving, endless devotion. God is unable to withdraw his love from you—because he is unwilling to. He truly loves you. You might try to destroy every part of yourself through drugs, alcohol, abuse, violence, guns, deprivation, anger, greed, hate or just plain stupidity. And don't be fooled, you can indeed lock yourself into a psychological or an emotional place where you will forbid God's love to come near you. But if you will admit to even the faintest flicker of courage

416

and let him touch you with his love, just as much as the size of a mustard seed, the tiniest chink in your armour, he will rescue you with such a profound assurance and love for you that will be as virginal and pure as the day he first heard about you in his home in Divinington.

These words, with their negligible impact, transform into actual contact, real revelation deep within you that you can't deny, from this very Thought Adjuster who is attending your life. It is one thing to hear the message, "God loves you and so do I," or "Jesus loves you, he died for your sins," and a whole other thing for that love to make a difference in our lives. And if it doesn't make a difference, then the message remains forever simply empty words for us flapping in the wind like some Tibetan prayer flag whose power is dormant until it sprouts inside a hungry person's soul.

Love stimulates, motivates and pours out of the Thought Adjuster's every activity with us. He has a love for us which is never exhausted and never made obsolete—his love is as fresh and new for us today as it was on the thrilling day of his arrival.

Converting the Thought Adjuster's love into currency we can use

For many of us though, we find it difficult to experience God's love, to find it meaningful, reachable. We struggle to convert it into the currency of faith and personal growth. The gulf between the world in which we live and have our being, and the heavens and all its power, sometimes just seems to be way to wide and mysteriously unapproachable.[34] In lieu of love, and to some extent broken-hearted because God's love was not as easy a matter as our simple hearts had expected, many of us turn to lesser gods like wealth, relationships, self importance, religious practices or the exploration of the psychic and the mental—whose outcomes are more tangible.

Can you find your own way into the Thought Adjuster's love and make it your own?

If not, then ask him for it. Ask him to demonstrate it. Ask God your Thought Adjuster to give rise to the presence of his love for you both inside your body and mind, and in an independent witness outside you, someone else. Trust me, God is here for the partnering—he *will* oblige you, it's in his most cherished plan for you. Your problem is not that his love isn't there, but that you've never had the inclination to draw on it and really indulge it with him. How often have you said to yourself, "It's Saturday in a few days. Father, how about you and I just absolutely go wild in your love for the whole day? Let's really get in there and really slosh around. Let's rub ourselves all over with it and drink it and eat it and breath it with complete joyful abandon for the whole day. Then we can be normal again on Sunday—but let's make Saturday *our* day Daddy!" You'll hear him say, "Sure—let's do that!"

If you're not that kind of a person, then turn to Jesus for your example. He gave us a perfect example of the Thought Adjuster's love, when he showed us the Father's love in his own life and in his teachings. He still shows us that same love when he shapes us in his image as our local universe Father.

Jesus gave us a way to love others. That way is to love others as the Father who is in Jesus loves Jesus—which translates as the way that Jesus loves us. His way of loving us is the Father's way of loving us. One of the greatest joys that facilitates progress in the path of sonship and the development of Adjuster fusion, is to love others with the love of our own Thought Adjuster, our Father. The Urantia papers tell us that our Adjuster has affection for us,[35] and that the greatest manifestation of the divine love for us is seen in the fact of his bestowal. But the best example of his love that we will ever encounter, is seen in the bestowal life of his Son Michael as he lived the ideal spiritual life on Earth as Jesus of Nazareth.[36]

The way that the Thought Adjuster loves us becomes currency for us when once we want to deliver his grace and blessing to others, as did Jesus.

Flesh type of Love and Spirit type of love

Our human love frequently binds us to the flesh. Our human love often ends up with us hating the sinner and being sullied by the sin. Our human love exhausts us in our own self-importance.[37] Am I talking to someone here? Have you noticed it—that we try our best with our own kind of loving and we frequently end up sleeping with the enemy.

Unlike our worldly kind of love, our Thought Adjuster's love saves the sinner, and his law destroys the sin.[38] The greatest gift that we can give to God is the commitment of our will, whereas the greatest gift we can give to another human being is to feed their hunger for truth and their thirst for righteousness—for God—by giving them the gift of the living bread and water of life. This gift is God's kind of love and its spiritual fruit: patience, kindness, loving service, unselfish devotion, courageous loyalty, sincere fairness, enlightened honesty, undying hope, confiding trust, merciful ministry, unfailing goodness, forgiving tolerance, and enduring peace.[39] Jesus said to us all that, when we go abroad to tell all nations the good news of this gospel, he will go before us, and his Spirit of Truth shall abide in our hearts. His abiding peace is a very real strength and inspiration as we manifest these fruits of the spirit of our sonship with God.

The transformation in us from our original worldly love to this kind of divine love is the heart of spiritual growth. The Urantia papers tell us that we may enter the kingdom as a child, but the Father requires that we grow up, by grace, to the full stature of spiritual adulthood and that if professed believers do not bear these fruits of the divine spirit in their lives, they are dead—the Spirit of Truth is not in them; they are useless branches on the living vine, and they soon will be taken away.[40] That statement isn't meant to be a threat, I'm sure, but it does highlight the fact that there is indeed a cut-off point between the worldly and the spiritual and it is exclusively centred around allowing God's love to rule in our hearts over and above our human love. Whilst our human love is excellent, and who among us hasn't cherished the love of another person, or freely given it, it is incapable of ferrying us into the eternal until our human love itself is given the divine wings of the Thought Adjuster's love.

What becomes of paramount importance to the son of God who is actively pursuing the career of the Finaliter, not mere passing knowledge but life-giving importance like oxygen to a deep sea diver, is to know deeply in their own soul how Jesus loved with the love of his Thought Adjuster. We know that our Thought Adjuster is saturated with the beautiful and self-bestowing love of the Father of spirits, and that he truly and divinely loves us, even as he longs for us to attain his divinity of love.[41] Let's together identify in the Urantia papers some of the instances when Jesus loved with our Father's kind of love. Once we see it, we will know it in ourselves. Once we know it, our Father's kind of love will rise up in our own lives quite naturally—only believe and do not doubt.

Jesus, the person

As a child, Jesus loved God in a way that provided him access: he was able to "talk with my Father who is in heaven" and, while he may not have been perfectly sure about the answer, he acted on what he felt his Father surely would have communicated to him.[42]

Jesus' love was reflected in several Old Testament scriptures,[43] such as, "Create in me a clean heart, O Lord;"[44] "The Lord is my shepherd; I shall not want;"[45] "You should love your neighbour as yourself;"[46] "For I, the Lord your God, will hold your right hand, saying, fear not; I will help you;"[47] and "Neither shall the nations learn war any more."[48]

Jesus was truly loved by his youthful associates because he was fair and sympathetic.[49] As an adult, people were mystified with his personality, charmed by his gracious manner: they fell in love with the man.[50]

Jesus spread good cheer everywhere he went. He was full of grace and truth. His associates never ceased to wonder at the gracious words that proceeded out of his mouth. Gracefulness can be cultivated, but graciousness is the aroma of friendliness, which emanates from a love-saturated soul.[51]

Jesus and family

Jesus bestowed himself fully on his family and as a result he deeply loved them with an extraordinary devotion and a great and fervent affection.[52]

He loved and respected his father and mother, saying that, "they who love me so much should be able to do more for me and guide me more safely than strangers who can only view my body and observe my mind but can hardly truly know me."[53] For a period, Jesus suffered great mental distress as the result of his constant effort to adjust his personal views to the beliefs of his parents. His conflict was between two great commands to which he espoused loyalty. One was: 'Be loyal to the dictates of

your highest convictions of truth and righteousness.' The other
was: 'Honour your father and mother, for they have given you
life and the nurture thereof.' Despite this conflict between the
spirit and the world however, he continued to adjust and find
solutions in an increasingly harmonious blend of personal
convictions and family obligations. Family became "a masterful
concept of group solidarity based upon loyalty, fairness,
tolerance, and love."[54]

Jesus deeply loved Mary, his mother. The very first miracle
that emerged from his love's desire, whereby one hundred and
twenty gallons of water was turned into the finest of wines, was
the direct result of his love for his mother. In one moment, Jesus
was saying, "My good woman, what have I to do with that?"
And the next moment he was comforting her, saying, "Most
gladly would I do what you ask of me if it were a part of the
Father's will." And the rest is history![55]

Jesus' love was nurtured in a wise home whose love life and
the loyal devotion of true religion exerted a profound reciprocal
influence upon each other—glorifying the home.[56] Long after
he left his family home, Jesus counselled Jacob saying that a,
"good and true father not only loves his family as a whole—as
a family—but he also truly loves and affectionately cares for
each individual member."[57]

Jesus and matters of the heart

In the evening classes that he made available to believers
during one of the preaching tours, Jesus taught: that anger might
be seen as the failure of the spiritual nature to gain control of our
combined intellectual and physical natures; that anger indicated
our lack of tolerant brotherly love plus our lack of self-respect
and self-control; that anger depleted our health, debased our
mind, and handicapped the Thought Adjuster's efforts to teach
our soul.

He cited Jewish scripture about anger, "Surely vexation kills
the fool, and jealousy slays the simple;"[58] "Those who are slow
to anger calm contention"[59] while "one who has a hasty temper
exalts folly."[60] "A soft answer turns away wrath, but a harsh
word stirs up anger."[61] "Those with good sense are slow to
anger."[62] "He that hath no rule over his own spirit is like a city
that is broken down, and without walls."[63] "Wrath is cruel,

anger is overwhelming."[64]

He further taught about letting our hearts be so dominated by love that our Thought Adjuster will have little trouble in delivering us from the tendency to give vent to those outbursts of animal anger which are inconsistent with the status of divine sonship.[65]

Jesus appealed to people whose hearts were cold toward God's love, revealing that the unselfish glories of Paradise were not possible of reception by a thoroughly selfish creature of the realms of time and space; that even the infinite love of God could not force the salvation of eternal survival upon any mortal creature who did not choose to survive; and he quoted from the Hebrew scriptures, saying, "I have called and you refused to hear;[66] I stretched out my hand, but no man regarded.[67] You have set at naught all my counsel,[68] and you have rejected my reproof, and because of this rebellious attitude it becomes inevitable that you shall call upon me and fail to receive an answer. Having rejected the way of life, you may seek me diligently in your times of suffering, but you will not find me."[69, 70]

Jesus taught that you cannot compel men to love the truth. Many teachers are blind guides. The blind lead the blind, both falling into the pit. He said that man is only defiled by that evil which may originate within the heart, and which finds expression in the words and deeds. Do you not know it is from the heart that there comes forth evil thoughts, wicked projects of murder, theft, and adulteries, together with jealousy, pride, anger, revenge, railings, and false witness? And it is just such things that defile men, and not ceremonial impropriety.[71]

Jesus' love invites us into a great repentance of sins, as great as was received by the woman who washed his feet with her tears and wiped them with the hair of her head and kissed his feet unceasingly and anointed them with precious lotions. Her many sins, having been forgiven, led her to love much; but those who have received but little forgiveness sometimes love but little.[72]

Jesus did not presume upon the Father's love. He declared that the heavenly Father is not a lax, loose, or foolishly indulgent parent who is ever ready to condone sin and forgive recklessness. Said Jesus, "My Father does not indulgently condone those acts and practices of his children which are self-destructive and suicidal to all moral growth and spiritual progress. Such sinful practices are an abomination in the sight of God."[73]

Concerning doubt and unbelief, Jesus taught, "Question not my Father's power of love, only the sincerity and reach of your faith. All things are possible to him who really believes."[74]

Jesus did not hesitate to appropriate the better half of a scripture while he repudiated the lesser portion. His great exhortation, "love your neighbour as yourself," he took from the scripture, which reads, "You shall not take vengeance against the children of your people, but you shall love your neighbour as yourself."[75] Jesus appropriated the positive portion of this scripture while rejecting the negative part. Jesus simply would not accept explanations of worship and religious devotion, which involved belief in the wrath of God, or the anger of the Almighty. As a young boy, looking appealingly into the eyes of his father, he said, "My father, it cannot be true—the Father in heaven cannot so regard his erring children on Earth. The heavenly Father cannot love his children less than you love me. And I well know, no matter what unwise thing I might do, you would never pour out wrath upon me nor vent anger against me. If you, my Earthly father, possess such human reflections of the Divine, how much more must the heavenly Father be filled with goodness and overflowing with mercy. I refuse to believe that my Father in heaven loves me less than my father on Earth."[76]

He even opposed negative or purely passive non-resistance. Said he, "When an enemy smites you on one cheek, do not stand there dumb and passive but in positive attitude turn the other; that is, do the best thing possible actively to lead your brother in error away from the evil paths into the better ways of righteous living." Jesus required his followers to react positively and aggressively to every life situation. The turning of the other cheek, or whatever act that may typify, demands initiative, necessitates vigorous, active, and courageous expression of the believer's personality."[77]

Jesus' love was concerned with the walls of prejudice, self-righteousness, and hate. He wanted them all to crumble before this preaching of the Father's love for all men.[78]

Jesus' love was not impatient. He instructed his apostles to take up their regular duties until "the hour of the kingdom comes," and study for their future work for three hours every evening while a change was wrought in their hearts by the Father.[79]

Jesus' love caused him to absolutely refuse to defend himself. He taught his apostles not to resist evil and not to combat injustice or injury. He gave warning against retaliation, revenge, the idea of getting even, holding of grudges, the idea of an eye for an eye and a tooth for a tooth, private and personal revenge, assigning these matters to civil government, on the one hand, and to the judgment of God, on the other. He taught us to love our enemies, remembering the moral claims of human brotherhood; the futility of evil: a wrong is not righted by vengeance, by fighting evil with its own weapons; and having faith, confidence, in the eventual triumph of divine justice and eternal goodness.[80]

Despite the rejection and crucifixion of Jesus, the Father and his Creator Son have never ceased to love the Jews. God is no respecter of persons, and salvation is for the Jew as well as for the gentile.[81]

Jesus frequently told and retold the parable of the prodigal son and the story of the Good Samaritan as a way of teaching the love of the Father and the neighbourliness of man.[82]

Jesus was above all, human. He loved, but he also grieved.[83]

Jesus and community

Jesus deeply pitied and loved his community, the Jewish people. Whilst he maintained a great respect for the sincere Pharisees and the honest scribes, he increasingly developed a righteous resentment of the presence in the Father's temple of the politically appointed priests—the hypocritical Pharisees and dishonest theologians.[84] He exercised a strong and peculiarly fascinating influence on both friends and foes in the community, multitudes following him for weeks, just to hear his gracious words and to witness his simple life. Devoted men and women loved Jesus with a well-nigh superhuman affection and the better they knew him the more they loved him. Even today, the more we come to know this God-man, the more we love and follow after him.[85]

Jesus and loving people

Jesus loved people. He said to Ganid, his young Indian student, "No man is a stranger to one who knows God." The Urantia papers expand on this by saying that when once a person is not a stranger, the door is open to knowing their problems and to learning to love them. Should we love all people and their problems straight off? No, not at all. To be genuine, to love authentically, we cannot expect love to miraculously appear out of thin air. Rather, we must grow with the person. We must give freely of ourself and be shaped by them, just as we shape them. Only when we grow with someone can we learn to love them.[86]

Before ever he entered into public ministry, the majority of persons Jesus met were attracted to him. He was interested in his fellows; he had learned how to love them and watched for the opportunity to do something for them, which he was sure they wanted done.[87] Jesus' usual technique of social contact was to draw people out and into talking with him, by asking them questions. The interview would usually begin by his asking them questions and end by them asking him questions. Those who derived most benefit from his personal ministry were overburdened, anxious, and dejected people. They gained much relief because of the opportunity to unburden their souls to a sympathetic and understanding listener. He always offered practical and immediately helpful suggestions to correct their real difficulties. He spoke words to provide immediate comfort and consolation. Invariably would he tell these distressed people about the love of God and impart the information, by various and sundry methods, that they were the children of this loving Father in heaven.[88]

Who can forget the way Jesus' love intervened between the chap who was mistreating his wife? His words brought dignity back into human life, and his smile brought the victory. His love and understanding and intervention placed marriage and child rearing on its proper spiritual footing when he said:

"My brother, always remember that man has no rightful authority over woman unless the woman has willingly and voluntarily given him such authority. Your wife has engaged to go through life with you, to help you fight its battles, and to assume the far greater share of the burden of bearing and rearing your children; and in return for this special service it is only fair that she receive from you that special protection which man can give to woman as the partner who must carry, bear, and nurture the children. The loving care and consideration which a man is willing to bestow upon his wife and their children are the measure of that man's attainment of the higher levels of creative and spiritual self-consciousness. Do you not know that men and women are partners with God in that they co-operate to create beings who grow up to possess themselves of the potential of immortal souls? The Father in heaven treats the Spirit Mother of the children of the universe as one equal to himself. It is Godlike to share your life and all that relates thereto on equal terms with the mother partner who so fully shares with you that divine experience of reproducing yourselves in the lives of your children. If you can only love your children as God loves you, you will love and cherish your wife as the Father in heaven honours and exalts the Infinite Spirit, the mother of all the spirit children of a vast universe."[89]

Who can forget the way Jesus loved the boy who was running away? His love was so inviting that in no time the boy wanted to overcome his obstacles and fly on the wings of his new found courage and love in being a son of God.[90]

Jesus' righteousness is a dynamic love—fatherly-brotherly affection. It is not the negative or thou-shalt-not type of righteousness. Fatherly love has singleness of purpose, and it always looks for the best in the individual; that is the attitude of a true parent. To see God—by faith—means to acquire true spiritual insight. And spiritual insight enhances Adjuster guidance, and these in the end augment God-consciousness. And when you know the Father, you are confirmed in the assurance of divine sonship, and you can increasingly love each of your brothers and sisters in the flesh, not only as a sibling—with a sibling's love—but also as a father—with fatherly affection.[91]

Jesus' gospel

Jesus' love was his message. It was always the fact of the

heavenly Father's love and the truth of his mercy, coupled with the good news that man is a faith-son of this same God of love.[92]

Jesus' loved God as a Father-friend.[93]

Jesus had a love that was, like ours, able to be human or divine. He loved his people and fairly believed in winning them—and the whole world—to his new spiritual kingdom, even as the expected Jewish Messiah. He also had the desire to live and work as he knew his Father would approve, to conduct his work on behalf of other worlds in need, and to continue, in the establishment of the kingdom, to reveal the Father and show forth the Father's divine character of love.[94]

This dilemma challenges all of us as we grow in the likeness of our Father's love: should we proceed with the things that we ourselves love and believe will be victorious and fruitful, or should we put it all aside in order to demonstrate our Father's will and his kind of love. The son of God, having proven its worth to himself or herself, will eventually settle only for the latter.

Jesus always taught his followers to manifest fatherly love rather than brotherly love. Brotherly love would love your neighbour as you love yourself, and that would be adequate fulfilment of the "golden rule." But fatherly affection would require that you should love your fellow mortals as Jesus loves you.[95]

Jesus did not expect his followers to achieve an impossible manifestation of brotherly love, but he did expect them to so strive to be like God—to be perfect even as the Father in heaven is perfect—that they could begin to look upon their fellows as God looks upon his creatures and therefore could begin to love people as God loves them—to show forth the beginnings of a fatherly affection.[96]

Jesus had a love that could instruct on the chief purpose of all human struggling—perfection—even divine attainment. Always he admonishes us, "Be you perfect, even as your Father in heaven is perfect." This was a love greater than loving one's neighbours as one's self—brotherly love. He rather admonished his apostles to love people as he loved them—to love with a fatherly as well as a brotherly affection.[97]

Regarding the Father's love that he demonstrated, Jesus said, "You are the child, and it is your Father's kingdom you seek to enter. There is present that natural affection between every normal child and its father which insures an understanding and loving relationship, and which forever precludes all disposition to bargain for the Father's love and mercy. And the gospel you are going forth to preach has to do with a salvation growing out of the faith-realization of this very and eternal child-father relationship."[98]

Jesus's love, and his person, is celebrated among us when we share the wine and bread of the supper of the remembrance that he established, for he said, "And as often as you do this, do it in remembrance of me. And when you do remember me, first look back upon my life in the flesh, recall that I was once with you, and then, by faith, discern that you shall all some time sup with me in the Father's eternal kingdom. This is the new Passover which I leave with you, even the memory of my bestowal life, the word of eternal truth; and of my love for you, the outpouring of my Spirit of Truth upon all flesh."[99]

Jesus' love actually serves you, and calls you by its example into allegiance to a new commandment, "That you love one another even as I have loved you. And by this will all men know that you are my disciples if you thus love one another."[100]

Jesus' demonstration of the Father's love proved that salvation should be taken for granted by those who believe in the Fatherhood of God. His love showed a way for us to cut through the selfish desire for personal salvation to find the unselfish urge to love for love's sake and for sonship's sake. The unselfishness of God exposes the concept of atonement and sacrificial salvation as being wholly unlike his love.[101]

Jesus likened his love as a vine that was growing in his Father's vineyard. We who love him are the branches on that vine and through us his love will flow and will cause us to bear fruit. We who love him abide in him, and he in us and, because of his life-giving love, we bear much fruit of the spirit and experience the supreme joy of yielding this spiritual harvest. When we abide in him and his words live in us, we become able to commune freely with him, and then his living spirit so infuses us that we may ask anything at all that his spirit wills and be completely assured that the Father will give us what we ask for. The Father of Thought Adjusters can be glorified—by Jesus' love being in a great many of us, and by our bearing the fruit of his love. The fruit of his love in us is that we love one another, even as he loves us.[102]

Jesus and the apostles, disciples and ministry

He loved and trusted his "personal associates"—the apostles—as friends, telling them, "I love you," and instructing them to be patient, gentle, ever obedient to the Father's will, ready for the call of the kingdom, prepared for trouble and much tribulation and yet expectant of a full joy and great blessing.[103] Jesus directed the apostles to go forth, as John had, preaching the gospel and instructing believers in the "good tidings of the kingdom of heaven," and that they must show forth love, compassion, and sympathy that was an expression of the enthronement of God in their hearts.[104]

Jesus taught them to preach the forgiveness of sin through faith in God without penance or sacrifice, and that the Father in heaven loves all his children with the same eternal love.[105]

Jesus taught that for workers in the kingdom, mercy always should determine their judgments and love their conduct.[106] Jesus' love and unselfishness impressed and shaped John, the "apostle of love" who, for years, at the close of services only said, "My little children, love one another."[107]

Jesus taught that despite his own love for people, the doing of the works of God was not for him to determine. The transformations of grace were wrought in response to the living faith of those who are the beneficiaries.[108] But he said, "I tell you that, even when a cup of cold water is given to a thirsty soul, the Father's messengers shall ever make record of such a service of love."[109]

Jesus taught that many souls can best be led to love the unseen God by being first taught to love their brethren whom they can see. And it was in this connection that new meaning became attached to the Master's pronouncement concerning unselfish service for one's fellows, "Inasmuch as you did it to one of the least of my brethren, you did it to me."[110]

Jesus had such a love that he was willing to lay down his life for his enemies, a love greater than any which had hitherto been known on Earth.[111] Jesus' love is forever nailed to the cross that represents the highest form of unselfish service and the supreme devotion of the full bestowal of a righteous life in the service of wholehearted ministry, even to the death. On the cross, Jesus' love did not die, it was exalted. Jesus truly inspires all of us to exercise the same kind of love.[112]

To the minister of the Father's love, Jesus says, "Give up your intolerance and learn to love men as I have loved you. Devote your life to proving that love is the greatest thing in the world. It is the love of God that impels men to seek salvation. Love is the ancestor of all spiritual goodness, the essence of the true and the beautiful."[113] "Then take good care of my sheep. Be a good and a true shepherd to the flock. Betray not their confidence in you. Be not taken by surprise at the enemy's hand. Be on guard at all times—watch and pray."[114] "Feed my sheep. Do not forsake the flock. Be an example and an inspiration to all your fellow shepherds. Love the flock as I have loved you and devote yourself to their welfare even as I have devoted my life to your welfare."[115]

Jesus taught, "If you would serve me, serve my brethren in the flesh even as I have served you. And be not weary in this well doing but persevere as one who has been ordained by God for this service of love. When you have finished your service with me on Earth, you shall serve with me in glory. Cease doubting; you must grow in faith and the knowledge of truth. Believe in God like a child but cease to act so childishly. Have courage; be strong in faith and mighty in the kingdom of God."[116]

Jesus taught, "If, therefore, you serve me with a whole heart, make sure that you are devoted to the welfare of my brethren on Earth with tireless affection. Admix friendship with your counsel and add love to your philosophy. Serve your fellow men even as I have served you. Be faithful to men, as I have watched over you. Be less critical; expect less of some men and thereby lessen the extent of your disappointment."[117]

Jesus and wealth creation and distribution

Jesus taught on how love can be ensnared by wealth, "Take heed and keep yourselves free from covetousness; a man's life consists not in the abundance of the things, which he may possess. Happiness comes not from the power of wealth, and joy springs not from riches. Wealth, in itself, is not a curse, but the love of riches many times leads to such devotion to the things of this world that the soul becomes blinded to the beautiful attractions of the spiritual realities of the kingdom of God on Earth and to the joys of eternal life in heaven."[118]

Jesus' love provided for feasts for the poor and the unfortunate, whilst he made it clear that indiscriminate kindness may be blamed for many social evils. No apostolic funds were to be given out as alms except upon his request or upon the joint petition of two of the apostles—his love was as wise as serpents but as harmless as doves. Regarding social conduct, he taught patience, tolerance, and forgiveness. Jesus repeatedly refused to lay down laws regarding marriage and divorce,[119] just as he offered no solutions for the non-religious problems of his own age nor for any subsequent age.[120]

Jesus taught the rich Roman Stoic concerning his duty to man and his loyalty to God, on a very personal basis. He spoke of inherited wealth; discovered wealth; trade wealth; unfair wealth; interest wealth; genius wealth; accidental wealth; stolen wealth; trust funds and earned wealth. He spoke about the concept of being a steward of these ten divisions of wealth, before God and in the service of men, but made it plain that he was not in the business of dictating to people how they should regard their wealth. The rich man however, perceiving great wisdom and goodness in Jesus, set off to follow his counsel.[121] Jesus' love made him a steward of all things. He counted all things as the Father's—even Nebadon, that great universe of his creation. Wealth creation and management, he perceived, was able to be elevated from a worldly view and placed at the disposal of the will of God in one's life. Consciousness around wealth creation and management thereby became integral to the path to Adjuster fusion—irrespective of whether a little or a lot of wealth was involved. The consciousness of the human is one of being a steward for the Thought Adjuster's wise and good use of that wealth.

It is an extraordinary thing when we let go our own mortal hold on our wealth creation and management and pass it squarely over to our Thought Adjuster. This action is not uninformed, blind, hopeless, or a grasping at an endless wishing tree of some kind. This is a decision that the will of God invites us into. When we respond, suddenly our Adjuster is unbelievably real for us and his recommendations are a blessing of immense proportions never otherwise gained.

Jesus and the cross

The Urantia papers tell us that, "The cross forever shows that the attitude of Jesus toward sinners was neither condemnation nor condonation, but rather eternal and loving salvation. Jesus is truly a saviour in the sense that his life and death do win men over to goodness and righteous survival. Jesus loves men so much that his love awakens the response of love in the human heart. Love is truly contagious and eternally creative. Jesus' death on the cross exemplifies a love which is sufficiently strong and divine to forgive sin and swallow up all evil-doing. Jesus disclosed to this world a higher quality of righteousness than justice—mere technical right and wrong. Divine love does not merely forgive wrongs; it absorbs and actually destroys them. The forgiveness of love utterly transcends the forgiveness of mercy. Mercy sets the guilt of evil-doing to one side; but love destroys forever the sin and all weakness resulting therefrom. Jesus brought a new method of living to Urantia. He taught us not to resist evil but to find through him a goodness which effectually destroys evil. The forgiveness of Jesus is not condonation; it is salvation from condemnation. Salvation does not slight wrongs; it makes them right. True love does not compromise nor condone hate; it destroys it. The love of Jesus is never satisfied with mere forgiveness. The Master's love implies rehabilitation, eternal survival. It is altogether proper to speak of salvation as redemption if you mean this eternal rehabilitation."[122]

Have you ever wanted your own life to be rid of some great problem?—or a problem in the life of someone whom you love deeply? Then look to Jesus and his love, for by the power of his personal love for men, Jesus could break the hold of sin and evil. He thereby set men free to choose better ways of living. Jesus portrayed a deliverance from the past which in itself promised a triumph for the future. Forgiveness thus provided salvation. Jesus lived out the truth that the beauty of divine love, once fully admitted to the human heart, forever destroys the charm of sin and the power of evil.[123]

The Urantia papers appeal to us to make sure that we see in the cross the final manifestation of the love and devotion of Jesus to his life mission of bestowal upon the mortal races of his vast universe; to see in the death of the Son of Man the climax of the unfolding of the Father's divine love for his sons of the mortal spheres; to see the cross portraying the devotion of willing affection and the bestowal of voluntary salvation upon those who are willing to receive such gifts and devotion; to see that there was nothing in the cross which the Father required— only that which Jesus so willingly gave, and which he refused to avoid.[124]

Summary

Pentecost, with its spiritual endowment, equips us with spiritual weapons to conquer the world with unfailing forgiveness, matchless good will, and abounding love, to overcome evil with good, to vanquish hate by love, to destroy fear with a courageous and living faith in truth and to be active and positive in a ministry of mercy and in manifestations of love.[125] The religion of Jesus is a new gospel of faith to be proclaimed to struggling humanity. This new religion is founded on faith, hope, and love.[126] This, then, is the love that Jesus lived by. This, then, is the love that Christ Michael has for us today when we sonship with him. This, then, is the love that your own Thought Adjuster has for you today as you sonship with him.

Enjoy! Dare to believe and not doubt! Life is beautiful!

Meeting growing needs

I have long benefited from the fact that the Thought Adjuster looks ahead to the needs of his child. I would invite you to benefit from that assurance too, as it applies to yourself, your children and those for whom you care.

When we are five he knows what we will need as we grow into puberty at twelve. When we are eighteen, he knows what we will need in order to grow into being thirty. When we are fifty, he knows what we will need as we grow later on into our old age.

He knows what we need in order to grow across a variety of

interests, and into levels of diverse depths.

Past; future; depth; communication; and healing

We live in a matrix of five existential needs: our past; our future; our depth; our communication with others; and our change and healing. He knows, or can find out along the way, what we need in order to be at peace with our past. He knows what we need in order to be confident about our future. He knows what we need in order to be capable, courageous and valid in our communications with others; He knows what we need in order to bring empowered change and healing to others, and in order to be faithful as we surrender ourselves to receiving empowering change and healing for ourselves. He knows what we need in order to be sincere as we progress in our communion with him and his values.

He knows what won't bring us into communion with him, no matter how much we pursuit it. He knows what threatens our future and keeps us awake all night. He knows what won't change or heal us, just as he knows what it is about us that won't change or heal anyone else. He knows how we deal with our past, and what of it looms over our life and disturbs our tranquillity. He knows how we manage these core needs and how their mismanagement can manifest as psychosomatic discomfort and disease in us. He knows how these needs are linked into our progress in the kingdom of heaven and how they are linked into our death.

God our Adjuster, knows what pursuits will never amount to much in our lives. He knows what will break us, and what will destroy us. He knows what activities will never bring us health, wealth or happiness just as he knows what will bring us into green pastures and what we would benefit from doing in those pastures. He knows the potentials of our circumstances, when it is useful to stick around and when it is time to move on. He also knows that unless we grasp the values he is constantly bringing into our mind, values we can adopt that will encourage us to make decisions about changing direction, he might watch us wither and wilt as we go down the wrong track.

The Thought Adjuster also knows the thrill when we do in

fact grasp onto his values, his desire for good and growth into his likeness. Can you imagine that? At some stage in your life, you have been the source of thrilling joy to the great and mighty Thought Adjuster who attends your life.

Let God access you

One thing I want to say here—don't make your Thought Adjuster so God Almighty that you can't pack a picnic lunch and just go sit with him and have a good heart to heart chat about things. If you don't do that, or you won't do that because you insist that you are too nothing and God is so everything, then get off that tramcar today and take a hike in the real world. Your Adjuster has not journeyed umpteen million light years to have you go into some dizzy self-importance trip about him being too awesome for you to personalise in your life. He wants to be your best friend. He wants you to fall in love with him so deeply that he can whisper into your heart and mind the very things that he's longing to tell you. He actually wants to be so intimate with you and have you so confident with him that you'll let him stand right in front of you and talk with you in Spirit like another person would. He definitely wants to be your best friend. Say that aloud to yourself three times now:

"The Thought Adjuster who came all the way from Divinington to be God for me doesn't feel very close to me right now, but he is my best friend and we are entering a new communion of love together."

"The Thought Adjuster who came all the way from Divinington to be God for me doesn't feel very close to me right now, but he is my best friend and we are entering a new communion of love together."

"The Thought Adjuster who came all the way from Divinington to be God for me doesn't feel very close to me right now, but he is my best friend and we are entering a new communion of love together."

I met a fellow once who was absolutely flabbergasted that I communicated with God. It was way out of reach to him. He was an American reader of the Urantia papers but he was philosopher, an intellectual, and he never lived by faith. You'll remember the prophet Ezekiel. It's recorded in the Bible that Ezekiel wrote this:

"The hand of the Lord came upon me, and he brought me out by the spirit of the Lord and set me down in the middle of a valley; it was full of bones. He led me all around them; there were very many lying in the valley, and they were very dry. He said to me, 'Mortal, can these bones live?' I answered, 'O Lord God, you know.' Then he said to me, 'Prophesy to these bones, and say to them: "O dry bones, hear the word of the Lord. Thus says the Lord God to these bones: I will cause breath to enter you, and you shall live. I will lay sinews on you, and will cause flesh to come upon you, and cover you with skin, and put breath in you, and you shall live; and you shall know that I am the Lord.""'127

Now, this American chap was like those old dry bones. He really needed someone to "speak the word of the Lord" into the dry bones that his religion had become. I tried, maybe others had tried before me, but Jesus told us that you can't tell the deaf. He said that we'd meet people with ears who can't hear, and eyes who can't see. A fellow like that needs to repent and get off his high horse. He needs to step back down on the ground and smell the roses—because that's where our Adjuster is, that's where God is, on the ground. Too many people need to repent of what their own ideas have done to their religion, and pull the plug on that whole development, and let God's understanding get a foot in the door.

You have to ask yourself, if your religion isn't about communion with God, what on Earth is it all about? It's nothing. It's empty. It's just a bunch of hot air going up and coming down, pulling here and shoving there. And at the end of the day it doesn't amount to a hill of beans. If your religion is only your ideas about God, *your* beliefs, then there's no wonder your life's a mess. Your religion needs to be *God's* ideas about *you*, not your ideas about God. If God is in your life, you can tell it because he manifests himself all around you. He's in your heart. He's in your mind. He's in your decisions. He's in your words. He's in your actions. He's in your blessing that you bring to others every day. If God is in your life he is constantly telling you who you are in his eyes. That's how he adjusts you. That's why he's called an Adjuster.

If he isn't in your life like that brother and sister, then you'd better starting speaking the "word of the Lord" into yourself and get with his program. Drop your limiting thought that you're doing the best you can. Kick out of your house the really dumb idea that God's doing everything he can for you in your current situation—obviously he can double what he's doing, at least! if you'll just get yourself out of the way and let him. Keep your excuses to yourself. Put down your grudge and the chip on your shoulder. Get down on your knees in humility and ask his forgiveness and receive it and let God be the centre of your religion, instead of your own self worth being at its core. Get up and step on around that mess on the ground. Then join the alive ones and cross on over into the promised ground that he came to bring you into day after day.

Now let's move on.

God has a plan you can follow

It is a great blessing to firstly know that God who is indwelling you, knows you thoroughly and has a plan for your needs to be met, and secondly, that you can change course at any time in your life to agree with that plan as he makes you aware of it or as you think fit.

The Urantia papers say that cooperation with our Thought Adjusters is not a particularly conscious process on our part, and that our cooperation is more easily known to us through our motives and decisions, our faithful determinations and our supreme desires.[128] In my own life, I like to talk with him, to commune with him, as did Jesus—I learned that from Jesus. Even though we do commune together, the day to day cooperation I experience is not something I keep my mind on. I just let everything to do with the machinery of our relationship run in my Father's way. Jesus came to decisions and understandings about his ministry in the Perean Hills after his baptism, and the Urantia papers tell us that he would "quietly begin the proclamation of the kingdom, and trust his Father (the Personalised Adjuster) to work out the details of procedure day by day."[129] I learned from Jesus doing that. When I do the same as that, I leave it to my Father to faithfully manage our whole relationship.

For example, I leave it to him to tell me when he needs my attention in order to change plans, or if I need to deal with an impending problem that I have overlooked. Sonship should be a relaxed thing; not a tense thing; it should not make us anxious but rather it should relax us. We shouldn't be anxious over our cooperation with our Adjuster. If you haven't got the vaguest idea about cooperating with your Thought Adjuster, then settle for a program of being clean hearted, sincere and cheerful. If you will bring into your life those three things, responding to the spiritual thought within you concerning which aspects of your life to deal with week by week, I guarantee you that you will be cooperating with your Thought Adjuster.

The basic map of life that my Father has shown me has at its core, the development of the human self-identity. It's not a particularly elaborate map, but it meets a considerable range of needs. His fundamental interest lies in two things: accurate communication and the delivery of appropriate information to us and to our Seraphim of destiny. These two effectively nurture self identity at any stage of life, in any circumstance—given that the human mind is still functional with a sense of "I" around which decisions can be formed and, by which, will can be exerted.

An aside note here is that, where there is no sense of self, and no will, there is no transmission of Adjuster activity possible between the human and God. An example of this is in many drug-induced experiences. They invalidate the Adjuster's efforts with his human child because the drug-induced person can so wholly forfeit their will to the chemical over-control of the drug. This is particularly so with heroin and other opiates. Another example is the over-control by so-called spirits that some people crave in things like voodoo and witchcraft, where spirituality at its best is the occasion of the complete surrender of their own identity and will to some kind of "other than I" based psychological phenomenon and psychic manifestation.

Let me say to you with confidence dear reader that, even if you think that such things are better in your life than not having them, if you will let this practice go and ask God your Thought Adjuster who is higher than this practice to keep that force at bay and out of your heart and mind, then he will establish in you a communion between himself and you that will bring you life and rewards and benefits that these other practices cannot—and do all this through the type of communion that will still let you access the assurances of prophecy that you like so much. You

438

have everything to gain and nothing to lose by doing this with God. Let go your stained and hurting heart now, and receive God's pure and clean heart in its place. Go on in peace now.

The foundations of communication

Fundamental to the map, my Father showed me the power of the communication system in our bodies and its development through infancy. This was integral to the stages of self-identity development—with every different level of self-identity comes new horizons, new challenges and new growth in our ability to share the mind of God.

There is a basic communication system in the human body and it can be perceived in the chest. By it we know three things, "Yes;" "No;" and "Uncertainty". Uncertainty can mean, "I need more information before I can come to a definite conclusion." Uncertainty always wants to come to a definite conclusion, one way of the other, and does not want to remain in a state of uncertainty.

Kinesiology[130] and Applied Physiology[131] are two modalities for learning and healing that employ the same type of consciousness in the body and identify the yes/no signal through indicator muscles.

You don't have to do this exercise of course, but if you want to then there's a way to experience your own equivalent of this communication system. When questions that have a yes/no answer are asked you, you wait for your chest area to deliver feelings as the answer. That means simply paying attention to the feelings you experience in your chest in response to questions that are asked. You'll feel a certain feeling when you are answering "yes," and a different feeling when you are answering "no," and an entirely different answer again when you're answering "uncertainty" to yourself. Ok, here we go. Without answering in words, and paying attention to the feelings that come into your chest, answer these questions:

1. Are you a male?
   (Notice the feeling and then read the next question.)
2. Are you female?
   (The feeling will be different from the feeling that arose for question 1.)
3. Is today Tuesday where you are?

439

4. Are you born again?
5. Do you own a copy of the Urantia papers?
6. Is the boomerang usually made from Eucalyptus wood?
7. Is it raining in Jerusalem right now?

That exercise is quite meditative, you'll agree. If you did that exercise with any kind of sensitivity, you probably experienced the full range of feelings from 'yes' to 'no' and to 'maybe'. From it, it's easy to see that at our most basic and least sophisticated level of consciousness, we receive information and make a personal decision from it. Basically, we experience life first in terms of it being true or false.

A sequence of changes in self-identity

Now, when a baby is born (and I'll use a baby boy for brevity in language) and grows up to the age of around two years, he is a total sponge for any and all information. In a sense, the infant is saying only "yes" to everything that happens. Everything is true for him. If Dad comes home drunk and bashes Mum, that's true for him, that's they way you do things. If Dad holds Mum's hand over dinner and says a prayer of thanks to God, then that's the way you do things, that's what's real and true. There's no argument coming from the boy.

Decision making is primitive. That all changes when the child learns to say "no," and later learns the value of how his "yes" and his "no" are able to enhance the pain or the pleasure in its life. "Do I want this soft fluffy thing? Yes: it makes me feel good!" "Do I want that funny tasting mushy stuff in my plate? No: it makes me feel uncomfortable," and so forth.

The child advances in the ability to employ his communication system across ever increasingly demanding decisions and wider horizons, culminating in his early days at school. At five years then, the child's reality suddenly expands when he mixes with other kids that he's never met before. Suddenly he has considerable objectivity on his own life, he is reflected in the kids around him and he can know himself more succinctly. He freely indulges his pleasure and vents his frustration without a second thought until he starts to reflect upon its value. He's never done that before. Reflection is a new thing. It is only a matter of months before he makes his first moral choice, and the Thought Adjuster who will be God for him arrives into his mind.[132]

He will develop his psychic feelings through the years six to puberty at around twelve. At twelve he is treated as an adult by the local universe administration and he will be offered the opportunity to make a decision which identifies that adulthood—he will make a decision about his spiritual allegiance.

Commensurate with this spiritual decision and his puberty, his self identity will rapidly change. He can reproduce the species: nature has completed its task. He now grows awkwardly out of his childhood and into his adolescence and, like a young eagle who has all the equipment but none of the experience, he will quickly try to develop three features in imitation of his parents or guardians. He will seek his own food. He will seek his own nest. He will seek his own partner, mate. How well he achieves that will depend very much on what he absorbed when he was a "yes"-only creature in his first couple of years, and how well he can influence his judgements about survival and shelter and mating during his years to puberty. Just about everything in his life though, will be judged by the values he claimed about himself from conception to puberty. Most of what happens from then on in his life will be based on those first basic judgements and values. Even when he gets born again and gets the Thought Adjuster's heart of flesh where once there was a heart of stone,[133] and even when he gets baptized in the Holy Spirit and fire and tongues, he will repeat those same early judgements and values unless he makes a concerted effort to undermine their influence in his life and changes the behaviour patterns they have established.

Is it any wonder we are addicted like our parents were? Or cruel; or absent; or violent; or afraid; or neglected; or perpetually abused; or abusive; or rejected; or ashamed; or abandoned? Is it any wonder that we find these things to be in our lives like such deep hooks in us that we find it impossible to tear them out of us and change who we are and what happens to us in life? Why, everything that we once were, once fully embrace these bizarre values and agreed with them as we saw those we loved showing us how they operated. And we had little means of arguing against them.

But there *is* a means now. That means is to actively adopt the

Father's view of you as being his son—whether you're male or female—and pursuing the path of perfection just like Jesus did, like I have, and like many others have.

The origins of that path are summed up in a simple prayer by the Psalmist who, out of the quiet sincerity of his own desperation said, "Create in me a clean heart, O God, and put a new and right spirit within me."[134]

The clean heart is made in us through the work of the Holy Spirit. The right spirit he is asking for, is the renewing of our mind so that it becomes like the mind of God—being influenced by the adjusting God who dwells within us so that we think the same values that he thinks.

When we look into Jesus and his personality, we can easily find that he managed the five existential needs we all have, very well indeed. He wasn't at all neurotic and afraid, small minded and petty. He was at peace with his past; confident about his future; capable with his communication to others; gentle and kind in his bringing healing and change to others and receiving it from the Father for himself; and constantly in communion with God in the fullness of perfect sonship with God. We see no traces of the problems that came into his life through Mary and Joseph or their ancestors—the sins of the Fathers.

Jesus is our hope. The Urantia papers confirm for us some amazing facts about our becoming like Jesus:

"Jesus was the perfectly unified human personality. And today, as in Galilee, he continues to unify mortal experience and to co-ordinate human endeavors. He unifies life, ennobles character, and simplifies experience. He enters the human mind to elevate, transform, and transfigure it. It is literally true: 'If any man has Christ Jesus within him, he is a new creature; old things are passing away; behold, all things are becoming new.'"[135]

"If your own mind does not serve you well, you can exchange it for the mind of Jesus of Nazareth, who always serves you well.[136]

"Because of the presence in your minds of the Thought Adjuster, it is no more of a mystery for you to know the mind of God than for you to be sure of the consciousness of knowing any other mind, human or superhuman. Religion and social consciousness have this in common: They are

442

predicated on the consciousness of other-mindness. The technique whereby you can accept another's idea as yours is the same whereby you may 'let the mind which was in Christ be also in you.'"[137]

When the adolescent reaches around twenty years of age, he will make a spiritual decision that will set his life course for the next twenty years as he ventures forward, out of one phase of the development of his identity and into the next. In the first twenty years of life, God is a provoker of thoughts and ideas and values in us, he is God the Thought Changer. Now at the age of twenty and on in until he is forty, God will adjust those ideas and values in him, ever bringing them on line with those of his own nature by a process of distillation. This is his time for growing through trial and error on the broader playing field of the whole world's pool of ideas and values. During this period of time, God is God the Thought Adjuster. Then, lastly from the age of forty to sixty and older, God leads him by the tried and tested ideas and values. Like an old dog to whom it is sometimes difficult to teach new tricks, he will be led into greater depth of meaning and value in a life which is now built upon the values he has proven to himself throughout his twenties and thirties. In the light of the way that God leads the person increasingly into his ways, by the method of mutual consent, God now has become God the Thought Controller.[138] Should a person fail to be led, God cannot arbitrarily control him in any way whatsoever. "The freewill of man is supreme in moral affairs."[139]

As you grow older you'll find that it is not difficult to exhaust the values and ideas that commonly rule the world. This is particularly so if you get a taste of the west and the east, the rich and the poor, the ancient and the modern, the manual and the electronic, the personal and the group, the simple and the complex in our societies. You may well have come to a point in your life when you felt as if you were in fact learning the things of heaven. The Urantia papers actually confirm that to us, telling us that we will learn all the values in the Mansion Worlds before settling our universe citizenship with that crowning glory called Adjuster fusion—perfect God-mindedness in the sphere in which we live.

The Urantia papers that detail life on the mansion worlds,

give us an understanding about the achievements in life that we catch up on before we are accepted into citizenship in the wider universe, and Adjuster fusion. Many things that we have difficulty with here on Earth, we are able to come to finality over in the mansion worlds after our death. Significantly, there is a type of mentality, a way of processing information and of understanding the higher things of sonship with God, which the Mansion World dweller calls Mota.

This then is a brief outline of a map that I employ in the comprehension of my own position in life's timeframe; my Father's motives for increasing my adoption of his values as I traverse that timeframe; and the position of others who might visit me for some help as they traverse their timeframes.

I commend to you that you develop in your own life, some kind of a cohesive view on this life and the next that works well for you. The Urantia papers say that cooperation with God would see us choosing to respond to his divine leading and sincerely basing our human life on the highest consciousness of truth, beauty, and goodness, and then coordinating these qualities of divinity through wisdom, worship, faith, and love. Whilst this is true and easy to prove in our lives, having some kind of a life map is really invaluable because it helps us to position the application of these qualities into a larger mosaic.

If we sew lots of little squares of truth, beauty and goodness together so that they form larger squares of wisdom, worship, faith and love, it is only when we stand back from our work that we can see how the whole quilt is shaping up to be an image of our life from the point of conception to the point of Adjuster fusion.

And it all hangs on the fact that our Father has a plan for us, in every stage of our life, and if ever we are lost or in need, we should suspend our activities and give him full opportunity to reveal it to us and to empower us with it. The key to cooperating with his plan is often not the question, "What do I want to do?" but rather "Who do I want to be?" His plan is often not a course of activities so much as a course of action that will enable you to embrace higher or broader or deeper values. Trying that approach for yourself may bring the results you have wanted.

Notes

1. Facilitated every three years by The Urantia Book
   Fellowship, e-mail ubinfo@ubfellowship.org or on
   the Internet at http://urantiabook.org/ or mail to 529
   Wrightwood Avenue, Chicago, Illinois 60614 USA;
   tel. 1(877)3355669.
2. Paper 31 The Corps Of The Finality.
3. 26:5.3 {That, then, is...}
4. 31:0.4 {During the present...}
5. 31:0.5 {One or more...}
6. 31:0.7 {The Finaliters maintain...}
7. 14:6.9 {Paradise is the...}
8. 163:3.2 {When Peter and...}; Mark 10:27
9. 5:1.9 {The fact that...}; 101:1.7 {Thus it may...}
10. 135:11.1 {John had a...}
11. 136:8.3 { Throughout all this...}
12. 153:1.3 {The Master well...}
13. 153:1.3 {The Master well...}
14. 157:2.2 {When Jesus had...}
15. 176:1.1
16. 168:4.3 {1. Prayer is an...}
17. 178:2.3 {David Zebedee, through...}
18. 168:4.3 {9. Do not hesitate...}
19. Ephesians 6:13
20. 168:1.9 {When Martha and...}
21. I had been ordained by the Abbot of Kong Meng San
    Phor Kark See in Singapore, in the Lin Chi sect of
    Chinese Buddhism, on December 10th 1976, and the
    monk name he offered me was Sek Kong Un—which
    is pronounced oon as it foot—and means "Cool
    Heart."
22. 168:1.9 {When Martha and...}
23. For further reading, see:
    Hunter, C.& F. 1981. "How to heal the sick." Hunter
    Books, Kingwood Texas. http://www.cfhunter.org/;
    Roberts, O. 1995. "Expect a miracle." Word
    Publishing, London. http://www.oru.edu/;
    Osborn, T.L. 1951-1992. "Healing the sick." Harrison
    House, Tulsa Oklahoma;

Jorgensen, O. 1998. "Supernatural: The life of William Branham," (in three books). Tucson Tabernacle, Arizona. http://www.Biblebelievers.org/; Lliardon, R. 1996. "Smith Wigglesworth: The complete collection of his life teachings." Albury Publishing, Tulsa Oklahoma.

24. See the chapter titled, "Death and resurrection."
25. 100:1.2 {Some persons are…}
26. 110:3.4 {I cannot but…}
27. 113:2.5 {The angels develop…}
28. Isaiah 61:1-2
29. John 14:12
30. 34:7.1 {Evolutionary mortals inhabiting…}
31. 108:1.2 {Although we do…}
32. 63:0.2 {Andon is the…}; 63:7.2 {On Jerusem both…}; 108:1.2 {Although we do…}
33. 110:0.2 As far as…}
34. 34:7 {The Spirit and the Flesh}
35. 107:7.3 {We have often…}
36. 2:5.10 {But the love…}
37. 48:6.10 {You will learn…}
38. 2:6.8 {God loves the…}
39. 193:2.2 {Peace be upon…}
40. 193:2.2 {Peace be upon…}
41. 107:6.2 {The Adjuster is…}
42. 123:6.9 {Because of this…}
43. 159:5.1
44. Psalm 51:10
45. Psalm 23:1
46. Leviticus 19:18
47. Isaiah 41:13
48. Isaiah 2:4; Micah 4:3
49. 124:2.5 {Perhaps his most…}
50. 164:2.3 {When this little…}
51. 171:7.1
52. 129:0.2 {The Son of Man…}
53. 129:0.2 {The Son of Man…}
54. 124:4.9 {Throughout this and…}
55. 137:4 {The wedding at Cana.}
56. 177:2.6 {It is our…}

57. 142:2.2 {Prayer is entirely...}
58. Job 5:2
59. Proverbs 15:18
60. Proverbs 14:29
61. Proverbs 15:1
62. Proverbs 19:11
63. Proverbs 25:28
64. Proverbs 27:4
65. 149:4.1
66. Jeremiah 7:13
67. Proverbs 1:24
68. Proverbs 1:25
69. Proverbs 1:28
70. 146:2.5 {4. There is a...}
71. 153:3.5 {Jesus then directed...}
72. 147:5.4 {When Simon saw...}
73. 147:5.9 {But Jesus earnestly...}
74. 158:5.2 {When Jesus has...}
75. Leviticus 19:18
76. 125:0.6 {Though many of...}
77. 159:5.4 {Jesus did not...}
78. 172:1.3 {Jesus talked with...}
79. 137:6.5 {Jesus instructed them...}
80. 140:8.2 {1. Doing the Father's...}
81. 175:2.3 {How cruel and...}
82. 169:1.16 {Many, many times...}
83. 163:3.3 {As they went...}
84. 126:0.3 {The story of...}
85. 149:2.12 {On both friends...}
86. 130:2.6 {Ganid was, by...}
87. 130:7.2 {When Ganid inquired...}
88. 132:4.2 {Always the burden...}
89. 133:2.2 {And then in...}
90. 130:6 {The young man who was afraid.}
91. 140:5.10 {4. Happy are the...}
92. 132:4.2 {Always the burden...}
93. 143:6.4 {The theme of...}
94. 136:4.9 {In all this...}
95. 140:5.1
96. 140:5.3 {Jesus did not...}

97. 140:5.11 {And then Jesus...}
98. 140:10.4 {This same evening...}
99. 179:5.9 {When Jesus had...}
100. 180:1.1
101. 188:4.9 {All this concept...}
102. 180:2.1
103. 137:6.5 {Jesus instructed them...}
104. 137:7.13 {While Jesus later...}
105. 138:8.2 {Jesus taught them...}
106. 140:6.9 {Then asked Nathaniel...}
107. 139:4.6 {Those characteristics of...}
108. 150:9.2 {But they jostled...}
109. 159:2.1
110. 155:3.4 {Increasingly they learned...}
111. 188:5.7 {The cross makes...}
112. 188:5.9 {The cross is...}
113. 192:2.1
114. 192:2.3 {After they had...}
115. 192:2.4 {When they had...}
116. 192:2.9 {Jesus next talked...}
117. 192:2.10 {Then said the...}
118. 165:4.1
119. 140:8.4 {3. Social attitude...}
120. 140:8.15 {The Master offered...}
121. 132:5 {Counselling the rich man.}
122. 188:5.2 {The cross forever...}
123. 188:5.3 {Jesus, by the...}
124. 188:5.11 {Make sure, then...}
125. 194:3.11 {Pentecost, with its...}
126. 194:3.2 {Many things which...}
127. Ezekiel 37:1-6
128. 110:3.6 {You must not...}
129. 136:9.8 {Jesus of Nazareth...}
130. See Krebbs, Charles, Dr., & Brown, J., 1998. A Revolutionary Way of Thinking. Hill of Content. Melbourne.
131. See Utt, Richard, 1991. Applied Physiology Acupressure formatting for Brain Physiology. Applied Physiology Publishing. Tucson AZ.
132. See the chapter titled, "Thought Adjuster arrival: how

I got "saved."
133. Ezekiel 11:19
134. Psalm 51:10
135. 100:7.18 {Jesus was the...}
136. 48:6.6 {3. Mind Planners...}
137. 102:4.1
138. 107:0.7 {On the evolutionary...}
139. 66:8.6 {the doctrine of...}

❦

Chapter 33

Sonship and doing the will of God

In 1993, a man came to the door one evening. He was literally doubled over in pain. He was only thirty or so, but he was doubled over like an old man. As I stood in the doorway, he looked up at me and pleaded, "Rob, you've got to help me. I am in so much pain that I can't move. I can't stand up straight. My spine. My spine. Can you give me some acupuncture or something? Can I just come in and lay down for a while?"

I brought him in and he made it onto the treatment couch, lying on his side. We discussed his case briefly. He said that he had had lower spine injury, then surgery, then a failed spinal fusion, which just complicated and messed up the whole thing. This day his pain had become so unbearable, and he didn't want to get back into using heroin to kill the pain, so he had come around to see me.

I, of course, had little to work with but my faith. I had little faith in acupuncture to relieve so gripping a pain.

As he lay there on the treatment couch, I let my Father's mind merge with mine. He is always eager to help, and ever ready to let his mind merge with ours. And so his mind merged with my mind, and I became conscious of something about this fellow.

"I see that you are thinking of going down the coast, to visit with your sister and friends. Is this true?" I asked him.

"Yes, it is," he replied.

"God showed me that. The mind of God holds that prophecy about you, and he shared it with me."

"He also showed me," I continued as I saw his Adjuster's desire for him as it was held in my own Father's mind, "that if you will by faith draw on the fact that God is your Father and that you are his son, you will find healing for your pain."

Straight away he said encouraging words:

"Rob, you know I'm a Jew. My family are Jews. Both my parents were in camps."

Then he looked into my eyes with a real sense of love as he continued.

"But I also love Jesus Christ. I gave my heart to Jesus at a Christian meeting last year. I know he's got healing for me, I just don't know how to get it."

I didn't know he'd found Jesus in his life until he told me.

"Look at me sincerely now," I said, to get his undivided attention.

He looked at me, wincing with the pain in his back, which sent fiery hot darts through his hip and his legs, and made the muscles in his neck and back cramp with tension. He was still doubled over, unable to straighten up, even though he was lying down on the treatment couch.

"I told you something that God showed me about you. And you said it was true. He also told me that if you will use the faith that comes to you by being his son, the faith that accompanies sonship with God, then he has healing for you and you can make that healing your own," I told him.

"OK. I understand," he said, and he thought for a moment to comprehend what that meant. Then he opened his eyes and said, "I believe that Rob. God is my Father. I am his son."

"Then God has healing for you," I affirmed. "And if you believe that, then you're going to slip off this treatment couch right now and stand to your feet and raise your hands high up above your head and God's healing is going to pour on down all over you and your pain will vanish. Because he said it would."

When that healing moment comes about in a human being, it is a moment of faith. The stresses of managing busy daily lives keep many people locked into the mental realm as they juggle and evaluate concepts to come to quality decisions. For many other people, the stresses and tensions of conflicting emotions keep them locked into the realm of emotions. While we stay locked in to the mental realm, or the emotional realm and, for that matter the psychic realm, we cannot access the realm of faith—they are incompatible and self-excluding. Faith is a response in trust, a whole body decision on our part to trust and go for it. All the others are a self-evaluation process, and God is commonly left out in the dark.

When you are told something about yourself that nobody could know unless you told them: and then the same person tells you that God gave them that information about you: then you think that the person is in contact with the mind of God. When that person then tells you that he or she can perceive that God has healing for you, if that's true in the mind of God, then there suddenly emerges a spark of faith in your body and mind and feelings. Suddenly God's world is available to you, where only a moment ago it was not. Suddenly you shift into the place in yourself where you can merge with God and receive from him, where a moment ago you could not. In that moment, when faith arises in you, you break through your customary realms and go beyond mere knowledge about healing and you make the real subjective connection to the potential interaction that God has for you. That connection is faith for action between God and you. At that instant, a bridge between the world with its pain and heaven with its remedy comes into existence. Then, in that moment of faith, if you act on that belief in God's healing for you by doing something you couldn't do a moment ago, fully believing that if you act believing that what you've asked for in faith will then manifest for you, then God's healing flows right on into you and you are perfectly healed.

How faith works

The principle is in Jesus' words; read them as if for the first time now, and see these faith-action moments in them—the clean heart; the request for what you want; the asking in faith to receive what you want; the guarantee that you will receive it; and the appropriating it by acting as if it is therefore yours by the asking, because it actually *is* yours for the asking when you believe it is. Jesus said:

"Truly I tell you, if you say to this mountain, 'Be taken up and thrown into the sea,' and if you do not doubt in your heart, but believe that what you say will come to pass, it will be done for you. So I tell you, whatever you ask for in prayer, believe that you have received it, and it will be yours. 'Whenever you stand praying, forgive, if you have anything against anyone; so that your Father in heaven may also forgive you your trespasses.'"[1]

"OK," he said. "I'm coming off the couch. I want his healing."

He creaked his way off the couch and, still doubled up, landed on his feet on the floor beside near where I was standing. The pain was still with him.

"Now, just stand up," I said.

And he did.

From out of nowhere, the pain subsided enough for him to

simply stand upright.

"Now raise your hands high above your head and thank God for your healing," I said. And he lifted his hands until they were a little above shoulder height, when it seemed his weight went more firmly on his hips.

"I can't," he said. "There's still pain there," he said.

I knew God had a full healing for his pain and so I just went right on, saying to him, "Lift your hands up high and let your mind's eye imagine that you are hanging onto God with your hands, and that he is holding you up. Just believe in him to do what he said he would do."

I felt it was important to help him through the last moment of doubt that pain brings. As soon as he did that, his whole body relaxed. He smiled. After a while, his arms lowered slightly. He said out loud,

"Oh God! Thank you for my healing. Thank you Father. Thank you Jesus."

Something good was obviously happening for him. Tears of relief trickled down his face. He quietly continued mouthing words of thanks to God. He slowly rolled his neck in a wide arc. Then he gently twisted himself at the waist. Then he lowered his arms and gracefully leaned over and touched his toes. Then he straightened up and stood upright.

I wanted to anchor the fact of his healing by giving him the opportunity to tell people other than just me. That's always so important, because later on, when the human mind can get to doubting and destroying all the good in this kind of an experience, he has the added reinforcement of the experience of other people's reactions to his healing which help support his on going claim to healing and change. Strange as it seems, people can doubt or be fooled into losing their healing. Charles and Francis Hunter wrote a very helpful little book on this topic, helpful to the spiritual healer and the patient alike.[2]

"Come with me into the kitchen," I said. "I want the people to see you."

We walked off into the kitchen of that house where a few of the people who were undergoing withdrawal for heroin were sitting around having their dinner.

As soon as he walked into the room, cutlery dropped onto plates. Eyes stared at him, wide open. They had peeked around

453

into the hall and seen him when he came to the front door, doubled up in agony. Now here he was not twenty minutes later standing upright and free of pain. He smiled at them, relaxed in their company, still aglow with the anointing of God on him, having from time to time come through this place as a resident in need of detox himself, and he said, "God just healed me. Christ just took away all my pain."

He looked to see that they comprehended that fact. He beamed at them with such a shine on his face, the glow of Christ's victory, that it was hard for them not to know something pretty dramatic had just happened with him. They slowly closed their gaping mouths and adjusted their looks of astonishment and nodded their heads as if to say, "Yeah, we know." Then he spoke to them for a few minutes about his faith in Jesus, and sonship with God, and we walked out to the front door and he rejoined his life.

I saw him about eighteen months later. That healing lasted him for about fifteen months apparently, until he had an accident and brought on more stress in his life. It was his weak point perhaps—every time he couldn't deal with life, he'd cripple himself through that part of his body. But he said that even though his back "played up" from the most recent accident, he still never has had the kind of pain and debility he'd endured for years up until that evening he received his Father's healing.

Healing is such an easy way to see the manifestation of the will of God

The wonderful thing about this case is the ease with which the will of God was facilitated. I have often thought that healing is such an easy way to see the manifestation of the will of God. The simple test of spiritual life being active or non-active is in whether the will of God is manifesting in your life.

Was it a miracle?

No. No physical laws were adjusted in order to manifest the healing.

In order to do the will of God do you have to produce miracles?

No, of course not. The will of God manifests in every arena

of life, every day, without miracles ever happening. The will of God is all about the manifestation of spiritual values rather than unusual events.

Does healing like this work every time and in all cases?

No.

Why not?

I have no idea: it's a case by case matter. It is never a case of the will of God failing to work its influence over material life— healing, change and a better value to pursue is always there for a person. Rather, it seems to me that life is underwritten by complex forces and it is not always easy for alignment to occur between the human being and the will of God. If such alignment was easy, there would obviously be a lot more healing going on, and considerably more people doing the will of God in the world.

Learning about doing the will of God

There is much we can learn about the doing of the will of God. The first consideration is that the will of God is something that we do actually learn to do, it's not that we will automatically grow into its doing. First, by hearing about it, we get an appetite for it, we grow into wanting to do it. Then we learn how to identify it. Then we do it, on a trial and error basis. Then we do it with significantly more confidence and whole outcomes.

As we learn these things, we increasingly take our mind off our own mind and put it onto the nature of the value in the mind of God our Thought Adjuster.

This is, so to speak, like sitting by a pond. At first we are busy thinking and preoccupied with our own thoughts. Eventually, our thoughts still and we gaze around at the pond and its surroundings and the things on its surface. Still later, we find that we can see into the depths of the pond, counting the large pebbles on the sandy floor in its shallows. We begin to know the pond itself. It is becoming a part of us. We feel the ripples on the surface as much as we feel the murkiness in which the reeds have their roots: with feelings that are deep within us, too deep for words and thought.

We are becoming a part of it somehow, we know not how. It is as if the pond begins to knows us.

As we and the pond deepen our knowing of each other, our secrets are opened to each other. Our past and our future. Our communication and our change. Our communion with life itself. These become the common property of the other.

We become a union, a single mind, a single will—the will of man and the will of the pond. At any time, we can be man or man-pond.

Our study has brought us a great depth of joy, even the joy that springs forth in us from the pond. It is a joy that we never knew when we were man alone. Our joy flows over into the lives of others, like the rains that spill the waters over the banks to form little ponds in their lives. We hope they will find the joy we have found, when they pause to sit by their pond.

And so, the will of God is studied and learned, like anything else throughout life on Earth. The magnificent thing about the will of God is that the life which is in the Thought Adjuster becomes our property. We own it. As he owns all that is in us.

Do you know the feeling of ownership about which I am speaking? You will recognise it when I describe it further. It is like the feeling that one has when one's parent is dying and one visits that loved one in hospital. One experiences an ownership of that dear person, because so very much of one's life has been lived in that person. A nurse comes by, or a doctor, and tries to do something for your parent. You know from the depth of every fibre in your being that your parent would never like that kind of a thing done. And you protest. You defend the rights of that parent to have things done a different way—because you are so much a part of them that it is like it is you yourself.

To be this intimate with your Thought Adjuster has a beautiful realness to it. You don't need faith then; your sonship has reached divine proportions that far transcend the flesh. Your bridge, once a stringy, wobbly thing of no account, has become a landfill. Where once the gap was like the Grand Canyon, jagged and deep, now because of the land fill that has been going on the shores of Earth and the shores of heaven commingle and there is between them only the waters of a little brook trickling across their sands. You can step across and barely get your feet wet.

Our study of the will of God teaches us, "That you may be strengthened with power through His spirit in the inner man;"

456

"'filled with all the fullness of God,' 'for all those who are led by the spirit of God are the sons of God.'"[3]

The will of God concerns values, power and persons

The will of God concerns values, and the power of those values over other values that compete for our attention. It is, for example, necessary to learn about the flesh and the spirit, and the bridge between the two, if the will of God is to be real in our life.[4] To study the spirit is to learn about God's role as it concerns the will of God. To study the flesh and our movement from the flesh to the spirit is to learn about our role.

There are very many early experiences when we think we are in the will of God but ultimately, as we mature in our individual spiritual capacity to learn, we will discover that the will of God involves the Spirit of Truth—Jesus and Christ Michael; the Holy Spirit—Mother Spirit of Nebadon; and the Thought Adjuster who indwells us—God the Father. The exquisite co-ordination of these three personal ministries delivers to us a single God, and a single "will of God" with which to concern ourselves. And this single "God" delivers us into the wider universe and brings us to a consciousness of interacting morally and wilfully with the others who inhabit Michael's vast universe.

At some point, we will find these deity persons as individuals, and we will find the will of the Father and the Son and the Spirit in them separately, and still they are perfectly unified and coordinated as if they were just one.

There is a significant shift in the will of God becoming our personal property so to speak, where once it was only ever in the domain of God who was outside us. Living like this is the difference between when we are kids, for example, and we send our wishes off into the wide blue yonder on the wings of our hope that somebody somewhere called God might find them. This kind of a God isn't a part of us. When God's will happens in our life during this phase of our life, it seems almost accidental. It is more hoped for than planned.

Doing the will of God with Jesus in our hearts

Given this, how is it that we grow closer to God so that the will of God is something that we can actually participate in? Let's start with Jesus, who did the will of God so perfectly.

The Urantia papers tell us that although the Spirit of Truth was given to all people at Pentecost, it is not automatically influential in all people. What makes its function and power accessible to people is almost wholly limited "by man's personal reception of that which constitutes the sum and substance of the mission of the bestowal Son." This means that the person will need to hear about Jesus, and then receive him into their heart.

The Holy Spirit's ability to do a work in that person is partly dependent then upon the human attitude, decisions and co-operation of the will of that person.[5]

When you receive Jesus into your own heart, it is because you believe him, you believe in him, you genuinely love him, and because you yield yourself to the transformation that occurs in you when you are led by the Father's teachings in his life. You receive into your heart both Jesus of Nazareth the Son of Man, the human, and Christ Michael the Son of God, the Creator Father-Son.

When you receive Jesus like this, the power and function in your life, of the Spirit of Truth, becomes coordinated with the Holy Spirit. Then, "the Spirit bears witness with your spirit (the Adjuster) that you are a child of God,"[6] and God can act in your life through a channel of faith which was not present before. Where once there was only the channel for intellectual knowledge about God and of truth, now there is the presence of faith by which the person can do the will of God as Jesus did the will of God—in power and in the Holy Spirit.[7] The difference is the difference between life and death.

> "Those who have received and recognised the indwelling of God have been born of the Spirit. 'You are the temple of God, and the spirit of God dwells in you.' It is not enough that this spirit be poured out upon you; the divine Spirit must dominate and control every phase of human

experience."[8]

What prevents people from doing the will of God?

What prevents people from doing the will of God?

We have a dual nature comprising the inheritance of animal tendencies—the flesh—and the high urge of spirit endowment—the Spirit.[9]

> "The Spirit never drives, only leads. If you are a willing learner, if you want to attain spirit levels and reach divine heights, if you sincerely desire to reach the eternal goal, then the divine Spirit will gently and lovingly lead you along the pathway of sonship and spiritual progress."[10]

Without your specific intention and decision to willingly receive what the spirit offers you, of course, you will remain fixated on the animal tendencies in your nature—the flesh. You will lock yourself into the realm of emotions, and life for you will be a struggle to find peace among endless conflicting emotions. Or, if you lock yourself into the mental realm, you will lock yourself into the ordering and re-ordering of your collection of concepts, like Scrooge McDuck endlessly counting away in his money vault, where each coin is a different concept.

If, on the other hand, you are locked into the realm of the fleshly lusts of the body, then you will spend your days indulging your senses and their pleasures. If you are locked into the psychic, your attention will be locked into the transference and perception of data that is derived from outside the realm of the five senses. It is always you who decides on the array of resources with which you will live. Unless the will of God is actively pursued, everything else is the pursuit of self and its experience potential.

The flesh does not inherently bear the fruit of the divine Spirit— the beautiful harvest of the co-operation between the Spirit of Truth and the Thought Adjuster in our life.[11] The flesh cannot and does not do the will of God. We are told that in a more normal world, we wouldn't experience such "acute conflicts between the spirit and the flesh which characterise the present-day Urantia races," and that we need to "put forth positive efforts" to move from the flesh to the spiritual,[12] to bring the spirit to victory in this "constant warfare" between the flesh and the spirit.[13]

The Urantia papers tell us the reason why our flesh nature is so strong and so seemingly dominant. It is because the:

"Caligastia upheaval precipitated world-wide confusion and robbed all subsequent generations of the moral assistance which a well-ordered society would have provided. But even more disastrous was the Adamic default in that it deprived the races of that superior type of physical nature which would have been more consonant with spiritual aspirations."[14]

The divine plan was for us to have had physical natures that were much more "naturally spirit responsive."[15]

The Urantia papers encourage us in our pursuit of the will of God, and show us the way to victory, saying:

"Notwithstanding this double disaster to man's nature and his environment, present-day mortals would experience less of this apparent warfare between the flesh and the spirit if they would enter the spirit kingdom, wherein the faith sons of God enjoy comparative deliverance from the slave-bondage of the flesh in the enlightened and liberating service of wholehearted devotion to doing the will of the Father in heaven. Jesus showed mankind the new way of mortal living whereby human beings may very largely escape the dire consequences of the Caligastic rebellion and most effectively compensate for the deprivations resulting from the Adamic default. 'The spirit of the life of Christ Jesus has made us free from the law of animal living and the temptations of evil and sin.' 'This is the victory that overcomes the flesh, even your faith.'"[16]

"Those God-knowing men and women who have been born of the Spirit experience no more conflict with their mortal natures than do the inhabitants of the most normal of worlds, planets which have never been tainted with sin nor touched by rebellion. Faith sons work on intellectual levels and live on spiritual planes far above the conflicts produced by unrestrained or unnatural physical desires. The normal urges of animal beings and the natural appetites and impulses of the physical nature are not in conflict with even the highest spiritual attainment except in the minds of ignorant, mistaught, or unfortunately overconscientious persons.[17]

"Having started out on the way of life everlasting, having accepted the assignment and received your orders to advance, do not fear the dangers of human forgetfulness and mortal inconstancy, do not be troubled with doubts of failure or by perplexing confusion, do not falter and question your status and standing, for in every dark hour, at every crossroad in the forward struggle, the Spirit of Truth will always speak, saying, 'This is the way.'"[18]

The bridge between the spirit and the flesh

At a practical level on this matter of working with the Holy Spirit and the will of God, my Father once revealed to me that the gulf between man and God is great. But, he added, man's healing by spiritual practices is only limited by two things: his own vision of himself, and the influences of sin that were introduced to the world by Caligastia the Devil which were set in motion to deliberately rob man of his faith in God. This of course is backed up when you read the papers on the Lucifer Rebellion and learn that Lucifer indeed wanted a whole universe to worship him as God, in place of Michael and the Father. Ever since, he has been called the father of lies; the deceiver; the one who brings only disease, death and destruction. The person who pursues the will of God will inevitably stand face to face with these forces and overcome them.

My Father said that because of the activities of the Thought Adjuster and the Spirit of Truth in the higher reaches of the human mind, and the presence of the Holy Spirit Mother around the more material environment of the person, all of the influences of sin and evil are easily able to be overcome by the person who wants to overcome them.

The only real problem lies in creating the bridge between the flesh and the divine Spirit.

Then, there's helping the person to have a clean heart—the Holy Mother Spirit will help them to do that too; she prepares the way in liaison with the Thought Adjuster.

That's done by helping a person to come to receive Jesus—and Christ Michael will help you to do that anyway.

Lastly there's helping them to believe that God heals, and that his healing is personally available to them, "by my grace and through their faith," he said.

With these in place, they can partake of the perfect will of God for their life because the bridge between man and God is able to be crossed by both man and God alike.

Nothing is impossible for God, but he won't violate your unbelief

Now, that bridge-crossing process sounds really simple and straightforward on paper. Does not everyone who has ever said a prayer for the dying child or loved one wish it were so simple? But it's not always achievable in practice. As I mentioned already, life is underwritten with complex forces that often make alignment with God on a specific task difficult. Oh sure, nothing is impossible with God—but that's true for the willing and pure hearted person. But Jesus, for example, wasn't always able to have people cross that bridge from the flesh to the spirit. There were probably numerous occasions when this occurred— which is ludicrous when you think about it, for here is the Creator Son, the Michael of an entire universe in the midst of his own creatures, his own children whom he adores, even today in the year 2000, and they have the gumption to argue with him and reject him! Truly the Bible is right about the average person's response to divine goodness when it recorded that:

> "He was despised and rejected by others; a man of suffering and acquainted with infirmity; and as one from whom others hide their faces he was despised, and we held him of no account."[19]

Mark tells us that when Jesus was in his hometown of Nazareth, the locals were stirred up against him:

> "Then Jesus said to them, 'Prophets are not without honour, except in their hometown, and among their own kin, and in their own house.' And he could do no deed of power there, except that he laid his hands on a few sick people and cured them. And he was amazed at their unbelief."[20]

This example from Jesus' life shows us how the unbelief in our flesh can keep us separate from the power of our Adjuster's divine will to help us. Obviously Jesus healed some of the sick but the sense is that there were many more people who could have received from God but who didn't.

Can people work for the kingdom of God and do no miracles of healing or other extraordinary events? Why, certainly they can. Jesus sent out over a hundred workers, including the twelve Apostles, and that group who did such magnificent work, the women's evangelistic corps.

"He promised to visit them often during this time. In the course of this month these twelve groups laboured in Gerasa, Gamala, Hippos, Zaphon, Gadara, Abila, Edrei, Philadelphia, Heshbon, Dium, Scythopolis, and many other cities. Throughout this tour no miracles of healing or other extraordinary events occurred."[21]

That's a month long crusade involving eleven towns and cities and over a hundred workers, and not a single extraordinary event occurred.

The will of God works in expectant and faith-dominated people

On the other hand, the Urantia papers tell us that for five months from May to October of A.D. 28, an enormous camp was established near Bethsaida. A kind of tent village sprang up and several thousand people passed through it. Its population varied from five hundred to fifteen hundred people. In an area nearby the main group of tents, the sick were tented under the supervision of a Syrian believer-physician named Elman. He was assisted by twenty-five young women and a dozen men and, during the four months of this hospital's existence, both Jesus and they made contact with at least a thousand patients who left there in a state of recovery. They were treated with the known material medical practices as well as with the spiritual practices of prayer and faith encouragement. The authors note their belief that, during this time, no so-called miracles of supernatural healing occurred.[22] They described the healings saying:

"Many of the cures effected by Jesus in connection with his ministry in behalf of Elman's patients did, indeed, appear to resemble the working of miracles, but we were instructed that they were only just such transformations of mind and spirit as may occur in the experience of expectant and faith-dominated persons who are under the immediate and inspirational influence of a strong, positive, and beneficent personality whose ministry banishes fear and destroys anxiety."[23]

Expectant and faith-dominated persons. That sounds like the attitude of this fellow who came to me doubled over in pain.

A strong, positive, and beneficent personality whose ministry banishes fear and destroys anxiety. That's the role that I undertook as I met his healing needs by helping him to cross that bridge between the flesh and the spirit; helping him to use the faith that came to him through the co-operation between the Spirit of Truth and his Thought Adjuster—the faith that had become his by receiving Jesus into his heart: the faith that enabled him to appropriate the healing that God had for him.

Faith opens the door for goodness

In Jesus' demonstration of the Father's will throughout the records in the Bible and the Urantia papers, I came to learn through my own experience that it is faith that opens the door to healing. Faith isn't the healer, mind you. Faith opens the door to another power, and divine Good comes in and does the healing. You'll remember the woman with the issue of blood who touched the hem of Jesus' robe and was healed in herself.[24]

"When Jesus heard this, he took the woman by the hand and, lifting her up, said: 'Daughter, your faith has made you whole; go in peace.' It was her faith and not her touch that made her whole."[25]

Material Medicine

There's an example right out of the life of Jesus that shows how faith opened the door to healing.

Where there is no faith, the practices of material medical science like surgery and drugs, therapy and manipulation might help.

It's important to remember that the Father's will may direct a person specifically toward the care provided by material medicine. Also, material practices almost miraculously from time to time seem to be wielded by faith-holding physicians;

their faith immeasurably helping the outcome that divine Good was able to manifest.

Material medical sciences can also institutionalise organisations with such unbelief that healing faith becomes an archenemy. Health care is the watchword, but healing, with all its gracious connection to the will of God and the manifestation of divine Good, is squeezed out by the human politics, the budget, selfish preferment, ambition, and the spiritual separation from all that Jesus stood for. Thank God for science and medical advances, pain relief, material expertise in surgery, molecular and x-ray diagnosis and pathology. They do contribute so much that is good, irrespective of the flesh or the spirit attitudes of their practitioners. But thank Jesus for the healing that the flesh so needs which the material sciences can't duplicate or reach.

Spiritual healing ever stands as a testimony to the fact of faith, the power of divine Goodness, the co-operation between the Spirit of Truth and the Thought Adjuster and the Holy Spirit, and the power of sonship with God.

Goodness and healing are so readily available

A young lady called around home last night for dinner. It so happened that she had been horse riding a few days earlier and had had a fall. She had tremendous trouble walking because she was very stiff in her thighs and legs and she also had pain in her lower back.

At a certain point in the evening, after we had eaten, I thought about helping her discomfort and so I said to her:

"Do you know that Christ can help you out with your pain? Jesus' spirit, that came to all people at Pentecost, mingles with the Spirit of the Father who resides in all of us, and by his will, when we ask him, he heals us."

"You know about Jesus," I continued. "In his ministry he healed people everywhere. Miracles happened around him. His healing is instant. One moment you are unwell and the next moment you are well. You'll see that now. I'm going to pray, to ask Jesus to bring his healing into you in the form of the power of the Holy Spirit, then you're going to get off your stool and walk around this kitchen about two times."

Then I looked into my Father's will to find out how long it would take before the impact of the anointing would change her condition.

"I think that by the time you've walked around this kitchen one and a half times, the healing anointing will have done its work," I said.

Would you like me to pray for this healing in you?" I asked.

"Oh yes, I certainly would," she replied. "I am so sore that I can barely walk. You saw how I hobbled in. Why, I could barely walk down the stairs into the kitchen."

I placed my right hand on her upper chest, and my left hand on her lower back, and then I spoke with Christ Michael, saying:

"Lord Jesus, please send your Holy Spirit power now. Let it come from heaven and touch Melissa. Let it be all over her like warm honey."

Then I perceived it beginning to flow and I said:

"Thank you Father. Yes, I see it coming now. Here it comes, here it comes."

Then I felt it making contact with her and going deep within her.

"There it is Father. Yes, it's making contact with her now," I said as I watched its outpouring. Then I saw it goes right down to her toes. "And there it is Melissa, going right on down to your feet."

After about a minute of letting the anointing do its work, I said to her:

"I'm not going to stop the anointing from doing its work. It's going to keep working for a little while longer now. But I want you to step off the stool now and walk on around this kitchen. Let the anointing keep working in you."

She stepped down off the stool. She looked like she didn't quite know what to expect. Off she walked, around the kitchen table.

She walked around once. Then she walked around again. As she walked around the second time she stopped half way around and looked at her partner and Mary my wife and me, saying:

"This is unbelievable. It's incredible. I am walking like I have no pain and stiffness at all."

"That's Jesus for you Melissa," I said. "He's a wonderful

healer. Now keep on walking."

On the third time that she walked around the kitchen I asked her to raise her hands, to twist her spine, to touch her toes—all those things that she said she couldn't do only minutes before.

"Do something that you definitely know you couldn't do before," I said.

Well, she was one happy girl. She couldn't stop telling her boyfriend about how she felt, and how surprised she was that the pain had vanished so quickly and how her mobility was restored so effortlessly.

"There's one final testing ground," I said.

"I saw you inch your way down those steps from the dining room to the kitchen when you came in. Take off your shoes now and run up those stairs."

She gave me a glance as if to say that she hadn't run up stairs since she was a kid, but she slipped out of her shoes and in a few moments had hurtled up the stairs and was walking around the dining room. Then she walked back down again into the kitchen and put her shoes back on.

"How is it for you," I asked.

She put her hand on her lower back, then said:

"Well, it's all great. My back is still a little sore, but that's to be expected 'cos that's where I landed when I fell off the horse. But the rest is great. It's like it never ever happened."

As she said mentioned the part about her back being a little sore still, I noticed something separate that needing healing and so I moved to address it.

"Melissa, your back is a different thing. It's weird, I know, but it's easiest to call it a spirit of something or other. It's a bit like you have an attitude stuck in there that's causing your pain. We'll get it out right now."

I called it out, saying:

"Spirit of whatever you are, come out now. Leave her."

Within seconds, the pain had gone. She bent over and touched her toes and rotated her hips to find no pain at all.

"People can lose their healing," I said. "As you drive home, or if you wake up in bed tonight, or during the day tomorrow, if the pain tries to come back you have to treat it like that spirit is trying to take a hold in you again.

"It's not a spirit like how some people think there are spirit-demons running all around the place and entering into people and making them sick," I said. "The Urantia papers tell us that there's no such a thing since Jesus' Spirit of Truth came into the world at Pentecost. But there is the capacity for the person to fall back from the spirit into the flesh and to reintroduce that flesh type problem where it left off at the time the spiritual healing became available to them. In a person with a good background in spiritual growth, the healing more easily holds up. In a person with little familiarity with keeping the flesh in their life at bay, the healing can be snatched away. Mary and I have been involved in presenting workshops that cover that topic, the flesh and the spirit and bridging the two, and have found people really benefit from that kind of knowledge and experience. So watch for it in your life."

"OK. I understand that. Thanks Rob," she said. "I'll do that."

Now the interesting thing about this little case is not that the pain was a record-breaking case of medical miracles: for it was not. It is more a case of how available and ever ready God is to bring healing to us. We're sitting around after dinner. The idea comes to heal the person of some crippling swelling and a back pain brought on by falling off a horse. So we do that and she recovers on the spot and we continue what we were doing. The point is that so many times, we are in the company of someone who has a health problem, and we walk on past our rights as sons of God to open the bridge between the flesh and the spirit and to bring Jesus' type of healing to that person by the will of their own indwelling Thought Adjuster.

Sonship service to another person, such as healing, builds faith. Faith builds bridges. Bridges become landfills. Land fills lead to Adjuster fusion. All of this builds peak meaning for life, magnificent self esteem, true character, victory over the world and eventual mastery of our Father's call for us to be perfect as he is perfect.

Think about this and, if you will, bring blessings more frequently to people as you pass by. By doing this, you exercise and practice the doing of the will of God. And in doing the will of God, you grow your sonship with God. Such growth, brought about by such doing of the will of your own Thought Adjuster, is the answer to the desire deep in your soul for increased spiritual growth and realness. There is no greater and, perhaps surprisingly, no more available door to your spiritual growth.

God's two plans for you

Once you get even the most rudimentary skills in exercising God's will over something, you never look back. It changes the way you find solutions in your life, and it definitely changes the way you are thankful for life. The will of God cuts across all problems to effect a change in you as a person. This doesn't necessarily affect your physical circumstances, but it well may. Your Father's will has two plans open to it only.

One plan is to bring you into union with him so that your peace is restored. Once your peace is restored, he knows you will be able to bear with the situation until physical change, or death, releases you from it. And you will bear with it well, because you will have your own Father's presence of mind, dignity.

Plan one

An example of this is that just yesterday I was sitting in an office in a men's maximum-security prison. I was told a fellow wanted to see me. Knowing what this particular fellow's emotional state was likely to be like, I picked up my cup of hot water and went out to meet him. My cup of water would tell him that whatever was going on in his life was not something that was more menacing than couldn't be dealt with over a relaxing social moment with him.

We sat on a metal bench, on the walkway that looked through a wire fence with razor wire atop it, across about a hundred metres of grass compound. On the other side of the compound was the unit he lived in. Beyond it some distance, through more fences and razor wire, was the high grey perimeter wall. Further off beyond it was the city haze and the tallest of the buildings in the central business district.

He was very agitated. His speech was loud, theatrical, calling attention to the officer nearby who must have questioned him about seeing me, because he was yelling out abuse after abuse with very intimidating ferocity.

Sitting in a jail with the freedom of the will of God at your disposal in the midst of both kinds of prisoners, those who seek God's goodness and those who hate the world, there is a certain resemblance to the time of Jesus on the cross. This fellow's attitude reminded me of the unrepentant thief who sought to defeat the world rather than find salvation from it. He had called to Jesus as he hung nearby, saying, "If you are the Son of God, why do you not save yourself and us?"[26] The answer to that question of course is that Jesus is more interested in showing us how to be free from death itself, rather than how to be free of mere politics and the judiciary. Similarly, in a prison, there is nowhere to go; there are only two avenues of activity open: hate the world more or find salvation from the world; there really isn't a middle road.

The prisoner who was sitting next to me was in the attitude of the brigand who hated the world, but I knew that the peace of God could swing him over to the attitude of the thief on the cross who sought and received salvation from Jesus.

I let him speak out his anger for a while, occasionally adding something to the conversation, waiting for a moment to break the flow. Then I looked into his eyes and said his name, and this invitation:

"I wish the peace of Jesus upon you right now."

He stopped what he was about to say and just looked at me.

"I wish the peace of Jesus upon you right now," I repeated, making sure he grasped what I had said.

"Jesus! Ha!" he laughed. "Yes. Jesus. The peace that passes all understanding," he said. He knew the Bible. "We all could do with a lot more of that peace," he said in a raised tone, as if to make sure the officer near at hand would take heed of that message. But as he continued speaking, the peace of Jesus rose up in him and the power of the Holy Spirit's comfort enshrouded us and he quickly became calm and whole again, just like that.

His abusiveness stopped. He lowered his voice. He became personally sensitive to my company. It was as if the stress of his problems evaporated and he could simply be himself again. His spirit was topped up, renewed-for those who live by the spirit are renewed by the spirit in no different a manner than how our car consumes its fuel and is replenished. If it is not replenished, it does not run. If we do not replenish our spirit, we function in the flesh or else we function with a great burden on our spirit.[27] This prisoner was merely suffering from spiritual depletion.

He was an interesting man with a painful background. He was released from prison two months later. He had a reputation for being "the man" in prison. Prisoners called him "king." He was a philosopher turned evangelist in his own way, a little crazy from time to time, with a history as a standover man. Around four months after this moment of prayer together, he was shot dead. He had found Jesus in prison, that I know because we prayed together, but he still had a lot of enemies who needed to settle with him. Some people said he had changed for the better.

But for now, once he was secured in the Father's peace given to him for that occasion, we wished each other farewell with a "God bless you." I returned to my office: he to his own struggle.

The power of plan one

The power of God in our lives changes everything. Ecclesiastes,[28] like Guatama after whom Buddhism is named, taught that this world in which we live and have our being is like dust, without substance, a mere mirage when compared with the realness and power of the First Source and Centre of all life, God. It took me many years to spiritually grasp the fact that nothing that we perceive in the world with our material senses is its own cause—that everything is created by something else and is therefore simply an effect without spiritual substance.

When we do the will of God, however, we introduce causes into the material world which are of a different nature from the causes that keep Ecclesiastes' world in motion. God's causes are different because they are, in a sense, sovereign over the whole system of causation in our lives.

Most causes, most things we do in life, are like throwing a cup of water into a wave that is about to break on the sea shore. The cup of water does not influence the wave's course of action. Why? Because the cup of water becomes a part of the wave and is simply carried along with it. It becomes the wave and adds to whatever the wave is doing. God's causes, on the other hand, turn the tide of events.

God's causes have authority over the causes of the world. The authority is a power to influence the causes of the world, to initiate changes-changes to health, prosperity, circumstances, benefits and so forth. The power in God's causes rests entirely in the fact that the creator can enter into its substance of that which he created and cause it to respond to divine goodness. When we do the will of God, we provide a way for God's goodness to influence the heart of the matter in question.

I'll give you an example. Suppose I have a well of water and I dip a bucket into it and draw up a bucket full of well water. Now suppose that over here nearby I have a well of the Holy Spirit and I dip a bucket into it and I draw up a bucket full of Holy Spirit. Now lets look at the characteristics of the contents in each bucket. The water is clear, wet and cool. The Holy Spirit is divinely true, beautiful and good. They both bring life, but the life they nourish is different. Now let's suppose we position an angry young man in between both buckets and let them influence the man. It is reasonable to expect that the man will start to simmer down in the presence of the Holy Spirit. He will become peaceful, his good side will resurface and he will become joyful.

Now suppose that he drinks from both buckets. The water will quench his thirst and sustain his mortal life. What kind of impact do you think the Holy Spirit will have once it gets inside him?

It will sustain his eternal life.

Plan two

I mentioned that your Father's will has two plans open to it only, and that one plan is to bring you into union with him so that your peace is restored. Once your peace is restored, he knows you will be able to bear, grow and be useful in the kingdom with the situation until physical change, or death, releases you from it. The other plan changes your circumstances.

I once had been sentenced to a military labour camp for a short period of time. On the sixth evening I prayed, asking God to deliver me from that place.

On the following day, I had a mild injury that enabled me to spend just about all of my sentence in the Naval Base Hospital instead of undergoing the rigours of prison. Life is full of these kinds of experiences where, as a result of prayer, one is delivered into better conditions.

Of the two plans, deeper personal integrity or a change in circumstances, people who do not live closely to God and his will often struggle to identify which plan to exercise. This is especially true when they are too rattled to think that spiritual peace is going to amount to much, and that a radical change in circumstances is the best option. Generally, however, we often benefit from staying put and letting our character grow out of difficult circumstances, as we draw ever more deeply from our spiritual well to meet our needs. Sometimes, we benefit from a change in our circumstances that comes about by other changes that go on around us. Occasionally, we benefit by simply walking away from the whole situation and picking up somewhere else, but when it becomes a lifestyle we lose integrity.

Very few of us have a model of change that enables the eradication of the forces of evil surrounding either ourselves or our circumstances—for the candidate for Adjuster fusion, such a model is imperative. I will be focussing more on this strategy in one of my next books.

Each person must find their own way through the complexity and diversity of situations and personal positions, but the Spirit of Truth is *always* there within, whispering, suggesting, hinting, "This is the way: walk therein."[29]

Knowing that there is not any one particular thing that God's will might say to you across every situation, it is valuable to know that the doing of the will of God has parameters to it that are unique to you, your situation, the values involved and the plan to lead you to higher ground.

The doing of the will of God is also the most deeply personal experience you will ever know. Deeper than sex; deeper than child birth; deeper than debt and deeper than riches; deeper than emotions and deeper than thoughts: deeper than all things human. Yet, doing the will of God is the plainest experience, the least embellished, the most ordinary. In an ironic sense, doing the will of God is too deep for the shallow person; too ordinary for the complex person; too plain for the fancy person; too unselfish for the person obsessed with gain and loss. The will of God beckons you to wholly and very literally make a gift of yourself to God, so that he then can be a gift that you bring to another person and the world. He is your gift to someone you love, but you yourself first must be a gift of love yourself, given over without reservation to him. There is something profoundly deep in all this, and yet it is profoundly plain and simple.

What, then, is the will of God? How do we identify it? How do we do it? And how do we do it so that it eventuates into Adjuster fusion?

What, then, is the will of God?

An answer to 'what, then, is the will of God?' is that, the will of God is what the Thought Adjuster who indwells our mind—God—wants for any situation. It's that simple. If I ask you a question like, "You're having a problem with your partner: what do you want to do in that situation?" You'll evaluate the situation, come to a conclusion about the values you are considering, develop an action plan and then you'll answer the question. All of this represents a case of your will being done. Were we to ask God the same kind of question, "This person has a problem with their partner: what do you want to have happen in that situation?" This is a case of God's will.

My Father showed me one way to identify his will and to make it manifest in my life, and I'll show it to you now. You don't have to do it of course, but if you choose to do it, you will more than likely experience the will of God in action in your own life just like I do.

An exercise in experiencing the will of God

The exercise involves a real problem you have or have had in your life.

It involves you finding where that problem exists in your torso, the part of your body from the top of your hips to the bottom of your neck. It also involves you feeling or seeing or perceiving the kind of image or feeling that your problem is couched as, at that place in your body. Then it involves you holding your attention on that part of your body and asking God to remake it into *his version* of that same problem. After that, it involves you doing a juggling act of keeping your attention on the place in your body where your problem is anchored and at the same time relaxing your hold on the problem and watching or feeling God your Thought Adjuster totally remake that image or feeling. Then, after it's been done, you have to give your thanks to your Thought Adjuster. Lastly, you have to reflect back onto the problem as it is in real life for you, and notice the incredible differences in how it is for you now—now that you have got God's version of the problem working for you instead of only your own version of the problem.

OK. That's sounds like it's pretty easy to do, doesn't it? A couple of words here, then.

Yes, God has a view of your problem. That's pretty obvious to us because when ever we pray, we are asking for God's version of life to take over our situation. Obviously he can't do that unless he has a very clear and tried and tested view on our situation or experience. Remember this one fact all your life: God absolutely knows the best thing for you to do at any time in your life and if you do that thing you will always act at your maximum best.

Yes, God can remake your version or your memory of it or how you are behaving as a response to the problem. Do you know why I'm so sure he can do that? It's because all he has to do is change your mind about the problem. You've changed your mind about hundreds of things. It's easy for you to change your mind. One second you're travelling in this direction about something, and the next second you think about the situation and you don't want to pursue it any more and bingo! You've changed your mind and you're heading in a whole other direction. Well, all God has to do is to give you something that you like more than what you've already got, and you'll change your mind. It's incredibly simple, and it's that easy. And he'll always give you something that he knows for sure is going to be better for you than what you've already got. All you have to do is let him do it—and that's like letting a pigeon walk over and eat some seeds being thrown on the ground: of course the little thing is going to walk over there and eat them. He loves to eat seeds!

Lastly, two things about the transformation of the image that you are holding in yourself and the image that God will give you in its place.

The transformation is like having two photographs, one behind the other. Your problem experience is the one in front. What happens is that God's version or perception of your problem situation is in back of your problem and when you ask for his version to come in and totally replace your version of it, it's like the two photographs become one photograph. The image in your problem photo starts to change and become fluid. The lines and colours and feelings in it start to bend and shrink or grow or change shape. In a matter of a couple of seconds, the old image is replaced totally by the new image, God's image of it.

At that point, you can understand how you had one kind of perspective on the problem, but God had a whole other perspective on the problem. Where, your perspective on the problem kept you without a solution for it, it was painful or not nice to be around, and you had no alternatives but to live in it as problem—God's image of it is first of all free, you had a choice now, it is OK to be around or to resolve or to leave behind.

It is absolutely true, in all ways and in every way, that where God's Spirit is, there is liberty.[30] That means that, when you have God's version of your problem, when God's ideals are in place in you for that situation, when we can act with the reinforcement of God's values at those times when you would ordinarily have acted with only human capabilities, then you experience real freedom. With freedom comes opportunities, options, growth, health, prosperity, progress and all of this can spill over into the lives of those people who were involved in our problem.

Therefore, this is an exercise in the experience of liberty through the will of God. This exercise is an exercise that is exclusively between you and your Thought Adjuster.

Exciting isn't it?

There are seven steps in this exercise.

OK. Let's begin.

Step one: identifying a problem to change

Take a moment to think about a very real problem you have in your life. It can be a problem you are currently having, or a problem that you once had. Who does it involve? Is it between you and people at work? Or people in your family? Or a stranger? Or an ability you may lack? Think about who is involved in the problem then give it a title and write the name of that problem down on paper.

That's step one completed: you have identified a problem with which to work.

Step two: locating your problem in your body

Step two involves you finding where that problem exists in your torso, the part of your body from the top of your hips to the bottom of your neck. In particular you will work with the front and sides of your body and not the back of your body.

Close your eyes and as you do your next five breath exhalations, say these words in your thoughts, "Body, you are relaxing with each breath now."

Next, you are going to feel for tension, even subtle and hardly perceptible tension, that occurs in your torso when you ask this question, "Body, please reveal where my problem 'and name the problem you wrote down on paper' resides in you."

Next, wait and notice that tension, or that feeling that arises quite spontaneously as a result of your question.

Around this time, you might be saying to yourself, "I'm not really sure if it's this one or that one. In fact I'm getting all confused about what exactly I am feeling." But that's OK and quite normal in people who have not done this before. Just go with your "hunch" so to speak, and touch the part of your torso that you think, "Yeah, it's probably this part of me."

The experience is residing in your body somewhere. It could be in your skin. It could be deeper in your muscles. It could be across a small patch of area about the size of a small coin or a golf ball. Touch that part of your body that you believe is the area that is holding the problem experience.

That's step two completed: you have identified the location of the problem where it resides within you.

Step three: perceiving your problem within your body

Next you will identify your problem itself. Some people see their problem. Some people hear their problem. Some people feel their problem. That's what makes us all different.[31]

Try seeing your problem deep inside that part of your torso you are touching. If an image doesn't appear quickly to you then try feeling for it. If the exact same feeling you ordinarily feel in your problem isn't forthcoming then try listening for the sounds in your problem. Hear if those sounds are there. Is somebody arguing? Shouting? Being intimidating?

This may also help you to locate your problem. If it isn't there in that spot, it may clarify for you that it's actually in another spot. So go there, touch that part of your body, and see or feel or hear for it there.

That's step three completed: you have perceived your problem *as it is within you*.

Step four: asking God to give you his version of your problem

Perceiving your problem *as it is within you* is really valuable because, when God's perception of your problem changes your perception of your problem, you can actually observe it taking place.

Step four involves you asking God to replace your perception of your problem with his version of your problem—which obviously isn't a problem any longer because God just doesn't have problems!

While you hold your attention on the image or feeling or sound of your problem at the part of your body you are touching, ask God in your thoughts to remake *your version* of it into *his version* of that same situation.

Note that step four and the next step, step five, can happen really quickly—the asking can be very quickly followed by the receiving because your Thought Adjuster lovingly doesn't waste time—so you might like to run these two steps together without interruption.

That's step four completed: you have held your problem still with your attention on it, and you have asked God to give you his version of it.

Step five: receiving God's version of your problem

Next, you need to keep your attention on your problem within your body and at the same time you need to relax your problem and watch or feel or hear God your Thought Adjuster totally remaking it.

God does this every time. If you have any trouble perceiving the change, it'll be because you can't keep your attention on the problem and perceive it changing or else you get stuck and can't relax to allow God's image to fully remake your own image.

I have met a few people like that when I have been praying with them, or helping them out in counselling sessions. I usually talk them through it and they relax and then in an instant, God's image is fully there. It's a little like giving birth to a baby, a new thing. Sometimes there's a little bit of resistance and it seems as if we can't get the whole thing through in one go.

If this happens for you, then trust more and say to God, "Father, I'm stuck. Release me please so I can receive your version of my problem fully."

Once the image of your problem has been completely remade, then take a few moments to enjoy it. Inspect it. Feel how different it makes you feel about the situation. Relax into this new way of perceiving things. Feel OK about being this confident in the situation.

This completes step five: you have received God's version of your problem and it has fully remade your version of your problem and you are celebrating the renewal he has brought to you.

Step six: give thanks to your Father

After the make over of your problem has been done, you'll want to give your thanks to your Thought Adjuster. Notice that you feel the joy and the freedom of being free from this problem solely because of the actions of your Thought Adjuster, and give him the praise and the glory. You have to admit to yourself that on your own, you couldn't have come up with such a perfect solution. Be sure and tell your friends and your work mates and others that you contact, "My Thought Adjuster helped me to solve my problem. God is wonderful!" That's giving God the glory. They may even ask you to help them to solve one of their own problems, and you can show them.

That's step six completed: you have perceived that you changed your problem situation as it is for you, with God's help and you have given him thanks and praise and all the glory for this often impossible task.

Step seven: taking the new you into the real world

The last step is to take this new you into the world. Reflect back onto the problem as it is in real life for you, and notice the incredible differences in how it is for you now—now that you have got God's version of the problem working for you instead of only your own version of the problem. Notice your freedom from the problem, and prepare to engage the people in the problem with a whole new power and victory.

Sometimes the problem doesn't go away in the lives of others, you simply leave it, but you leave as a free person. Do you remember the words of Kenneth Hagin, "Die if you want, to but don't die sick!"

Sometimes the problem was a past wound, and now healing starts in full. Sometimes the problem is current and you'll meet with people who are involved in the problem, and you'll approach the whole situation differently now.

That's step seven completed: you have taken your changes into the world and found your problem is no longer a problem and that by God's grace it is a magnificent solution that is filled with life and vitality for you.

You might like to recycle through to step one again, and find another problem.

You might also like to build this practice into your daily life as a part of your own internal hygiene program. It has excellent interfaces with meditation, prayer, reading, personal growth, ministry and helping others as you pass by.

God's will includes Michael, Mother Spirit and the Thought Adjuster Father

The recognition and doing of God's will can seem to get complicated by the involvement of the wills of more than one divine person of Deity. When we're little, we think of God as being just a one off person or force. As we become familiar with the revelation in the Urantia papers though, we find out that the will of God is actually the ideals in the minds of more than one person or force. Where once we just had "God," now we are stretched to adapt to something that often doesn't sit too comfortably in us. We can't go back to the old sense of "God" but we have to go through a whole new birthing process as we learn about these people to whom the term "God" actually always pointed.

God is a term that is the will of our Thought Adjuster—God the Father; but it also includes the will of Christ Michael—the Spirit of Truth; the will of Mother Spirit—the Holy Spirit; and the combined ministry of the Father and the Son and the Holy Spirit all in one.

In the birthing process whereby we are uplifted to the extent that we can realistically include these divine persons in our sense of who and what God is, we can start out quite lost and confused, wondering who's doing what and when and how. It can all get really messy and confusing given the amount of information in the Urantia papers on these divine persons. The main problem is that where once we had a feeling of God inside us that matched whatever we thought about God, now, with the introduction of Michael and Mother Spirit and the confusions in Christianity's traditional identification of the Holy Spirit as being a male force, our inner feeling can seem as if it is fragmented and for a time it can feel like we have lost track of God.

But not for long. These persons of God quickly come to help us through this hiccup in the growth of our spiritual consciousness. It's a big leap to go from a single person of God to meeting the actual persons that parent us. And they are like loving parents who are helping their little baby to know them, to feel at home with them, and to receive their blessings as quickly as possible. They literally want you to know them. They want you to do their will, their ideals in your life. They are not holding back and neither are they cheap or skimpy in their contributions to our lives. They are absolutely capable; absolutely prosperous; absolutely positive; absolutely fearless; absolutely parent-like toward us; absolutely there for us, if we will consciously invite them in and allow them to stay on a day by day basis.

Although there are different persons who make up the sense of "God" that we experience, essentially the will of either the Son or the Spirit can be found in the will of the Thought Adjuster.

His will and jurisdiction over you is sovereign.

That means that, unless you have a personal relationship with Christ Michael or Mother Spirit, you may as well count everything that you identify as God, as being your Thought Adjuster—God the Father. If you know Michael and Mother Spirit, you will increasingly have the opportunity to commune with each of them as separate individuals. Interestingly though, you will never see them as having a will which is not their way of doing the Father's will. The will of Michael is the Father's way of doing things. The will of Mother Spirit is the way the Infinite Spirit of the Father does things, and she will do them in ways that are congruent with Michael's organisational requirements for a whole universe. So, all in all, the Father's will is predominant.

Why include Michael and Mother Spirit in what we experience as God?

Why bother with including Michael and Mother Spirit in what we experience as God?

Oh, that's easy. As you grow spiritually, you grow as a universe citizen. It is as if you live on levels of citizenship other than this native world. It's not that you don't want to be a universe citizen, a morontia citizen, it's that it just happens. As you run out of the spiritual things that can add growth to you on Earth, you naturally start to become a person of the next highest world: in our case that's the mansion worlds. It happens just like the changes we go through with our bodies, like learning to walk, and talk, and socialise, and puberty, and partnering: we don't have a choice because it's in the growth pattern that is given to us by God. Actually, in real terms, our growth pattern is given to us by Michael—it's his universe into which we were born![32]

The great thrill is that when at last you do meet Michael, it's absolutely fantastic!

Another great thrill is that when you finally get to meet Mother Spirit, you'll identify her by her exquisite and divine motherliness; it's simply unbelievable!

In meeting them, in finding your actual childship in them, what they call your sonship in them, suddenly having a God who comprises the Father, Son and Holy Spirit is in fact an easy thing to live with. Mind you, the transformation which is wrought in you by such encounters is like the transformation from the caterpillar to the butterfly—spiritually, you bear almost no resemblance to the old you.

What many Christians call the Holy Spirit is usually not Mother Spirit alone, but the combined action of a number of spiritual persons and forces that the Urantia papers refer to as God the Supreme. This involves the Thought Adjuster, the Guardian angel, the Spirit of Truth and the Holy Spirit. All of these persons are correlated into a single meaningful ministry, which is why we can be led to they think that Jesus and the Holy Spirit are the same person and event.[33] In addition, the Urantia papers tell us that the Universe Mother Spirit, "acts as the universe focus and centre of the Spirit of Truth as well as of her own personal influence, the Holy Spirit."[34]

Our personal experience of the will of God is made out of faith, reasoning and wisdom. Faith comes to us by the Thought Adjuster and the cosmic mind. Our ability to reason with our soul's intelligence comes to us from the Holy Spirit. Our ability to be spiritually wise, to develop spiritual philosophy, comes to us from the Spirit of Truth.[35] Without these divine associations, we are not at all different from any animal or insect or being who can not consciously choose to do the will of God as compared with the will of nature—the two are dissimilar in that the former is pulled by God's central gravity and always spans the universes, whilst the latter is always local to the native planet and subservient to the gravity of birth, old age, decay and death.

Prayer is the province of Michael

In practical terms, we worship the Father—our Thought Adjuster; we pray with the Son—Michael—and we live out our daily lives in fellowship with the power and agents—such as angels—of the Holy Spirit.[36]

Concerning prayer being the province of Michael, when I was in communion with Mother Spirit on one occasion, she said quite emphatically to, "Never pray to me about the things which are rightfully the domain of Michael. Commune with me; speak with me; love me, for I am your mother: you are my son and I love you: but take all your prayer requests to Michael. Be assured that he will convey them to me for execution."

I had never had that kind of a message in my spiritual life until I was able to present myself personally in both her presence of mind and Michael's presence of mind when I prayed. Before that time, my prayer was simply to a generic God, the Father I guess, and often there was more distance than communion.

I only ever once went to her in prayer, and she immediately corrected me. But in the long run, it doesn't matter a whole lot for most people until they make real face to face contact with Michael and Mother Spirit in person—and that will definitely occur for you, if not here then on the mansion worlds.

We don't get our prayers answered any better or worse for knowing that it is Christ Michael who receives our prayer and who initiates the forces to have it fulfilled. The Urantia papers pay considerable attention to the nature of prayer and worship and the distinguishing features in practical terms as they affect us in daily life. As long as you meet the basic requirements of effective prayer, your prayer will be effective.

What is sad, is that people who pray and who receive help from Christ Michael, the only source of prayer response in this universe, are frequently in contempt of his sons and daughters of other faiths whose prayers are reaching the same Christ Michael. If you could have the veil lifted from your eyes and see the prayers of the six billion people on Earth being received by Christ Michael every day, you would see his executive action over every single one of them. You would see his grace given back into the lives of those people through the power and activities of the agents of the Holy Spirit, the co-creator of his universe, Mother Spirit. It would make you recognize the pettiness in the religious differences that cause the people of this world to wage war and division among themselves. You would be renewed by the unifying power that is within the author of our faith and the hearer of our prayers. Knowing Michael and his relevance to all human prayer, you would quickly live in the light of his forgiveness; you would forgive your neighbour and love him or her, and you would act in ways that increase divine light and life in this world for Michael's sake and for the world's sake. You would immediately become a part of the solution and leave off being a part of the problem in the world. You would lift up the name of Michael of Nebadon and you would lift up the Urantia papers and you would lift up the experience of sonship with God and its unifying power for good.

Changing to whom we pray

It takes a while for a person to swing their worship over to the Father, and their prayer exclusively over to the Son, particularly if the person has a spiritual life that has been built up around worshipping Jesus and prayer to Our Lady.

A Buddhist lady in Penang, Malaysia once asked me if it would matter if she changed praying from one aspect of God to another aspect of God—from Amitabha to Kwan Yin. In telling her that her sincere prayer would be heard by the appropriate aspect of God, I replied to her what the Urantia papers would have replied:

> "You must judge your fellows by their deeds; the Father in heaven judges by the intent."[37]

I continued instructing her that God acts on the intention of our heart's desire, not our words, nor even the God to whom we think you are praying. Obviously our Father is not in the business of neglecting people who don't call him by a certain name, or who have faith in him by holding onto a primitive idol or tradition. Obviously he is in the business of helping people to grow into the full consciousness of his close and personal Parenting; and obviously he is in the business of instructing us to get along fragrantly and courteously with all his children.

I also instructed her about how Jesus taught about prayer having criteria to meet for it to become effective. I said it needed to be unselfish, in that her prayer should be for the welfare of the Father's efforts in the life of his child. She should believe by faith, she should truly recognise that her prayer is real and had real consequences. She should be sincere, intelligent and that she should trust the Father's choice of outcomes.[38] She was very pleased with that answer and said that she would do that from then on.

How I worship and pray and minister

Personally, I distinguish between prayer and communion with my divine Parents. You know what it's like to be with someone who could give you the world, but you never ask them for a thing because you don't want your needs to get in the way of your love filled time with them. Sometimes, you just have to have fun with God.

There are other times when you are worshipping in spirit the Father who is adored and worshipped.

There are other times that you are being equipped for mission: these are usually filled with prayer.

There are other times when I am ministering my Parents' grace and power, developing the fruit of the spirit, and these times are often a combination of dialogue with my divine Parents and my requesting and my commanding—all the aspects of the identification of God's will and the doing of it in a ministry setting.

During these times I will be involved with the Father, with the Son, with the Holy Spirit, possibly with the Guardian Seraphim, possibly with the combined ministry of all of them together as a single unified "person"—God the Supreme, and sometimes I will be in a state of one-mindedness, like Adjuster fusion mindedness, where my Father and I are one. All within the same occasion. For other people, of course, it may be different, but that is how these things are for me.

Marrying Mary

God's will is *his desire for a certain situation or circumstance*, where God's desire means the kind of *value and meaning he sees is possible to be present in that situation* which, when it is in place, will bring it on line with his own character, as that character is able to be found within human beings.

Let's unpack that sentence.

On a certain day in 1983, I had a need to progress in my life and I asked God for help in focussing our journey together. I went to him to find his desire for a certain situation or circumstance.

I knew he would have a value and meaning he sees is possible to be present in that situation.

How did I know?

He always has one. That's what makes him God.

I knew that he would be able to see what I could make out of my life better than I could see that. Whatever he could see would be something I could grow with.

I knew that whatever he could help me with would be something that would help me because it would *bring it on line with his own character.* In other words, it would be a good thing; a true thing; a beautifying thing; a thing too valuable for me to resist.

I also knew that it would be something that I walk into with God that would increase my Godly character. In other words, if I walked followed his guidance, I would increase my being like him and so would those with whom I would be involved. That covers the last part of that statement: *when it is in place, will bring it on line with his own character, as that character is able to be found within human beings.*

I quietened myself, cleansed my heart, and brought myself into a state of mind where I could proceed with this holy and sacred event. And when I had reached that kind of a place, I asked God really simply:

"Please give me some direction. I have left the monastery and gone to America and now to Australia. I feel I should return to my monastery in Singapore. Please help me to find your way for me."

At that time in my life, I was only a couple of months back in the west. I still thought and pretty much lived like an itinerant Buddhist monk. I wasn't fitting into daily life too well. I missed the intensity of spiritual focus in India, but I was hungry for more spiritual experience within my own culture. I was living with a few people who were sanyassins of Bhagwan Rajneesh who was then in Oregon, but I think I was more hungry for Christ than eastern meditation and energy practices. I know I wasn't looking for a Guru. I know one thing though, I had exhausted the path on which I had been travelling and I was in need of a complete renewal.

I didn't know God then as intimately as I do now. I knew him more as Buddha Nature than as my Father. It would be ten years before I would experience sonship with him like I did in Kong Meng San temple in Singapore. I had absolutely no idea what lay ahead of me. My tools were simple and lay in prayer. I knew I could ask him and he would answer my prayer within three days. I knew I could trust myself to uphold the spiritual drive of his will for me. I knew I would do absolutely anything he put before me. And I knew I could trust him impeccably.

As soon as I asked my question, he replied:

"Is there anything in your life that you have not fully satisfied?"

I was then thirty-four years old. I searched back through my life experiences. I had not had an enlightenment experience, but since reading the Urantia papers more thoroughly, it didn't seem to be something that I was unsatisfied with.

I looked through the experiences with Christian contemplatives. The door felt so fully closed in that area that it simply felt irrelevant in my life.

In this way, I plumbed the years I had lived, uncovering leaf after leaf, journey after journey, topic after topic.

At the end of my search, I really found nothing that I hadn't felt satisfied and complete. I reviewed all of the things I had wanted to do as a kid, and I had completed them all. I reviewed all the things I had wanted to do as an adult, and they had been completed also. So I went back to God.

"I didn't find anything," I said.

"Look more deeply," he said.

So I did. I found myself looking in a way that was still deeper, more focussed, more still.

Finally, there it was. I found something that I was not completely satisfied in. It was like a shiny little penny at the bottom of a thousand-foot deep, dry well shaft.

I must admit that I was a little surprised to see it there. I reflected on something similar to it, in order to confirm that what I was perceiving was in fact correct. And then I confirmed it.

I was, in a sense, the opposite side of the coin to the universal love I had found through Christ on the day I experienced a spiritual death on the cross in his name. Now, here was this other thing, about which I didn't know a whole lot at all, nor even wanted a whole lot, I might add.

Personal love.

Loving someone personally.

Years later, I reflected on how the eastern religious experience focuses on universal love and how Jesus' religion focuses on personal love, falling in love with the stranger and the enemy in deeply personal and responsible ways. But on this day of the birth of my renewal, I had no such an understanding. To me, universal love was the acme of spiritual truth and personal love was almost like a handicap, a weakness, and, to the monk such as I saw myself to be, unnecessary baggage that cluttered one's spiritual focus.

Boy! Was I ever wrong. And boy! Was I ever right! Yet somewhere down the track a ways, these two extremes came together and married right into each other and then blossomed out the other side of what they had become.

I was astonished.

"God, you can't be for real," I said. "You can't mean for me to get involved with personal love. Surely not. Can you? Are you? Is that what you are saying?"

And then, like God can do ever so easily, he just never answered. Ha!

Well, I spent the next few hours mulling over this project. It was very foreign to me. I thought about the aspects of personal love. Eventually it became clear that if I was to pursue this path it would involve marriage. Why, I didn't even know anyone I could marry! I thought back on a couple of friends of earlier years, but they had gone their own ways.

I had to start from scratch.

I took out paper and a pencil and started to write down the kinds of things that I wanted in a woman that I would marry. I knew that when I had my list drawn up and took it to God, he would fill the bill. I had had too much experience with him to doubt that.

I amassed something close to sixty different criteria that the person would have to meet in her character and in her potential growth. They were mostly all spiritual requisites. Central to all of them was that she would need to be able to relate to the Urantia papers and to grow in the religion of Jesus. Everything else grew as branches out of that single vine.

Underlying all of these criteria, was one that insisted she be the kind of woman who would give her entire life up to the doing of God's will and that nothing would stand between her and her love for God.

Another criteria, close to that one, was that she would have the wherewithal to have faith in God to grow both she and I into the fullness of Adjuster fusion in the context of this marriage together and that she would always willingly choose to call on God as a mediator in times of difference and argument.

As I wrote down these criteria, the grace and comfort of the Holy Mother Spirit came upon me. Her anointing power softened me. It turned me from being a project writer to a person who was sympathetic to the task and a bit more personal than I had been when I started writing. And the last of the criteria was one that said:

"If the person is not like this now, as she is wherever she is, then she will want to grow into all of this; and I will help her, just as she will help me to grow into the things she will bring into our love."

When I completed the list, I reviewed it. It wasn't a wish list for hot sex and partying. It was a very sincere list, a sort of Adamson meets Ratta[39] kind of thing, although it wasn't really on that scale of events. Finally, satisfied with the task ahead, I took it back to God.

I then knew it was in place. It was a live order, out there in God-land. It would cause the angels to be set in motion. Co-ordination, perhaps planned for months, if not years before, would become mobilised. Somewhere out there in the world, a young woman would be steered into a wholly new path. There is a certain magic to love, isn't there? Somewhere, out there in God-land, a new spiritual path would be opened up for me. And I have to admit, the search for spiritual life was more on the agenda than falling in love.

God answers prayer in three days

It was common for certain changes to occur over a three day span. Day one was when the change is initiated. On day two, every part of the change process disappeared and underwent a generative, creative process out of sight and consciousness. Then, on day three, it re-emerged as the new change.

If I prayed, I knew the outcome would be secured on or before the third day. If it wasn't complete on the third day, then I would review the stage that had been developed, check to see if further prayer was required to launch it into another period of growth or if the power to develop was still present and active.

At that time in my life, I lived by that process, linking it somewhat loosely to the fact that three Earth days are one local universe "heavenly" day,[40] and that whatever we bind on Earth is bound in heaven and whatever we ask for on Earth is given from heaven.

On the next day, Mary was brought to my home with a mutual friend.

He was visiting Melbourne for a few days, and just had to visit with me. He was staying with his cousin, and his cousin was involved with Mary in a marriage that had already fallen apart.

It's fair to say that Mary and I had absolutely nothing in common.

Whatever it was that our Father saw in matching us up was clearly hidden in his grace some place, because it sure wasn't up front and slapping either of us in the face a whole lot.

A year later, after only a few contacts, there was still no romance from my side whatsoever, and there was considerable questioning of God saying, "Are you sure God? No one else has turned up in my life. No one! You can't surely mean Mary?" But he never answered me on that topic.

During that period, I visited my mother while she was dying. I expressed to her that I thought I would marry Mary. She smiled and said something like, "That's nice Rob," as she wished me well with whatever journey I was on. She was going on a whole other journey, she wouldn't be a part of it. It couldn't mean a whole lot to her really. A couple of days later, she died.

A couple of months later, I returned to Kong Meng San monastery in Singapore. I really was fed up with my efforts to find a relevant spiritual life within western culture and had made plans to visit my abbot and then travel on to a hermits' monastery in Korea. Mary did not figure into my plans at all. Almost a year had transpired and I did not know what to make of my plan with God. Perhaps my renewal was just not real at all. Perhaps it had just died in the water and lay dissolving at the bottom of the bay.

But God is faithful to his word and his plan.[41]

I flew out of Melbourne with a sense of leaving behind a mistaken venture.

When I walked around the temple grounds, however, I instantly knew that my days in that kind of environment were over as well. The idea of continuing to Korea was plainly

491

incorrect. Now I was in a funny spot. I had nothing behind me and nothing ahead of me. I needed a quantum leap.

After a couple of days, I thought about spending time in the Philippines. I was at a bit of a loss what to do and I thought that, seeing as I am in the neighbourhood and I been curious about to the kinds of healing practices in those islands, I might just go over there and learn about them.

Filipino healing

I arrived in Manila, took an inexpensive hotel downtown and started inquiries where I could meet a healer—the kind that pull stuff out of people's bodies—and learn those practices.

I prayed. I expected the result within three days, and within that time, after an encounter with a pretty weird person and her healing ministry, using the term very loosely, the cab driver said that she knew someone, "The best in all of the Philippines," she touted.

"But I don't think he will teach you. He's never taught anyone, not even Filipinos. He has sons that he has taught but that's all. Nobody else. Especially not a foreigner."

At my request, she made a phone call and then came back to me wide-eyed and shocked.

"He wants me to bring you around to his house in the morning. He says that he will teach you," she said. "Wow!" she exclaimed. "He has never done that in twenty-five years. The man is a legend in our country. He has never done this to anyone, and here you come along and he hasn't even seen you and he wants you to live in his house and teach you. Who are you mister?" she asked.

"Nobody. I just want to learn this kind of healing," I replied, leaving out the part about also currently being totally without direction.

I went to the phone at her request and spoke with the healer and agreed to meet him the following morning.

I stayed with him and his family for several weeks. Every morning, seven days a week, he and his family opened their house to his healing ministry from around 6am until 10.30am.

I learned about "Albulario" healing with him, what they call Christian prayer healing, but I never practised it on anyone.

It was an unusual and refocussing time for all of us. It was a time of making my commitment to follow Jesus in person.

During my stay with them in Parañaque, Metro Manila, among the many surprises that were in that journey, two things of substance happened. I watched a fellow from Akron, Ohio who was on Manila television. He was filmed during a healing meeting in China. His gift was for deaf-mutes, and he was in an institution for deaf and dumb children. One by one they were led onto the stage and one by one, without fail, he came to each child and said, "Satan, in Jesus name," then he clapped his hands simultaneously with stating the next words, "come out!"

Then he cupped a hand around the child's ear and said the word, "Baby."

And the child would say, "Baby."

Then he would cup his hand around the ear of the other ear and again say, "Baby."

And the child would again say, "Baby."

Child after child, was suddenly free of their deafness and able to speak.

Watching this man work filled me with wonder and the desire to find the kind of spirituality that he had. That was the first thing of substance that happened for me while I lived with this family.

The second thing was that during this time, I fell in love with Mary. Distance does make the heart grow fonder. I phoned her from the post office and I was thrilled to hear that she had feelings for me too. From that time I planned to return to Melbourne to meet up with her, and continue working with God on his plan for renewal in me.

God is faithful. And what's so great about God's kind of faithfulness, is that it endures while we take the long and necessary way to our goal. God never forgets the substance of our prayer, even while we are doubting it and even discarding it.

Eventually, I returned to Melbourne, looking for a way into Christ. Jesus Christ was my future. Mary was my friend. I now knew for a certainty that she was God's choice of partner for me, and I pledged myself to his will for my loving her.

Upon my return, I let the Philippines experience settle and turned to explore the meaning and experience of the Christian Church, and studied at Theology College. Toward the end of that time, Mary and I became engaged and after a few months we were married by my tutor in evangelism and Old Testament—two years after the prayer was made that brought Mary and I together.

Whilst sharing the mind of God, I planned to give Mary her engagement ring at the altar of St. John's Anglican Church, Malvern. The priest of that Church was then my lecturer in Romans at Ridley Theological College and we had been attending his church for most of the year. At the Sunday morning service, he unexpectedly called the entire congregation into a huge circle in order to do some kind of Pentecostal thing. I saw my chance and took Mary by the hand and speadily led her to the altar where we would link hands with others. Whilst there, somehow anointed and sanctified from the rest of the goings on for a few moments while the priest organised and enthused everyone else, I proposed to Mary.

Thank you Father for the opportunity; and for every little thing that you take care of.

The journey, thus far, I counted as the fulfilment of the will of God.

We will celebrate our fourteenth wedding anniversary next week, on January 25. I can truly say that everything I wrote on my list that morning has been fulfilled in Mary and me over these past years: she is an extraordinary person and daily I thank my Father for my time with her. This was time, not without difficulty; not without pain; not without surrender and giving and chameleonic transformations; not without the human struggle for God's values to have sovereignty and then victory over our hearts and the things we caused to happen each day. I have often laughingly reflected that my marriage was pre-empting my time with a member of the Univitatia,[42] so great were our differences.

This period, too, I count as the fulfilment of the will of God. We have achieved the value that God had in his mind for us sixteen years ago. More than that, God counts it as his will being done; and that's more important to me.

In retrospect I can see that our Father wanted to achieve two children who loved each other so much through him, that they would freely give of themselves to his interests, and taught to minister his Son's and his Daughter's care for others. His way of doing that was to take two extreme opposites, bind them together with his grace, and grow them into the production of a wholly new kind of fruit bearing branch in Christ Michael.

I am so very satisfied that my Father was able to achieve the desire in his heart. May he find his satisfaction in your life too, dear reader. Is there some thing that you have not satisfied in your own life that you might bring to your Father for his help?

God has a value just waiting for you to claim it

We have looked at what the will of God is. God's will is his desire to bring value and meaning into a situation which, when it is in place, will bring the situation on line with his own character, as that character is able to be found within human beings.

The term situation means everything we encounter. There is no need in life that our Thought Adjuster does not have a saving and growing and regenerating value for. If there was, then we would be the Adjuster!

Are we doing well in life? God has a value by which we will do even better.

Are we burdened? God has a value that will lift that burden off us and break its hold over us so that we do not bring it back onto us.

Are we broken? God has a value that will mend us.

Are we wounded? God has healing.

Are we poor? God has prosperity that we can make our own.

Are we ignorant? God has knowledge and learning.

Are we foul-mouthed and uncouth? God has cleansing soap for our minds that washes us so clean and so lovingly that we find ourselves gladly using it every day.

Are we lowly? God has values that will build up our self-esteem and our courage and our conviction.

Are we addicted to drugs or alcohol or sex or instability or gambling or violence or co-dependency or prostituting ourselves or standing over others with our intimidation and our weapons of despair and hatred? God our own Father has values that will take that shackle off us and destroy it and lead us into new strength.

Are we tired of our life and our isolation? God our Father has values and connections to bring us into new life.

Are we tired of the flesh and desirous of the spirit? God has the power and the values that he will pour out on us so that we can make them our own and live in his righteousness with power from on high.

This is his plan for us. This is his will for us. This is his vision for us. This is his ambition for us, as he grows us up in sonship with him into the fullness of his own stature and glory. His presence in us is sufficient evidence of this. Call on him then, and let he who has the model plan for your life and he who is subservient to your will,[43] exercise his great victory in your life with you. Live. Do not die. Live, dear one, but live by him, letting him show you how to identify his values and his will for you.

How do we identify God's will for any situation?

The will of God is obviously different for Michael than it is for an angel, and different again for a human being, Why? Not that it isn't perfect. Oh, no. But rather because the level of glory that God can bring into the life of all three is vastly different. We, as humans, with our little perspectives and responsibilities, can only be filled with a little glory. Angels, with wider perspectives and larger responsibilities, can be filled with much more glory. Michael, with his huge perspective and vast responsibilities, is filled with tremendous glory. And though there are billions upon billions of beings who are filled with God's glory, still his glory is neither depleted nor even reduced.

Now let's look at how we identify his will in any situation.

God is a special somebody who has a desire for a special outcome in any given situation in your life. Remember that sentence. God is a special somebody who has a desire for a special outcome in any given situation in your life. Type it out on your computer as a poster and paste it on your computer screen and above the kitchen sink! God is a special somebody who has a desire for a special outcome in any given situation in your life!

And so do you.

The chances are pretty good that the desired outcome, and the power to bring about the outcome, will be different for you and for God. It's a good thing to know that your desired outcome isn't necessarily the best outcome possible for the situation.

God's outcome, however, is almost totally dependent upon you making a way for it to happen. That way might involve prayer.

Be faithful and unswerving in prayer

There is the story about the little boy who prayed a lot about every little thing that happened in his life. He seemed to have so many needs, and he prayed about them all, endlessly.

As he grew up, he stopped praying because he never saw his prayers fulfilled. He had so many, you'd have thought that one of them would be fulfilled at least.

Then one night, he dreamed a dream.

In the dream he went to heaven and he was led into a huge room. While he was standing there he saw lots of angels coming in and registering books. Occasionally, very occasionally, he'd see an angel come in and take a book off one of the millions of shelves, check it out at the desk, and disappear out the door. Angels just flooded into the room, often carrying whole stacks of books in their arms.

He asked the angel at the desk:

"What goes on up here?"

The angel gently looked up at him and replied, "Sir, this place is where God keeps all the prayer plans that were written up to bring people into divine victory, but that the people didn't start; or they started and then stopped; or they started and then changed their mind and prayed about something else to happen in their life. We keep them all up here in this library. In heaven, this is called the room of unwanted prayers."

He awoke and recalled the revelation in his spirit, and, from that time onwards the fellow always took his prayers seriously. He always waited for them to run their full course before modifying them. He never added too many to the stack at one time. He wrote down every major thing he prayed for so that he could watch it coming into fulfilment. Over time, he was glorified by God because he became a master of prayer. He also counselled others about being faithful with their own prayer requests too. He became a real example to people and was much loved for the way he helped them to understand the simplicities of effective prayer.

Kittens

Prayer is linked to God's will and through the vision of God's outcome that can come to us through prayer, it is one way that we can identify God's will.

The experience of communion with God brings about prayer that is like two kittens coming together beside the fire on a cold night. One kitten is curled up beside the fire and the other kitten walks nearby. She looks around for the best spot on the floor in front of the fire, and of course it is taken by the first kitten. So then she looks for the best place to snuggle into him.

She snuggles in. A little wriggle here. A little squirm there. After a few moments we have two kittens snuggled up by the fire.

After a while, the fire has warmed both of them and they arouse and stretch and yawn, first one and then the other. Then they snuggle up a bit more. Their fur mixes. Their purring mixes. Their breathing mixes. Their relaxation mixes. They may as well be a single cat because they are so intertwined in each other in front of the fire.

Then, after a while, when a certain completeness dawns, one kitten will become alert, stretch, yawn, flex its claws, then roll away from the other kitten. It will look around, wash itself, and then stroll away to sit some place nearby, perhaps not so close to the fire. Later on, the other kitten will do the same, to another place.

Like this, the mind of man and the mind of God merge in a time of prayer, dialogue together in total intimacy, then conclude and part only to repeat the action at the next prayer time. Yet, even in their parting, there remains a rapport that lingers throughout the day and night.

God's will is in his vision

God best conveys an image of his ideal to us when we are in loving communion with him. The person who is not habitually in loving communion with him will only receive an image or word of his instruction of guidance at a time of crisis in their life, and many might miss even that slim glimpse from him.

It is common for people to say words or thoughts of request to God, but never expect him to talk back or convey a message of hope or an image of an outcome. Such people are too busy to listen, to watch and to feel for his gentle touch and word; or the Holy Spirit is not alive in them; or they think so poorly of themselves that God could never really do anything for them directly—which is simply not true, for he would if they'd let him.

Be still. Be self-composed: just you, uncluttered by thoughts and concerns of others. Ask God, and then be sensitive to what arises in your mind and thoughts and feelings and impulses, then decide wisely upon those. You don't have to be Christ delivering the beatitudes to hear from God. He is your Father. It is enough for you to be still and expect him to communicate with you somehow.

As a rule, treat your prayer time sincerely. Imagine the person you esteem the most on Earth. Now imagine being in a room alone with him or her, away from the clammer of the world and the clutter of your own life. Then imagine asking him or her for this thing that you know is really precious to him or her also.

Prayer, like worship, is the most sacred and respectful thing that we do.

God's value, verses a prediction

If your Thought Adjuster manages to impart into your mind an image of the way some situation is going to work out, then that's prediction. That prediction, however, doesn't mean that the outcome or even the image is God's will. What is God's will in it, is only the fact that you received the image from him. He wanted you to have that image. Prediction, in this sense, only means that God has imparted a vision to you of the outcome as he sees it happening if no one changes anything in it: not as he has an ideal for it to be changed in some way or another. The two are different.

God can know and see what will become of a circumstance in your life, but so too perhaps can an astrologer, a clairvoyant, a medium or channeller and a fatalistic diviner. There is nothing necessarily of God's ideal imparted in such knowledge. That's like saying, "I see you going on holiday to France or to Japan or to Brazil," and having been told that, you think that because it's extrasensory information that it is automatically the will of God. But it's not. It's only an image of the outworking of humanly contrived events.

If, on the other hand, we look to God's ideal for a situation, we might then say, "OK if I accept that I'm going to that place on holiday: Father, how would you like me to best spend my time there, for I want to do things that will increase our love and Adjuster fusion? Reveal to me the kind of fruit of the spirit you'd like to produce with me in that place please."

Do you see the difference? That's a whole other ball game.

Doing the will of God liberates you from being snagged on lifeless prediction, as you submit your will to having it reinforced by the will of your Thought Adjuster. You will deliberately turn from man's ways to God's ways. You will permit God to be a part of your life in all things.

The problems that many clairvoyants and channellers have is that, twenty years down the track, they haven't grown towards Adjuster fusion a whole lot. Oh sure, they may have developed their skills in prediction. And they probably know the unseen world better than they know the seen world. But when have they converted their life over to the doing of God's will? God's ideal? When have they come to a love so divine that they would give their life for their enemy? When have they acted with the mind of this mighty Adjuster?

Communicating with our Thought Adjuster

When you seek the will of God, then, in response to your seeking, your Thought Adjuster will impart a vision or image to you, or he may simply dialogue with you if you are capable of being with him in that manner, and he will impart to you the values that he would love to see put into action for that occasion. Then, you are dealing directly with the will of God and not merely his knowledge.

When given the opportunity by the human will, the Thought Adjuster trains his child in effective communication. It is a learning process. Having noticed how people can learn this kind of an experience, I have conducted training courses to foster in people those things that help such communication. Generally, however, when receiving God's vision for some situation in life, it depends upon him imparting values to you in the form of a picture. There is, however, an important transition that a person makes between recognising the image and recognising the value that is being portrayed by the image. Such a transition quite frequently requires personal growth and familiarity with this means of communication between one's Thought Adjuster and oneself. That kind of growth benefits from a whole approach to spirituality—worship, work and play—and time.[44]

The Urantia papers speak of the difficulties facing Thought Adjusters as they try to communicate with us, and how the currents of our materiality wash away their message.[45]

Feed yourself with divine images

The Urantia papers tell us that the Thought Adjuster's communication is by image and word.

They also speak of the Adjuster fusion type of mind state, when a person is at one with the Thought Adjuster and there is no need for communication.[46]

The Tibetan Buddhists have a practice like this, the union of the human and the Thought Adjuster's minds. It is called Dzogchen, or Mahamudra.[47] In Japanese Zen practice, it is called Shikantaza.

The candidate for Adjuster fusion is many times trained in this state of reality as we increasingly identify and fuse our mind and will with the mind and will of our Thought Adjuster. This is the mind wherein we command rather than request; create rather than seek; declare rather than ask; impart power rather than draw power toward ourself; transcend rather than join; assume a whole subjectiveness rather than adopt a division of self and other, subject and object division; express divine love with no need of love being requited; think and act in a God-like manner, and as God[48]—when our entire subjectivity vanishes and all is objective.

Our being like God is important to God. Jesus told John:

"The kingdom of heaven consists in these three essentials: first, recognition of the fact of the sovereignty of God; second, belief in the truth of sonship with God; and third, faith in the effectiveness of the supreme human desire to do the will of God—to be like God. And this is the good news of the gospel: that by faith every mortal may have all these essentials of salvation."

These three essentials are stages of experience that one can cycle through on wholly new levels or reality, ever inwards and upwards, from basic fleshly ignorance all the way to our perfection, Adjuster fusion. At every level they have an enhanced face about them, yet their truth is perennial.

There is little evidence in either the Urantia papers or the New Testament to indicate the manner in which Jesus developed communication with his Thought Adjuster, only that he did, and to the point of perfection.[49]

We need to be clear about the scope of the Urantia papers on this kind of topic. They are not a textbook on all of the developmental strategies that can exist between humanity and our Thought Adjusters. That is way too exclusive an approach that would deny and frustrate most of us.

Experientially, however, both Michael and our Father Adjuster teach us the way.

For example: I believe in Jesus. I believe what he says about the kingdom of heaven. I believe that he perfected his communication with his Thought Adjuster, God. Believing this about him, I follow him and his ways to the best of my ability. My Thought Adjuster believes in him too. And that's what counts. Many times, I employ his way of thinking in place of my own.

As I love him more and more and grow in familiarity with his ways and thankfulness for his goodness, my own Thought Adjuster can impart to me images and words through that channel of love that I have for Jesus. The images and words given me from my Thought Adjuster will reaffirm the words and the images of Jesus' life and teachings and experiences that I have in my mind.

My Thought Adjuster will build on the images that I develop. He won't build on the images of hate and loathing and fear that a person may have in them; he can only build on the images of love and truth and beauty and Godliness that he or she authentically reveres. Therefore, it is important to feed our minds and our spirits with the spiritual food we need to feed our Thought Adjuster. That food is knowledge that we love to know about and love to feed from.

The prophet Hosea spoke for his Thought Adjuster, saying:

"My people are destroyed for lack of knowledge; because

you have rejected knowledge, I reject you from being a priest to me. And since you have forgotten the law of your God, I also will forget your children."

It is important to tell others of the knowledge that God provides for them. We can see from this passage that Hosea's Thought Adjuster does not at all take kindly to a person holding back his knowledge from his children. The priest is someone who is commissioned to provide others with God's information and, in this instance, this particular priest is guilty of refusing to do that. Can you imagine that happening in our day and age? What would it be like to hold back the Urantia papers or the Bible from people? What kind of evil would be in the hearts of people like that? Reading further in Hosea, his Adjuster is saying that heaven definitely won't help them! Yet, it happens, doesn't it? God's teachings are actively, deliberately denied people.

It is important to feed ourselves on Godly images and words, lest we are starved and become destroyed for lack of knowledge. If someone won't feed you, then you start feeding yourself.

How do we do that? Well, a little listening to others can go a real long way and sometimes the best thing if you're thirsty, is to go to the spring and put your lips to the source of that refreshing drink. Be with your Thought Adjuster, and let him be with you. It won't take you too long at all before the Holy Spirit settles on you and you find God's peace and his images and his words start to rise up in you.

Once you build up his presence with you, then feed that presence as much as you want to with books and tapes and videos and personal encounters with others who are faith-filled and speak your kind of spiritual language.

I once worked at a place where I had to drive thirty-five minutes each way. I recorded four or five tapes for the car, reading from various papers, and listened to them hour after hour after hour, drive after drive. There was almost never a time when they weren't playing and with every time I heard the same tape again, the Thought Adjuster was able to take me deeper and deeper into his kind of word and image and value. It's a praiseworthy practice, that one.

An exercise in imagery

Try this if you want. Trust God and say:
"Father, please give me an image of yours about something in my life."

Then wait, and watch—or feel. Give him time to build up in you a sense of you doing something, or being somewhere. It won't take him long at all. He's already seen the script of this book you're reading: he's knows this sentence was coming.

Enjoy each other.

God's will is in his Word

When you think about a person that you know, a friend, and you want to know what they want you to do, their intention, how do you find out that information?

One way to go about it is to ask them directly. "Please tell me what you want so I can help you have that happen."

Another way is they can tell you before you even asked. "My friend, I would really like such and such to happen."

Another way is that it is in the things they have told others. Let's say that you want to buy your female friend a gift for her birthday and she has told one of her friends that she really needed a certain item. When her friend tells you about this, you know that you can trust their conversation and go ahead and buy that gift for her, knowing that it is something that your friend actually does want.

This way of knowing what your friend wants is by her giving her word to her friend. You know what she wants because it is in her word.

Either way, in all of these ways, the way we know what she wants is through her word, her communication.

For God and us it is the same. God's will is in his word, in his communication.

The big question then is, how do we find out what he is communicating about a certain situation?

Let's look at these two ways: God is in his Word when: 1) he tells you directly; or 2) he tells you indirectly via someone else.

When does God tell you directly what he wants?

He tells you during your time of prayer. He tells you by the inner witness of his word to your inner person. He tells you in the occasional dream in which he can get his actual message through to you.

How does God tell you directly what he wants?

He tells you in your thought, through words and images. He tells you in your body through feelings, imagery and a wordless knowing. He tells you in your soul, your inner and higher consciousness, through a knowing that is a precursor to thought.

For God to communicate with you, he must use mind or your spirit or your body.

For God to communicate with you, he also must use imagery that is based on your sense-based experience plus the values that you can already relate to. If you receive an image into your mind with no meaning attached, it may not be from God but rather from your own unconscious desires. If you experience something that you think is from God, but you can't relate to it, it may be something that you will relate to shortly after other experiences have occurred, or else, again, it may well be something emerging from your sub-consciousness.

Unless God or one of his agents says something like a direct command to you—"Run!" "Stop, now!" "Go left! Now!" "Act! Now!" and so forth—he will mostly communicate values to you. It is from values alone that we choose a better way.

Christianity has built an entire spiritual approach around the concept that God is in his word, and reinforces that concept by ascribing the entire Old and New Testaments as being literally written by the Holy Spirit.

Some people flounder on that concept, even some Christians, for any number of reasons.

The Urantia papers tell us that Jesus didn't believe that kind of small view of the scriptures, only that they were a repository of some of the world's spiritual values. He drew from them quite selectively, according to his needs. They did not represent to him a single coherent story of the origins and history of man and his relationship with God any more than they represented a true and appropriate portrait of himself and his ministry as the incarnated Created Michael of the universe of Nebadon. But they were the best that humanity had developed at that stage of their million years of development. As poor as they might seem to be to post-Pentecost humanity who have the enormous benefit of the Urantia papers, they were a tremendous blessing to disenfranchised humanity and a credit to Machiventa Melchizedek and his ministry team.[50]

For God to be in his word, we must understand that God's word is a promise through which we can experience an affinity with him by literally experiencing him in his word.

God is God when silent as well as when speaking: both are dynamic forms of communication. Only our sense of a loss of contact with God is experienced as God not communicating.

An exercise in experiencing God's word

Let's take a word from the New Testament that says:
"The one who comes from above is above all; the one who is of the Earth belongs to the Earth and speaks about Earthly things. The one who comes from heaven is above all."[51]

If we believe that a Thought Adjuster brought a value into the mind of a living human being, and that person uttered that statement and lived by it's truth, then we can also believe that our Thought Adjuster could say that very same statement and help us to live by it's truth also. Our Thought Adjuster and the Thought Adjuster of that person are not operating off two different divine realities, now are they?

If you agree with that, and re-read those words, you'll feel in yourself the spiritual truth they can convey to you.

To enhance their meaning, try this for example.

Change the words "The one who comes from above," to "My Adjuster who comes from above." Then also change the words, "The one who comes from heaven," for "My Father who comes from heaven." Then add in a statement about how he links to you, such as, "and he makes me like himself." Then say the whole statement aloud, three times, slowly, listening for its truth. You'll find yourself transformed by his mind, the mind that comes to your mind through words about what is true and real for him. Try it, but say it as if it's being spoken to you:
"Your Adjuster who comes from above is above all, and he makes you like himself;
the one who is of the Earth belongs to the Earth and speaks about Earthly things.
Your Father who comes from heaven is above all."

Now try it in its original context, as it referred to Jesus:

"Jesus who comes from above is above all, and he makes you like himself;
the one who is of the Earth belongs to the Earth and speaks about Earthly things.
Your Father who comes from heaven is above all."

Now try it in a Urantia papers type of context, as it refers to Mother Spirit:

"Mother Spirit who comes from above is above all, and she makes you like herself;
the one who is of the Earth belongs to the Earth and speaks about Earthly things.
Your Mother who comes from heaven is above all."

Now try it in another Urantia papers context, as it refers to Michael of Nebadon:

"Christ Michael who comes from above is above all, and he makes you like himself;
the one who is of the Earth belongs to the Earth and speaks about Earthly things.
Your Father who comes from heaven is above all."

God is in his word. We find him in his word. We become like him when we fill ourselves with his word. God's word carries values that transform us and make us Godly as we bring those values into our lives—the fruit of the spirit is the evidence of God's values in our lives.

The Bible is so filled with the kinds of passages that our Thought Adjuster can employ to convey divine truths about our relationship with him that it's easy to see how people say that the whole Bible is the word of God.

The Thought Adjuster will obviously do this just as well or even better in the Urantia papers for the student of that revelation. The more progressive students of the Urantia papers have been finding that for years.

God's word and God's image have the power to transform us according to his character, solely if it has his presence and power with it. Without God's personal presence, words ascribed to God are simply sounds or characters on paper. Just as the word about you, the description of you, is not your word, so too, the word *about* God is not the same as the word *of* God.

God is never separate from his word, his communication.

God's values cut across the whole spectrum of human life

with the power of sovereignty. God's word heals us, because it binds the power of the fleshly values and initiates the sovereignty of the creator's values. God's word breaks the chains of poverty and debt and lack, because it binds those material forces, arrests their continuance, and empowers people's lives with his values of prosperity. God's word brings people into Jesus' kingdom of heaven, because it cuts through insincerity and unbelief and doubt and delivers the human child to his and her divine parent.

The doing of the will of God therefore is the doing of the values that God has in mind for your kind of need. *How* you do that will, is by letting his values work for you and adopting them as your own.

God's comfort comes from our Mother

God's comfort is not his word but his word is always comforting. The comfort we mostly experience is brought to us from our Mother, the Holy Spirit.

Do you remember how it was for Jesus in the garden at Gethsemane? He was in need of a sign from God, and of comfort and of strength. A mighty angel came to his side and spoke with him, comforting and strengthening him by the power of the Holy Spirit and by the power of truth.[52] He always taught that truth will make you free.[53] Now, Jesus is experiencing God's word and it is making him free. Free from what? Free from the world and its stress and limited perspective. We read further[54] that Jesus took that comfort and strength and used it to know God's will clearly: that the humanly orchestrated events that would lead to his arrest would maintain their momentum. He then moved on deeper with God, to deal with those events. This event was one of the last recorded divine ministries to which he was subject in the flesh, before his ascension, orchestrated by the will of his Adjuster and through the ministry of his own universe co-creator, Mother Spirit. The angels and the archangels are of her alone.

You can receive the comfort Mother Spirit brings by appealing to her directly, saying, "My dear Mother. Please be with me right now." She will help you in your genuine time of distress.

Thought Adjuster communication software

Back around 1990, when I was working with drug users and ex-prisoners who were withdrawing from heroin and amphetamines, I found that they very often had difficulty talking about their own private concerns. It seemed that they needed some kind of a program that they could work through their own issues confidently and in their own privacy. I brought this problem to my Thought Adjuster and together we worked out a way to help.

Over the next few months together, we developed a little software package for the computer. It contained hundreds of references to different scriptures, and even non-scriptural texts and concepts. The aim was to provide the person with a God-given reference that would answer their questions.

It required a communication system that would enable the Thought Adjuster of the person to communicate with the person's nervous system in a way that bi-passed their self-consciousness, yet in a way that they could identify. The communication system we settled on was developed to enable the person to sit at the keyboard and punch in a key for the "yes" signal and a different key for the "no" signal that they received from their Thought Adjuster.

My Father told me that this would be something that any Thought Adjuster could do with his human child. I've never seen a person use it and be dissatisfied with it yet, so maybe he's right about that.

The way the software worked was this. The person typed in their question. The software led them through a series of questions and their Thought Adjuster answered each question with either a "yes" or a "no" answer in their physical body. They then typed in each answer. After six specific questions were answered, the software led the person to the answer the Thought Adjuster had identified as closely matching their problem. At the push of a button, the program printed out both the question and the answer.

A large number of people gained considerable benefit from the program, not the least of which was the confirmation that God is with them, interested in them, and able to communicate to them, if only through their body. The program is exceptionally good for people who really have trouble identifying the will of God for their circumstances, particularly because it doesn't involve superstition and evil—it is something that is strictly between one's Thought Adjuster and one's self.

When I want to know what the will of God is

When I want to know what the will of God is for a certain situation, sometimes I commune with my Thought Adjuster's mind, giving both he and myself time to adjust to our communion together. Then, I simply look into his mind. That won't mean anything to you unless you can already do it, I guess.

When I do this, the communication to me of the values he has for any situation will be by an image or in words.

Today, a friend of ours just left the house. She was talking with her sister and Mary about the possibility of getting married. I looked into God's mind and saw her in her white gown at the time of her wedding ceremony. Her Father already had a vision of her wedding day. It was there for the receiving.

Is a vision for someone's situation always there for the asking just like that? No, not always. The conditions for receiving it are totally dependent upon a state of holiness on my part: it is a sacred moment. When the holiness is not present, I need to make it so in order to gather my focus in him.

Also, I have noticed in times when healing and change have been requested of God, that the process of finding confirmation of his will can take time. So I watch and feel, and I wait for him. Suddenly, if it is going to arrive—and sometimes it doesn't, or doesn't to my awareness of it—it arrives. When this happens, sometimes it is as if the process has involved a chain of permissions, requests for action being passed up the line, then styling of the outcomes, shaping them for the person concerned and the ongoing plans with their Adjuster and guardian seraphim. Yet, there are other occasions when God's image or word on his desire for the person or situation is right there, sort of jumping out of its skin to get into the action.

Sometimes, when a healing is required, it takes a little time for the power for change to break through into the material world and act on the physical body. For example, there is a kind of anointing power that comes from God that is like molten, warm honey. I see it arriving into the contact with the physical body when it is about one foot away from the body. It seems to me to be coming from some other higher dimension, a thinner and less material dimension, because as it arrives it thickens up and takes this form of soft flowing honey. It then only takes a second before it makes contact with the physical body, but having made contact it penetrates right inside as if it can influence all parts of the body: skin, muscles, tendons, blood, bones and marrow and presumably the genetic coding.

In this way, when I am working with this kind of healing experience, I literally watch it in my spirit coming about in the patient. I haven't met many people who see the proceedings of change come about. I've heard of a few, and most of them are Christians with a healing ministry. Frequently, when I am helping a person with a problem, I will touch their body in different places as I trace the complaint back to the will of God as it resides in their diaphragm area or the area just below their navel. When I do this, I watch the impact of the intervention as it is reflected in the their physiology according to the principles of Chinese medicine: meridians and extra-meridian locations. As a physician at that time, I am a someone who is doing the will of God and who is seeking the will of God in the person as it resides beneath the person's problem. My aim is to then draw the will of God into the problem. Healing and change occur on the basis that in the face of God, falsehood must depart.

To look into God's mind is not like using your own mind to remember something. One's personal memory is a completely different aspect of mind from that which interfaces with the mind of one's Thought Adjuster, or communes with Michael or Mother Spirit. Similarly, to view the proceedings of the Holy Spirit, one does not use their ordinary everyday mortal mind. One's higher consciousness is involved.

The Bible calls this encounter the anointing of God. Christians ascribe the words of the prophet Isaiah to Jesus, and Jesus himself used Isaiah's prophecy to announce his own ministry:

> "The spirit of the Lord God is upon me, because the Lord has anointed me; he has sent me to bring good news to the

oppressed, to bind up the brokenhearted, to proclaim liberty to the captives, and release to the prisoners; to proclaim the year of the Lord's favour, and the day of vengeance of our God; to comfort all who mourn;[55]

With the added perspective of the Urantia papers, we can see that for Jesus, the "spirit of the Lord God," was his Personalised Thought Adjuster.[56] The "good news" that he brought to the oppressed, was a teaching about his actual relationship with his Father—sonship with God. The "anointing" he received from his Father was the authentic union of his human mind with the mind of his Adjuster—such union then providing the word and the image and the knowing of the will of the Father in him. The "sending" of Jesus by his Father, was his commissioning to be exclusively about the Father's business. In this way, Jesus' personal works of the spirit were wrought by the united wills of this Adjuster and himself as one will, and the manifestation of ministry out-workings wrought by the Holy Spirit Mother and her angels and workers.

If you would do anything good in your life, claim the anointing: for by it alone do you have the power from on high to be victorious in life by means of God's righteousness.

At other times when doing the will of God, there are occasions when I find that I am distinct from my Thought Adjuster. I will consult him; he will communicate to me his perspective. There are occasions when this goes on within me, in my "inner person" so to speak. There are occasions when in fact he is like a distinct individual who is standing in front of me, and we dialogue the one to the other as two dear friends who have travelled a great distance to be with each other.

There is another an aspect of liaison with the mind of God, in which I am not at all separate from this Thought Adjuster. To all intents and purposes, we are one. To me, it has two distinct features. One is that I feel completely augmented by divine mind: there is nothing to identify the Adjuster as an individual who is separate from me: there is something present in me to indicate that I am no longer exclusively mortal. The second feature is that, for me, the entire world becomes a single matrix with no apparent separation of self from the world. This is to say that the whole world, at that time, emerges from within the divine me. At this time, the objects around about are of the same substance as divine mind. There is a certain perfection about the unity between this mind and the objects in the world that brings it altogether as a single and wholly subjective reality.

This is the Adjuster fusion type of mind. It is this mind that best communicates with Michael and Mother Spirit. It is this mind that increasingly claims universe citizenship as a morontia being, in very real terms. It is this mind that knows the mind of Jesus of Nazareth.

The moon in the puddle is not the moon in the heavens

One word of caution. The words that I am writing are simply descriptions and you as a reader shouldn't latch on to them too tightly. If doing the will of God seems a daunting and impossible thing for you still, I want to settle you down and reassure you. Your own experience is so unique that, when you are doing the will of God and someone asks you about it, you will probably use completely different words from the ones I use. In spirit, we'll be the same, but our descriptions will be different. Just have faith. In younger years, I could never have dreamed at all about the amount of contact that I've had with God in my life. I am nobody special; in fact I'm probably somewhat ordinary. Just have faith. I know it's sometimes hard. If you are willing though, you *will* attain this mind. I say this, despite your current thoughts and doubts, because your Thought Adjuster has a single mission for you at present. It includes many things, among which is your attainment of this kind of mind so that you might increasingly do the will of God. Adjuster fusion *is* your immediate destiny.

How do we do God's will?

How we identify God's will, that is, what it is exactly that God wants to do in a particular situation, has a lot to do with how we actually do God's will.

Doing the will of God is a concept we use for the liaison of our mind with the mind of the Thought Adjuster partner who indwells us. This liaison is a transitory station on the way to a greater mindedness, call Adjuster fusion, wherein the similarity of mind is so identical that the Adjuster is behaving humanly and the human is behaving Adjusterly, so to speak. The two are without form and there is disclosed in the human heart all the heart of the Thought Adjuster. In this way the human feels and thinks and believes what the Thought Adjuster would think and feel and believe were he God incarnate as a human being—both God and Man, as was Jesus during his ministry years.

There is a great transformation that has occurred in the human who can be like his or her Thought Adjuster like this. The transformation represents what people call spirituality, but most people who are transformed in this way tend to call it their own growth. Many of the world's concepts about spirituality no longer appear relevant by this stage. Even the term spirituality has gone through a transformation whereby it loses all its idealism and hope and becomes a matter of fact term that alludes to the behaviour that streams forth from this dual mind which has been made one by grace, faith and considerable experience and mastery of mind itself.

Knowing this, the doing of God's will can be different for the innocent little girl and the teenage boy and the twenty-five year old young man and the thirty-five year old woman and the forty-five year old man and the sixty-five year old woman. How we do God's will at each of these stages of life is obviously going to be different because of the different perspectives and different values involved at each stage.

An exchange of values

The doing of the will of God concerns the exchange of values. We exchange values with each other, the human and the Thought Adjuster. We seek his value and we let it be ours. The will of God is not so much concerned with turning left, parking over there, walking through that door and not walking through this door over here, but *why* God would be recommending such an action. Whilst such things occur in the life of the person who receives communications in their mind, the will of God is best conceived of as being our adoption of a value, much like how we see a movie and certain features of the characters or the places impress us so significantly that we adopt them in our life for a while. Why the characters did such and such, is the heart of the matter, not that they did it. They could have done any number of other things in order to claim and express the same value. When we grasp the "why" of the Adjuster's partnership with us, his motivation, the how-to pretty much flows out of that into our lives in a straightforward and adaptable manner.

Our Thought Adjuster is constantly conveying values to us. It's not the same value all the time of course. For example, he is not imparting to us, "Love thy neighbour," twenty-four hours a day. Rather, he is keeping in our mind, between our own thoughts, a Thought Adjuster version of our thoughts, our speculations, our hopes, our aspirations, and the grounds for our decisions as we move throughout our day.

He will cloak these thoughts with a sense of other-than-us around them, so we can identify that they are not generated by ourself but that another is communicating in our mind. Or he will cloak them with a pedigree that tells us that these thoughts are no different from those in our normal stream of consciousness.

Sometimes, it's really valuable to perceive that the impressions in our mind are his. By that means, we know we are in dialogue with our creator. Sometimes, it's absolutely vital that we think the impressions in our mind are ours. That way, we can gather our own perspective and integrity. Sometimes, we confuse our own mental voice for his voice, and vice versa: but these are problems that each of us needs to work out for ourselves as were progress in learning and practising how to do the will of this God who accompanies us.

The exception to this streaming of values to us, is when we have a momentous problem or wound on our minds and he is prompting us to take heed of a certain course of action. But the course of action is the way of achieving the value that he perceives to be the ideal remedy in the situation. Suicidal people have been told, "Gather some of the things that are the most valuable to you and give them to the poor, in God's name, and your life will change for the better." They did and it did. Bankrupt people have been told, "Give freely to God, and you will quickly recover." They did, and they did. Sick people have been told, "Believe, and now stand up and walk." They did and they did. But you can see that behind all of this ministry to the person who is in a desperate state, there is the value to keep them alive and healthy *according* to their relationship with their Thought Adjuster. Simply keeping them alive, or solvent, or healthy isn't the value that is being imparted so much as getting them into the kingdom of heaven and keeping them there so that they can continue their journey toward Adjuster fusion. What use is it to God that his child rejects him but remains healthy, wealthy, happy and wise in the world? None whatsoever. In the end, the disappointed Thought Adjuster will wing his way back to Divinington alone. God always wants the very best for his child and the best starts with sonship.

Your Adjuster wants not to rule our decisions but rather to provide our will with values that will encourage us to seek greater goodness, deeper truth, more inclusive beauty, bolder courage, more sensitive a sympathy and compassion, more empathy with the pain of others, more confidence in the victory of the anointing of God that Jesus knew—fusion mindedness.

The will of God is not expected to dominate our pursuits for good relations with all the people that we meet. The will of God is not a proposition by God to win our affections or a promise to answer our prayers, many of which are simple expressions of frustration on our part rather than actual prayer. The will of God is not a measure that is designed to supplant argument in our inner turmoil for justice, nor to change our heart's concerns for the things that trouble us. The will of God is not a tool for change, like psychotherapeutic methodologies. The will of God is instead the view of God and, if we adopt it and let it wash over us and influence our thinking, and should we act on this new and enhanced reason for doing a certain thing, we will find ourself encouraged by the higher ideal for which we have a vision; uplifted by the power of augmentation through liaison with the mind of our Adjuster; confident of victory because God transcends the world and the ideal we now hold in our mind is bound to be victorious over the world; transcendent, in that we perceive the values of others in relationship, as being of the world and to some extent often impotent, harmless, material, temporary, fruitless; harnessing the energy of the new life that is in our idealistic mind, we will bestow a charge upon the world by our increased perspective and our delight in bringing to life higher values, deeper meaning, more personal realness, and enhanced love and capacity for goodness and truth—beauty.

Fit for a noble guest

Saying all this, it is not easy to describe a formula for *how* to do the will of God. The human mind is so apt to intellectualise a formula that by the time it has learned to act according to the formula's prescription, we are far removed from the original circumstances when we needed it.

There are, however, a number of pointers that are valuable to consider.

For example, the will of God is not designed to force us to act in a certain way. It is designed to be a fragrant rose nearby us. Surely you will choose to stoop over and smell its beautiful perfume. But the choice is always yours. You might ignore it completely. You might walk on by after giving it a mere glimpse. You might reach out and touch its petals without inhaling its perfume, or you might stop, clear your mind and gather your attention, fondling its leaves and petals and, almost as an act of worship, you might bring your nose to its heart and become one with its perfume. The decision has always remained yours—the rose is the same rose throughout.

The first step in doing the will of God is knowing the origins and motives and powers of God your Father. These are no more personally presented than in the principles that Jesus lived by.

The formula for how to do the will of God is simple: do what Jesus did.

How do you know what Jesus did? Read the New Testament or read the fourth section of the Urantia papers or read both.

But, let's say that you don't understand them, or don't want to turn to a book for your instructions. Then, you will need to use your mind, and use it very well and very carefully.

Many of us shun scriptures and traditional religious practices because we fear being misled by the human addition to sacred things thought to be more pure in the heart of God himself. So we head off for the mind and heart of God essentially with no map and a Jerry-can full of our hopes as fuel. We often overlook the grossness of our own mind. We certainly overlook the fact that the human mind doesn't translate the motives of the divine minded Thought Adjuster without considerable sensitivity and skilled cooperation. The more animalistic nature in our character immeasurably restricts our ability to use our mind effectively in our pursuit of God. For example, our dietary habits, our use of intoxicants, our involvement with behaviours and pursuits that stress our nervous system and fragment our self esteem, all immensely handicap our desire to find God's will and intentions as they reside directly within God. We can easily become numbed, confused, overburdened, neurotic, medicated mast-less vessels trying to dance the Swan Lake ballet with all the poise and grace and strength of some Russian prima donna. But, instead, we are floundering gooses who are off balance, misled and self-styled drifters. Not that we want to be; our path has made us so.

In many people's homes we find fine cutlery and crockery that we would use when an honoured guest dines with us. We would also find the toilet cleaning equipment we use for other purposes that we don't want the noble guest to see. For some of us who have no spiritual map about how to proceed towards the doing of the will of God, our lives become like the cleaning gear yet we are hoping to become the fine cutlery. If we would travel alone, without a map that tells us to first have a pure heart toward God, let these words be a guide to you at least from this day forward. Without a pure heart toward God, we will never see God: not ever.

Meeting God in the Scriptures

For those of us who look to scriptures to find the will of God, the Thought Adjuster will empower us at the time that we and he meet in the same value.

An example of this is the Benedictine exercise of *sacred reading—lectio divina*. You select a passage to read. You mouth the words as you read them, just loud enough to hear the air forming the words. You note when you come upon a part of the passage that alerts your mind to something personally valuable or sensitive. You contemplate that part of the passage. As you contemplate it, you meet with God in his value that is contained therein, and it speaks to you. Knowing the value, letting it transform the previous value you held, when next you behave in that area of your life, you will find yourself doing the will of God for he has brought your character in line with his own, so to speak.

The Father does not place a great burden upon humanity to go out and study the fine print of the doing of the will of God like some great onerous task. In the long run, he is going to have more success with the child who has long practised doing the will of God without even knowing it is being done. Why? Because, when his human son of God gets into personal difficulty, he or she will have much more to fall back on in their own ingenuity and strength of character.

Meeting God beyond the Scriptures

There does come a time, however, when the son of God is led to ways of doing the will of God which transcend the known scriptures. Jesus showed that fact to us.

It is not that the scriptures are found to be wholly erroneous, it is that they are seen to be reflections of one's own spirit-filled experience in an Adjuster fusion minded reality. The transformation of conscious that has occurred in the son of God is in the source of authority: where once, the scripture provided us with divine authority, now the divine authority comes to us entirely from our relationship with this Thought Adjuster whom we call our Father.

Jesus quoted the scriptures from time to time, but he did not look to them for his authority. He looked to the direct contact that he had with his Thought Adjuster, the Father, for all of his authority.

How do we know this?

We need only look to the scriptures that recorded it so.

For example, Mark 1:22 tells us that "he taught them as one having authority, and not as their scribes." Mark 1:27 records that the people were, "all amazed, and they kept on asking one another, 'What is this? A new teaching—with authority! He commands even the unclean spirits, and they obey him."[57] When people debated with him regarding his authority, he said, "For which is easier, to say, 'Your sins are forgiven,' or to say, 'Stand up and walk'?" Then he demonstrated his authority by saying, "But so that you may know that the Son of Man has authority on Earth to forgive sins"—he then said to the paralytic—'Stand up, take your bed and go to your home.' And he stood up and went to his home."[58] He gave the authority he had, to the twelve apostles and, "began to send them out two by two, and gave them authority over the unclean spirits."[59]

When he was in Jerusalem, the chief priests, and the scribes, and the elders asked him about the authority with which he ministered saying, "'By what authority are you doing these things? Who gave you this authority to do them?' Jesus said to them, "I will ask you one question; answer me, and I will tell you by what authority I do these things. Did the baptism of John come from heaven, or was it of human origin? Answer me.' They argued with one another, 'If we say, 'From heaven,' he will say, 'Why then did you not believe him?' But shall we say, 'Of human origin'?"—they were afraid of the crowd, for all regarded John as truly a prophet. So they answered Jesus, 'We do not know.' And Jesus said to them, 'Neither will I tell you by what authority I am doing these things.'"[60]

How do we do the will of God?

We do what Jesus did.
What did Jesus do?

What did Jesus do?

Jesus spent time of lone communion with himself and his Father's immediate presence—the Personalised Adjuster. When he faced any new or serious decisions, Jesus would withdraw for communion with his own spirit that he might seek to know the will of God.[61]

This tells us that we can expect to be nurtured by our ever patient Thought Adjuster in the desire for communion with him. We will then find ourselves deliberating with him over our concerns, and his, in the privacy of our own time and place. It is a wonderful time when we first make plans with God, to achieve some certain task, when we can affirm to ourselves that that's exactly what's happening. Then, at that time, we know for certain the power of sonship with God—it is in our communion together. Later on, we will find our sonship manifesting as the outcome that we planned together.

Jesus vigorously defended his policy to do the will of his Paradise Father, and we will definitely need to do the same on a daily basis. The Urantia papers tell us that, "he turned upon Peter and the other apostles, saying: 'Get you behind me. You savour of the spirit of the adversary, the tempter. When you talk in this manner, you are not on my side but rather on the side of our enemy. In this way do you make your love for me a stumbling block to my doing the Father's will. Mind not the ways of men but rather the will of God.'"62

Many people have a religious life that is based on things being wholly positive, good, true and beautiful—particularly those people who follow the New Age philosophies. Such a philosophy usually has a very poor defence system because, being very passive, it frequently steers itself away from any capacity to be pro-active. As soon as we move out of a spirituality in which it only contains those things that come to us while we are passive, and move into a spirituality, which is dynamic, and achiever focussed, we suddenly find that we need an impeccable defence line. All of a sudden, everybody and their dog, it seems, wants to rob us of our spirituality. They want it dead in the water. They want it for themselves. They want to corrupt it so that it looks like them. They want to abuse it. They want to do just about everything to it except honour it. At that time it becomes obvious that Jesus was absolutely crystal clear about his policy. He had a wall of defence that was as solid as steel and if you came near it you would get a taste of his razor wire as he cut you to ribbons. Christians are not too far off the mark when they teach us to develop practices that have us shielding our spiritual policies against evil and sin and iniquitous forces in the world. Without such skills in defence, all of our good efforts become eroded and undermined.

If you want to be the friend of a great spiritual person like Jesus, firstly honour the fact that he will cut you out of his will just like that, when you tamper with his convictions about his sonship with his Father. And so should every one who is learning from him do the same.

Do you know that there are many of us who are ashamed to tell people that we read the Bible, or the Urantia papers, or that we follow Christ, of that God is our Father? Can you imagine that? Imagine how easy it is for the Peter's of that moment with Jesus, to simply talk us out of our spiritual faith, and leave us back in the flesh as if we never counted for anything in the eyes of God. Imagine how weak is our spiritual will. Imagine how shadowy and timid a character we have become and how unlike the authority of sonship we are. Imagine how far away would be the prospect of doing the will of God when we are like that. Imagine how our Thought Adjuster would be wishing all day and everyday that we would gather enough sincerity to at least defend his cause for partnering us.

How we do the will of God also involves being an active member of the spiritual brotherhood of man.[63] We have confessed our faith in the fatherhood of God, and thereby we declare our wholehearted dedication to the doing of the will of God. Such sons of God are the most cherished men and women on the Earth. Without them, the will of God cannot manifest among humanity. Without them, we have no reliable elders. Without them, human spiritual value cannot take root in the Earth and bring this universe to the glorious stage of Light and Life. When you meet another son of God, you are seeing the Father's light on Earth. Such a man or woman, girl or boy, is worthy of our respect and our care and our deep love and our deep concern—for are they not our Father's variation on we ourself? Are they not children of the mighty Michael and Mother Spirit?

From this we can see that how we do the will of God involves not only communion with God, but the development of God's philosophy as well.

Jesus showed us that we should always have faith in our Father's ability to prevail in the end. Even in the face of betrayal, Jesus trusted his Father. When David Zebedee tried to tell Jesus about how Judas was plotting to have him arrested, Jesus said, "Only doubt not in your own heart that the will of God will prevail in the end."[64]

The power that is in sonship with God

It's important to know that the *power* of sonship with God, is not in your philosophy, nor in your gifts of the spirit, nor in your Church, nor in your fruits of the spirit. The power in your sonship is the absolute fact that, in your life, and by *your* will, God will prevail.

Mary and I have from time to time come to an impasse in our lives when we have both wanted to do something different on the same occasion. To break the impasse, we simply agreed with each other that our Father had total, uninhibited, free reign to provide whatever he wanted for us.

On one occasion, it was a pilgrimage to Israel. From out of nowhere, on the tenth day after we asked him for help, we were taking communion in St. George's Cathedral about ten minutes walk from the Damascus Gate through which Jesus once carried his cross to Golgotha. It was a life changing experience, one that we ordinarily wouldn't have chosen.

On another occasion, the turning of the century from 1999 to 2000, we gave our plans over to him again. During the same day, he conveyed to me not to prepare the evening meal, for what he had planned for us would not only include entertaining us for the New Year celebrations, but also feed us. It turned out wonderfully. We waited all day and there was not sign at all. God is never early: but he is never late. At 6.30pm, the phone rang and we were invited out to a wonderful evening. Interestingly, we both were able to do the things we wanted to do, at the same place and event, despite our different wishes. And the food was truly wonderful.

Try it yourself. Give God a day of your life. Or, give him an encounter between you and someone else. I ran a number of groups wherein I sent people off to encounter other people. The outcomes were life changing for them. Your Father is always full of great surprises. Best of all: he always prevails.

The peace

How we do the will of God is again shown to us by Jesus as it concerns the peace that he gives us. The peace is an emblem of the power and position of our Father, the authority we have in the world and the sense of potential victory with which we ever live. Jesus shows us that it is unlike the joys and satisfactions of the material world, and so, in response to our Father's inner promptings, we will wean ourselves out of relying upon the will of God to be involved in the conquest of such joys and satisfactions unless they are involved in the process of securing higher spiritual value. Total peace, that wholly washes over us and rises up within us, which is not based upon some ephemeral temporary will of the wisp material joy and satisfaction can only come to us by the will of our Father. It is gifted to us, not made by our hand. No amount of will power can manufacture it; no amount of optimism can generate it. The peace of Jesus comes by Jesus.[65]

Sonship with God creates a desire to dedicate the whole life to the doing of our Father's will. Our heart is purified by that desire and for that desire's outworking. Our selfishness once was the lamplight of our survival. Now it is transformed, and not overnight but by experience over time and with differing circumstances and values. Sonship anchors us in an eternal loyalty to our Father's recognition, of the extraordinary beauty that exists in others' well being. We live literally in the light of the Spirit of Truth, the power of the Holy Spirit, the communion with the Father, and the fellowship with other sons of God—and in all this we find ourselves growing and changing rapidly as we move from being mortals of Urantia, to morontia beings who are sons of Michael and Mother Spirit.[66] How do we do the will of God? We live as ordinary morontia sons of God live.

How we do the will of God is by seeking first the kingdom of God, and seeking it in all things. Jesus taught us to do this: to seek out how the Father's values might be put into the busy scenes of life. When we look into his family prayer, we see his desire for the kingdom to come: that is, he actively sought the values of his Thought Adjuster and Paradise Father and put them in place in the world through his life on a daily basis.[67]

It is important to remember, as we consider the various ways in which we might put into the world the values of our Father, to not be daunted by the task. Sometimes we think that it was easy for Jesus because he was the Son of God and a Creator Michael, but that we are mere mortals and hopelessly equipped in comparison. It is important to remember that Jesus was an unusual character, without doubt, but he put his power and divinity aside in order to be a man who is under the sovereignty of the power and divinity of our Father. Jesus did not achieve the doing of the will of God by arduous asceticism, or long meditative practices, or prayer and fasting. He simply understood his life from the point of view of being with God as he understood it. We should not think that long complex exercises and religious practices will bring us into the doing of the will of God. "Jesus of Nazareth was a religious man who, by faith, achieved the knowing and the doing of the will of God; he was the most truly religious man who has ever lived on Urantia."[68] If we want to, we can be like him. He will help us, when we love him, and when we understand his motives for doing what he did, *when we are understanding him in the atmosphere of God's presence.*

The religion of Jesus and the religion of Paul

To understand the will of God, and its doing, when we are not in God's atmosphere, his communion, is little understanding at all. First find the kingdom, Jesus said, and then all else flows out of it. First receive God's forgiveness, and then, being in the kingdom, presume to commune with your Father, and all else will flow from him to you.

Jesus and Paul both did the will of God as they perceived it. The Urantia papers tell us that "Jesus founded the religion of personal experience in doing the will of God and serving the human brotherhood; Paul founded a religion in which the glorified Jesus became the object of worship and the brotherhood consisted of fellow believers in the divine Christ."[69] They each represent the two legitimate ways of understanding Jesus. They are both poles apart. They will both impact on how we do the will of God.

Ultimately, the life of Christ which is in us,[70] as Paul calls it, flows out of our born-again spirit and into our consciousness to produce the fruit of the Spirit according to our choices and decisions. This life of Christ flows out because it is the life of Michael of Nebadon our universe Father. It flows out because the Father is in us and also in Michael as he flows into us. Knowing that Jesus Christ is the Son of God who was sent from heaven by the will of God to reconcile the world to the Father, is not essentially incorrect at all—for that is exactly what he began.

The difference between living the religion of Jesus and living the religion that Paul lived is that Paul's religious experience, outside of it not being an example that demonstrated the Adjuster fusion Jesus showed us, that he never knew Jesus the man. Paul keeps Jesus in a lofty domain that is remote from the person who sincerely wants to know how the human Jesus dealt with the problems of being a human being. It is one thing to be saved from a situation—that is like feeding the starving—and a whole other thing to work out one's salvation with one's Father—which is like giving the starving the tools to feed themselves.

It is wonderful to see the Son of God on Earth as a man. That vision has ferried humanity through two thousand years. But what it is so much a greater thing to see Jesus dealing with making a living, navigating family matters, social injustices, personal love, close friendships, betrayal, humiliation, shame, and most spectacularly even death itself—the hub of all life's search for meaning.

This great difference is the focal point of the gift of the Urantia papers to us from our Michael and Mother, from the Ancients of Days, from our Father, from Gabriel, from the authors themselves, and in the name of the most extraordinary plan to raise up sons of God from every nation under the sun: sons, just like Jesus.

It is a fact that Jesus had his own religion and that his gospel was not some predefined heavenly rule that he brought from heaven to Earth, but rather it was the truth that he found in his own religious living as a man. It is the hope of every one of our ancestors who now prospers in their own sonship in the mansion worlds and constellations, all the way down the generation since Andon and Fonta, your own relatives—even the distant 'mother' of yours who was on the Earth during the years that Jesus lived—that we might discern the magnificence of the religion of Jesus, and find it alive in our blood and flesh and water and spirit.

Would you do the will of God? Then how you do that is plainly before your eyes: do like Jesus did in the way that you and *your* Father do that. Have faith in your own personal religion. Grow it up by the green pastures and cool waters of his example. You will surely be victorious and, at the end of your life on Earth, you will be much pleased with yourself and with your own Father's delight in a life well lived.

The difference between the religion of Jesus and the religion of Paul is never more clearly seen than in the fact that Jesus did not live Paul's religion.

Of course, Paul did not live Jesus' religion either; and Paul's New Testament invitation is more into his own religion than into the religion that Jesus lived out in the flesh.

Christianity may well have been short-sighted on that point. It is time to live the religion that Jesus lived.

What is that religion?

The religion of Jesus is the perfect sharing of the mind of God, as a son and Father.

Notes

1. Mark 11:23-25
2. Hunter, C. & F. 1991. "How to receive and maintain a healing." Hunter Books, Kingwood, Texas.
3. 34:6.10 {The purpose of...}
4. 34:7 {7. The spirit and the flesh.}
5. 34:5.5 {Though the Spirit...}
6. 34:6.12 {And when such...}
7. 34:6.6 {The dead theory...}
8. 34:6.7 {Those who have...}
9. 34:6.9 {In every mortal...}
10. 34:6.11 {The Spirit never ...}
11. 34:7.1 {The flesh, the...}
12. 34:7.2 {Evolutionary mortals inhabiting ...}
13. 34:7.3 {The mortals of...}
14. 34:7.4 {The Urantia peoples...}
15. 34:7.5 {Urantia mortals are...}
16. 34:7.6 {Notwithstanding this double...}
17. 34:7.7 {Those God-knowing...}
18. 34:7.8 {Having started out...}
19. Isaiah 53:3
20. Mark 6:4-6
21. 159:0.2 {On this Thursday...}
22. Paper 148 {Training evangelists at Bethsaida.}
23. 148:2.2 {Many of the...}
24. Mark 5:25-34
25. 152:0.3 {When Jesus heard...}
26. 187:4.1
27. 44:5.8 {7. The teachers of...}
28. Ecclesiates 3:20
29. 148:6.10 {Job was altogether...}
30. 2 Corinthians 3:17 KJV
31. For further reading on perception and secular personal growth, see authors such as Milton H. Erickson, Anthony Robins, Richard Bandler and John Grinder.
32. 101:2.10 {Revelation as an...}
33. 113:4.6 {The ministering personality...}; 194:2.11 {Since the bestowal...}
34. 34:4.4. { The Universe Mother ...}

35. 101:3.2 {Faith-insight, or spiritual...}
36. 5:3.5 {When you deal...}
37. 140:6.4 { Then said Simon...}
38. 144:3.7 {Jesus taught that...}
39. 77:5 {Adamson and Ratta}
40. 33:6.9 {The day in...}
41. Mark 11:22; Romans 4:20
42. 43:7 {The Univitatia}
43. 110:2.1; 107:7.4 {Why then, if...}
44. 110:6.4 {When the development...}
45. 109:5 {Material handicaps to Adjuster indwelling};
    110:3.1 {Adjusters are playing...}
46. 110:7.8 {During mortal life...}
47. For further reading, for example, see:
    Berzin, A., (Translator and editor). 1978. "The
    Mahamudra: Eliminating the darkness of ignorance—
    the ninth Karmapa Wang-Ch'ug Dor-je." Library of
    Tibetan Works & Archives, Dharamsala India.
    Also see, for example:
    Chogyal Namkai Norbu, "Dzogchen: the self-
    perfected state." Snow Lion Publications, New York.
48. 140:10.9 {John asked Jesus...}; 1:2.3 {The actuality
    of...}
49. 136:2.2 {When Jesus of...}
50. Paper 93; Genesis 14:18
51. John 3:31
52. 182:3.2 {The Master remained...}; Luke 22:43
53. 162:7.2 {If my words...}; John 8:32
54. 182:3.4 {And then, for...}
55. Isaiah 61:1-2
56. 136:2.3 {Ordinarily, when a...}
57. Mark 1:27
58. Matthew 9:5-7
59. Mark 6:7
60. Mark 11:27-33
61. 136:4.8 {The forty days...}
62. 158:7.4 {Peter spoke thus...}
63. 170:5.9 {The kingdom, to...}
64. 178:2.3 {David Zebedee, through...}
65. 181:1.7 {Jesus gives peace...}

66. 194:3.19 {The coming of...}
67. 196:0.8 {The faith of...}
68. 196:1.1 {Jesus' devotion to...}
69. 196:2.6 {Jesus founded the...}
70. Romans 1:5; 8:2; 8:11; 1 Corinthians 1:30; Galatians
    2:20

Chapter 34

What should I believe?

Our beliefs and practices directly shape every feature of our life. Our current life is a repository of our past beliefs and practices. It stands to reason that if we change our current beliefs and practices, our life will change—for the worse or for the better. It also stands to reason that our beliefs and practices will contribute to what happens when we die. Generally speaking, the Christian thinks their beliefs and practices will take them to heaven and not to hell. The Buddhist thinks that their beliefs and practices will take them to a better rebirth or out of the cycle of reincarnation altogether. The Atheist thinks that his or her beliefs and practices don't count for anything because he or she is not expecting to have a personal future beyond the moment of death. The person who believes and practices the religion of Jesus and who is informed by the Urantia papers thinks that they will be resurrected in the Mansion Worlds, or will experience Adjuster fusion and bi-pass death.

Everybody's every decision is valuable—individually and collectively. Decisions shape our beliefs and practices and they in turn shape our decisions. Both our beliefs and our practices are in a constant state of flux. We all believe what we believe because we expect greater benefit in our lives. We flee pain and we gravitate to pleasure-even at a spiritual level: for there are most definitely things we reject or embrace spiritually. We ever seek pleasurable increase and shun painful decrease.

For example, if we want to change something in our lives, we need only perceive it to be a painful and troublesome thing, and to increase our consciousness of how pleasurable is its alternative.

There are a great many things that we draw on to fashion and shape our beliefs and practices. The Urantia papers can not and do not hold every answer to our life needs, any more than does the Bible or the Koran or the Bhagavad Gita.

The building blocks of life are the reason of science, the wisdom of philosophy and the faith of personal spiritual experience.[1] These building blocks, however, don't exist in a vacuum: they are inextricably a part of the whole human experience, as it is for any human being at any time or place on Earth.

It is realistic to consider what exactly the Urantia papers are able to contribute to the whole pool of knowledge and experience from which we are able to build our own personal science, philosophy and faith.

For example, if you want to experience actual spirituality, how will the Urantia papers help you?

If you are sick and you want healing, how will the Urantia papers help you?

If you are bankrupt; if you are poor and you want prosperity; if you want a wife or a husband who will stick by you and really make a go of life with you; if you are desperate to flee your circumstances: how will the Urantia papers help you?

If you are suicidal, substance dependent, bound up in depravity, addicted to sex or food or violence or the Internet or television or pornography or rituals or wealth, and you want to be free of that slavery, how will the Urantia papers help you?

If you are a prisoner to something and you are hungry to progress and escape it, then it is a realistic and reasonable question to ask what the fifth epochal revelation can do for you-just as people asked Jesus what he could do for them.

Similarly, if you are not bound up but rather you live a good life with a pure heart and you want to excel, it's your right to expect something as momentous as a fifth epochal revelation to be able to answer your need for guidance, insight, power and righteousness and growth.

Being with Jesus in the Perean hills

Consider Jesus of Nazareth coming up out of the river Jordan at the time of his baptism. He knew of a certainty that he was the Michael of Nebadon. Obviously, if we had any of these needs I mentioned, and we stood in his presence, we couldn't possibly expect them to remain unchanged.

We would expect that our faith would be quickened by being in his presence. We would expect the hold our needs had on us to be loosened in his presence. We would expect to be remade, reinvented, renewed.

We would expect that many of the emotions and attitudes that were formed during our struggle with that oppression over the years would simply fall away. It is reasonable to expect our cynicism to vanish, our doubt, pessimism, contempt and nervousness to dissipate, simply by being close to someone in whom there was so much divine victory.

It is reasonable to expect that we would leave considerable personal baggage in the Jordan and that he would not bring both our concerns and us into the kingdom of heaven. Obviously, that which has no life in the shared mind—the mind of the human and the mind of the Thought Adjuster—would be filtered out.

He would walk us across the Jordan with him, and take us out into the Perean hills, leaving our loathsome bondage in the river's waters to be washed down into the Dead Sea, the sea of sins as it is called.

As he commenced to commune with the Father, he would bring us into that place where we would, being wholly free of our worldly burden, begin to commune with the God indwelling us also. Being with him would change all of our previous frustrations about finding God. With Jesus, the Father would suddenly be so unmistakably available to us.

He would have lifted us up, by our faith and through the Father's grace and power, and placed us in that place of honour where we could claim our rightful place as his son, and a son of his Father also.

With this sonship would come your individuality. From your location on the heights and in the wilderness of the Perean hills, you would notice your freedom from links to the world and its corrupting influences and pressures. You would have had the darkness of the world drawn out of you and off you so that you could receive Jesus' kind of pure heart. And you would see God.

In the company of God, you would think through, like Jesus thought through, the things that matter to you. Your finances. Your family. Your lifestyle. Your relationships. Your values. Your deeper ambitions. And, best of all, you would secure for yourself a pledge of union with your Father in your own mind and heart and soul, that the world would never more be able to corrupt or assault.

Reinventing your beliefs and practices

You would have reinvented your beliefs; cutting the root of

what they once were; and you would have sown the seeds that would adjust your practices accordingly.

Coming out of the hills and leaving behind this time of solitude with your Father, you would guard your life and your pure heart, and the Father would guard it with you. You would nurture your new beliefs and your new practices; keeping them divinely alive by keeping them within the mind that you and your Father now share.

You would thus be a new creature, a valiant ambassador of another realm—even the domain in which the Father and the son share the same mind, the kingdom of heaven. You would be at peace in the world because you would be not of the world but rather of your own Father. Similarly, you would have ease with the world because you would be living according to your Father's nature rather than the nature of the world, the nature of the flesh, and the nature of thought—these things that have no root.

You would thus look into the nature of the world and see that it is held in the bondage of spiritual darkness, ignorance about God, and endless negativity. Then you would look at people and you would see the origin and perpetuity of their misery.

You would clearly see beyond superstition, traditions that breed fundamentalism, fear and rank idealism. You would see clearly the machinations of the two laws in the world—the law of the flesh and the law of the spirit. You would see how people give themselves little choice yet bind themselves to the particular law they serve.

You would see that the law of the flesh brings the fruit of illusions, and perpetuates and fuels endless hunger, while tantalizing the nervous system. You would see the law of the spirit brings the fruit of realness and lasting personal satisfaction because it is good.

You would see that it is by the power of words that these seeds are sown and harvested. You would see that the world is a matrix. of principles and power, wholly governed at a supernatural level and at a material level by the spoken word.

You would recognise that the power of the flesh leads at best to moral civility: whilst at worst it engenders evil, rage, stagnation, depression, hopelessness, decay, disease, sin, destruction, death and the illusion that nothing can be changed.

You would recognise that the power of the spirit leads to Godliness, the power from on high, goodness, truth, beauty, peace and dignity in the least of its portions.

You would then realise the power of having the broadest possible knowledge base upon which God can impart his on going revelation to you. You would know for a fact that your eternal growth is dependent upon knowledge in the presence of the power of the shared mind—the mind of man and the mind of God. You would be hungry to know the full dimension of the kingdom of heaven about which your friend Jesus spoke so often—as it is in the human heart, the material world, and the heavenly worlds. This would engender in you a deep appreciation for the potentials that are within the Urantia papers.

This time with Jesus, and this encounter with your Father in the solitude of your own sincerity, equips you for wholly new beliefs and practices, wholly new perspectives. It may well prepare you for setting your divine Father free to minister on Earth through your own good life, your prayer and the desires of your beautiful heart which mirror those in his own heart.

The Urantia papers offer a new perspective

The Urantia papers shift the focus of belief provided by every traditional religion, including Christianity. They challenge us to include, reject, ignore or suspend judgement on additional information provided to humanity. They also open up new dimensions of our spiritual experience of Personal Deity. They provide the basis for a wholly new philosophical view on life. The Urantia papers free the individual believer from the effects of believing in ways that are addictive, superstitious and impoverishing. They set in place the origins and after-death destiny of the human race and clarify what actually matters in the righteous life and what doesn't.

Unequivocally, the Urantia papers place the life and teachings of Jesus of Nazareth as the cornerstone of the purpose for the whole revelation.

The Urantia papers tell us that we are sons of God, and give us Jesus as the perfect example of that sonship. The Urantia papers tell us that the willing heart will definitely hear the call to perfection and will be led into a communion with the Spirit of the Paradise Father, the indwelling Thought Adjuster. The

Urantia papers tell us that we shall be born again of this Spirit, endued with power from on high, and that we shall be perfect like our Father. The Urantia papers tell us that we shall ascend the universe of universes; that we shall attain to Paradise; that we shall attain Finality and Trinitization; that we shall perhaps, in the undisclosed future for humanity; be the glorified sovereigns of entire universes.

Nothing that has gone before in the history of life on Earth can compare with the breadth and depth and height of the revelation that is brought to us by the Urantia papers.

Living with wholly new beliefs

It thus becomes obvious that the experience of sonship with God will lead the devotee of Jesus' religion to the Urantia papers. It also becomes obvious that the Son of God will develop beliefs that will bear only a fragmentary likeness to many other beliefs on Earth.

In the course of faith being born in us through our belief in the principles of the Urantia papers, we learn to communicate our experiences and their value through our ideas. Much that is contained in the expression of our faith and values is anchored to names and places that exist only in the Urantia papers. Yet, in all this, these aspects are no different from the journey into the religious experience in any other faith.

Difficulties always arise when discussing interfaith issues like beliefs and values. The Urantia papers include a portrait of Jesus and Ganid in discussion over the virtues and aims of the world's leading religions.[2] Whilst these discussions are interesting, I recall discussing what the Urantia papers had to say about Buddhism with an American friend who was a monk in a Tibetan order. We both were monks at that time and we both had read the Urantia papers from cover to cover. We reflected on just how different the authors' description of Buddhism was when compared with how we found it through the living of it.

I would imagine that the same is true for the faithful of all the other faiths portrayed in that section of the Urantia papers.

It is important therefore, I believe, to avoid making the words of the Urantia papers into a religion or into a religious opinion. That kind of fundamentalism runs contrary to the authors aims of sparking individuality and diversity rather than a hybrid collection of monotypical drones.

The essence, the truth, the foundation of every authentic religious person, is not an authority given them by the scriptures. Nor is it their intellectual grasp on universe realities. Rather, it is the authority given them by the literal presence of the Father's perfection in them, whose evidence is the fruit of his spirit—sonship. If you are authentically spiritual, then you have sonship with God—and the fruit of your sonship is the fruit of the spirit. If you are a son of God, you will know that your sonship is a free gift that is daily offered to you by your Father, through his graciousness, and that you receive it moment by moment by faith. If you have sonship with God, you will be sharing the mind of God, for such is sonship: the mind of God and the human mind in communion. If you have sonship with God, you will know his total love for you; and you will share that love as it comingles with your own love.

Discovering divine truth in others

Personally, one's own beliefs and practices are a matter between oneself and one's Thought Adjuster—a deeply private matter. Socially, however, it is very healthy to recognize how other's beliefs compare with one's own, if for no other reason than to view them with some sense of objectivity.

I have long felt that the study of other's spiritual experience and its religious roots, is comparable to studying the language and customs of others.

It is a very small world within which one lives if only one culture has been experienced. The problem arising from this smallness is that its views are often far too narrow to deal with the current problems of living in a way that can give one's Thought Adjuster sufficient scope to exercise the kinds of growth in universal values that is in his heart to do. It's like your Thought Adjuster has just made you a multi-millionaire, but you only have a bank in your small town that trades in withdrawal amounts of one hundred dollars per day. Which reality do you want to live with?

Even as I write this, I imagine that there are Buddhists around the world who want to maintain their Buddhist faith and yet complement their faith with gains derived from the Urantia papers. So too, there are Muslims, Christians, Jews, Shinto and

Confucianists doing likewise. The extraordinary thing about the Urantia papers is that they contribute to each of these wonderful faiths, a dimension of science and philosophy and personal spiritual experience that can not be gained through any other means. And, I believe, that contribution is enormous.

The Urantia papers devote around forty percent of the revelation to Jesus and his being the Son of God on Earth as a son of God. My experiences with the Father, Christ Michael and Mother Spirit convince me that the believer who takes up sonship with God through the Urantia papers will inevitably study Christianity at some level in their life. That's where they'll find Jesus alive in other people, where they may not yet find him so alive among students of the Urantia papers. That's where they'll find the first two thousand years of his Spirit of Truth in action. That's where they'll find Christ Michael and Mother Spirit and the Indwelling Father, albeit not necessarily under those names. That's where they'll see the ascending human spirit struggling to bring into daily life on this planet, the values within the pursuit of individual and community perfection—with all its humanness and the miracle of faith.

It is, however, a completely foolish proposition to suppose that our Father, Michael, Mother Spirit and their various ministering groups are not equally active in the life of every other human being on Earth and in the faiths to which they belong. The fruit of the spirit is plainly visible across the world, across cultures, and across faiths. The Father lives in the heart of every believing son of God—and the fruit of the spirit is not present without sonship.

When I was completing the documentation involved in becoming an ordained Buddhist monk, one of the forms had a question on it that asked me to indicate my religion. I found it amusing that Buddhists really don't care about one's religious background. Christianity, on the other hand, can be so completely intolerant of other faiths that they wage war upon themselves just as quickly. I have always thought that there was something diseased about all that—if not getting something your own way makes you so upset, could it be that the thing you want is against the goodness of God?

The Urantia papers give a clear presentation of how people aren't really meant to agree on everything to the letter. God has magnificent plans to stimulate the growth of diversity in the world.

Given this, it is relatively safe to say that those people who have encountered Jesus over the past two thousand years also follow the Father's trend toward diversity if they can escape the shackles that bind a man to fundamentalism.

Despite the immense differences in beliefs, customs and practices among believers in Jesus around the world, there is a common thread that links all believers together in him. That single essence is the fact that Jesus is Lord, Universal Sovereign. According to the Urantia papers, that translates over into the concept that Michael of Nebadon is a Master Michael and sovereign of all Nebadon in his own right. Most Christians would probably have trouble swallowing that idea because it's source is outside the Biblical tradition, even though Christ himself is obviously larger than the Biblical tradition. Yet, despite the bones in the chicken soup, Michael's Lordship remains the bridge between Christians and devotees of the Urantia papers—far more so than the concept of the Fatherhood of God.

That's a strange thing to say, because one would think that if we all loved God the Father we would all get along. But that's not the case at all. Our differences and troubles are deeper than merely believing in God. We would only get along if we had an ample vision of the Father's destiny for us. That destiny is given us by the life of Jesus and by the Fatherhood of Michael of Nebadon. It is not given us so clearly and so well by the life of any other person throughout all history. Christianity does so poorly with itself and its neighbours because of a lack of vision about the individuals in its numbers—a vision that engenders the Father's love among them. So too, with all warring groups.

What to believe

It is never healthy to tell people what to believe. There are many good reasons why we each must grow our own beliefs and draw from within our own experiences. In the course of my encounter with God and the Urantia papers, for example, it has become apparent to me that there are certain truths that I believe are available to us all, and they concern sonship with God.

The son of God will live by the revelation that is his or hers through sharing the mind of God.

The son of God will have direct sonship with Christ Michael, Mother Spirit and the Paradise Father whose spirit indwells him or her and stimulates, adjusts and eventually leads thought—where thought is the name given to one's beliefs and their value.

The son of God will increasingly be like his or her divine Parents. The evidence of this will be in their wanting to follow the Father's mandate to be perfect as is he, and in creating the fruit of his Spirit.

The son of God has no previous personal existence and does not reincarnate on Earth, as that concept is taught in Hinduism and Buddhism—no person does. The son of God will increasingly live on Earth as a joint Earth-Morontia citizen and will pass from this their native planet to Mansonia. The son of God will not as Christianity teaches, return to a glorified Earth upon the return of Christ—his return will not initiate such events.

The son of God will have power by the Spirit of Truth and by sharing the Father's mind that will give victory over evil, sin and all the legacy of Caligastia's corruption.

It's important to note here that I said *all* the legacy of Caligastia's corruption: for that is what is contained in the Spirit of Truth.

The son of God will love like a father, care like a mother, and be a friend to you like an elder brother or sister—through sharing the mind of God as did Jesus.

Anyone who wants to be a son of God will immediately be so, by fiat of the Father himself. Anyone who wants citizenship in the local universe will receive this by fiat of Michael and Mother Spirit of Nebadon.

All else that is spiritual for us in the Urantia papers—and in fact all goodness, truth and beauty on Earth—is built on these types of principles.

❦

Notes

1. 103:9.8 {Science (knowledge) is...}
2. Paper 131 {The World's Religions.}

❦

Chapter 35

The birth of a son of God

Sonship is obviously different for every person. Different for the female; different for the male. Different for the youngster; different for the mature religionist. Different for the Jew and for the Gentile, as they say. Different for the person who grows up with the Urantia papers only; and different for the person who comes to the Urantia papers from another or a mix of faiths.

I am hoping that this book will bring all these diverse people to drink from the Urantia papers in a new and more personal light. I truly hope that the reader will find Michael and Mother Spirit and our Father and Adjuster fusion far more easily by encountering them through me.

I do expect that, as a result of this book being published and—as funds become available—it is translated into other languages, many other people will write about their particular journey in sonship with God, and that many of those will add other dimensions that my view alone can contribute.

Our great hope, of course, is that a great many views will be published. The more the better: for in them, our Father's plan for diversity prospers and we are all greatly advantaged. With diversity, we find that the normal more often includes us and our individuality: we have less struggle with humanity and are more available to our Father.

Every son of God has a contribution to make. You dear reader, as you read these words, can prosper enormously from the fact that as a son of God you can offer us all something of our Father, and of yourself. You are such a valued person. You probably have no idea how much you do count. Right now, for example, you are the answer to some one's prayers. Someone has prayed and you can bring into that person's life the thing their Father is giving them—just as someone will bring into your life the things you prayed for. That's really special. You have something to give into our fellowship, and something to receive from it, day after day. I pray that you well leave the mark of your goodness among us. Each of us has something of our Parents to share with us.

One of the most unexpected and extraordinary features of sonship with God that I have encountered, and I hope that it has come through in this book, is the amazing and superb realness and closeness of the persons of God the Father, Michael of Nebadon and Mother Spirit—the Holy Spirit.

Buddhism taught me that all things and beings manifest themselves within my Mind. Christianity taught me that Deity manifests objectively, as a separate person who is distinct from me and my mind. The Urantia papers taught me that the persons of Deity are individual people who manifest both objectively and subjectively.

Their appearance is their presence. Their presence is known by our Spirit. Our Spirit learns to perceive, then to understand, then to trust, then to obey and act. Eventually, inevitably, our Spirit can fully receive the presence of our divine Parents.

Church of Christ Michael

In 1997, after many experiences of them, in my inner person and objectively as persons in whose company I was standing, I again commenced holding regular worship and healing services in Melbourne. I was quite convinced that the Parents of Deity could be as real for other people as they were for me. Over the months, we all found that indeed they were. People from traditional Christian backgrounds, people from New Age backgrounds, people from Urantia papers backgrounds—all met these Parents of Deity in the real way that I had met them.

We were a small group, a pretty ordinary bunch really even though among our number was a fellow who was seated on the Anglican synod in Victoria; a lady who was an Elder at a Uniting Church; another lady who was a member of a motorcycle outreach ministry; a fellow who was the coordinator of a drug rehab; and others. We were plain people however, who were deeply in love with Jesus and God. The meetings were very open and relaxed and invited free spiritual expression for all. We didn't gather to judge and form religious rules. We were in every way what is called a primitive Church, and we had praise, worship and devotional music; spontaneity and great depth of prayerfulness; and sensitivity to the move of God throughout the whole service. We always began with an hour of study of both the Urantia papers and the Bible—so that the Urantia papers could the better interface with existing human spiritual realities—then we would share a lunch together. I preached, led people into the Father's forgiveness, and did whatever I perceived in Michael's will regarding healing, change, comfort and transformation. I also did whatever was right to do in this fusion mindedness that our Adjuster brings upon us.

During this period of time of pastoring the small fellowship in Melbourne, I introduced people to the experience of sonship with God through a spiritual encounter with Michael of Nebadon, Mother Spirit, and of course the Father. I wanted to give them the source of things upon which Adjuster fusion is based—the living experience of Jesus' gospel.

Internet chat-line communion

I had long behaved spiritually in ways that transcended space, and had an idea of leading people into sonship with God in the same manner yet through a prayerfulness that could be maintained over an Internet chat line. My thinking was pretty simple really and it went as follows: Michael is Spirit and he comes to people in Spirit. The way to encounter him is in prayerful communion. I know how to bring people into that kind of prayerful communion in such a way that they can encounter Michael. Surely, my ability with prayer, and Michael's own will to reveal himself to his child and thus create sonship with God for that person, could make something work for both Michael and the person. If it could happen with Michael, it could also happen with the Father and with Mother Spirit.

I met an American lady through email; an avid student of the Urantia papers; extraordinary for her devotion to the quest for Adjuster fusion—Carol Davidson. She lives in Arizona.

She had a friend, who is now also my friend, Dede, and she lives in New Jersey. We arranged to meet in an Internet chat room one day when we could coordinate the different time zones. The encounter was extraordinary. As we spoke about our lives and experiences, we all could experience faith, and God's grace, and the Holy Spirit happening among us just like we were in Church together. Yet, here we were a half a world apart. I was in Australia and they were on the East Coast of America and in the Arizona desert near Mexico.

This meeting led to others joining us and eventually an Internet chat room in the *#Urantia* room on *Starlink: US, TX,*

WitchitaFalls was established. Carol also established a mail list for subscribers. We met regularly, bringing people into sonship with God. The most fascinating thing was that Michael and Mother Spirit and the Father would manifest to people where they were at their computers in whatever part of the world they happened to be. People were from Australia, Finland, Canada and in different parts of the United states of America. It was a real global communion, a real sharing of God's mind across the nations.

In the course of writing this book recently, I happened to enter the chat room one day to find a couple of people there, Carol and Roy. I have never met them in the flesh but I have chatted with them before. What followed then, was my leading Judith, a visitor to the chatroom, into sonship with Michael and Mother Spirit. You might be interested to follow the dialogue. I have entered the occasional comment along the way, but other than that, it is a record of the transcript log pretty much as it happened.[1]

If you have never been involved in a chat room conversation before, each line represents one person typing on their computer keyboard and then sending the message off into the Internet to be received on every one else's screens almost instantly. Often, they'll be typing away and then they'll stop and read what others have written, and then comment on something a couple of lines up in the text. The conversation doesn't flow like a play script, but you'll get the gist of the meeting pretty easily.

The participants' names have been included with their consent, and the transcript is used in this book with their permission.

The :) or :))) is a way a person indicates they are smiling. <G> means a grin, and LOL means laughing out loud.

The log starts:

*** Rob has joined #urantia: Session Time: Fri Jan 0200:00:00 2000.

<Rob> Hi there.

<Carol> Rob, how wonderful.

<Judith> Hi.

<Carol> Meet Judith.

<Judith> Hi Rob :) Nice to meet you.

[Roy pastes in a graphic of a church building.]

<Rob> Hi Roy :)))))) We're meeting in God's place...I can
      tell !!
<Roy> :)
<Carol> :)
<Judith> :) Yep enough for a congregation. <G>
<Roy> Hello Rob.
<Rob> Nice to be with you again Roy.
<Carol> Judith, Rob is my mentor.
<Rob> Hello Judith.
<Judith> Hi Rob.
<Judith> nice to meet you.
<Judith> Oh Lord! really?
<Rob> you too
<Carol> We were just talking about fusion, Rob
<Rob> OK...the little pearl!
<Carol> Judith has decided to go for it :)
<Judith> :)
<Rob> Bless you...and bless your Father Judith.
<Roy> Did she?
<Judith> Thanks :)
<Judith> Of course
<Roy>! :)
<Judith> You think I was just typing?
<Judith> :)
<Roy> OK, I look forward to our date.
<Judith> Right then :) So I'll tell you what happens.
<Rob> Where do you live Judith?
<Judith> Toronto
<Judith> And you?
<Rob> Melbourne Australia

*[I have edited out a few lines of small talk that would be of no
interest to the reader.]*

<Rob> Judith, do you read the Urantia papers?
<Judith> Of course :)
<Rob> How have they impacted in your life?
<Judith> Very, very, majorly! :) Just this year, I see a lot of

things coming to fruition. :) I've been very blessed :)
Carol, you wanna recount my day to him and see
what he thinks? :)

<Carol> I don't think he would be interested is a normal day,
more or less. I think the main thing was that tonight
you voiced your desire to attain Adjuster fusion from
Earth.

<Judith> Okay :) well...

<Rob> Judith, what do you think of Adjuster fusion?

<Judith> Well, my whole life I've always thought that union
would God would happen after death but since
reading the Urantia papers I learned otherwise. But
even then I thought why not stay on Earth as long as
possible to influence as many lives as possible. But
then Carol got me thinking about aiming to fuse from
Earth and we were talking about people who tried.

<Rob> Ha ha ha ... stick around Carol long enough and I tell
you, you'll think you were so much like God it'll
dazzle you!

<Judith> LOL

<Carol> No comment :)

<Judith> People who tried to fuse and what the formula is for
fusion, and Carol said only through Michael. I was
just saying before you came on that we have a perfect
recipe in the Bible. Enoch's father Methuselah
walked with God over 500 years and he fused. He
never died. Neither did Moses. Well Methuselah is
the better example as I think Moses died first and
then was taken. Methuselah walked right into heaven.
So the key is constant communication with God
everyday, every hour.

<Rob> Did you read in the Urantia papers Judith, where
Michael and Satan had an argument over the control
of Moses after he died?

<Judith> Hmmm I remember; yes; yes. But recount it. It's
been a while.

<Rob> I think Moses didn't Adjuster fuse but died, whereas
Enoch and Elijah fused.

<Judith> Yes, that's what I meant. You are right. Moses did
die first like I thought but he was taken after. There

was no body, I think. Old Methuselah is Enoch's father and the oldest man that ever lived in the Bible. But Enoch fused too. I need to look at it again.

<Rob> Constant communication with God every day is a powerful formula for knowing the will of God and becoming like it. Is this what you intend to do?

<Judith> Yes, that's what I intend to do. But I've been doing it on and off for years. I mean, when I was a kid, all I ever did was talk to God. I was one weird kid. LOL

[I have edited out a few lines of small talk that would be of no interest to the reader.]

<Rob> Maybe Carol will be around on the planet for 365 years before fusing :)))

<Carol> :)

<Judith> By the way, my faith background is Seventh Day Adventist.

<Judith> LOL. No way! I would hate living that long!

<Rob> I'll bet Carol hopes it's less than 80 years and not 365 years :))

<Judith> Yep! Well I had a dream a long time back that I lived to 120 years and it was so weird! I mean all my family has lived to at least 100

<Rob> 120! Wow.

<Judith> LOL

<Judith> Yep

<Judith> One old great aunt is hitting 105 now. Feisty as ever. :)

<Carol> Judith, how well do you know Michael, since you've got to ask him?

<Judith> There is always room to know Michael more, but I believe I know him pretty well. I mean after talking to him since babyhood... I stopped for a while during early teens. I thought that too, but I found there was a deeper connection than I'd known...so...but the connection always grows deeper.

<Carol> I ask because, he could reach me better since I knew more about who he was, etc.

<Judith> I believe there is no end to it.

546

\<Carol\> There was a definite experience for me. In fact, I got it right here on #urantia with Rob.

\<Judith\> Well I know you're further along than me in that.

\<Judith\> Really?? Tell me.

\<Carol\> He told me of his experience and I wanted it.

\<Judith\> :) That sounds interesting.

\<Carol\> So I asked him if I had the same kind of connection to Michael that he had, and he looked into my Spirit I guess, and said I didn't, but that Michael was poised ready to come in if I wanted to ask him into my heart. So I just asked.

\<Roy\> fusion is a personal event, as personalities we are unique, so each path to fusion must be unique. There can be no fixed formula to achieve fusion.

\<Carol\> And I had a mighty feeling of his power. And for the next two days all I could do was cry. And I could feel Michael and Mother Spirit hovering over me. And I could even talk to them and hear them, believe it or not :)

\<Judith\> Pretty powerful :)

\<Carol\> Others have also received it. You've heard Carlie talk about it also. She's also a Michael son.

\<Judith\> Yes I know :)

\<Carol\> Rob, any comments?

\<Judith\> Well my life's been full of miracles from beginning to end.

\<Roy\> And a lot of trips for new batteries.

\<Judith\> LOL

\<Roy\> :)

\<Judith\> Well Roy there is no perfect recipe

\<Rob\> I imagine that if you died tonight Judith, you'd know for certain that you'd go to heaven? That right?

\<Judith\> of course! :)

\<Judith\> Especially in these past few months: there's been a major power build up around me :) and in me :) I never feared I would not make it.

\<Rob\> Doesn't the Holy Spirit have a magnificent way of cleaning our hearts, washing our lives, and sorting our all the jitters from our younger days?

\<Judith\> Definitely!!! And the thing is the WAY he does it is incredible!

<Rob> What way are you talking about Judith?

<Judith> :) Well to make a long story short, basically you know when you get stuck in a loop and then all of a sudden its like the lights go on and then the whole puzzle finally click into place completely. :)

<Judith> and everything starts falling into place :) Just like that: no effort of mine.

<Rob> By grace through faith?

<Judith> Before, there was so much effort in getting things to work, but now it just gets done. :) cause the lesson got learned :)

<Judith> Yep

[At this point, introductions and chitchat is over as far as I am concerned, and I want to get down to the Father's business. Firstly, I wanted to know the level of intimacy that Judith had with Michael.]

<Rob> Did you ever meet Jesus face to face Judith?

<Judith> Once when I was a kid. :) I used to dream a lot about him too. But when I got older, I was just feeling his presence. I mean, I've had enough things happen to me that everyone who has known me long enough would declare I am protected.

<Rob> Isn't he wonderful?

<Judith> Yes he's very, very wonderful.

[Her reply told me that she had never met Jesus or Christ Michael, and in fact probably never suspected that she even could. I next wanted to find out whether she had developed a relationship with God that placed him as sovereign over her morals, ethics and philosophy, as against simply believing in God and that God is wonderful and a protector and so forth, but that belief not amounting to much transformation and character development in her actual life.]

<Rob> Did you ever do anything that you knew he wanted you to do...and when you did it, it really glorified God?

<Judith> And most wonderful is he still remembered a deep prayer I had from when I was a kid. :)

<Rob> What kind of a prayer was it?

<Judith> LOL well I wrote him a letter!!!! LOL And then I prayed that he would answer my request. And he did, many, many years later. :) You know what Urantia papers say...

<Rob> Oh we all do that don't we Carol—write God a letter. :)))

<Carol> Yep

<Judith> That prayers are like recorded and then, when the conditions are right then they arc granted. :)

<Judith> Well, Carol I told you I've been in incubation :) but not for long. :)

<Carol> :)

<Judith> Urantia papers power is really manifesting more than ever now. :)

[At this point, I commune with her Thought Adjuster and identify his intention for her in the coming days and weeks. As a result, I want to sound out if she is anticipating a change in spiritual consciousness. Is she expecting God to do some new thing in her life? Is she expecting God to heal some past wound or tragedy, so that she can move on? What exactly is she expecting God to do in the immediate future?]

<Rob> Judith, if God could bless your life right now, in a really special way, what would he have to do for you?

<Judith> Umm...

<Judith> He's already done it! :)

<Rob> Wonderful :)))

<Judith> Yep :)

<Judith> Well, its just a matter of time now :) That's it. I mean, for everything that happens I have the confidence that it's for a good purpose.

<Carol> Were you talking experiences or events, Rob?

<Judith> good question :)

[I can see that she might be anticipating God to do something

in her life, but it needs a bit of a nudge to get through to her that he wants to do something pretty special right now, on-line.]

<Rob> If I can be frank now...
<Rob> Judith, your Father wants to do some things for you, and he's showing me that he does. And they're really deep things.
<Judith> :) I know. :) But I'm so overwhelmed by what he's already done for me...that I keep thinking he's really enjoying this. :)

[I think to myself that this person is a full teacup, there's no more room for a fresh infilling of tea. I compliment her politely but then indicate that she is full of herself and not full of God.]

<Rob> Oh good...then I don't need to go on.
<Judith> Well go on anyways; it's good to have words to confirm. :)
<Rob> Oh Judith, you sound like you've got all your great big cup can hold right now anyways.

[I listen to her reply, and I again gently open the door for her Adjuster.]

<Rob> Judith, if God could bless your life right now, in a really special way, what would he have to do for you?
<Roy> longer life batteries
<Judith> LOL yeah :) Well, I tell you.
<Judith> LOL
<Roy> LOL
<Judith> Yeah!
<Roy> Excuse me?

[I see that the conversation is going nowhere and I am about to exit the room. She is not grasping the Thought Adjuster's outreach to her. I turn my attention and commune with her Thought Adjuster with an attitude of shrugging my shoulders and saying: 'All the best Father, I'm out of here.' But he

pleads with me to try a little harder. I decide to give it a fully focussed attempt. At this point, I am not interested in anything but connecting her to Michael and Mother Spirit, and so I steer the conversation accordingly.]

<Rob> Do you know the greatest thing that God can give a
          person?
<Judith> I think I'm gonna buy a kinetic watch!
<Judith> LOL
<Judith> Fusion? :)
<Rob> No. You have to think really hard on this one.
<Judith> I am. :)
<Rob> Ha ha ha ha ha ha ha. OK, I'll tell you.
<Judith> Can't you hear the cogs turning? LOL
<Rob> LOL
<Roy> I know. The answer is, each other.
<Judith> Okay tell Rob.
<Roy> Each other. The greatest thing that God can give a
          person is each other.
<Judith> LOL Really??
<Judith> Well is it Rob? :)

[Now, you have to remember that I want her to be a hungry vessel so that her Thought Adjuster can give her something wholly new.]

<Rob> The greatest thing that God can do for someone is to
          empty them completely of everything that they have
          ever known about God so that God can completely
          replenish them.
<Judith> What??? :)
<Judith> Oh yes, I see.
<Rob> And fill them anew with a wholly new infilling
<Judith> Yes
<Rob> You see, in that way, God gets you all to himself.
          Nothing stands in between you and God.
<Judith> LOL
<Carol> Been there on that one, and he is right.
<Rob> It is like the baby skin and the mama's skin and they
          connect through and through.

<Judith> Well that's where I'm heading.
<Judith> :)
<Rob> Judith ... it's not much of a gift from me, but that's
        my gift to you tonight.
<Judith> Thanks :) Much appreciation. :)
<Rob> Now the interesting thing is that your Thought
        Adjuster, wants to bring you this very gift in person,
        and he wanted me to explain it to you, which I've
        done.
<Judith> I know. I know already. Okay :)
<Judith> Yeah you are so right. That reconfirms it!
<Judith> :)
<Rob> :)

*[What Judith said, affirmed to me that she had been receiving
her Thought Adjuster's ministry to her, but that it was still only
knowledge and it was not yet mixed with her faith... She
needed to move out of her involvement with God being an idea
that he was going to upgrade her spiritual life, to really
connecting to him in an actual experience of the upgrade. That
shift upward and inward was about to happen: I could see it.
Judith was propelled into God's faith domain, the domain of
communion with her Thought Adjuster's values, at the moment
that she recognised the link between what I had said regarding
her Thought Adjuster, and the previous plans he had
communicated to her. Here was I, an unknown and complete
stranger, telling her the things that her Thought Adjuster had
been communicating to her. That spark ignited her faith.
From her new position in faith, she then said "Yeah, you are
so right. That confirms it!"
The instant her faith was aroused, I perceived her Thought
Adjuster starting his move. His mind connected with her
conscious mind and made a union with her sense of self. I
perceived that she was feeling a shift of consciousness, and
that she would have been feeling a real connection with God. I
spoke about what she would be experiencing at this time, in
terms of sonship with God.]*

<Rob> You are a son of God in the terms of the Urantia
        papers Judith...

*[As I spoke wrote those words to her on the chat-line, I saw in
her Thought Adjuster's mind, an image that he wanted
Michael of Nebadon to join with his mind in Judith.
I turned my attention to commune with Christ Michael and I
confirmed his intention to present himself to Judith. So, I
announced that to Judith.
Now remember, Judith has never before encountered Christ
Michael or Mother Spirit. What you are reading is wholly new
territory for her.]*

<Rob> And shortly, Christ Michael will bring you into a new
　　　 presence with him also...he is showing it to me...
<Judith> Really?? :) I was just figuring out how to be a
　　　 Michael son :)
<Rob> A new infilling of Christ himself.
<Judith> I can't imagine a human not being a son of God. :)

*[I recognise that Judith is still in her thinking mind, and I
want to move her more into her capacity for spiritual
perception if she is to receive Michael in any way that she can
recognise.]*

<Rob> Judith, close your eyes for a few moments...your
　　　 Father wants to draw near and bless you mightily.

*[At this point I felt Judith's Thought Adjuster move into her
mind with such a physical force that I felt her heart touched by
him, with the result that his joy sprang up within her heart.
She then confirmed that a few seconds later.]*

<Judith> Yes I feel it. :)
<Rob> God just touched your heart Judith. Literally.
<Judith> I've been getting these jolts all afternoon and
　　　 now...was really...what a day!
<Judith> I'm so charged I don't think I'm sleeping tonight! :)
　　　 And I didn't at all last night. (gasp!)
<Rob> "With my mouth I say these words: 'I love you child.
　　　 You are my daughter, a son of God. Our minds are
　　　 united," says God your Father to you Judith.

<Rob> He is explaining a new kind of connection that he has
        made within your mind and soul in which he can
        literally "be" in you and with you.
<Judith> I'm so full of joy, my cup overfloweth. :)

*[I perceived her mind to be in the fusion-minded state with her
Thought Adjuster, and I described it to her in order to give her
feedback and assurance. In this way, I am able to help in the
birthing process as a new son of the Father, and son of
Michael and son of Mother Spirit is born into morontia
citizenship.]*

<Rob> You can feel this new connection, because you can
        feel somehow whole and spiritually complete. It's not
        like before; somehow bigger; larger; more universal;
        sort of silvery and clear; inside your body and outside
        it all at the same time.
<Judith> yes :)
<Rob> This is the mind of the Thought Adjuster Judith.
<Judith> Wow! :)

[Remember that Judith is in Toronto, Rob is in Melbourne,
Carol is in Arizona and Roy is in California and it is 6pm
Melbourne time on a Friday evening.]

<Rob> This mind will eventually become like your mind,
        wholly.

*[At this point, I want to check and see if Carol has yet
developed the sensitivity and focus to keep up with these
spiritual events going on for Judith, but she says that she is
not in the loop. I also want to ensure that she'll be around for
further mentoring with Judith in the immediate future, to help
Judith settle into sonship with someone she trusts that she can
talk to about anything at all.]*

<Rob> Carol, are you connected?
<Carol> No.
<Rob> Ease on in if you want to...you will be mentoring
        Judith about this new mind I think.

<Judith> She has been already. :)

[At this point, still being in communion with Christ Michael and Judith's Thought Adjuster, I perceive Michael directly and I see him leaving some distant location on his way to be with Judith. whether he is doing that in person, or simply sending his attention in the same way that I am doing with Judith and her Adjuster, is totally irrelevant because, to all intents and purposes, when he connects to her face to face, he may as well be standing right in front of her.
As I speak to her, there are pauses between what I say, as I watch and participate in the events as they unfold.]

<Rob> Judith... Michael is on his way to you. [pausing and watching]
<Rob> coming now... [pausing and watching]

[I notice that her Thought Adjuster has stilled her mind completely. He has prepared the way for her to receive Christ Michael. What magnificent coordination between the Father and the Son!]
<Rob> Feel the stillness? [pausing and watching]
<Rob> The way is being cleared for him.
<Judith> Yes :)
<Rob> He is coming to you, I saw him leave. [pausing and watching]
<Rob> His spirit, where he is in Salvington right now, is going to burst through the universe and meet you. [pausing and watching]

[I see Christ Michael a ways off. It will be a few more moments before he is sufficiently material to engage Judith's mind.]

<Rob> Here he comes. [pausing and watching]
<Rob> Don't fuss Judith. [pausing and watching]
<Rob> Nearly here. [pausing and watching]
<Rob> This is the Father of your life Judith; the creator who has given you the opportunity of life.
<Judith> :)

[All around is stillness; as if the Thought Adjuster has still the whole world; as if the sea that was turbulent has been stilled to a glassy shimmering calm. I can identify that her Thought Adjuster is holding her body and mind and spirit focussed to receive Christ Michael.
Then, in an instant, he greets me directly. I wasn't expecting this!]

<Rob> Now he has met me. He is waiting. He is right here with me.
<Rob> He asked me to say when...so to speak...how gracious of him.

[I quickly think of Judith and convey my impression to Michael, not in the least taking seriously that the creator of Nebadon is waiting upon me to give him the word to proceed to reveal his fatherhood to Judith. Then, in an instant, Michael left my presence and went to Judith where she was in Toronto.]

<Rob> There...Christ is coming to you Judith... [pausing and watching] Fully enjoy now. [pausing and watching]
<Judith> I feel Him.
<Judith> :)

[At this point, Judith is engrossed in her spiritual experience of Michael. I know that she can completely leave us out of the communication loop, and that is her privilege to do if she chooses, but I invite her to keep us in contact if she wants to, by typing in whatever is going on for her.]

<Rob> You can type what is happening if you like, or you can just bathe in him. [pausing and watching and waiting to see if Judith types anything for the chat room.]
<Judith> He said, "This is the first day of the rest of your life." :)
<Judith> I'm bathing in him. :)

[At this point, a magnificent communion spreads out from

Michael and our Thought Adjusters, connecting us all in their grace and love. In a leisurely manner, I type out simple statements from my heart, while Judith continues to enjoy her sonship with Michael.]

<Rob> Jesus I love you.
<Rob> Michael I love you.
<Rob> Father I love you.
<Carol> I feel him too.
<Rob> I will do your will Father,
<Rob> I offer you my whole life, from here to Paradise and
      beyond.
<Rob> Thank you for the opportunity of my life Michael.

[Next we receive the physical evidence of Judith's encounter with Christ Michael.]

<Judith> I'm crying... :) *[pause]*
<Judith> Shaking. *[pause]*
<Judith> Thank you Father! :) I've waited for this so long!
      [pause]

[This is an exciting moment for all of us!]

<Roy> :)
<Rob> Glory to God !!! A child is born in heaven and on
      Earth !!!

[After a while of letting her experience Michael, and just giving herself fully to him, Mother Spirit made herself known to me and indicated that she was available to reveal her holy and divine Motherhood to Judith.]

<Rob> Judith. Please ask for your universe mother, the Holy
      Spirit, to now reveal herself to you through Jesus
Christ. *[pausing and watching]*
<Judith> OK :)
<Judith> How? Mother is something I've not really had a
      chance to really know.

[But Judith's "OK" was enough, and I saw Mother Spirit making her way into Judith's consciousness.]

<Rob> Here she comes. *[pausing and watching]*
<Rob> There she is! *[pausing and watching]*
<Rob> What a glory! *[pausing and watching]*

[In a few moments, Mother Spirit had made contact with Judith. I described the way that Mother Spirit was engaging her, and while I was sending my message to the chat room, Judith also confirms what I was saying about the way Mother Spirit was encountering her.]

<Rob> What a mother! She wraps herself all around, and within.
<Judith> She does! God!
[Judith stopped typing to embrace Mother Spirit. I was excited about the encounter and so I kept on typing things as I perceived them.]
<Rob> New!!!! And AMAZING!!!
<Rob> And She's a Mother ... even your Mother :))))))))))
<Rob> What a wonderful thing to behold.
<Rob> Who ever would have guessed that we had a universe Mother and a universe Father also? [pausing and watching]
<Judith> a whole family!

[Considerable time then passes in silence. Our screens sit quietly awaiting Judith's communication.
After a while of perceiving what's going on in the fusion mind that is shared between Judith and her Thought Adjuster, I make comment in order to maintain the communion links between us.]

<Rob> Judith, this is the experience of the Father (Thought Adjuster), the Son (Jesus Christ your Father) and the Spirit (Holy Spirit...the Mother Spirit) *[pausing and watching]*
<Judith> I feel very full now. :)
<Rob> Yes...fullness is sonship with God at a universe level

and also at an infinite level.

<Rob> You feel your entire mind and being to be renewed by these divine parents.

<Judith> My hands have just warmed up for the first time all day!

<Judith> This is for real!

<Judith> I feel them here beside me.

<Judith> I never thought I could have Mother Spirit too.

<Rob> Don't we wish it was all this easy for us Carol, when it happened?

<Carol> Yep!

<Judith> Before, Mother Spirit was so distant, I could never really reach her.

<Carol> No longer

<Rob> Judith, you cannot Adjuster fuse without her.

<Judith> I knew God all my life, and the Holy Spirit. But not as my Mother.

<Rob> Now, for the first time in your life, you are being equipped for Adjuster fusion because you have been filled by God with their Parenthood.

<Judith> So when I learned in the Urantia papers...

<Judith> Now I know. :)

<Judith> This is so incredible!

<Judith> All these things happening to me in these last few weeks!

[Her birth into sonship—her conversion experience—is now complete. She is in the hands of the Father and the Son and the Holy Spirit. She has Carol there on line to talk to her about these kinds of matters. I decide to go off line.]

<Rob> I am going to go now Judith. Carol will be with you. God bless you Judith.

<Carol> Thank you Rob. :)

<Rob> Good night.

<Rob> Good night Carol.

<Carol> Nite.

<Roy> Night Rob...

<Rob> Love you all.

<Judith> My deepest thanks to you Rob.

<Rob> Truly, it was the house of God tonight. Thank you my
      dear Parents for your never ending grace.
<Judith> Amen! :)
<Rob> :))
*** Rob has left #urantia.

Jesus is knocking

This is the end of the transcript. What a lovely experience it was for all of us, especially for Judith. Four of us were on an Internet chat line and yet able to commune prayerfully across the world from Toronto to Melbourne to Phoenix and California. I have done this on a number of occasions and on other chatlines as well. Moreover, the Thoughts Adjusters provided a shared mind so that prayerfulness could be powerful among us and keep us focussed. Oh, but wasn't it a magnificent blessing dear reader, that Christ Michael and Mother Spirit themselves should actively seek out their human daughter in Toronto and birth her into a whole new dimension of spirituality.

And they will do this with you if you will only believe and, in faith, ask. The book of Revelation 3:20 tells us that Jesus is standing at the door of our hearts, knocking. He promises that if we hear his voice, to open the door, because he will come in to us and eat with us, and we with him. But the door has only one handle, and it's on our side of the door. He can't come in unless we let him in. Do that. Listen for his voice, and let him in. How do you do that? It's as simple as wanting to, dear one: you just want to and you say, "Jesus, please come in, and stay."

❦

Epilogue

This, then, is sonship as I have encountered it. It obviously involves the Urantia papers and the Bible and the personal experience of sharing the mind of God. I hope you will put aside the chicken bones and keep sipping the soup. Sonship is the finest soup, in anyone's language.

If you have journeyed with me through this entire book then you have read about many things new to you, and perhaps you have wondered if you could do them in your life also.

I want to confirm that, yes, you could do all this and more if you will use the keys to the kingdom. Those keys are your sharing the mind of God, like Jesus did, and, believing in Jesus' religion of sonship with God. Through such real contact with God your Father, you can have an unswerving faith that you will do and have whatever you have seen in the mind of God—the will of God.

If you have enjoyed reading this book half as much as I have enjoyed living it and writing it, then you have probably thought of someone you know who would also enjoy it. Get them a copy soon, and let's both be partners in spreading Christ Michael's new light—sonship with God and the Urantia papers—to the people across all the nations of this Earth. Let's bless the world together with our Father's grace and love through them.

You may also want to help the Thought Adjusters in the world by placing copies in the libraries and reading rooms that come to mind for you. Many a person you will never meet will be touched by your kindness and sense of mission for God's growing love on earth. If the wellspring is not there, the thirsty cannot drink. If it is there, others will love what you love.

As you go about your daily life in this new millenium, remember that the Son of God once lived among us and showed us human spiritual perfection. Live by the truth that God is your Father, and that you are his son or daughter, that all other people are therefore spiritually your brothers and sisters. Receiving this with an attitude that the Father's forgiveness *is* your salvation, and all else in your eternal spiritual life springs forth from it.

❧

So said in faith: so done by grace

My dear Michael, this whole book is my prayerful communion with you. My vision of the ideal in your mind is that you will raise up a great many sons of God from the men and women and boys and girls who are spiritually touched by it. This is my seed and I am sowing it in your will Father, as you have given it to me so to do. By your will then Michael, let the thousand-fold harvest now begin and be unstoppable, for your kingdom in this new stream of the sons of God. This, truly, is the kingdom of heaven: the love-filled fellowship among people who share the mind of God.

I have shown them some of your ways, Father. And I have shown them some of the ways you have revealed to me in my life with you. Bless them all, my Father. Feed their desire for your righteousness and anoint their faith with the mind of your human perfection, Adjuster fusion.

With this great work spread before us—the bringing of a whole people of faith into sharing the mind of God—Father watch over the spread of the teachings of sonship in the Urantia papers, that the life in its spirit, and not just its letter, might be imparted to the reader. Watch over, Father, the long life of those who will bring your blessings into the world by their lives: there shall be a great many of these victorious ones who abide in you, as you abide in them—some of whom will be the Governors General of this dear world in the age to come.

So said in faith: so done by grace.

❦

Most bookshops will order a copy of *The Urantia Book* upon request. Copies are also available directly through distributors such as:

Urantia Foundation
533 Diversey Parkway, Chicago, Illinois 60614.
Telephone USA 773-525-3319 (or free call within the USA on 1-800-urantia);
Email: urantia@urantia.org
Internet: http:// http://www.urantia.org/

The Urantia Book Fellowship
529 Wrightwood Avenue, Chicago, Illinois 60614 USA;
Tel. 1(877)3355669;
Email: ubinfo@ubfellowship.org
Internet: http://urantiabook.org/

❧

The Urantia papers are on the Internet and are available for free download at a number of sites. Search the web with your favourite browser, or go to "Ask Jeeves" at http://www.askjeeves.com/ and type in the word *Urantia* to see the listings in a number of search engines.

❧

Michael Foundation produced, among other books, a copy of the fourth section of the Urantia papers, titled "Jesus—a new revelation."

Michael Foundation
3333 S. Council Road
Oklahoma City, Oklahoma, 73179 USA;
Tel. 1(405)745 7707;
Email: michaelfoundation@ibm.net

❧

How to order copies of "Sonship and the Urantia papers: sharing the mind of God"

Please send me ____ copies of *Sonship and the Urantia papers: sharing the mind of God* at Aus$49.50 (GST included) PLUS Aus$16 postage for 1 copy or Aus$100 postage for 10 copies. International delivery is approximately 21 working days.

Name _____

Number and Street _____

City _____

State _____Post Code _____

Contact Phone Number or Email address (for confirmation of order received)

_____

Total in Australian dollars: $ _____

Send this order form and your International Bank Check to:
Robert Crickett,
P.O.Box 6067, Hawthorn West, Victoria 3122 Australia.

Or, to pay by direct bank transfer, please fax this form to notify us of your order on Melbourne Australia 3-98539237 (or email us) then arrange an International money transfer at your bank to:
Robert Crickett,
National Australia Bank: 445 Toorak Road, Toorak Victoria 3142 Australia: Account number:083453-474169254. For all foreign exchange, please add $5 per book for bank transfer fees charged by Australian banks upon arrival.
For further enquiries, and to first confirm that stock is currently available, email sonship@gravity.net.au

❧

Berzin, A. (Translator and editor). 1978. "The Mahamudra: Eliminating the darkness of ignorance—the ninth Karmapa Wang-Ch'ug Dor-je." Library of Tibetan Works & Archives, Dharamsala India.

Chang, Garma C. C. 1959. "The Practice Of Zen." Harper & Row. New York.

Chogyal Namkai Norbu. "Dzogchen: the self-perfected state." Snow Lion Publications, New York.

Davidson, C. 2000. "Adjuster fusion and the Urantia papers: perfect union with God." P.O.Box 802, Scottsdale AZ 85252-0802.

Godman, D. 1985. "The Teachings Of Sri Ramana Maharshi." Arkana, London.

Hunter, Charles & Frances 1981. "How to heal the sick." Hunter Books, Kingwood Texas. http://www.cfhunter.org/;

Jorgensen, Owen. 1998. "Supernatural: The life of William Branham," (in three books). Tucson Tabernacle, Arizona. http://www.Biblebelievers.org/

Krebbs, Charles, Dr., & Brown, J. 1998. "A Revolutionary Way of Thinking. Hill of Content. Melbourne. Email: map@enternet.com.au

Lliardon, R. 1996. "Smith Wigglesworth: The complete collection of his life teachings." Albury Publishing, Tulsa Oklahoma.

McMullan, Harry. 1999. "Index To The Urantia Book" Michael Foundation: S 3333 Council Rd Oklahoma City, OK.

Michael Foundation. 1999. "Jesus—a new revelation." 3333
S. Council Road, Oklahoma City, Oklahoma, 73179
USA; Tel. 1(405)745 7707; Email:
michaelfoundation@ibm.net

Morose, Ray. 1998. "The Heart Of Silence." P.O.Box 60
Ocean Shores, NSW Australia 2483.

Osborn, T.L. 1951-1992. "Healing the sick." Harrison House,
Tulsa Oklahoma;

Pullinger, Jackie. 1980. "Chasing the Dragon" Hodder and
Stoughton, London.

Pullinger, Jackie. 1989. "Crack In The Wall." Hodder and
Stoughton, London.

Roberts, O. 1995. "Expect a miracle." Word Publishing,
London. http://www.oru.edu/;

Schloegl, I. 1976. "The Zen Teaching Of Rinzai." Shambhala.
Berkley.

Utt, Richard. 1991. "Applied Physiology: Acupressure
formatting for Brain Physiology." Applied Physiology
Publishing. Tucson AZ.